Edward Gibbon

The Works of Edward Gibbon

History of the decline and fall of the Roman empire. Volume 1

BAMBOO BOOKS

Edward Gibbon

The Works of Edward Gibbon

History of the decline and fall of the Roman empire.
Volume 1

Original published in 1906
Republished by Bamboo Books, 2021
Cover Design: Bamboo Books

ISBN: 978-5-519-70781-7

THE WORKS OF EDWARD GIBBON

HISTORY OF ROME

VOLUME I

NEW YORK
FRED DeFAU & COMPANY
PUBLISHERS

THE HISTORY

OF THE

DECLINE AND FALL OF THE ROMAN EMPIRE

BY

EDWARD GIBBON

EDITED BY

J. B. BURY, M.A.

WITH AN INTRODUCTION

BY

THE RT. HON. W. E. H. LECKY

VOL. I

NEW YORK
FRED DE FAU & COMPANY
PUBLISHERS

Norwood Press

CONTENTS OF THE FIRST VOLUME

CHAPTER I

The Extent and Military Force of the Empire, in the Age of the Antonines

CHAPTER II

Of the Union and Internal Prosperity of the Roman Empire in the Age of the Antonines

CHAPTER III

Of the Constitution of the Roman Empire, in the Age of the Antonines

CHAPTER IV

The Cruelty, Follies, and Murder of Commodus — Election of Pertinax — His attempts to reform the State — His Assassination by the Prætorian Guards

CHAPTER V

Public Sale of the Empire to Didius Julianus by the Prætorian Guards — Clodius Albinus in Britain, Pescennius Niger in Syria, and Septimius Severus in Pannonia declare against the Murderers of Pertinax — Civil Wars and Victory of Severus over his three Rivals — Relaxation of discipline — New Maxims of Government

CHAPTER VI

The Death of Severus — Tyranny of Caracalla — Usurpation of Macrinus — Follies of Elagabalus — Virtues of Alexander Severus — Licentiousness of the Army — General State of the Roman Finances

CHAPTER VII

The Elevation and Tyranny of Maximin — Rebellion in Africa and Italy, under the Authority of the Senate — Civil Wars and Seditions — Violent Deaths of Maximin and his Son, of Maximus and Balbinus, and of the three Gordians — Usurpation and Secular Games of Philip

CHAPTER VIII

Of the State of Persia after the Restoration of the Monarchy by Artaxerxes

CHAPTER IX

The State of Germany till the Invasion of the Barbarians, in the Time of the Emperor Decius

LIST OF ILLUSTRATIONS

INTRODUCTION [1]

BY W. E. H. LECKY

The history of Gibbon has been described by John Stuart Mill as the only eighteenth-century history that has withstood nineteenth-century criticism; and whatever objections modern critics may bring against some of its parts, the substantial justice of this verdict will scarcely be contested. No other history of that century has been so often reprinted, annotated, and discussed, or remains to the present day a capital authority on the great period of which it treats. As a composition it stands unchallenged and conspicuous among the masterpieces of English literature, while as a history it covers a space of more than twelve hundred years, including some of the most momentous events in the annals of mankind.

Gibbon was born at Putney, Surrey, April 27, 1737. Though his father was a member of Parliament and the owner of a moderate competence, the author of this great work was essentially a self-educated man. Weak health and almost constant illness in early boyhood broke up his school life, — which appears to have been fitfully and most imperfectly conducted, — withdrew him from boyish games, but also gave him, as it has given to many other shy and sedentary boys, an early and inveterate passion for reading. His reading, however, was very unlike that of an ordinary boy. He has given a graphic picture of the ardour with which, when he was only fourteen, he flung himself into serious but unguided study; which was at first purely desultory, but gradually contracted into historic lines, and soon concentrated itself mainly on that Oriental history which he was one day so brilliantly to illuminate. "Before I was sixteen," he says, "I had exhausted all that could be learned in English of the Arabs and Persians, the Tartars and Turks; and the same ardour led me to guess at the French of D'Herbelot, and to construe the barbarous Latin of Pocock's 'Abulfaragius.'"

His health, however, gradually improved, and when he entered Magdalen College, Oxford, it might have been expected that a new period of intellectual development would have begun; but Oxford had at this time sunk to the lowest depth of stagnation, and to Gibbon it proved extremely uncongenial. He complained that he found no guidance, no stimulus, and no discipline, and that the fourteen months he spent there were the most idle and unprofitable of his life. They were very unexpectedly cut short by his conversion to the Roman Catholic faith, which he formally adopted at the age of sixteen.

This conversion is, on the whole, the most surprising incident of his calm and uneventful life. The tendencies of the time, both in England and on the Continent, were in a wholly different direction. The more spiritual and emotional natures were now passing into the religious revival of Wesley and Whitefield, which was slowly transforming the character of the Anglican Church and laying the foundations of the great Evangelical party. In other quarters the predominant tendencies were towards unbelief, scepticism, or indifference. Nature seldom formed a more sceptical intellect than that of Gibbon, and he was utterly without the spiritual insight, or spiritual cravings, or overmastering enthusiasms, that produce and explain most religious changes. Nor was he in the least drawn towards Catholicism on its æsthetic side. He had never come in contact with its worship or its professors; and to his unimaginative, unimpassioned, and profoundly intellectual temperament, no ideal type could be more uncongenial than that of the saint. He had, however, from early youth been keenly interested in theological controversies. He argued, like Lardner and Paley, that miracles are the Divine attestation of orthodoxy. Middleton convinced him that unless the Patristic writers were wholly undeserving of credit, the gift of miracles continued in the Church during the fourth and fifth centuries; and he was unable to resist the conclusion that during that period many of the leading doctrines of Catholicism had passed into the Church. The writings of the Jesuit Parsons, and still more the writings of Bossuet, completed the work which Middleton had begun. Having arrived at this conclusion, Gibbon acted on it with characteristic honesty, and was received into the Church on the 8th of June, 1753.

The English universities were at this time purely Anglican bodies, and the conversion of Gibbon excluded him from Oxford. His father judiciously sent him to Lausanne to study with a Swiss pastor named Pavilliard, with whom he spent five happy and profitable years. The theological episode was soon terminated. Partly under the influence of his teacher, but much more through his own reading and reflections, he soon disentangled the purely intellectual ties that bound him to the Church of Rome; and on Christmas Day, 1754, he received the sacrament in the Protestant church of Lausanne.

His residence at Lausanne was very useful to him. He had access to books in abundance, and his tutor, who was a man of great good sense and amiability but of no remarkable capacity, very judiciously left his industrious pupil to pursue his studies in his own way. "Hiving wisdom with each studious year," as Byron so truly says, he speedily amassed a store of learning which has seldom been equalled. His insatiable love of knowledge, his rare capacity for concentrated, accurate, and fruitful study, guided by a singularly sure and masculine judgment, soon made him, in the true sense of the word, one of the best scholars of his time. His learning, however, was not altogether of the kind that may be found in a great university professor. Though the classical languages became familiar to him, he never acquired or greatly valued the minute and finished scholarship which is the boast of the chief English schools; and careful students have observed that in following Greek books he must have very largely used the Latin translations. Perhaps in his capacity of historian this deficiency was rather an advantage than the reverse. It saved him from the exaggerated value of classical form, and from the neglect of the more corrupt literatures, to which English scholars have been often prone. Gibbon always valued books mainly for what they contained, and he had early learned the lesson which all good historians should learn: that some of his most valuable materials will be found in literatures that have no artistic merit; in writers who, without theory and almost without criticism, simply relate the facts which they have seen, and express in unsophisticated language the beliefs and impressions of their time.

Lausanne and not Oxford was the real birthplace of his intellect, and he returned from it almost a foreigner. French had become as familiar to him as his own tongue; and his first book, a somewhat superficial essay on the study of literature, was published in the French language. The noble contemporary French literature filled him with delight, and he found on the borders of the Lake of Geneva a highly cultivated society to which he was soon introduced, and which probably gave him more real pleasure than any in which he afterwards moved. With Voltaire himself he had some slight acquaintance, and he at one time looked on him with profound admiration; though fuller knowledge made him sensible of the flaws in that splendid intellect. I am here concerned with the life of Gibbon only in as far as it discloses the influences that contributed to his master work, and among these influences the foreign element holds a prominent place. There was little in Gibbon that was distinctively

English; his mind was essentially cosmopolitan. His tastes, ideals, and modes of thought and feeling turned instinctively to the Continent.

In one respect this foreign type was of great advantage to his work. Gibbon excels all other English historians in symmetry, proportion, perspective, and arrangement, which are also the preëminent and characteristic merits of the best French literature. We find in his writing nothing of the great miscalculations of space that were made by such writers as Macaulay and Buckle; nothing of the awkward repetitions, the confused arrangement, the semi-detached and disjointed episodes that mar the beauty of many other histories of no small merit. Vast and multifarious as are the subjects which he has treated, his work is a great whole, admirably woven in all its parts. On the other hand, his foreign taste may perhaps be seen in his neglect of the Saxon element, which is the most vigorous and homely element in English prose. Probably in no other English writer does the Latin element so entirely predominate. Gibbon never wrote an unmeaning and very seldom an obscure sentence; he could always paint with sustained and stately eloquence an illustrious character or a splendid scene: but he was wholly wanting in the grace of simplicity, and a monotony of glitter and of mannerism is the great defect of his style. He possessed, to a degree which even Tacitus and Bacon had hardly surpassed, the supreme literary gift of condensation, and it gives an admirable force and vividness to his narrative; but it is sometimes carried to excess. Not unfrequently it is attained by an excessive allusiveness, and a wide knowledge of the subject is needed to enable the reader to perceive the full import and meaning conveyed or hinted at by a mere turn of phrase. But though his style is artificial and pedantic, and greatly wanting in flexibility, it has a rare power of clinging to the memory, and it has profoundly influenced English prose. That excellent judge, Cardinal Newman, has said of Gibbon, "I seem to trace his vigorous condensation and peculiar rhythm at every turn in the literature of the present day."

It is not necessary to relate here in any detail the later events of the life of Gibbon. There was his enlistment as captain in the Hampshire militia. It involved two and a half years of active service, extending from May, 1760, to December, 1762; and as Gibbon afterwards acknowledged, if it interrupted his studies and brought him into very uncongenial duties and societies, it at least greatly enlarged his acquaintance with English life, and also gave him a knowledge of the rudiments of military science, which was not without its use to the historian of so many battles. There was a long journey, lasting for two years and five months, in France and Italy, which greatly confirmed his foreign tendencies. In Paris he moved familiarly in some of the best French literary society; and in Rome, as he tells us in a well-known passage, while he sat "musing amidst the ruins of the Capitol while the barefooted friars were singing vespers in the Temple of Jupiter" (which is now the Church of the Ara Cœli), — on October 15, 1764, — he first conceived the idea of writing the history of the decline and fall of Rome.

There was also that very curious episode in his life, lasting from 1774 to 1782, — his appearance in the House of Commons. He had declined an offer of his father's to purchase a seat for him in 1760; and fourteen years later, when his father was dead, when his own circumstances were considerably contracted, he received and accepted at the hands of a family connection the offer of a seat. His Parliamentary career was entirely undistinguished, and he never even opened his mouth in debate, — a fact which was not forgotten when very recently another historian was candidate for a seat in Parliament. In truth, this somewhat shy and reserved scholar, with his fastidious taste, his eminently judicial mind, and his highly condensed and elaborate style, was singularly unfit for the rough work of Parliamentary discussion. No one can read his books without perceiving that his English was not that of a debater; and he has candidly admitted that he entered Parliament without public spirit or serious interest in politics, and that he valued it chiefly as leading to an office which might restore the fortune which the extravagance of his father had greatly impaired. His only real public service was the composition in French of a reply to the French manifesto which was issued at the beginning of the war of 1778. He voted steadily and placidly as a Tory, and it is not probable that in doing so he did any violence to his opinions. Like Hume, he shrank with an instinctive dislike from all popular agitations, from all turbulence, passion, exaggeration, and enthusiasm; and a temperate and well-ordered despotism was evidently his ideal. He showed it in the well-known passage in which he extols the benevolent despotism of the Antonines as without exception the happiest period in the history of mankind, and in the unmixed horror with which he looked upon the French Revolution that broke up the old landmarks of Europe. For three years he held an office in the Board of Trade, which added considerably to his income without adding greatly to his labours, and he supported steadily the American policy of Lord North and the Coalition ministry of North and Fox; but the loss of his office and the retirement of North soon drove him from Parliament, and he shortly after took up his residence at Lausanne.

But before this time a considerable part of his great work had been accomplished. The first quarto volume of the "Decline and Fall" appeared in February, 1776. As is usually the case with historical works, it occupied a much longer period than its successors, and was the fruit of about ten years of labour. It passed rapidly through three editions, received the enthusiastic eulogy of Hume and Robertson, and was no doubt greatly assisted in its circulation by the storm of controversy that arose about his Fifteenth and Sixteenth Chapters. In April, 1781, two more volumes appeared, and the three concluding volumes were published together on the 8th of May, 1788, being the fifty-first birthday of the author.

A work of such magnitude, dealing with so vast a variety of subjects, was certain to exhibit some flaws. The controversy at first turned mainly upon its religious tendency. The complete scepticism of the author, his aversion to the ecclesiastical type which dominated in the period of which he wrote, and his unalterable conviction that Christianity, by diverting the strength and enthusiasm of the Empire from civic into ascetic and ecclesiastical channels, was a main cause of the downfall of the Empire and of the triumph of barbarism, gave him a bias which it was impossible to overlook. On no other subject is his irony more bitter or his contempt so manifestly displayed. Few good critics will deny that the growth of the ascetic spirit had a large part in corroding and enfeebling the civic virtues of the Empire; but the part which it played was that of intensifying a disease that had already begun, and Gibbon, while exaggerating the amount of the evil, has very imperfectly described the great services rendered even by a monastic Church in laying the basis of another civilisation and in mitigating the calamities of the barbarian invasion. The causes he has given of the spread of Christianity in the Fifteenth Chapter were for the most part true causes, but there were others of which he was wholly insensible. The strong moral enthusiasms that transform the character and inspire or accelerate all great religious changes lay wholly beyond the sphere of his realisations. His language about the Christian martyrs is the most repulsive portion of his work; and his comparison of the sufferings caused by pagan and Christian persecutions is greatly vitiated by the fact that he only takes account of the number of deaths, and lays no stress on the profuse employment of atrocious tortures, which was one of the most distinct features of the pagan persecutions. At the same time, though Gibbon displays in this field a manifest and a distorting bias, he never, like some of his French contemporaries, sinks into the mere partisan, awarding to one side unqualified eulogy and to the other unqualified contempt. Let the reader who doubts this examine and compare his masterly portraits of Julian and of Athanasius, and he will perceive how clearly the great historian could recognise weaknesses in the characters by which he was most attracted, and elements of true greatness in those by which he was most repelled. A modern writer, in treating of the history of religions, would have given a larger space to comparative religion, and to the gradual, unconscious, and spontaneous growth of myths in the twilight periods of the human mind. These, however, were subjects which were scarcely known in the days of Gibbon, and he cannot be blamed for not having discussed them.

Another class of objections which has been brought against him is that he is weak upon the philosophical side, and deals with history mainly as a mere chronicle of events, and not as a chain of causes and consequences, a series of problems to be solved, a gradual evolution which it is the task of the historian to explain. Coleridge, who detested Gibbon and spoke of him with gross injustice, has put this objection in the strongest form. He accuses him of having reduced history to a mere collection of splendid anecdotes; of noting nothing but what may produce an effect; of skipping from eminence to eminence without ever taking his readers through the valleys between; of having never made a single philosophical attempt to fathom the ultimate causes of the decline and fall of the Roman Empire, which is the very subject of his history. That such charges are grossly exaggerated will be apparent to any one who will carefully read the Second and Third Chapters, describing the state and tendencies of the Empire under the Antonines; or the chapters devoted to the rise and character of the barbarians, to the spread of Christianity, to the influence of monasticism, to the jurisprudence of the republic, and of the Empire; nor would it be difficult to collect many acute and profound philosophical remarks from other portions of the history. Still, it may be admitted that the philosophical side is not its strongest part. Social and economical changes are sometimes inadequately examined and explained, and we often desire fuller information about the manners and life of the masses of the people. As far as concerns the age of the Antonines, this want has been amply supplied by the great work of Friedländer.

History, like many other things in our generation, has fallen largely into the hands of specialists; and it is inevitable that men who have devoted their lives to a minute examination of short periods should be able to detect some deficiencies and errors in a writer who traversed a period of more than twelve hundred years. Many generations of scholars have arisen since Gibbon; many new sources of knowledge have become available, and archæology especially has thrown a flood of new light on some of the subjects he treated. Though his knowledge and his narrative are on the whole admirably sustained, there are periods which he knew less well and treated less fully than others. His account of the Crusades is generally acknowledged to be one of the most conspicuous of these, and within the last few years there has arisen a school of historians who protest against the low opinion of the Byzantine Empire which was held by Gibbon, and was almost universal among scholars till the present generation. That these writers have brought into relief certain merits of the Lower Empire which Gibbon had neglected, will not be denied; but it is perhaps too early to decide whether the reaction has not, like most reactions, been carried to extravagance, and whether in its general features the estimate of Gibbon is not nearer the truth than some of those which are now put forward to replace it.

Much must no doubt be added to the work of Gibbon in order to bring it up to the level of our present knowledge; but there is no sign that any single work is likely to supersede it or to render it useless to the student; nor does its survival depend only or even mainly on its great literary qualities, which have made it one of the classics of the language. In some of these qualities Hume was the equal of Gibbon and in others his superior, and he brought to his history a more penetrating and philosophical intellect and an equally calm and unenthusiastic nature; but the study which Hume bestowed on his subject was so superficial and his statements were often so inaccurate, that his work is now never quoted as an authority. With Gibbon it is quite otherwise. His marvellous industry, his almost unrivalled accuracy of detail, his sincere love of truth, his rare discrimination and insight in weighing testimony and in judging character, have given him a secure place among the greatest historians of the world.

His life lasted only fifty-six years; he died in London on January 15, 1794. Gibbon's autobiography is one of the best specimens of self-portraiture in the language, reflecting with pellucid clearness both the life and character, the merits and defects, of its author. He was certainly neither a hero nor a saint; nor did he possess the moral and intellectual qualities that dominate in the great conflicts of life, sway the passions of men, appeal powerfully to the imagination, or dazzle and impress in social intercourse. He was a little slow, a little pompous, a little affected and pedantic. In the general type of his mind and character he bore much more resemblance to Hume, Adam Smith, or Reynolds, than to Johnson or Burke. A reserved scholar, who was rather proud of being a man of the world; a confirmed bachelor, much wedded to his comforts though caring nothing for luxury, he was eminently moderate in his ambitions, and there was not a trace of passion or enthusiasm in his nature. Such a man was not likely to inspire any strong devotion. But his temper was most kindly, equable, and contented; he was a steady friend, and he appears to have been always liked and honoured in the cultivated and uncontentious society in which he delighted. His life was not a great one, but it was in all essentials blameless and happy. He found the work which was most congenial to him. He pursued it with admirable industry and with brilliant success, and he left behind him a book which is not likely to be forgotten while the English language endures.

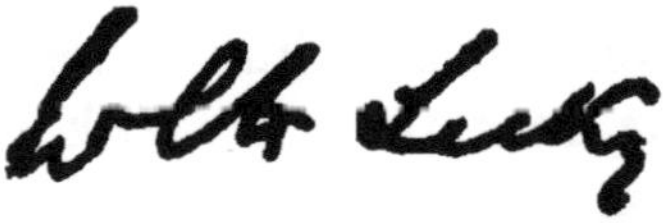

PREFACE OF THE AUTHOR

It is not my intention to detain the reader by expatiating on the variety, or the importance of the subject, which I have undertaken to treat; since the merit of the choice would serve to render the weakness of the execution still more apparent, and still less excusable. But, as I have presumed to lay before the Public a *first* volume only[1] of the History of the Decline and Fall of the Roman Empire, it will perhaps be expected that I should explain, in a few words, the nature and limits of my general plan.

The memorable series of revolutions, which, in the course of about thirteen centuries, gradually undermined, and at length destroyed, the solid fabric of human greatness, may, with some propriety, be divided into the three following periods:

I. The first of these periods may be traced from the age of Trajan and the Antonines, when the Roman monarchy, having attained its full strength and maturity, began to verge towards its decline; and will extend to the subversion of the Western Empire, by the barbarians of Germany and Scythia, the rude ancestors of the most polished nations of modern Europe. This extraordinary revolution, which subjected Rome to the power of a Gothic conqueror, was completed about the beginning of the sixth century.

[1] The first volume of the quarto, which is now contained in the two first volumes of the octavo edition.

II. The second period of the Decline and Fall of Rome may be supposed to commence with the reign of Justinian, who by his laws, as well as by his victories, restored a transient splendour to the Eastern Empire. It will comprehend the invasion of Italy by the Lombards; the conquest of the Asiatic and African provinces by the Arabs, who embraced the religion of Mahomet; the revolt of the Roman people against the feeble princes of Constantinople; and the elevation of Charlemagne, who, in the year 800, established the second, or German Empire of the West.

III. The last and longest of these periods includes about six centuries and a half; from the revival of the Western Empire till the taking of Constantinople by the Turks and the extinction of a degenerate race of princes, who continued to assume the titles of Cæsar and Augustus, after their dominions were contracted to the limits of a single city; in which the language, as well as manners, of the ancient Romans had been long since forgotten. The writer who should undertake to relate the events of this period would find himself obliged to enter into the general history of the Crusades, as far as they contributed to the ruin of the Greek Empire; and he would scarcely be able to restrain his curiosity from making some enquiry into the state of the city of Rome during the darkness and confusion of the middle ages.

As I have ventured, perhaps too hastily, to commit to the press a work, which, in every sense of the word, deserves the epithet of imperfect, I consider myself as contracting an engagement to finish, most probably in a second volume,[1] the first of these memorable periods; and to deliver to the Public the complete History of the Decline and Fall of

[1] The Author, as it frequently happens, took an inadequate measure of his growing work. The remainder of the first period has filled *two* volumes in quarto, being the third, fourth, fifth and sixth volumes of the octavo edition.

the Western Empire. With regard to the subsequent periods, though I may entertain some hopes, I dare not presume to give any assurances. The execution of the extensive plan which I have described would connect the ancient and modern history of the World; but it would require many years of health, of leisure, and of perseverance.

BENTINCK STREET,
February 1, 1776.

P.S. — The entire History, which is now published, of the Decline and Fall of the Roman Empire in the West abundantly discharges my engagements with the Public. Perhaps their favourable opinion may encourage me to prosecute a work, which, however laborious it may seem, is the most agreeable occupation of my leisure hours.

BENTINCK STREET,
March 1, 1781.

An Author easily persuades himself that the public opinion is still favourable to his labours; and I have now embraced the serious resolution of proceeding to the last period of my original design, and of the Roman Empire, the taking of Constantinople by the Turks, in the year one thousand four hundred and fifty-three. The most patient reader, who computes that three ponderous volumes [1] have been already employed on the events of four centuries, may, perhaps, be alarmed at the long prospect of nine hundred years. But it is not my intention to expatiate with the same minuteness on the whole series of the Byzantine history. At our entrance into this period, the reign of Justinian and the conquests of the Mahometans will deserve and detain our attention, and the last age of Constantinople (the Cru-

[1] [Containing chaps. i. to xxxviii.]

sades and the Turks) is connected with the revolutions of Modern Europe. From the seventh to the eleventh century, the obscure interval will be supplied by a concise narrative of such facts as may still appear either interesting or important.

BENTINCK STREET,
March 1, 1782.

ADVERTISEMENT TO THE NOTES[1]

DILIGENCE and accuracy are the only merits which an historical writer may ascribe to himself; if any merit indeed can be assumed from the performance of an indispensable duty. I may therefore be allowed to say that I have carefully examined all the original materials that could illustrate the subject which I had undertaken to treat. Should I ever complete the extensive design which has been sketched out in the preface, I might perhaps conclude it with a critical account of the authors consulted during the progress of the whole work; and, however such an attempt might incur the censure of ostentation, I am persuaded that it would be susceptible of entertainment as well as information.

At present I shall content myself with a single observation. The Biographers, who, under the reigns of Diocletian and Constantine, composed, or rather compiled, the lives of the emperors, from Hadrian to the sons of Carus, are usually mentioned under the names of Ælius Spartianus, Julius Capitolinus, Ælius Lampridius, Vulcatius Gallicanus, Trebellius Pollio, and Flavius Vopiscus. But there is so much perplexity in the titles of the MSS., and so many disputes have arisen among the critics (see Fabricius Biblioth. Latin. l. iii. c. 6) concerning their number, their names and their respective property, that for the most part I have quoted them without distinction, under the general and well-known title of the AUGUSTAN HISTORY.

[1] [Which in the first quarto edition of vol. i. were printed at the end of the volume.]

ADVERTISEMENT TO THE FIRST OCTAVO EDITION

The History of the Decline and Fall of the Roman Empire is now delivered to the public in a more convenient form. Some alterations and improvements had presented themselves to my mind, but I was unwilling to injure or offend the purchasers of the preceding editions. The accuracy of the corrector of the press has been already tried and approved; and perhaps I may stand excused if, amidst the avocations of a busy writer, I have preferred the pleasures of composition and study to the minute diligence of revising a former publication.

Bentinck Street,
April 20, 1783.

PREFACE TO THE FOURTH VOLUME OF THE QUARTO EDITION

I NOW discharge my promise, and complete my design, of writing the History of the Decline and Fall of the Roman Empire, both in the West and the East. The whole period extends from the age of Trajan and the Antonines to the taking of Constantinople by Mahomet the Second; and includes a review of the Crusades and the state of Rome during the middle ages. Since the publication of the first volume, twelve years have elapsed; twelve years, according to my wish, "of health, of leisure and of perseverance." I may now congratulate my deliverance from a long and laborious service, and my satisfaction will be pure and perfect, if the public favour should be extended to the conclusion of my work.

It was my first intention to have collected under one view the numerous authors, of every age and language, from whom I have derived the materials of this history; and I am still convinced that the apparent ostentation would be more than compensated by real use. If I have renounced this idea, if I have declined an undertaking which had obtained the approbation of a master-artist,[1] my excuse may be found in the extreme difficulty of assigning a proper measure to such a catalogue. A naked list of names and editions would not be satisfactory either to myself or my readers: the characters of the principal Authors of the Roman and Byzantine History have been occasionally connected with the events which they describe; a more copious and critical enquiry might indeed deserve, but it would demand, an elaborate volume, which

[1] See Dr. Robertson's Preface to his History of America.

might swell by degrees into a general library of historical writers. For the present I shall content myself with renewing my serious protestation, that I have always endeavoured to draw from the fountain-head; that my curiosity, as well as a sense of duty, has always urged me to study the originals; and that, if they have sometimes eluded my search, I have carefully marked the secondary evidence, on whose faith a passage or a fact were reduced to depend.

I shall soon visit the banks of the lake of Lausanne, a country which I have known and loved from my early youth. Under a mild government, amidst a beauteous landskip, in a life of leisure and independence, and among a people of easy and elegant manners, I have enjoyed, and may again hope to enjoy, the varied pleasures of retirement and society. But I shall ever glory in the name and character of an Englishman: I am proud of my birth in a free and enlightened country; and the approbation of that country is the best and most honourable reward for my labours. Were I ambitious of any other Patron than the Public, I would inscribe this work to a Statesman, who, in a long, a stormy, and at length an unfortunate administration, had many political opponents, almost without a personal enemy: who has retained, in his fall from power, many faithful and disinterested friends; and who, under the pressure of severe infirmity, enjoys the lively vigour of his mind, and the felicity of his incomparable temper. LORD NORTH will permit me to express the feelings of friendship in the language of truth: but even truth and friendship should be silent, if he still dispensed the favours of the crown.

In a remote solitude, vanity may still whisper in my ear that my readers, perhaps, may enquire whether, in the conclusion of the present work, I am now taking an everlasting farewell. They shall hear all that I know myself, all that I could reveal to the most intimate friend. The motives of action or silence are now equally balanced; nor can I pronounce, in my most secret thoughts, on which side the scale will preponderate. I cannot dissemble that twelve ample octavos must have tried, and may have exhausted, the indulgence of the Public; that, in the repetition of similar attempts, a successful Author has much more to lose, than he can hope to gain; that I am now descending into the vale of years; and that the most respectable of my countrymen, the men whom I aspire to imitate, have resigned the pen of history about the same period of their lives. Yet I consider that the annals of ancient and modern times may afford many rich and interesting subjects; that I am still possessed of health and leisure; that by the practice of writing some skill and facility must be acquired; and that in the ardent pursuit of truth and knowledge I am not conscious of decay. To an active mind, indolence is more painful than labour; and the first months of my liberty will be occupied and amused in the excursions of curiosity and taste. By such temptations I have been sometimes seduced from the rigid duty even of a pleasing and voluntary task: but my time will now be my own; and in the use or abuse of independence I shall no longer fear my own reproaches or those of my friends. I am fairly entitled to a year of jubilee: next summer and the following winter will rapidly pass away; and experience only can determine whether I shall still prefer the freedom and variety of study to the design and composition of a regular work, which animates, while it confines, the daily application of the Author. Caprice and accident may influence my choice; but the dexterity of self-love will contrive to applaud either active industry or philosophic repose.

DOWNING STREET,
May 1, 1788.

P. S. — I shall embrace this opportunity of introducing two *verbal* remarks, which have not conveniently offered themselves to my notice. 1. As often as I use the definitions of *beyond* the Alps, the Rhine, the Danube, &c., I generally suppose myself at Rome, and afterwards at Constantinople: without observing whether this relative geography may agree with the local, but variable, situation of the reader or the historian. 2. In proper names of foreign, and especially of Oriental, origin, it should be always our aim to express in our English version a faithful copy of the original. But this rule, which is founded on a just regard to uniformity and truth, must often be relaxed; and the exceptions will be limited or enlarged by the custom of the language and the taste of the interpreter. Our alphabets may be often defective: a harsh sound, an uncouth spelling, might offend the ear or the eye of our countrymen; and some words, notoriously corrupt, are fixed, and, as it were, naturalised in the vulgar tongue. The prophet *Mohammed* can no longer be stripped of the famous, though improper, appellation of Mahomet: the well-known cities of Aleppo, Damascus and Cairo would almost be lost in the strange descriptions of *Haleb*, *Demashk* and *Al Cahira:* the titles and offices of the Ottoman empire are fashioned by the practice of three hundred years; and we are pleased to blend the three Chinese monosyllables *Con-fû-tzee* in the respectable name of Confucius, or even to adopt the Portuguese corruption of Mandarin. But I would vary the use of Zoroaster and *Zerdusht*, as I drew my information from Greece or Persia: since our connection with India, the genuine *Timour* is restored to the throne of Tamerlane: our most correct writers have retrenched the *Al*, the superfluous article, from the Koran; and we escape an ambiguous termination by adopting *Moslem* instead of Musulman, in the plural number. In these, and in a thousand examples, the shades of distinction are often minute; and I can feel, where I cannot explain, the motives of my choice.

INTRODUCTION

BY THE EDITOR

GIBBON is one of those few writers who hold as high a place in the history of literature as in the roll of great historians. He concerns us here as an historian; our business is to consider how far the view which he has presented of the decline and fall of the Roman Empire can be accepted as faithful to the facts, and in what respects it needs correction in the light of discoveries which have been made since he wrote. But the fact that his work, composed more than a hundred years ago, is still successful with the general circle of educated people, and has not gone the way of Hume and Robertson, whom we laud as "classics" and leave on the cold shelves, is due to the singularly happy union of the historian and the man of letters. Gibbon thus ranks with Thucydides and Tacitus, and is perhaps the clearest example that brilliance of style and accuracy of statement — in Livy's case conspicuously divorced — are perfectly compatible in an historian.

His position among men of letters depends both on the fact that he was an exponent of important ideas and on his style. The appreciation of his style devolves upon the history of literature; but it may be interesting to illustrate how much attention he paid to it, by alterations which he made in his text. The first volume was published, in quarto form, in 1776, and the second quarto edition of this volume, which appeared in 1782, exhibits a considerable number of variants. Having carefully collated the two editions throughout the first fourteen chapters, I have observed that, in most cases, the changes were made for the sake not of correcting misstatements of fact, but of improving the turn of a sentence, rearranging the dactyls and cretics, or securing greater accuracy of expression. Some instances may be interesting.

	First edition	*Second edition*
P. 2.	Instead of exposing his person and his legions to the arrows of the Parthians, he *satisfied himself with* the restitution of the standards and prisoners which *were* taken in the defeat of Crassus.	Instead of exposing his person and his legions to the arrows of the Parthians he *obtained, by an honourable treaty,* the restitution of the standards and prisoners which *had been* taken in the defeat of Crassus.
P. 12.	The peasant or mechanic, imbibed the useful prejudice . . . that, although the prowess of a private soldier, *might* escape the notice of fame, *it would be in his power* to confer glory or disgrace on the company, the legion, or even the army, to whose honours he was associated.	The peasant, or mechanic imbibed the useful prejudice . . . that although the prowess of a private soldier *must often* escape the notice of fame, his own behaviour might sometimes confer glory or disgrace on the company, the legion, or even the army, to whose honours he was associated.
P. 67.	The olive, in the western world, *was the companion as well as the symbol of peace.*	The olive, in the western world, *followed the progress of peace of which it was considered as the symbol.*
P. 75.	The *general* definition of a monarchy seems to be that of a state, &c.	The *obvious* definition of a monarchy seems to be that of a state, &c.
P. 77.	The present greatness of the Roman state, the corruption of manners, and the licence of the soldiers *added new weight* to the advocates of monarchy.	The present greatness of the Roman state, the corruption of manners, and the licence of the soldiers *supplied new arguments* to the advocates of monarchy.
P. 79.	*On the most important occasions,* peace and war were seriously debated in the senate.	*The most important resolutions of* peace and war were seriously debated in the senate.

	First edition	*Second edition*
P. 89.	However the latter [*i.e.* the name Cæsar], was diffused by adoption and female alliance, Nero was the last prince who could *claim so noble an extraction.*	However the latter was diffused by adoption and female alliance, Nero was the last prince who could *allege any hereditary claim to the honours of the Julian line.*
P. 93.	Which . . . had *just finished* the conquest of Judæa.	Which . . . had *recently achieved* the conquest of Judæa.
P. 136.	To ascend a throne *streaming* with the blood of so near a relation.	To ascend a throne *polluted* with the *recent* blood of so near a relation.
P. 141.	Severus, who *had sufficient greatness of mind to adopt* several useful institutions from a vanquished enemy.	Severus, who *afterwards displayed the greatness of his mind by adopting* several useful institutions from a vanquished enemy.

These are a few specimens of the numerous cases in which alterations have been made for the purpose of improving the language. Sometimes, in the new edition, statements are couched in a less positive form. For example: —

P. 11.	The legions themselves *consisted* of Roman citizens.	The legions themselves *were supposed to consist* of Roman citizens.
P. 99.	And he even condescended to give lessons of philosophy in a more public manner than *suited* the modesty of a sage or the dignity of an emperor.	And he even condescended to give lessons of philosophy in a more public manner than *was perhaps consistent with* the modesty of a sage or the dignity of an emperor.

There are also cases, where something is added which, without changing the general sense, renders a statement fuller, more picturesque, or more vivid. Thus: —

P. 31.	A sandy desert skirted along the doubtful confine of Syria, from the Euphrates to the Red Sea.	A sandy desert, *alike destitute of wood and water*, skirts along the doubtful confine of Syria, from the Euphrates to the Red Sea.

	First edition	*Second edition*
P. 61.	The spirit of improvement had passed the Alps and been felt even in the woods of Britain.	The spirit of improvement had passed the Alps and been felt even in the woods of Britain, *which were gradually leared away to open a free space for convenient and elegant habitations.*
P. 72.	The sciences of physic and astronomy were cultivated *with some degree of reputation;* but if we except the inimitable Lucian, *an* age of indolence passed away without *producing* a single writer of genius, *who deserved the attention of posterity.*	The sciences of physic and astronomy were *successfully* cultivated *by the Greeks; the observations of Ptolemy and the writings of Galen are studied by those who have improved their discoveries and corrected their errors;* but if we except the inimitable Lucian, *this* age of indolence passed away without *having produced* a single writer of *original* genius, *or who excelled in the arts of elegant composition.*

It may be noticed in this connection that at a later period Gibbon set to work to revise the second edition, but did not get further than p. 32 of the first volume.[1] His own copy with autograph marginal notes was exhibited last year, on the occasion of the Gibbon Centenary, by the Royal Historical Society, and is to be seen in the British Museum. The corrections and annotations are as follows:—

(P. 1 = 1 of this edition.) "To describe the prosperous condition of their empire." Read *times* for *empire*.

"And afterwards from the death of Marcus Antoninus." The following note is entered: "Should I not have given the *history* of that fortunate period which was interposed between two iron ages? Should I not have deduced the decline of the Empire from the Civil Wars that ensued after the Fall of Nero, or even from the tyranny which succeeded the reign of

[1] It is stated that there are also unimportant annotations in vols. iv. and vi.

Augustus? Alas! I should: but of what avail is this tardy knowledge? Where error is irreparable, repentance is useless."

(P. 2=1.) "To deduce the most important circumstances of its decline and fall: a revolution which will ever be remembered, and is still felt by the nations of the earth." These words are erased and the following are substituted: "To prosecute the decline and fall of the empire of Rome: of whose language, religion and laws the impression will be long preserved in our own and the neighbouring countries of Europe." To which an observation is appended: "N.B. Mr. Hume told me that, in correcting his history, he always laboured to reduce superlatives, and soften positives. Have Asia and Africa, from Japan to Morocco, any feeling or memory of the Roman Empire?"

(P. 2=2.) On the words "rapid succession of triumphs," note: "EXCURSION I. *on the succession of Roman triumphs*."

(P. 3=3.) On "bulwarks and boundaries," note: "Incertum metû an per invidiam (Tacit. Annal. i. 11). Why must rational advice be imputed to a base or foolish môtive? To what cause, error, malevolence, or flattery shall I ascribe the unworthy alternative? Was the historian dazzled by Trajan's conquests?"

(P. 6=6.) "On the immortality and transmigration of soul" (compare footnote). Note: "Julian assigns this Theological cause, of whose power he himself might be conscious (*Cæsares*, p. 327). Yet I am not assured that the religion of Zamolxis subsisted in the time of Trajan; or that his Dacians were the same people with the Getae of Herodotus. The transmigration of the soul has been believed by many nations, warlike as the Celts, or pusillanimous like the Hindoos. When speculative opinion is kindled into practical enthusiasm, its operation will be determined by the previous character of the man or the nation."

(P. 7=7.) "On their destroyers than on their benefactors." Note: "The first place in the temple of fame is due and is assigned to the successful heroes who had struggled with adversity; who, after signalising their valour in the deliverance of their country, have displayed their wisdom and virtue in foundation or government of a flourishing state. Such men as Moses, Cyrus, Alfred, Gustavus Vasa, Henry IV. of France, &c."

"The thirst of military glory will ever be the vice of the most exalted [characters . . . but he] lamented with a sigh that his advanced age, &c." All included within the brackets is erased, and the following substituted: "the most exalted minds. Late generations and far distant climates may impute their calamities to the immortal author of the Iliad. The spirit of Alexander was inflamed by the praises of Achilles: and succeeding Heroes have been ambitious to tread in the footsteps of Alexander. Like him the Emperor Trajan aspired to the conquest of the East; but the Roman lamented with a sigh," &c.

(P. 11 = 12.) "A just preference was given to the climates of the north over those of the south." Note: "The distinction of North and South is real and intelligible; and our pursuit is terminated on either side by the poles of the Earth. But the difference of East and West is arbitrary and shifts round the globe. As the men of the North, not of the West, the legions of Gaul and Germany were superior to the *South*-Eastern natives of Asia and Egypt. It is the triumph of cold over heat; which may, however, and has been surmounted by moral causes."

(P. 15 = 15.) "A correspondent number of tribunes and centurions." Note: "The composition of the Roman officers was very faulty. 1. It was late before a Tribune was fixed to each cohort. Six tribunes were chosen from the entire legion, which two of them commanded by turns (Polyb. l. vi. p. 526, edit. Schweighaeuser), for the space of two months. 2. One long subordination from the Colonel to the Corporal was unknown. I cannot discover any intermediate ranks between the Tribune and the Centurion, the Centurion and the manipularis or private leginary [*sic*]. 3. As the tribunes were often without experience, the centurions were often without education, mere soldiers of fortune who had risen from the ranks (eo immitior quia toleraverat, Tacit. Annal. i. 20). A body equal to eight or nine of our battalions might be commanded by half a dozen young gentlemen and fifty or sixty old sergeants. Like the legions, our great ships of war may seem ill provided with officers: but in both cases the deficiency is corrected by strong principles of discipline and rigour."

(P. 17, footnote 53 = 18, footnote 55.) "As in the instance of Horace and Agricola." These words are erased. Note: "quod mihi pareret legio Romana Tribuno (Horat. Serm. l. i. vi. 45), a worthy commander of three and twenty from the school of Athens! Augustus was indulgent to Roman birth, liberis Senatorum . . . militiam. auspicantes non tribunatum modo legionum sed et praefecturas alarum dedit (Sueton. c. 38)."

(P. 32, footnote 86 = 33, footnote 94.) "A league and a half above the surface of the sea." Note: "More correctly, according to Mr. Bouguer, 2500 toises (Buffon, Supplement, tom. v. p. 304). The height of Mont Blanc is now fixed to 2416 toises (Saussure, Voyage dans les Alpes, tom. i. p. 495): but the lowest ground from whence it can be seen is itself greatly elevated above the level of the sea. He who sails by the isle of Teneriff, contemplates the entire Pike, from the foot to the summit."

But Gibbon has his place in literature not only as the stylist, who never lays aside his toga when he takes up his pen, but as the expounder of a large and striking idea in a sphere of intense interest to mankind, and as a powerful representative of certain tendencies of his age. The guiding idea or "moral" of his history is briefly stated in his epigram: "I have described the triumph of barbarism and religion." In other words, the historical development of human societies, since the second century after Christ, was a retrogression (according to ordinary views of "progress"), for which Christianity was mainly to blame. This conclusion of Gibbon tended in the same direction as the theories of Rousseau; only, while Rousseau dated the decline from the day when men left Arcadia, Gibbon's era was the death of Marcus Aurelius.

We are thus taken into a region of speculation where every traveller must make his own chart. But to attempt to deny a general truth in Gibbon's point of view is vain; and it is feeble to deprecate his sneer. We may spare more sympathy than he for the warriors and the churchmen; but all that has since been added to his knowledge of facts has neither reversed nor blunted the point of the "Decline and Fall." Optimism of temperament may shut the eyes; faith, wedded to some "one increasing purpose" which it shrinks from grasping, may divert from the path of facts. But for an inquirer not blinded by religious prepossessions, or misled by comfortable sophistries, Gibbon really expounded one of the chief data with which the philosophy of history has to reckon. How are we to define progress? how recognise retrogression? What is the end in relation to which such words have their meaning, and is there a law which will explain "the triumph of barbarism and religion" as a necessary moment in a reasonable process towards that end, whatever it may be? Answers have been given since Gibbon's day, engaging to the intellect, but always making some demand on the faith — answers for which he would have the same smile as for Leo's Dogmatic Epistle. There is certainly some reason for thinking these questions insoluble. We may say at least that the meaning of the philosophy of history is misapprehended until it is recognised that its function is not to solve problems but to transform them.

But, though the moral of Gibbon's work has not lost its meaning yet, it is otherwise with the particular treatment of Christian theology and Christian institutions. Our point of view has altered, and, if Gibbon were writing now, the tone of his "candid and rational inquiry" would certainly be different. His manner would not be that of sometimes open, sometimes transparently veiled, dislike; he would rather assume an attitude of detachment. He would be affected by that merely historical point of view, which is a note of the present century and its larger tolerances; and more than half disarmed by that wide diffusion of unobtrusive scepticism among educated people, which seems to render offensive warfare superfluous. The man of letters admires the fine edge of subtle sarcasm, wielded by Gibbon with such skill and effect; while the historian is interested in an historical standpoint of the last century. Neither the historian nor the man of letters will any longer subscribe, without a thousand reserves, to the theological chapters of the "Decline and Fall," and no discreet inquirer would go there for his ecclesiastical history. Yet we need not hide the fact that Gibbon's success has in a large measure been due to his scorn for the Church; which, most emphatically expressed in the theological chapters, has, as one might say, spiced his book. The attack of a man, equipped with erudition, and of perfectly sober judgment, on cherished beliefs and revered institutions, must always excite the interest, by irritating the passions, of men. Gibbon's classical moderation of judgment, his temperate mood, was responsible, as well as foreign education and the influence of French thought, for his attitude to Christianity and to Mahometanism. He hated excess, and the immoderation of the multitude. He could suffer the tolerant piety of a learned abbé or "the fat slumbers of the Church"; but with the religious faith of a fanatical populace or the ardour of its demagogues his reason was unable to sympathise. In the spirit of Cicero or Tacitus he despised the superstitions of the vulgar, and regarded the unmeasured enthusiasm of the early Christians as many sober Churchmen regard the fanaticism of Islam. He dealt out the same measure to the opposite enthusiasm of Julian the Apostate.[1] His work was all the more effective, because he was never dogmatic himself. His irony should not be construed as insincerity, but rather as showing that he was profoundly — one might say, constitutionally — convinced of the truth of that sceptical conclusion which has been, in a different spirit, formulated precisely by the Bishop of Oxford; "there is no room for sweeping denunciations or trenchant criticisms in the dealings of a world whose falsehoods and veracities are separated by so very thin a barrier."

Thus Gibbon's attitude to religion, while it was conditioned by the intellectual atmosphere of Europe in that age, was also the expression of the man. When Dean Milman spoke of his "bold and disingenuous attack on Christianity,"[2] he made one of those futile charges which it would be impossible to prove and impossible to disprove; such imputations as are characteristic of theologians in the heat of controversy and may be condoned to politicians in the heat of electioneering, but in an historical critic are merely an impertinence.

It has sometimes been remarked that those histories are most readable which are written to prove a thesis. The indictment of the Empire by Tacitus, the defence of Cæsarianism by Mommsen, Grote's vindication of democracy, Droysen's advocacy of monarchy, might be cited as examples. All these writers intended to present the facts as they took place, but all wrote with prepossessions and opinions, in the light of which they interpreted the events of history. Arnold deliberately advocated such partiality on the ground that "the past is reflected to us by the present and the partyman feels the present most." Another Oxford Regius Professor remarked that "without some infusion of spite it seems as if history could not be written." On the other side stands the

[1] The influence of Gibbon's picture of Julian can be discerned in Ibsen's "Emperor and Galilæan."

[2] In a footnote to the Autobiography.

formula of Ranke as to the true task of the historian: "Ich will bloss sagen wie es eigentlich gewesen ist." The Greek History of Bishop Thirlwall, the English Constitutional History of Bishop Stubbs himself, were written in this spirit. But the most striking instances perhaps, because they tread with such light feet on the treacherous ashes of more recent history, are Ranke and Bishop Creighton. Thucydides is the most ancient example of this historical reserve. It cannot be said that Gibbon sat down to write with any ulterior purpose, but, as we have seen, he allowed his temperament to colour his history, and used it to prove a congenial thesis. But, while he put things in the light demanded by this thesis, he related his facts accurately. If we take into account the vast range of his work, his accuracy is amazing. He laboured under some disadvantages, which are set forth in his own Memoirs. He had not enjoyed that school and university training in the languages and literatures of Greece and Rome which is probably the best preparation for historical research. His knowledge of Greek was imperfect; he was very far from having the "scrupulous ear of the well-flogged critic." He has committed errors of translation, and was capable of writing "Gregory of Nazianzen." But such slips are singularly few. Nor is he accustomed to take lightly quotations at second hand; like that famous passage of Eligius of Noyon — held up by Arnold as a warning — which Robertson and Hallam successively copied from Mosheim, where it had appeared in a garbled form, to prove exactly the opposite of its true meaning.

From one curious inaccuracy, which neither critics nor editors seem to have observed, he must I think be acquitted. In his account of the disturbances in Africa and Egypt in the reign of Diocletian, we meet the following passage (vol. ii. chap. xiii. p. 160): —

> "Julian had assumed the purple at Carthage. Achilleus at Alexandria, and even the Blemmyes, renewed, or

> rather continued their incursions into the Upper Egypt."

Achilleus arose at this time (295–6 A.D.) as a tyrant at Alexandria; but that he made either at this date or at any previous date an incursion into the Upper Egypt, there is not a trace of evidence in our authorities. I am convinced however that this error was not originally due to the author, but merely a treacherous misprint, which was overlooked by him in correcting the proof sheets, and has also escaped the notice of his editors. By a slight change in punctuation we obtain a perfectly correct statement of the situation:—

> "Julian had assumed the purple at Carthage, Achilleus at Alexandria; and even the Blemmyes renewed, or rather continued, their incursions into the Upper Egypt."

I have no doubts that this was the sentence originally meant and probably written by Gibbon, and have felt no scruple in extirpating the inveterate error from the text.[4]

Gibbon's diligent accuracy in the use of his materials cannot be over-praised, and it will not be diminished by giving the due credit to his French predecessor Tillemont. The *Histoire des Empereurs* and the *Mémoires ecclésiastiques*, laborious and exhaustive collections of material, were addressed to the special student and not to the general reader, but scholars may still consult them with profit. It is interesting to find Mommsen in his later years retracting one of his earlier judgments and reverting to a conclusion of

[4] In some other cases I have corrected the text in this and the following volume. (1) vol. i. p. 69, n. 109; Sumelpur for Jumelpur, see Appendix 9. (2) vol. ii. p. 29, l. 8 from top; the reading of the received text "public" is surely a printer's error, which escaped detection, for "republic," which I have ventured to restore. (3) vol. ii. p. 55, l. 6 from foot, I have assumed an instance of "lipography." (4) vol. ii. n. 35, "Lycius" had been already corrected (see Smith's ed.) to "Lydius." Probably Gibbon had his Zosimus open before him when he wrote this note, and his pen traced Lycius

Tillemont. In his recent edition[5] of the Laterculus of Polemius Silvius, he writes thus: —

> "L'auteur de la Notice — peritissimi Tillemontii verba sunt (hist. 5, 699) — vivoit en Occident et ne savoit pas trop l'état où estoit l'Orient; *ei iuvenis contradixi hodie subscribo.*"

It is one of Gibbon's merits that he made full use of Tillemont, "whose inimitable accuracy almost assumes the character of genius," as far as Tillemont guided him, up to the reign of Anastasius I.; and it is only just to the mighty work of the Frenchman to impute to him a large share in the accuracy which the Englishman achieved. From the historical, though not from the literary, point of view, Gibbon, deserted by Tillemont, distinctly declines, though he is well sustained through the wars of Justinian by the clear narrative of Procopius.

Recognising that Gibbon was accurate, we do not acknowledge by implication that he was always right; for accuracy is relative to opportunities. The discovery of new materials, the researches of numerous scholars, in the course of a hundred years, have not only added to our knowledge of facts, but have modified and upset conclusions which Gibbon with his materials was justified in drawing. Compare a chapter or two of Mr. Hodgkin's *Italy and her Invaders* with the corresponding episode in Gibbon, and many minor points will appear in which correction has been needful. If Gibbon were alive and writing now, his history would be very different. Affected by the intellectual experiences of the past century he could not adopt quite the same historical attitude; and we should consequently lose the colouring of his brilliant attack on Chris-

because Lycia happened to occur in the very next line of his authority. I have followed Sir William Smith's precedent in dealing freely with the punctuation, and in modernising the spelling of a few words.

[5] In the Chronica Minora (M.G.H.), vol. i. 512 *sqq.* See vol. ii. p. 360.

tianity. Again, he would have found it an absolute necessity to learn what he insolently called that "barbarous idiom," the German language; and this might have affected his style as it would certainly have affected his matter. We dare not deplore Gibbon's limitations, for they were the conditions of his great achievement.

Not the least important aspect of the Decline and Fall is its lesson in the unity of history, the favourite theme of Mr. Freeman. The title displays the cardinal fact that the Empire founded by Augustus fell in 1461; that all the changes which transformed the Europe of Marcus Aurelius into the Europe of Erasmus had not abolished the name and memory of the Empire. And whatever names of contempt — in harmony with his thesis — Gibbon might apply to the institution in the period of its later decline, such as the "Lower Empire," or "Greek Empire," his title rectified any false impressions that such language might cause. On the continuity of the Roman Empire depended the unity of his work. By the emphasis laid on this fact he did the same kind of service to the study of history in England, that Mr. Bryce has done in his *Holy Roman Empire* by tracing the thread which connects the Europe of Francis the Second with the Europe of Charles the Great.

Gibbon read widely, and had a large general knowledge of history, which supplied him with many happy illustrations. It is worth pointing out that the gap in his knowledge of ancient history was the period of the Diadochi and Epigoni. If he had been familiar with that period, he would not have said that Diocletian was the first to give to the world the example of a resignation of sovereignty. He would have referred to the conspicuous case of Ptolemy Soter; Mr. Freeman would have added Lydiadas, the tyrant of Megalopolis. Of the earlier example of Asarhaddon Gibbon could not have known.

To pass from scope and spirit to method, Gibbon's historical sense kept him constantly right in dealing with his sources, but he can hardly be said to have treated them methodically. The growth of German erudition is one of the leading features of the intellectual history of the nineteenth century; and one of its most important contributions to historical method lies in the investigation of sources. German scholars have indeed pressed this "Quellenkunde" further than it can safely be pressed. A philologist, writing his doctoral dissertation, will bring plausible reasons to prove where exactly Diodorus ceased to "write out" Ephorus, whose work we do not possess, and began to write out somebody else, whose work is also lost to us. But, though the method lends itself to the multiplication of vain subtleties, it is absolutely indispensable for scientific historiography. It is in fact part of the science of evidence. The distinction of primary and derivative authorities might be used as a test. The untrained historian fails to recognise that nothing is added to the value of a statement of Widukind by its repetition by Thietmar or Ekkehard, and that a record in the Continuation of Theophanes gains no further credibility from the fact that it likewise occurs in Cedrenus, Zonaras or Glycas.

While evidence is more systematically arranged, greater care is bestowed on sifting and probing what our authorities say, and in distinguishing contemporary from later witnesses. Not a few important results have been derived from such methods; they enable us to trace the growth of stories. The evidence against Faustina shrinks into nothing; the existence of Pope Joan is exploded. It is irrelevant to condemn a statement of Zonaras as made by a "modern Greek." The question is, where did he get it? [a]

The difficult questions connected with the authorship and compilation of the Historia Augusta have produced a chestful of German pamphlets, but they did not trouble Gibbon.

[a] Gibbon had a notion of this, but did not apply it methodically. See in vol. ii. p. 227, note 59: "but those modern Greeks had the opportunity of consulting many writers which have since been lost." And see, in general, his Preface to the fourth volume of the quarto ed.

The relationships of the later Greek chronicles and histories are more difficult and intricate even than the questions raised by the Historia Augusta, but he did not even formulate a prudent interrogation. Ferdinand Hirsch, twenty years ago, cleared new roads through this forest, in which George the Monk and the Logothete who continued him, Leo Grammaticus and Simeon Magister, John Scylitzes, George Cedrenus and Zonaras, lived in promiscuous obscurity. Büttner-Wobst on one side, C. de Boor on the other, have been working effectually on the same lines, clearing up the haze which surrounds George the Monk — the time has gone by for calling him George Hamartolus. Another formidable problem, that of John Malalas — with his namesake John of Antioch, so hard to catch, — having been grappled with by Jeep, Sotiriadês and others, is now being more effectively treated by Patzig.

Criticism, too, has rejected some sources from which Gibbon drew without suspicion. In the interest of literature we may perhaps be glad that like Ockley he used with confidence the now discredited Al Wakidi. Before such maintained perfection of manner, to choose is hard; but the chapter on the origin of Mahometanism and its first triumphs against the Empire would alone be enough to win perpetual literary fame. Without Al Wakidi's romance they would not have been written; and the historian, compelled to regard Gibbon's description as he would a Life of Charles the Great based on the monk of St. Gall, must refer the inquirer after facts to Sprenger's Life of Mahomet and Weil's History of the Caliphs.[7]

In connection with the use of materials, reference may be

[7] In Mahometan history in general, it may be added, not only has advance been made by access to new literary oriental documents, but its foundations have been more surely grounded by numismatic researches, especially those of Mr. Stanley Lane-Poole. This scholar's recently published handbook containing tables and lists of the "Mohammadan" Dynasties is a guerdon for which students of history must be most deeply grateful. The special histories

made to a mode of proceeding which Gibbon has sometimes adopted and which modern method condemns. It is not legitimate to blend the evidence of two different periods in order to paint a complete picture of an institution. Great caution, for example, is needed in using the Greek epics, of which the earliest and latest parts differ by a long interval, for the purpose of portraying a so-called Homeric or heroic age. A notice of Fredegarius will not be necessarily applicable to the age of the sons and grandsons of Chlodwig, and a custom which was familiar to Gregory or Venantius may have become obsolete before the days of the last Merwings. It is instructive to compare Gibbon's description of the social and political institutions of our Teutonic forefathers with that of Bishop Stubbs. Gibbon blends together with dexterity the evidence of Cæsar and Tacitus, between whom a century had elapsed, and composes a single picture; whereas Bishop Stubbs keeps the statements of the two Romans carefully apart, and by comparing them is able to show that in certain respects the Germans had developed in the interval. Gibbon's account of the military establishment of the Empire, in the first chapter of his work, is open to a like objection. He has blended, without due criticism, the evidence of Vegetius with that of earlier writers.[8]

In the study of sources, then, our advance has been great, while the labours of an historian have become more arduous. It leads us to another advance of the highest importance. To use historical documents with confidence, an assurance that the words of the writer have been correctly transmitted is manifestly indispensable. It generally happens that our

of Mahometan Sicily and Spain have been worked out by Amari and Dozy. For the Mongols we have the overwhelming results of Sir Henry Howorth's learning and devotion to his "vasty" subject.

[8] It may be said for Gibbon, however, that even Mommsen, in his volume on the Provinces, has adopted this practice of blending evidence of different dates. For the historical artist, it is very tempting, when the evidence for any particular period is scanty; but in the eyes of the scientific historian it is indefensible.

texts have come down in several MSS., of different ages, and there are often various discrepancies. We have then to determine the relations of the MSS. to each other and their comparative values. To the pure philologist this is part of the alphabet of his profession; but the pure historian takes time to realise it, and it was not realised in the age of Gibbon as it is to-day. Nothing forces upon the historian the necessity of having a sound text so impressively as the process of comparing different documents in order to determine whether one was dependent on another, — the process of investigating sources. In this respect we have now to be thankful for many blessings denied to Gibbon and — so recent is our progress — denied to Milman and Finlay. We have Mommsen's editions of Jordanes and the Variæ of Cassiodorius, his Chronica Minora (still incomplete), including, for instance, Idatius, the Prospers, Count Marcellinus; we have Peter's Historia Augusta, Gardthausen's Ammianus, Luetjohann's Sidonius Apollinaris; Duchesne's *Liber Pontificalis;* and a large number of critical texts of ecclesiastical writers might be mentioned.[a] The Greek historians have been less fortunate. The Bonn edition of the "Byzantine Writers," issued under the auspices of Niebuhr and Bekker in the early part of this century, was the most lamentably feeble production ever given to the world by German scholars of great reputation. It marked no advance on the older folio edition, except that it was cheaper, and that one or two new documents were included. But there is now a reasonable prospect that we shall by degrees have a complete series of trustworthy texts. De Boor showed the way by his splendid edition of Theophanes and his smaller texts of Theophylactus Simocatta and the Patriarch Nicephorus. Mendelssohn's Zosimus, and Reifferscheid's Anna Comnena stand beside them. Haury promises a Procopius, and we are expecting from Seger a long-desired John Scylitzes, the greater part of whose text, though

[a] Especially the Corpus Ecclesiasticorum Latinorum.

existing in a MS. at Paris, has never been printed and can only be inferred by a comparison of the Latin translation of Gabius with the chronicle of Cedrenus, who copied him with faithful servility.

The legends of the Saints, though properly outside the domain of the historian proper, often supply him with valuable help. For "Culturgeschichte" they are a direct source. Finlay observed that the Acta Sanctorum contain an unexplored mine for the social life of the Eastern Empire. But before they can be confidently dealt with, trained criticism must do its will on the texts; the relations between the various versions of each legend must be defined and the tradition in each case made clear. The task is huge; the libraries of Europe and Hither Asia are full of these holy tales. But Usener has made a good beginning and Krumbacher has rendered the immense service of pointing out precisely what the problems are.[10]

Besides improved methods of dealing with the old material, much new material of various kinds has been discovered, since the work of Gibbon. To take one department, our coins have increased in number. It seems a pity that he who worked at his Spanheim with such diligence was not able to make use of Eckhel's great work on Imperial coinage which began to appear in 1792 and was completed in 1798. Since then we have had Cohen, and the special works of Saulcy

[10] Usener, Der heilige Theodosios, 1890. Krumbacher, Studien zu den Legenden des heiligen Theodosios, 1892. It is worth while to state briefly what the chief problem is. The legends of the saints were collected, re-handled, cleansed of casual heresy, and put into literary form in the tenth century (towards its close according to Vasilievski) by Symeon Metaphrastes. Most of our MSS. are derived from the edition of Symeon; but there are also extant, some, comparatively few, containing the original pre-Symeonic versions, which formed the chief literary recreation of ordinary men and women before the tenth century. The problem is to collect the materials for a critical edition of as many legends as have been preserved in their original form. When that is done, we shall have the data for fully appreciating the methods of Symeon. As for the text Krumbacher points out that what we want is a thoroughgoing study of the *Grammar of the MSS.*

and Sabatier. M. Schlumberger's splendid study of Byzantine sigillography must be mentioned in the same connection.[11]

The constitution and history of the Principate, and the provincial government of the early Emperors, have been placed on an entirely new basis by Mommsen and his school.[12] The Römisches Staatsrecht is a fabric for whose rearing was needed not only improved scholarship but an extensive collection of epigraphic material. The Corpus of Latin Inscriptions is the keystone of the work.

Hence Gibbon's first chapters are somewhat "out of date." But on the other hand his admirable description of the change from the Principate to absolute Monarchy, and the system of Diocletian and Constantine, is still most valuable. Here inscriptions are less illustrative, and he disposed of much the same material as we, especially the Codex Theodosianus. New light is badly wanted, and has not been to any extent forthcoming, on the respective contributions of Diocletian and Constantine to the organisation of the new monarchy. As to the arrangement of the provinces we have indeed a precious document in the Verona List (published by Mommsen), which, dating from 297 A.D., shows Diocletian's reorganisation. The modifications which were made between this year and the beginning of the fifth century when the Notitia Dignitatum was drawn up, can be largely determined not only by lists in Rufus and Ammianus, but, as far as the Eastern provinces are concerned, by the Laterculus of Polemius Silvius. Thus, partly by critical method applied to Polemius, partly by the discovery of a new document, we are enabled to rectify the list of Gibbon, who adopted the

[11] M. Schlumberger followed up this work by an admirable monograph on Nicephorus Phocas, luxuriously illustrated; and we are looking forward to the appearance of a companion work on Basil II.

[12] The first volume of Mr. Pelham's history of the Empire, which is expected shortly, will show, when compared with Merivale, how completely our knowledge of Roman institutions has been transformed within a very recent period.

simple plan of ascribing to Diocletian and Constantine the detailed organisation of the Notitia. Otherwise our knowledge of the changes of Diocletian has not been greatly augmented; but our clearer conception of the Principate and its steady development towards pure monarchy has reflected light on Diocletian's system; and the tendencies of the third century, though still obscure at many points, have been made more distinct. The year of the Gordians is still as great a puzzle as ever; but the dates of Alexandrine coins with the tribunician years give us here, as elsewhere, limits of which Gibbon was ignorant. While speaking of the third century, I may add that Calpurnius Siculus, whom Gibbon claimed as a contemporary of Carinus, has been restored by modern criticism to the reign of Nero, and this error has vitiated some of Gibbon's pages.

The constitutional history of the Empire from Diocletian forward has still to be written systematically. Some noteworthy contributions to this subject have been made by Russian scholars.

Gibbon's forty-fourth chapter is still not only famous, but admired by jurists as a brief and brilliant exposition of the principles of Roman law. To say that it is worthy of the subject is the best tribute that can be paid to it. A series of foreign scholars of acute legal ability has elaborated the study of the science in the present century; I need only refer to such names as Savigny and Jhering. A critical edition of the Corpus juris Romani by Mommsen himself has been one of the chief contributions. The manuscript of Gaius is the new discovery to be recorded; and we can imagine with what interest Gibbon, were he restored to earth, would compare in Gneist's parallel columns the Institutions with the elder treatise.

But whoever takes up Gibbon's theme now will not be content with an exposition of the Justinianean Law. He must go on to its later development in the subsequent centuries, in the company of Zachariä von Lingenthal and Heimbach. Such a study has been made possible and comparatively easy by the magnificent works of Zachariä, among whose achievements I may single out his restoration of the Ecloga, which used to be ascribed to Leo VI., to its true author Leo III.; a discovery which illuminated in a most welcome manner the Isaurian reformation. It is interesting to observe that the last work which engaged him even on his death-bed was an attempt to prove exactly the same thing for the military treatise known as the Tactics of Leo VI. Here too Zachariä thinks that Leo was the Isaurian, while the received view is that he was the "Philosopher."

Having illustrated by examples the advantages open to an historian of the present day, which were not open to Gibbon, for dealing with Gibbon's theme, — improved and refined methods, a closer union of philology with history, and ampler material, — we may go on to consider a general defect in his treatment of the Later Empire, and here too exhibit, by a few instances, progress made in particular departments.

Gibbon ended the first half of his work with the so-called fall of the Western Empire in 476 A.D. — a date which has been fixed out of regard for Italy and Rome, and should strictly be 480 A.D. in consideration of Julius Nepos. Thus the same space is devoted to the first three hundred years which is allowed to the remaining nine hundred and eighty. Nor does the inequality end here. More than a quarter of the second half of the work deals with the first two of these ten centuries. The mere statement of the fact shows that the history of the Empire from Heraclius to the last Grand Comnenus of Trebizond is merely a sketch with certain episodes more fully treated. The personal history and domestic policy of all the Emperors, from the son of Heraclius to Isaac Angelus, are compressed into one chapter. This mode of dealing with the subject is in harmony with the author's contemptuous attitude to the "Byzantine" or "Lower" Empire.

But Gibbon's account of the internal history of the Empire after Heraclius is not only superficial: it gives an entirely false impression of the facts. If the materials had been then as well sifted and studied as they are even to-day, he could not have failed to see that beneath the intrigues and crimes of the Palace there were deeper causes at work, and beyond the revolutions of the Capital City wider issues implied. The cause for which the Iconoclasts contended involved far more than an ecclesiastical rule or usage: it meant, and they realised, the regeneration of the Empire. Or, to take another instance: the key to the history of the tenth and eleventh centuries is the struggle between the Imperial throne and the great landed interest of Asia Minor;[13] the accession of Alexius Comnenus marked the final victory of the latter. Nor had Gibbon any conception of the great ability of most of the Emperors from Leo the Isaurian to Basil II., or, we might say, to Constantine the conqueror of Armenia. The designation of the story of the later Empire as a "uniform tale of weakness and misery"[14] is one of the most untrue, and most effective, judgments ever uttered by a thoughtful historian. Before the outrage of 1204, the Empire was the bulwark of the West.[15]

Against Gibbon's point of view there has been a gradual reaction which may be said to have culminated within the last ten years. It was begun by Finlay, whose unprosperous speculations in Greece after the Revolution prompted him to seek for the causes of the insecurity of investments in land, and, leading him back to the year 146 B.C., involved him in

[13] This has been best pointed out by C. Neumann.

[14] Chap. xlviii. *ad init.*, where a full statement of his view of the later Empire will be found.

[15] I need not repeat here what I have said elsewhere, and what many others have said (recently Mr. Frederic Harrison in two essays in his volume entitled *The Meaning of History*), as to the various services of the Empire to Europe. They are beginning to be generally recognised and they have been brought out in Mr. C. W. Oman's brief and skilful sketch of the "Byzantine Empire" (1892).

a history of the "Byzantine Empire" which embedded a history of Greece.[16] The great value of Finlay's work lies not only in its impartiality and in his trained discernment of the commercial and financial facts underlying the superficial history of the chronicles, but in its full and trustworthy narration of the events. By the time that Mr. Tozer's edition appeared in 1876, it was being recognised that Gibbon's word on the later Empire was not the last. Meanwhile Hertzberg was going over the ground in Germany, and Gfrörer, whose ecclesiastical studies had taken him into those regions, had written a good deal of various value. Hirsch's *Byzantinische Studien* had just appeared, and Rambaud's *l'Empire grec au xme siècle*. M. Sathas was bringing out his Bibliotheca Græca medii aevi — including two volumes of Psellus — and was beginning his Documents inédits. Professor Lambros was working at his Athens in the Twelfth Century and preparing his editio princeps of the great Archbishop Akominatos. Hopf had collected a mass of new materials from the archives of southern cities. In England, Freeman was pointing out the true position of New Rome and her Emperors in the history of Europe.

These tendencies have increased in volume and velocity within the last twenty years. They may be said to have reached their culminating point in the publication of Professor Krumbacher's History of Byzantine Literature.[17] The importance of this work, of vast scope and extraordinary accuracy, can only be fully understood by the specialist. It has already promoted and facilitated the progress of the study in an incalculable measure; and it was soon followed by the inauguration of a journal, entirely devoted to works on "Byzantine" subjects, by the same scholar. The *Byzan-*

[16] Since then a Greek scholar, K. Paparrigopulos, has covered the whole history of Greece from the earliest times to the present century, in his *Ἱστορία τοῦ Ἑλληνικοῦ ἔθνους*. The same gigantic task, but in a more popular form, has been undertaken and begun by Professor Lambros, but is not yet finished.

[17] Geschichte der byzantinischen Litteratur (565–1453), 1891.

tinische Zeitschrift would have been impossible twenty-five years ago, and nothing shows more surely the turn of the tide. Professor Krumbacher's work seems likely to form as important an epoch as that of Ducange.

Meanwhile in a part of Europe which deems itself to have received the torch from the Emperors as it has received their torch from the Patriarchs, and which has always had a special regard for the city of Constantine, some excellent work was being done. In Russia, Muralt edited the chronicle of George the monk and his Continuers, and compiled Byzantine Fasti. The Journal of the Ministry of Public Instruction is the storehouse of a long series of most valuable articles dealing, from various sides, with the history of the later Empire, by those indefatigable workers Uspenski and Vasilievski. At length, in 1894, Krumbacher's lead has been followed, and the *Visantiski Vremennik*, a Russian counterpart of the *Byzantinische Zeitschrift*, has been started under the joint editorship of Vasilievski and Regel, and is clearly destined, with the help of Veselovski, Kondakov, Bieliaiev and the rest of a goodly fellowship, to make its mark.

After this general sketch of the new prospects of later Imperial history, it will be useful to show by some examples what sort of progress is being made, and what kind of work has to be done. I will first take some special points of interest connected with Justinian. My second example shall be the topography of Constantinople; and my third the large field of literature composed in colloquial Greek. Lastly, the capital defect of the second half of Gibbon's work, his inadequate treatment, or rather his neglect, of the Slavs, will serve to illustrate our historical progress.

New light has been cast, from more than one side, on the reign of Justinian where there are so many uncertain and interesting places. The first step that methodical history had to take was a thoroughgoing criticism of Procopius, and this was more than half done by Dahn in his elaborate monograph. The double problem of the "Secret History" has stimulated the curiosity of the historian and the critic. Was Procopius the author? and in any case, are the statements credible? Gibbon has inserted in his notes the worst bits of the scandals which far outdid the convivium quinquaginta meretricum described by Burchard, or the feast of Sophonius Tigellinus; and he did not hesitate to believe them. Their credibility is now generally questioned, but the historian of Cæsarea is a much more interesting figure if it can be shown that he was the author. From a careful comparison of the Secret History with the works of Procopian authorship, in point of style, Dahn concluded that Procopius wrote it. Ranke argued against this view and maintained that it was the work of a malcontent who had obtained possession of a private diary of Procopius, on which framework he constructed the scandalous chronicle, imitating successfully the Procopian style.[18]

The question has been placed on a new footing by Haury;[19] and it is very interesting to find that the solution depends on the right determination of certain dates. The result is briefly as follows: —

Procopius was a malcontent who hated Justinian and all his works. He set himself the task of writing a history of his time, which, as the secretary of Belisarius, he had good opportunities of observing. He composed a narrative of the military events, in which he abstained from committing himself, so that it could be safely published in his own lifetime. Even here his critical attitude to the government is sometimes clear. He allows it to be read between the lines that he regarded the reconquest of Africa and Italy as calamities for those countries; which thus came under an

[18] I was seduced by this hypothesis of Ranke (Later Roman Empire, i. 363), but no longer believe in it.

[19] Procopiana, 1891.

oppressor, to be stripped by his governors and tax gatherers. But the domestic administration was more dangerous ground, on which Procopius could not tread without raising a voice of bitter indignation and hatred. So he dealt with this in a book which was to be kept secret during his own life and bequeathed to friends who might be trusted to give it to the world at a suitable time. The greater part of the Military History, which treated in seven Books the Persian, Vandalic, and Gothic wars, was finished in 545 A.D., and perhaps read to a select circle of friends; at a later time some additions were made, but no changes in what had been already written. The Secret History, as Haury has proved from internal evidence, was written in 550.[39] About three years later the Military History received an eighth Book, bringing the story down to the end of the Gothic war. Then the work came under the notice of Justinian, who saw that a great historian had arisen; and Procopius, who had certainly not described the wars for the purpose of pleasing the Emperor, but had sailed as close to the wind as he dared, was called upon to undertake the disagreeable task of lauding the oppressor. An Imperial command was clearly the origin of the De Ædificiis (560 A.D.), in which the reluctant writer adopted the plan of making adulation so fulsome, that, except to Justinian's vanity, he might appear to be laughing in his sleeve. At the very beginning of the treatise he has a sly allusion to the explosives which were lying in his desk, unknown to the Imperial spies.

Such is the outline of the literary motives of Procopius as we must conceive them, now that we have a practical certainty that he, and no other, wrote the Secret History. For Haury's

[39] One of the author's points is that Justinian was the real ruler during the nominal reign of Justin, who was an "ass." Hence he dates Justinian's administration (not of course his Imperial years) from 518. The consequence of this important discovery of Haury, which he has proved up to the hilt, is that the work was written in 550 (not, as before believed, in 559)—the thirty-second year of Justinian's administration.

dates enable us, as he points out, to argue as follows: If Procopius did not write the book, it was obviously written by a forger, who wished it to pass as a Procopian work. But in 550 no forger could have had the close acquaintance with the Military History which is exhibited by the author of the Anecdota. And moreover the identity of the introduction of the eighth Book of the Military History with that of the Secret History, which was urged by Ranke as an objection to the genuineness of the latter work, now tells decisively in favour of it. For if Procopius composed it in 553, how could a forger, writing in 550, have anticipated it? And if the forger composed it in 550, how are we to explain its appearance in a later work of Procopius himself? These considerations put it beyond all reasonable doubt that Procopius was the author of the Secret History; for this assumption is the only one which supplies an intelligible explanation of the facts.

Another puzzle in connection with Justinian lay in certain biographical details relating to that emperor and his family; which Alemanni, in his commentary on the Secret History, quoted on the authority of a Life of Justinian by a certain Abbot Theophilus, said to have been the Emperor's preceptor. Of these biographical notices, and of Justinian's preceptor Theophilus, we otherwise knew nothing; nor had any one, since Alemanni, seen the Biography. Gibbon and other historians accepted without question the statements quoted by Alemanni; though it would have been wiser to treat them with more reserve, until some data for criticising them were discovered. The puzzle of Alemanni's source, the Life of Theophilus, was solved by Mr. Bryce, who discovered in the library of the Barberini palace at Rome the original text from which Alemanni drew his information.[31]

[31] The Life of Justinian by Theophilus, in the *English Historical Review*. Vasil'ev has given an account of Mr. Bryce's article in the *Visantiski Vremennik*, i. 469 *sqq*.

It professes to be an extract from a Slavonic work, containing the Life of Justinian up to the thirtieth year of his reign, composed by Bogomil, abbot of the monastery of St. Alexander in Dardania. This extract was translated by Marnavich, Canon of Sebenico (afterwards Bishop of Bosnia, 1631–1639), a friend of Alemanni, and some notes were appended by the same scholar. *Bogomil* is the Slavonic equivalent of the Greek *Theophilus*, which was accordingly adopted by Alemanni in his references. Mr. Bryce has shown clearly that this document, interesting as it is in illustrating how Slavonic legends had grown up round the name of Justinian, is worthless as history, and that there is no reason to suppose that such a person as the Dardanian Bogomil ever existed. We are indeed met by a new problem, which, however, is of no serious concern to the practical purposes of history. How did Marnavich obtain a copy of the original Life, from which he made the extract, and which he declares to be preserved in the library of the monks who profess the rule of St. Basil on Mount Athos? Does the original still exist, on Mount Athos or elsewhere? or did it ever exist?

The wars of Justinian[22] in the west have been fully and admirably related by Mr. Hodgkin, with the exception of the obscure conquest of Spain, on which there is too little to be said and nothing further seems likely to come to light. In regard to the ecclesiastical policy of Justinian there is still a field for research.

As for the study of the great work of Anthemius, which brings us to the general subject of Byzantine art, much has been done within the last half century. Gibbon had nothing to help him for the buildings of Constantinople that could compare with Adam's splendid work which he consulted for the buildings of Spalato. We have now Salzenberg's luxurious work, *Alt-christliche Baudenkmale von Constantinopel*,

[22] The Persian and Lazic wars have been related in detail in my Later Roman Empire, vol. i.

published just fifty years ago by the Prussian government, with plates which enable us to make a full study of the architecture of St. Sophia. A few months ago a complete and scholarly English study of this church by Messrs. Lethaby and Swainson appeared. Other churches, too, especially those at Ravenna, have received careful attention; De Voguë's admirable work on the architecture of Syria is well known; but Strzygovski has only too good reason for complaining that the study of Byzantine architecture, as a whole, has not yet properly begun. A large work on the churches of Greece, which two English scholars are preparing, ought to do much to further the cause which Strzygovski has at heart, and to which he has made valuable contributions himself.[39] More progress is perhaps being made in the study of miniature painting and iconography; and in this field the work of the Russian student Kondakov is the most noteworthy.

The study of works of architecture in ancient cities, like Athens, Rome, or Constantinople, naturally entails a study of the topography of the town; and in the case of Constantinople this study is equally important for the historian. Little progress of a satisfactory kind can be made until either Constantinople passes under a European government, or a complete change comes over the spirit of Turkish administration. The region of the Imperial Palace and the ground between the Hippodrome and St. Sophia must be excavated before certainty on the main points can be attained. Labarte's *a priori* reconstruction of the plan of the palace, on the basis of the Cerimonies of Constantine Porphyrogennetos and scattered notices in other Greek writers, was wonderfully ingenious and a certain part of it is manifestly right, though there is much which is not borne out by a more careful examination of the sources. The next step was taken by a

[39] His new work on the reservoirs of Constantinople may be specially mentioned.

Russian scholar Bieliaiev who has recently published a most valuable study on the Cerimonies,[24] in which he has tested the reconstruction of Labarte and shown us exactly where we are, — what we know, and what with our present materials we cannot possibly know. Between Labarte and Bieliaiev the whole problem was obscured by the unscholarly work of Paspatês, the Greek antiquarian; whose sole merit was that he kept the subject before the world. As the acropolis is the scene of so many great events in the history which Gibbon recorded, it is well to warn the reader that our sources make it absolutely certain that the Hippodrome adjoined the Palace; there was no public space between them. The Augusteum did not lie, as Paspatês asserted, between the Palace and the Hippodrome,[25] but between the north side of the Hippodrome and St. Sophia.

On the trades and industries of the Imperial City, on the trade corporations and the minute control exercised over them by the government, new light has been thrown by M. Nicole's discovery and publication of the Prefect's Book, a code of regulations drawn up by Leo VI. The *demes* of Constantinople are a subject which needs investigation. They are certainly not to be regarded as Gibbon and his successors have regarded them, as mere circus parties. They must represent, as Uspenski points out in the opening number

[24] Byzantina. Ocherki, materialy, i. zamietki po Vizantiskim drevnostiam. 1891–3. I must not omit to mention Dr. Mordtmann's valuable Esquisse topographique (1892), and N. Destunis has made noteworthy contributions to the subject.

[25] With blameworthy indiscretion I accepted this false view of Paspatês, in my Later Roman Empire, without having gone methodically into the sources. I was misled by the fame won by the supposed "topographical discoveries" of this diligent antiquarian and by his undeservedly high reputation; this, however, is no excuse, and unfortunately the error has vitiated my account of the Nika revolt. I have gone into the theory of Paspatês in the *Scottish Review* (April, 1894), where he is treated too leniently. His misuse of authorities is simply astounding. I may take the opportunity of saying that I hope to rewrite the two volumes of my Later Roman Empire and correct, so far as I may be able, its many faults. A third volume, dealing with the ninth century, will, I hope, appear at a not too distant date.

of the new *Visantiski Vremennik*, organised divisions of the population.

A field in which the historian must wander to breathe the spirit and learn the manner of the mediæval Greek world is that of the romance, both prose and verse, written in the vulgar tongue. This field was closed to Gibbon, but the labours of many scholars, above all Legrand, have rendered it now easily accessible. Out of a large number of interesting things I may refer especially to two. One is the epic of Digenes Akritas, the Roland or Cid of the Later Empire, a poem of the tenth century, which illustrates the life of Armatoli and the border warfare against the Saracens in the Cilician mountains. The other is the Book of the Conquest of the Morea,[26] a mixture of fiction and fact, but invaluable for realising the fascinating though complicated history of the "Latin" settlements in Greece. That history was set aside by Gibbon, with the phrase, "I shall not pursue the obscure and various dynasties that rose and fell on the continent or in the isles," though he deigns to give a page or two to Athens.[27] But it is a subject with unusual possibilities for picturesque treatment, and out of which, Gibbon, if he had apprehended the opportunity, and had possessed the materials, would have made a brilliant chapter. Since Finlay, who entered into this episode of Greek history with great fulness, the material has been largely increased by the researches of Hopf.[28]

[26] The Greek and the French versions were published by Buchon, uncritically. A new edition of the Greek text is promised by Dr. John Schmitt.

[27] The history of mediæval Athens has been recorded at length in an attractive work by Gregorovius, the counterpart of his great history of mediæval Rome.

[28] For a full account of Vulgär-griechische Litteratur, I may refer to Krumbacher's Gesch. der Byz. Litt. Here it is unnecessary to do more than indicate its existence and importance. I may add that the historian cannot neglect the development of the language, for which these romances (and other documents) furnish ample data. Here the Greeks themselves have an advantage, and scholars like Hatzidakês, Psicharês, and Jannarês are in this field doing work of the best kind.

As I have already observed, it is perhaps on the Slavonic side of the history of the Empire that Gibbon is most conspicuously inadequate. Since he wrote, various causes have combined to increase our knowledge of Slavonic antiquity. The Slavs themselves have engaged in methodical investigation of their own past; and, since the entire or partial emancipations of the southern Slavs from Asiatic rule, a general interest in Slavonic things has grown up throughout Europe. Gibbon dismissed the history of the First Bulgarian Kingdom, from its foundation in the reign of Constantine Pogonatus to its overthrow by the second Basil, in two pages. To-day the author of a history of the Empire on the same scale would find two hundred a strict limit. Gibbon tells us nothing of the Slavonic missionaries, Cyril and Methodius, round whose names an extensive literature has been formed. It is only in recent years that the geography of the Illyrian peninsula has become an accessible subject of study.

The investigation of the history of the northern peoples who came under the influence of the Empire has been stimulated by controversy, and controversy has been animated and even embittered by national pride. The question of Slavonic settlements in Greece has been thoroughly ventilated, because Fallmerayer excited the scholarship of Hellenes and Philhellenes to refute what they regarded as an insulting paradox.[39] So, too, the pride of the Roumanians was irritated by Roesler, who denied that they were descended from the inhabitants of Trajan's Dacia and described them as later immigrants of the thirteenth century. Pič arose against him; then Hermuzaki argued for an intermediate date. The best Hungarian scholar of the day joined the fray, on the other side; and the contention became bitter between

[39] Fallmerayer's thesis that there was no pure Hellenic blood in Greece was triumphantly refuted. No one denies that there was a large Slavonic element in the country parts, especially of the Peloponnesus.

Vlach and Magyar, the Roumanian pretensions to Siebenbürgen — "Dacia irredenta" — sharpening the lances of the foes. The Roumanians have not come out of their "question" as well as the Hellenes. Hungary too has its own question. Are the Magyars to be ethically associated with the Finns or given over to the family of the Turks, whom as champions of Christendom they had opposed at Mohácz and Varna? It was a matter of pride for the Hungarian to detach himself from the Turk; and the evidence is certainly on his side. Hunfalvy's conclusions have successfully defied the assaults of Vámbéry.[30] Again in Russia there has been a long and vigorous contest, — the so-called Norman or Varangian question. No doubt is felt now by the impartial judge as to the Scandinavian origin of the princes of Kiev, and that the making of Russia was due to Northmen or Varangians. Kunik and Pogodin were reinforced by Thomsen of Denmark; and the pure Slavism of Ilovaiski[31] and Gedeonov, though its champions were certainly able, is a lost cause.

From such collisions sparks have flown and illuminated dark corners. For the Slavs the road was first cleared by Šafarik. The development of the comparative philology of the Indo-Germanic tongues has had its effect; the Slavonic languages have been brought into line, chiefly by the life-work of Miklosich; and the science is being developed by such scholars as Jagič and Leskien. The several countries of the Balkan lands have their archæologists and archæological journals; and the difficulty which now meets the historian is not the absence but the plenitude of philological and historical literature.

[30] In a paper entitled, The Coming of the Hungarians, in the *Scottish Review* of July, 1892, I have discussed the questions connected with early Magyar history, and criticised Hunfalvy's Magyarország Ethnographiája (1876) and Vámbéry's A magyarok eredete (1882). One of the best works dealing with the subject has been written by a Slav (C. Grot).

[31] Ilovaiski's work Istorija Rossii, vol. i. (Kiev period), is, though his main thesis is a mistake, most instructive.

A word may be added about the Hungarians, who have not been so successful with their early history as the Slavs. Until the appearance of Hunfalvy, their methods were antediluvian, and their temper credulous. The special work of Jászay, and the first chapters of Szalay's great History of Hungary, showed no advance on Katóna and Pray, who were consulted by Gibbon. All believed in the Anonymous Scribe of King Béla; Jászay simply transcribed him. Then Roesler came and dispelled the illusion. Our main sources now are Constantine Porphyrogennetos, and the earlier Asiatic traveller Ibn Dasta, who has been rendered accessible by Chwolson.[32] The linguistic researches of Ahlquist, Hunfalvy and others into Vogul, Ostjak and the rest of the Ugro-Finnic kindred, must be taken into account by the critic who is dealing with those main sources. The Chazars, to whom the Hungarians were once subject, the Patzinaks, who drove the Magyars from "Lebedia" to "Atelkuzu" and from "Atelkuzu" to Pannonia, and other peoples of the same kind, have profited by these investigations.

The foregoing instances will serve to give a general idea of the respects in which Gibbon's history might be described as behind date. To follow out all the highways and byways of progress would mean the usurpation of at least a volume by the editor. What more has to be said, must be said briefly in notes and appendices. That Gibbon is behind date in many details, and in some departments of importance, simply signifies that we and our fathers have not lived in an absolutely incompetent world. But in the main things he is still our master, above and beyond "date." It is needless to dwell on the obvious qualities which secure to him immunity from the common lot of historical writers, — such as the bold and certain measure of his progress through the ages; his accurate

[32] Chwolson, Izviestiia o Chozarach, Burtasach, Bolgarach, Madiarach, Slavaniach, i Rusach.

vision, and his tact in managing perspective; his discreet reserves of judgment and timely scepticism; the immortal affectation of his unique manner. By virtue of these superiorities he can defy the danger with which the activity of successors must always threaten the worthies of the past. But there is another point which was touched on in an earlier page and to which here, in a different connection, we may briefly revert. It is well to realise that the greatest history of modern times was written by one in whom a distrust of enthusiasm was deeply rooted.[33] This cynicism was not inconsistent with partiality, with definite prepossessions, with a certain spite. In fact it supplied the antipathy which the artist infused when he mixed his most effective colours. The conviction that enthusiasm is inconsistent with intellectual balance was engrained in his mental constitution, and confirmed by study and experience. It might be reasonably maintained that zeal for men or causes is an historian's marring, and that "reserve sympathy" — the principle of Thucydides — is the first lesson he has to learn. But without venturing on any generalisation we must consider Gibbon's zealous distrust of zeal as an essential and most suggestive characteristic of the "Decline and Fall."

[33] And who regarded history as "little more than the register of the crimes, follies and misfortunes of mankind" (see below, p. 98).

THE HISTORY OF THE DECLINE AND FALL OF THE ROMAN EMPIRE

CHAPTER I

The Extent and Military Force of the Empire in the Age of the Antonines

In the second century of the Christian era, the empire of Rome comprehended the fairest part of the earth, and the most civilised portion of mankind. The frontiers of that extensive monarchy were guarded by ancient renown and disciplined valour. The gentle, but powerful, influence of laws and manners had gradually cemented the union of the provinces. Their peaceful inhabitants enjoyed and abused the advantages of wealth and luxury. The image of a free constitution was preserved with decent reverence. The Roman senate appeared to possess the sovereign authority, and devolved on the emperors all the executive powers of government. During a happy period of more than fourscore years, the public administration was conducted by the virtue and abilities of Nerva, Trajan, Hadrian, and the two Antonines. It is the design of this and of the two succeeding chapters, to describe the prosperous condition of their empire; and afterwards, from the death of Marcus Antoninus, to deduce the most important circumstances of its decline and fall: a revolution which will ever be remembered, and is still felt by the nations of the earth.

The principal conquests of the Romans were achieved under the republic; and the emperors, for the most part, were satisfied with preserving those dominions which had been acquired by the policy of the senate, the active emulation of the consuls, and the martial enthusiasm of the people. The seven first centuries were filled with a rapid succession of triumphs; but it was reserved for Augustus to relinquish the ambitious design of subduing the whole earth, and to introduce a spirit of moderation into the public councils. Inclined to peace by his temper and situation, it was easy for him to discover that Rome, in her present exalted situation, had much less to hope than to fear from the chance of arms; and that, in the prosecution of remote wars, the undertaking became every day more difficult, the event more doubtful, and the possession more precarious and less beneficial. The experience of Augustus added weight to these salutary reflections, and effectually convinced him that, by the prudent vigour of his counsels, it would be easy to secure every concession which the safety or the dignity of Rome might require from the most formidable barbarians. Instead of exposing his person and his legions to the arrows of the Parthians, he obtained, by an honourable treaty, the restitution of the standards and prisoners which had been taken in the defeat of Crassus.[1]

His generals, in the early part of his reign, attempted the reduction of Æthiopia and Arabia Felix. They marched near a thousand miles to the south of the tropic; but the heat of the climate soon repelled the invaders and protected the unwarlike natives of those sequestered regions.[2] The northern

[1] Dion Cassius (l. liv. p. 736 [8]) with the annotations of Reimar, who has collected all that Roman vanity has left upon the subject. The marble of Ancyra, on which Augustus recorded his own exploits, asserts that *he compelled* the Parthians to restore the ensigns of Crassus.

[2] Strabo (l. xvi. p. 780), Pliny the elder (Hist. Natur. l. vi. 32, 35 [28, 29]) and Dion Cassius (l. liii. p. 723 [29], and l. liv. p. 734 [6]) have left us very curious details concerning these wars. The Romans made themselves masters of Mariaba, or Merab, a city of Arabia Felix, well known to the

countries of Europe scarcely deserved the expense and labour of conquest. The forests and morasses of Germany were filled with a hardy race of barbarians, who despised life when it was separated from freedom; and though, on the first attack, they seemed to yield to the weight of the Roman power, they soon, by a signal act of despair, regained their independence, and reminded Augustus of the vicissitude of fortune.[3] On the death of that emperor his testament was publicly read in the senate. He bequeathed, as a valuable legacy to his successors, the advice of confining the empire within those limits which nature seemed to have placed as its permanent bulwarks and boundaries; on the west the Atlantic Ocean; the Rhine and Danube on the north; the Euphrates on the east; and towards the south the sandy deserts of Arabia and Africa.[4]

Happily for the repose of mankind, the moderate system recommended by the wisdom of Augustus was adopted by the fears and vices of his immediate successors. Engaged in the pursuit of pleasure or in the exercise of tyranny, the first Cæsars seldom showed themselves to the armies, or to the provinces; nor were they disposed to suffer that those triumphs which *their* indolence neglected should be usurped by the conduct and valour of their lieutenants. The military fame of a subject was considered as an insolent invasion of the Imperial prerogative; and it became the duty, as well as interest, of every Roman general, to guard the frontiers intrusted to his care, without aspiring to conquests which

Orientals (see Abulfeda and the Nubian geography, p. 52). They were arrived within three days' journey of the Spice country, the rich object of their invasion. [See Mommsen, Römische Geschichte, v. p. 608 *sqq.*]

[3] By the slaughter of Varus and his three legions. See the first book of the Annals of Tacitus. Sueton. in August. c. 23, and Velleius Paterculus, l. ii. c. 117, &c. Augustus did not receive the melancholy news with all the temper and firmness that might have been expected from his character.

[4] Tacit. Annal. l. ii. [i. 11]. Dion Cassius, l. lvi. p. 832 [33], and the speech of Augustus himself, in Julian's Cæsars. It receives great light from the learned notes of his French translator, M. Spanheim.

might have proved no less fatal to himself than to the vanquished barbarians.[5]

The only accession which the Roman empire received during the first century of the Christian era was the province of Britain. In this single instance the successors of Cæsar and Augustus were persuaded to follow the example of the former, rather than the precept of the latter. The proximity of its situation to the coast of Gaul seemed to invite their arms; the pleasing, though doubtful, intelligence of a pearl fishery attracted their avarice;[6] and as Britain was viewed in the light of a distinct and insulated world, the conquest scarcely formed any exception to the general system of continental measures. After a war of about forty years, undertaken by the most stupid,[7] maintained by the most dissolute, and terminated by the most timid of all the emperors, the far greater part of the island submitted to the Roman yoke.[8] The various tribes of Britons possessed valour without conduct, and the love of freedom without the spirit of union. They took up arms with savage fierceness, they laid them down, or turned them against each other with wild inconstancy; and while they fought singly, they were successively subdued. Neither the fortitude of Caractacus, nor the despair of Boadicea, nor the fanaticism of the Druids, could avert

[5] Germanicus, Suetonius Paulinus, and Agricola were checked and recalled in the course of their victories. Corbulo was put to death. Military merit, as it is admirably expressed by Tacitus, was, in the strictest sense of the word, *imperatoria virtus*.

[6] Cæsar himself conceals that ignoble motive; but it is mentioned by Suetonius, c. 47. The British pearls proved, however, of little value, on account of their dark and livid colour. Tacitus observes, with reason (in Agricola, c. 12), that it was an inherent defect. "Ego facilius crediderim, naturam margaritis deesse quam nobis avaritiam."

[7] Claudius, Nero, and Domitian. A hope is expressed by Pomponius Mela, l. iii. c. 6 (he wrote under Claudius), that, by the success of the Roman arms, the island and its savage inhabitants would soon be better known. It is amusing enough to peruse such passages in the midst of London.

[8] See the admirable abridgment, given by Tacitus, in the Life of Agricola, and copiously, though perhaps not completely, illustrated by our own antiquarians, Camden and Horsley. [See Appendix 2.]

the slavery of their country, or resist the steady progress of the Imperial generals, who maintained the national glory, when the throne was disgraced by the weakest or the most vicious of mankind. At the very time when Domitian, confined to his palace, felt the terrors which he inspired, his legions, under the command of the virtuous Agricola, defeated the collected force of the Caledonians at the foot of the Grampian hills;[9] and his fleets, venturing to explore an unknown and dangerous navigation, displayed the Roman arms round every part of the island. The conquest of Britain was considered as already achieved; and it was the design of Agricola to complete and ensure his success by the easy reduction of Ireland, for which, in his opinion, one legion and a few auxiliaries were sufficient.[10] The western isle might be improved into a valuable possession, and the Britons would wear their chains with the less reluctance, if the prospect and example of freedom was on every side removed from before their eyes.

But the superior merit of Agricola soon occasioned his removal from the government of Britain; and for ever disappointed this rational, though extensive, scheme of conquest. Before his departure the prudent general had provided for security as well as for dominion. He had observed that the island is almost divided into two unequal parts by the opposite gulfs or, as they are now called, the Friths of Scotland. Across the narrow interval of about forty miles he had drawn a line of military stations, which was afterwards fortified, in the reign of Antoninus Pius, by a turf rampart, erected on foundations of stone.[11] This wall of Antoninus, at a small

[9] [There is no good ground for the identification of *mons Graupius* with the Grampian hills. The date of the battle was 84 or 85 A.D.; the place is quite uncertain.]

[10] The Irish writers, jealous of their national honour, are extremely provoked on this occasion, both with Tacitus and with Agricola. [Agricola's design was not carried out because Domitian refused to send the additional legion.]

[11] See Horsley's Britannia Romana, l. i. c. 10.

distance beyond the modern cities of Edinburgh and Glasgow, was fixed as the limit of the Roman province. The native Caledonians preserved, in the northern extremity of the island, their wild independence, for which they were not less indebted to their poverty than to their valour. Their incursions were frequently repelled and chastised; but their country was never subdued.[12] The masters of the fairest and most wealthy climates of the globe turned with contempt from gloomy hills assailed by the winter tempest, from lakes concealed in a blue mist, and from cold and lonely heaths, over which the deer of the forest were chased by a troop of naked barbarians.[13]

Such was the state of the Roman frontiers, and such the maxims of Imperial policy, from the death of Augustus to the accession of Trajan. That virtuous and active prince had received the education of a soldier, and possessed the talents of a general.[14] The peaceful system of his predecessors was interrupted by scenes of war and conquest; and the legions, after a long interval, beheld a military emperor at their head. The first exploits of Trajan were against the Dacians, the most warlike of men, who dwelt beyond the Danube, and who, during the reign of Domitian, had insulted, with impunity, the majesty of Rome.[15] To the strength and fierceness of barbarians they added a contempt for life, which was derived from a warm persuasion of the immortality and transmigration of the soul.[16] Decebalus, the Dacian king, approved

[12] The poet Buchanan celebrates, with elegance and spirit (see his Sylvæ, v.), the unviolated independence of his native country. But, if the single testimony of Richard of Cirencester was sufficient to create a Roman province of Vespasiana to the north of the wall, that independence would be reduced within very narrow limits.

[13] See Appian (in Procem. [5]) and the uniform imagery of Ossian's poems, which, according to every hypothesis, were composed by a native Caledonian.

[14] See Pliny's Panegyric, which seems founded on facts.

[15] Dion Cassius, l. lxvii. [6 *et sqq.*]

[16] Herodotus, l. iv. c. 94. Julian in the Cæsars, with Spanheim's observations.

himself a rival not unworthy of Trajan; nor did he despair of his own and the public fortune, till, by the confession of his enemies, he had exhausted every resource both of valour and policy.[17] This memorable war, with a very short suspension of hostilities, lasted five years; and as the emperor could exert, without control, the whole force of the state, it was terminated by the absolute submission of the barbarians.[18] The new province of Dacia, which formed a second exception to the precept of Augustus, was about thirteen hundred miles in circumference. Its natural boundaries were the Dniester, the Theiss, or Tibiscus, the Lower Danube, and the Euxine Sea. The vestiges of a military road may still be traced from the banks of the Danube to the neighbourhood of Bender, a place famous in modern history, and the actual frontier of the Turkish and Russian Empires.[19]

Trajan was ambitious of fame; and as long as mankind shall continue to bestow more liberal applause on their destroyers than on their benefactors, the thirst of military glory will ever be the vice of the most exalted characters. The praises of Alexander, transmitted by a succession of poets and historians, had kindled a dangerous emulation in the mind of Trajan. Like him, the Roman emperor undertook an expedition against the nations of the east, but he lamented with a sigh that his advanced age scarcely left him any hopes of equalling the renown of the son of Philip.[20]

[17] Plin. Epist. viii. 9.

[18] Dion Cassius, l. lxviii. p. 1123, 1131 [6 and 14]. Julian. in Cæsaribus. Eutropius, viii. 2, 6. Aurelius Victor in Epitome. [See Appendix 3.]

[19] See a Memoir of M. d'Anville, on the Province of Dacia, in the Académie des Inscriptions, tom. xxviii. p. 444-468. [The region east of the Aluta, corresponding to the modern Walachia, was not included in Dacia, but went with the province of Lower Mœsia. See Domaszewski, Epigr. Mittheilungen, xiii. p. 137. The limits of Dacia are incorrect in the map in this volume. They should follow the line of the Carpathians in the south-east and east, excluding Walachia and Moldavia.]

[20] Trajan's sentiments are represented in a very just and lively manner in the Cæsars of Julian. [The date of the beginning of the Parthian War is 114 A.D.]

Yet the success of Trajan, however transient, was rapid and specious. The degenerate Parthians, broken by intestine discord, fled before his arms. He descended the river Tigris in triumph, from the mountains of Armenia to the Persian gulf. He enjoyed the honour of being the first, as he was the last, of the Roman generals, who ever navigated that remote sea. His fleets ravished the coasts of Arabia; and Trajan vainly flattered himself that he was approaching towards the confines of India.[21] Every day the astonished senate received the intelligence of new names and new nations that acknowledged his sway. They were informed that the kings of Bosphorus, Colchos, Iberia, Albania, Osrhœne, and even the Parthian monarch himself, had accepted their diadems from the hands of the emperor; that the independent tribes of the Median and Carduchian hills had implored his protection; and that the rich countries of Armenia, Mesopotamia, and Assyria, were reduced into the state of provinces.[22] But the death of Trajan soon clouded the splendid prospect;[23] and it was justly to be dreaded that so many distant nations would throw off the unaccustomed yoke, when they were no longer restrained by the powerful hand which had imposed it.

It was an ancient tradition that, when the Capitol was founded by one of the Roman kings, the god Terminus (who presided over boundaries, and was represented according to the fashion of that age by a large stone) alone, among all the inferior deities, refused to yield his place to Jupiter himself. A favourable inference was drawn from his obstinacy, which was interpreted by the augurs as a sure presage that the

[21] Eutropius and Sextus Rufus have endeavoured to perpetuate the illusion. See a very sensible dissertation of M. Freret, in the Académie des Inscriptions, tom. xxi. p. 55.

[22] Dion Cassius, l. lxviii. [18 *et sqq.*]; and the Abbreviators.

[23] [117 A.D. A triumph in honour of this eastern expedition was celebrated after the emperor's death. On inscriptions he is called *Divus Traianus Parthicus*, instead of *Divus Traianus* (Schiller, Gesch. der röm. Kaiserzeit, i. 563).]

boundaries of the Roman power would never recede.[24] During many ages, the prediction, as it is usual, contributed to its own accomplishment. But though Terminus had resisted the majesty of Jupiter, he submitted to the authority of the emperor Hadrian.[25] The resignation of all the eastern conquests of Trajan was the first measure of his reign. He restored to the Parthians the election of an independent sovereign; withdrew the Roman garrisons from the provinces of Armenia, Mesopotamia, and Assyria; and, in compliance with the precepts of Augustus, once more established the Euphrates as the frontier of the empire.[26] Censure, which arraigns the public actions and the private motives of princes, has ascribed to envy a conduct which might be attributed to the prudence and moderation of Hadrian. The various character of that emperor, capable, by turns, of the meanest and the most generous sentiments, may afford some colour to the suspicion. It was, however, scarcely in his power to place the superiority of his predecessor in a more conspicuous light, than by thus confessing himself unequal to the task of defending the conquests of Trajan.

The martial and ambitious spirit of Trajan formed a very singular contrast with the moderation of his successor. The restless activity of Hadrian was not less remarkable when compared with the gentle repose of Antoninus Pius. The life of the former was almost a perpetual journey; and as he possessed the various talents of the soldier, the statesman, and the scholar, he gratified his curiosity in the discharge of his duty. Careless of the difference of seasons and of climates,

[24] Ovid Fast. l. ii. ver. 667. See Livy [i. 55], and Dionysius of Halicarnassus, under the reign of Tarquin.

[25] St. Augustin is highly delighted with the proof of the weakness of Terminus, and the vanity of the Augurs. See De Civitate Dei, iv. 29. [The loss of trans-Rhenane Germany was a previous instance of the retreat of Terminus.]

[26] See the Augustan History, p. 5 [i. 9]. Jerome's Chronicle, and all the Epitomisers. It is somewhat surprising, that this memorable event should be omitted by Dion, or rather by Xiphilin. [See Appendix 3.]

he marched on foot, and bareheaded, over the snows of Caledonia, and the sultry plains of the Upper Egypt; nor was there a province of the empire which, in the course of his reign, was not honoured with the presence of the monarch.[27] But the tranquil life of Antoninus Pius was spent in the bosom of Italy; and, during the twenty-three years that he directed the public administration, the longest journeys of that amiable prince extended no farther than from his palace in Rome to the retirement of his Lanuvian villa.[28]

Notwithstanding this difference in their personal conduct, the general system of Augustus was equally adopted and uniformly pursued by Hadrian and by the two Antonines. They persisted in the design of maintaining the dignity of the empire, without attempting to enlarge its limits. By every honourable expedient they invited the friendship of the barbarians; and endeavoured to convince mankind that the Roman power, raised above the temptation of conquest, was actuated only by the love of order and justice. During a long period of forty-three years their virtuous labours were crowned with success; and, if we except a few slight hostilities that served to exercise the legions of the frontier, the reigns of Hadrian and Antoninus Pius offer the fair prospect of universal peace.[29] The Roman name was revered among the most remote nations of the earth. The fiercest barbarians frequently submitted their differences to the arbitration of the emperor; and we are informed by a contemporary historian

[27] Dion, l. lxix. p. 115 [9]. Hist. August. p. 5, 8 [l. 10 and 16]. If all our historians were lost, medals, inscriptions, and other monuments would be sufficient to record the travels of Hadrian. [See Dürr, Die Reisen des Kaisers Hadrian, 1881.]

[28] See the Augustan History and the Epitomes. [Date: 138–161 A.D.]

[29] We must, however, remember that, in the time of Hadrian, a rebellion of the Jews raged with religious fury, though only in a single province. Pausanias (l. viii. c. 43) mentions two necessary and successful wars, conducted by the generals of Pius. 1st, Against the wandering Moors, who were driven into the solitudes of Atlas. 2d, Against the Brigantes of Britain, who had invaded the Roman province. Both these wars (with several other hostilities) are mentioned in the Augustan History, p. 19 [iii. 5].

that he had seen ambassadors who were refused the honour which they came to solicit, of being admitted into the rank of subjects.[30]

The terror of the Roman arms added weight and dignity to the moderation of the emperors. They preserved peace by a constant preparation for war; and while justice regulated their conduct, they announced to the nations on their confines that they were as little disposed to endure as to offer an injury. The military strength, which it had been sufficient for Hadrian and the elder Antoninus to display, was exerted against the Parthians and the Germans by the emperor Marcus. The hostilities of the barbarians provoked the resentment of that philosophic monarch, and, in the prosecution of a just defence, Marcus and his generals obtained many signal victories, both on the Euphrates and on the Danube.[31] The military establishment of the Roman empire, which thus assured either its tranquillity or success, will now become the proper and important object of our attention.

In the purer ages of the commonwealth, the use of arms was reserved for those ranks of citizens who had a country to love, a property to defend, and some share in enacting those laws which it was their interest, as well as duty, to maintain. But in proportion as the public freedom was lost in extent of conquest, war was gradually improved into an art, and degraded into a trade.[32] The legions themselves, even at the time when they were recruited in the most distant provinces,

[30] Appian of Alexandria, in the preface to his History of the Roman Wars [7].

[31] Dion, l. lxxi. Hist. August. in Marco [iv. 9, 12, 17, 20, 22, &c.]. The Parthian victories gave birth to a crowd of contemptible historians, whose memory has been rescued from oblivion, and exposed to ridicule, in a very lively piece of criticism of Lucian.

[32] The poorest rank of soldiers possessed above forty pounds sterling (Dionys. Halicarn. iv. 17), a very high qualification, at a time when money was so scarce, that an ounce of silver was equivalent to seventy pound weight of brass. The populace, excluded by the ancient constitution, were indiscriminately admitted by Marius. See Sallust. de Bell. Jugurth. c. 91 [86].

were supposed to consist of Roman citizens. That distinction was generally considered either as a legal qualification or as a proper recompense for the soldier; but a more serious regard was paid to the essential merit of age, strength, and military stature.[83] In all levies, a just preference was given to the climates of the north over those of the south; the race of men born to the exercise of arms was sought for in the country rather than in cities, and it was very reasonably presumed that the hardy occupations of smiths, carpenters, and huntsmen would supply more vigour and resolution than the sedentary trades which are employed in the service of luxury.[84] After every qualification of property had been laid aside, the armies of the Roman emperors were still commanded, for the most part, by officers of a liberal birth and education; but the common soldiers, like the mercenary troops of modern Europe, were drawn from the meanest, and very frequently from the most profligate, of mankind.

That public virtue, which among the ancients was denominated patriotism, is derived from a strong sense of our own interest in the preservation and prosperity of the free government of which we are members. Such a sentiment, which had rendered the legions of the republic almost invincible, could make but a very feeble impression on the mercenary servants of a despotic prince; and it became necessary to supply that defect by other motives, of a different, but not less forcible nature,—honour and religion. The peasant, or mechanic, imbibed the useful prejudice that he was advanced to the more dignified profession of arms, in which his rank and reputation would depend on his own valour; and that, although the prowess of a private soldier must often escape the notice of fame, his own behaviour might some-

[83] Cæsar formed his legion Alauda of Gauls and strangers; but it was during the licence of civil war; and after the victory he gave them the freedom of the city, for their reward. [It was really formed, B.C. 55; Suetonius, Jul. 24.]

[84] See Vegetius de Re Militari, l. i. c. 2–7.

times confer glory or disgrace on the company, the legion, or even the army, to whose honours he was associated. On his first entrance into the service, an oath was administered to him with every circumstance of solemnity. He promised never to desert his standard, to submit his own will to the commands of his leaders, and to sacrifice his life for the safety of the emperor and the empire.[35] The attachment of the Roman troops to their standards was inspired by the united influence of religion and of honour. The golden eagle, which glittered in the front of the legion, was the object of their fondest devotion; nor was it esteemed less impious than it was ignominious, to abandon that sacred ensign in the hour of danger.[36] These motives, which derived their strength from the imagination, were enforced by fears and hopes of a more substantial kind. Regular pay, occasional donatives, and a stated recompense, after the appointed term of service, alleviated the hardships of the military life,[37] whilst, on the other hand, it was impossible for cowardice or disobedience to escape the severest punishment. The centurions were authorised to chastise with blows, the generals had a right to punish with death; and it was an inflexible maxim of Roman discipline, that a good soldier should dread his officers far more than the enemy. From such laudable arts did the valour of the Imperial troops receive a degree of firmness and

[35] The oath of service and fidelity to the emperor was annually renewed by the troops, on the first of January.

[36] Tacitus calls the Roman Eagles, Bellorum Deos. They were placed in a chapel in the camp, and with the other deities received the religious worship of the troops.

[37] See Gronovius de Pecunia vetere, l. iii. p. 120, &c. The emperor Domitian raised the annual stipend of the legionaries to twelve pieces of gold, which, in his time, was equivalent to about ten of our guineas. This pay, somewhat higher than our own, had been, and was afterwards, gradually increased, according to the progress of wealth and military government. After twenty years' service, the veteran received three thousand denarii (about one hundred pounds sterling), or a proportionable allowance of land. The pay and advantages of the guards were, in general, about double those of the legions.

docility, unattainable by the impetuous and irregular passions of barbarians.

And yet so sensible were the Romans of the imperfection of valour without skill and practice, that, in their language, the name of an army was borrowed from the word which signified exercise.[38] Military exercises were the important and unremitted object of their discipline. The recruits and young soldiers were constantly trained, both in the morning and in the evening, nor was age or knowledge allowed to excuse the veterans from the daily repetition of what they had completely learnt. Large sheds were erected in the winter-quarters of the troops, that their useful labours might not receive any interruption from the most tempestuous weather; and it was carefully observed, that the arms destined to this imitation of war should be of double the weight which was required in real action.[39] It is not the purpose of this work to enter into any minute description of the Roman exercises. We shall only remark that they comprehended whatever could add strength to the body, activity to the limbs, or grace to the motions. The soldiers were diligently instructed to march, to run, to leap, to swim, to carry heavy burdens, to handle every species of arms that was used either for offence or for defence, either in distant engagement or in a closer onset; to form a variety of evolutions; and to move to the sound of flutes in the Pyrrhic or martial dance.[40] In the midst of peace, the Roman troops familiarised themselves with the practice of war; and it is prettily remarked by an ancient historian who had fought against them, that the effusion of blood was the only circum-

[38] *Exercitus ab exercitando*, Varro de Linguâ Latinâ, l. iv. [v. 87 ed. L. Müller]. Cicero in Tusculan, l. ii. 37. There is room for a very interesting work, which should lay open the connection between the languages and manners of nations.

[39] Vegetius, l. i. c. 11, and the rest of his first book.

[40] The Pyrrhic Dance is extremely well illustrated by M. le Beau, in the Académie des Inscriptions, tom. xxxv. p. 262, &c. That learned academician, in a series of memoirs, has collected all the passages of the ancients that relate to the Roman legion.

stance which distinguished a field of battle from a field of exercise.[41] It was the policy of the ablest generals, and even of the emperors themselves, to encourage these military studies by their presence and example; and we are informed that Hadrian, as well as Trajan, frequently condescended to instruct the inexperienced soldiers, to reward the diligent, and sometimes to dispute with them the prize of superior strength or dexterity.[42] Under the reigns of those princes, the science of tactics was cultivated with success; and as long as the empire retained any vigour, their military instructions were respected as the most perfect model of Roman discipline.

Nine centuries of war had gradually introduced into the service many alterations and improvements. The legions, as they are described by Polybius,[43] in the time of the Punic wars, differed very materially from those which achieved the victories of Cæsar, or defended the monarchy of Hadrian and the Antonines. The constitution of the Imperial legion may be described in a few words.[44] The heavy-armed infantry, which composed its principal strength,[45] was divided into ten cohorts, and fifty-five companies, under the orders of a correspondent number of tribunes and centurions. The first cohort, which always claimed the post of honour and the cus-

[41] Joseph. de Bell. Judaico, l. iii. c. 5. We are indebted to this Jew for some very curious details of Roman discipline.

[42] Plin. Panegyr. c. 13. Life of Hadrian, in the Augustan History [l. 14]. [Fragments of a speech which Hadrian delivered to his soldiers at Lambaesis in Africa have been found in an inscription, C. I. L. viii. 2532.]

[43] See an admirable digression on the Roman discipline, in the sixth book of his history [19–42].

[44] Vegetius de Re Militari, l. ii. c. 5, &c. Considerable part of his very perplexed abridgment was taken from the regulations of Trajan and Hadrian; and the legion, as he describes it, cannot suit any other age of the Roman empire.

[45] Vegetius de Re Militari, l. ii. c. 1. In the purer age of Cæsar and Cicero, the word *miles* was almost confined to the infantry. Under the Lower Empire, and in the times of chivalry, it was appropriated almost as exclusively to the men at arms, who fought on horseback. [This account of the army demands some corrections. See Appendix 4.]

tody of the eagle, was formed of eleven hundred and five soldiers, the most approved for valour and fidelity. The remaining nine cohorts consisted each of five hundred and fifty-five; and the whole body of legionary infantry amounted to six thousand one hundred men. Their arms were uniform, and admirably adapted to the nature of their service: an open helmet, with a lofty crest; a breast-plate, or coat of mail; greaves on their legs, and an ample buckler on their left arm. The buckler was of an oblong and concave figure, four feet in length, and two and a half in breadth, framed of a light wood, covered with a bull's hide, and strongly guarded with plates of brass. Besides a lighter spear, the legionary soldier grasped in his right hand the formidable *pilum*, a ponderous javelin, whose utmost length was about six feet, and which was terminated by a massy triangular point of steel of eighteen inches.[46] This instrument was indeed much inferior to our modern fire-arms; since it was exhausted by a single discharge, at the distance of only ten or twelve paces. Yet, when it was launched by a firm and skilful hand, there was not any cavalry that durst venture within its reach, nor any shield or corslet that could sustain the impetuosity of its weight. As soon as the Roman had darted his *pilum*, he drew his sword, and rushed forwards to close with the enemy. It was a short well-tempered Spanish blade, that carried a double edge, and was alike suited to the purpose of striking or of pushing; but the soldier was always instructed to prefer the latter use of his weapon, as his own body remained less exposed, whilst he inflicted a more dangerous wound on his adversary.[47] The legion was usually drawn up eight deep; and the regular distance of three feet was left between the files as well as ranks.[48] A body of troops, habituated to preserve

[46] In the time of Polybius and Dionysius of Halicarnassus (l. v. c. 45) the steel point of the *pilum* seems to have been much longer. In the time of Vegetius it was reduced to a foot or even nine inches. I have chosen a medium.

[47] For the legionary arms, see Lipsius de Militiâ Romanâ, l. iii. c. 2–7.

[48] See the beautiful comparison of Virgil, Georgic. ii. v. 279.

this open order, in a long front and a rapid charge, found themselves prepared to execute every disposition which the circumstances of war, or the skill of their leader, might suggest. The soldier possessed a free space for his arms and motions, and sufficient intervals were allowed, through which seasonable reinforcements might be introduced to the relief of the exhausted combatants.[49] The tactics of the Greeks and Macedonians were formed on very different principles. The strength of the phalanx depended on sixteen ranks of long pikes, wedged together in the closest array.[50] But it was soon discovered, by reflection as well as by the event, that the strength of the phalanx was unable to contend with the activity of the legion.[51]

The cavalry, without which the force of the legion would have remained imperfect, was divided into ten troops or squadrons; the first, as the companion of the first cohort, consisted of an hundred and thirty-two men; whilst each of the other nine amounted only to sixty-six. The entire establishment formed a regiment, if we may use the modern expression, of seven hundred and twenty-six horse, naturally connected with its respective legion, but occasionally separated to act in the line, and to compose a part of the wings of the army.[52] The cavalry of the emperors was no longer composed, like that of the ancient republic, of the noblest youths of Rome and Italy, who, by performing their military service on horseback, prepared themselves for the offices of senator

[49] M. Guichard, Mémoires Militaires, tom. i. c. 4, and Nouveaux Mémoires, tom. i. p. 293-311, has treated the subject like a scholar and an officer.

[50] See Arrian's Tactics [12]. With the true partiality of a Greek, Arrian rather chose to describe the phalanx of which he had read, than the legions which he had commanded.

[51] Polyb. l. xvii. [xviii. 15].

[52] Veget. de Re Militari, l. ii. c. 6. His positive testimony, which might be supported by circumstantial evidence, ought surely to silence those critics who refuse the Imperial legion its proper body of cavalry. [But his testimony must be treated with great caution.]

and consul; and solicited, by deeds of valour, the future suffrages of their countrymen.[53] Since the alteration of manners and government, the most wealthy of the equestrian order were engaged in the administration of justice, and of the revenue;[54] and whenever they embraced the profession of arms, they were immediately intrusted with a troop of horse, or a cohort of foot.[55] Trajan and Hadrian formed their cavalry from the same provinces, and the same class of their subjects, which recruited the ranks of the legion. The horses were bred, for the most part, in Spain or Cappadocia. The Roman troopers despised the complete armour with which the cavalry of the East was encumbered. *Their* more useful arms consisted in a helmet, an oblong shield, light boots, and a coat of mail. A javelin, and a long broad sword, were their principal weapons of offence. The use of lances and of iron maces they seem to have borrowed from the barbarians.[56]

The safety and honour of the empire was principally intrusted to the legions, but the policy of Rome condescended to adopt every useful instrument of war. Considerable levies were regularly made among the provincials, who had not yet deserved the honourable distinction of Romans. Many dependent princes and communities, dispersed round the frontiers, were permitted, for a while, to hold their freedom and security by the tenure of military service.[57] Even select troops of hostile barbarians were frequently compelled or persuaded to consume their dangerous valour in remote

[53] See Livy almost throughout, particularly xlii. 61.

[54] Plin. Hist. Natur. xxxiii. 2. The true sense of that very curious passage was first discovered and illustrated by M. de Beaufort, République Romaine, l. ii. c. 2.

[55] As in the instance of Horace and Agricola. This appears to have been a defect in the Roman discipline; which Hadrian endeavoured to remedy by ascertaining the legal age of a tribune. [For the *equites*, compare Mommsen, Staatsrecht, iii. 476–569.]

[56] See Arrian's Tactics [4].

[57] Such, in particular, was the state of the Batavians. Tacit. Germania, c. 29.

climates, and for the benefit of the state.[58] All these were included under the general name of auxiliaries; and howsoever they might vary according to the difference of times and circumstances, their numbers were seldom much inferior to those of the legions themselves.[59] Among the auxiliaries, the bravest and most faithful bands were placed under the command of prefects and centurions, and severely trained in the arts of Roman discipline; but the far greater part retained those arms, to which the nature of their country, or their early habits of life, more peculiarly adapted them. By this institution, each legion, to whom a certain proportion of auxiliaries was allotted, contained within itself every species of lighter troops, and of missile weapons; and was capable of encountering every nation with the advantages of its respective arms and discipline.[60] Nor was the legion destitute of what, in modern language, would be styled a train of artillery. It consisted in ten military engines of the largest, and fifty-five of a smaller size; but all of which, either in an oblique or horizontal manner, discharged stones and darts with irresistible violence.[61]

The camp of a Roman legion presented the appearance of a fortified city.[62] As soon as the space was marked out, the

[58] Marcus Antoninus obliged the vanquished Quadi and Marcomanni to supply him with a large body of troops, which he immediately sent into Britain. Dion Cassius, l. lxxi. [16].

[59] Tacit. Annal. iv. 5. Those who fix a regular proportion of as many foot, and twice as many horse, confound the auxiliaries of the emperors with the Italian allies of the republic. [See Appendix 4.]

[60] Vegetius, ii. 2. Arrian, in his order of march and battle against the Alani.

[61] The subject of the ancient machines is treated with great knowledge and ingenuity by the Chevalier Folard (Polybe, tom. ii. p. 233–290). He prefers them in many respects to our modern cannon and mortars. We may observe that the use of them in the field gradually became more prevalent, in proportion as personal valour and military skill declined with the Roman empire. When men were no longer found, their place was supplied by machines. See Vegetius, ii. 25. Arrian.

[62] Vegetius finishes his second book, and the description of the legion, with the following emphatic words: "Universa quæ in quoque belli genere

pioneers carefully levelled the ground, and removed every impediment that might interrupt its perfect regularity. Its form was an exact quadrangle; and we may calculate, that a square of about seven hundred yards was sufficient for the encampment of twenty thousand Romans; though a similar number of our own troops would expose to the enemy a front of more than treble that extent. In the midst of the camp, the prætorium, or general's quarters, rose above the others; the cavalry, the infantry, and the auxiliaries occupied their respective stations; the streets were broad and perfectly straight, and a vacant space of two hundred feet was left on all sides, between the tents and the rampart. The rampart itself was usually twelve feet high, armed with a line of strong and intricate palisades, and defended by a ditch of twelve feet in depth as well as in breadth. This important labour was performed by the hands of the legionaries themselves; to whom the use of the spade and the pick-axe was no less familiar than that of the sword or *pilum*. Active valour may often be the present of nature; but such patient diligence can be the fruit only of habit and discipline.[83]

Whenever the trumpet gave the signal of departure, the camp was almost instantly broken up, and the troops fell into their ranks without delay or confusion. Besides their arms, which the legionaries scarcely considered as an encumbrance, they were laden with their kitchen furniture, the instruments of fortification, and the provision of many days.[84] Under this weight, which would oppress the delicacy of a modern soldier, they were trained by a regular step to advance,

necessaria esse creduntur, secum legio debet ubique portare, ut in quovis loco fixerit castra, armatam faciat civitatem."

[83] For the Roman Castrametation, see Polybius, l. vi. [27 *et sqq.*] with Lipsius de Militiâ Romanâ, Joseph. de Bell. Jud. l. iii. c. 5. Vegetius, i. 21–25, iii. 9, and Mémoires de Guichard, tom. i. c. 1.

[84] Cicero in Tusculan, ii. 37 [16]. — Joseph. de Bell. Jud. l. iii. 5. Frontinus, iv. 1.

in about six hours, near twenty miles.[59] On the appearance of an enemy, they threw aside their baggage, and, by easy and rapid evolutions, converted the column of march into an order of battle.[60] The slingers and archers skirmished in the front; the auxiliaries formed the first line, and were seconded or sustained by the strength of the legions; the cavalry covered the flanks, and the military engines were placed in the rear.

Such were the arts of war, by which the Roman emperors defended their extensive conquests, and preserved a military spirit, at a time when every other virtue was oppressed by luxury and despotism. If, in the consideration of their armies, we pass from their discipline to their numbers, we shall not find it easy to define them with any tolerable accuracy. We may compute, however, that the legion, which was itself a body of six thousand eight hundred and thirty-one Romans, might, with its attendant auxiliaries, amount to about twelve thousand five hundred men. The peace establishment of Hadrian and his successors was composed of no less than thirty of these formidable brigades; and most probably formed a standing force of three hundred and seventy-five thousand men. Instead of being confined within the walls of fortified cities, which the Romans considered as the refuge of weakness or pusillanimity, the legions were encamped on the banks of the great rivers, and along the frontiers of the barbarians. As their stations, for the most part, remained fixed and permanent, we may venture to describe the distribution of the troops. Three legions were sufficient for Britain. The principal strength lay upon the Rhine and Danube, and consisted of sixteen legions, in the following proportions: two in the Lower, and three in the Upper Germany; one in Rhætia, one in Noricum, four in Pannonia, three in Mæsia, and two in Dacia. The defence

[59] Vegetius, l. 9. See Mémoires de l'Académie des Inscriptions, tom. xxv. p. 187.

[60] See those evolutions admirably well explained by M. Guichard, Nouveaux Mémoires, tom. i. p. 141–234.

of the Euphrates was intrusted to eight legions, six of whom were planted in Syria, and the other two in Cappadocia. With regard to Egypt, Africa, and Spain, as they were far removed from any important scene of war, a single legion maintained the domestic tranquillity of each of those great provinces. Even Italy was not left destitute of a military force. Above twenty thousand chosen soldiers, distinguished by the titles of City Cohorts and Prætorian Guards, watched over the safety of the monarch and the capital. As the authors of almost every revolution that distracted the empire, the Prætorians will very soon and very loudly demand our attention; but, in their arms and institutions, we cannot find any circumstance which discriminated them from the legions, unless it were a more splendid appearance, and a less rigid discipline.[67]

The navy maintained by the emperors might seem inadequate to their greatness; but it was fully sufficient for every useful purpose of government. The ambition of the Romans was confined to the land; nor was that warlike people ever actuated by the enterprising spirit which had prompted the navigators of Tyre, of Carthage, and even of Marseilles, to enlarge the bounds of the world, and to explore the most remote coasts of the ocean. To the Romans the ocean remained an object of terror rather than of curiosity;[68] the whole extent of the Mediterranean, after the destruction of Carthage and the extirpation of the pirates, was included within their provinces. The policy of the emperors was directed only to preserve the peaceful dominion of that sea, and to protect the commerce of their subjects. With these moderate views,

[67] Tacitus (Annal. iv. 5) has given us a state of the legions under Tiberius; and Dion Cassius (l. lv. p. 794 [23]) under Alexander Severus. I have endeavoured to fix on the proper medium between these two periods. See likewise Lipsius de Magnitudine Romanâ, l. i. c. 4, 5. [On the author's procedure here, see Appendix 4. On the Prætorian Guards see below, p. 133.]

[68] The Romans tried to disguise, by the pretence of religious awe, their ignorance and terror. See Tacit. Germania, c. 34.

Augustus stationed two permanent fleets in the most convenient ports of Italy, the one at Ravenna, on the Adriatic, the other at Misenum, in the bay of Naples. Experience seems at length to have convinced the ancients that, as soon as their galleys exceeded two, or at the most three ranks of oars, they were suited rather for vain pomp than for real service. Augustus himself, in the victory of Actium, had seen the superiority of his own light frigates (they were called Liburnians) over the lofty but unwieldy castles of his rival.[69] Of these Liburnians he composed the two fleets of Ravenna and Misenum, destined to command, the one the eastern, the other the western division of the Mediterranean; and to each of the squadrons he attached a body of several thousand marines. Besides these two ports, which may be considered as the principal seats of the Roman navy, a very considerable force was stationed at Frejus, on the coast of Provence, and the Euxine was guarded by forty ships, and three thousand soldiers. To all these we add the fleet which preserved the communication between Gaul and Britain, and a great number of vessels constantly maintained on the Rhine and Danube, to harass the country, or to intercept the passage of the barbarians.[70] If we review this general state of the Imperial forces, of the cavalry as well as infantry, of the legions, the auxiliaries, the guards, and the navy, the most liberal computation will not allow us to fix the entire establishment by sea and by land at more than four hundred and fifty thousand men: a military power which, however formidable it may seem, was equalled by a monarch of the last century, whose kingdom was confined within a single province of the Roman empire.[71]

[69] Plutarch. in Marc. Anton [66]. And yet if we may credit Orosius, these monstrous castles were no more than ten feet above the water, vi. 19. [They had two ranks of oars.]

[70] See Lipsius, de Magnitud. Rom. l. i. c. 5. The sixteen last chapters of Vegetius relate to naval affairs. [See Appendix 5.]

[71] Voltaire, Siècle de Louis XIV, c. 29. It must, however, be remembered, that France still feels that extraordinary effort.

We have attempted to explain the spirit which moderated, and the strength which supported, the power of Hadrian and the Antonines. We shall now endeavour, with clearness and precision, to describe the provinces once united under their sway, but, at present, divided into so many independent and hostile states.[72]

Spain, the western extremity of the empire, of Europe, and of the ancient world, has, in every age, invariably preserved the same natural limits; the Pyrenean mountains, the Mediterranean, and the Atlantic Ocean. That great peninsula, at present so unequally divided between two sovereigns, was distributed by Augustus into three provinces, Lusitania, Bætica, and Tarraconensis.[73] The kingdom of Portugal now fills the place of the warlike country of the Lusitanians; and the loss sustained by the former, on the side of the East, is compensated by an accession of territory towards the North. The confines of Grenada and Andalusia correspond with those of ancient Bætica. The remainder of Spain — Gallicia, and the Asturias, Biscay, and Navarre, Leon, and the two Castilles, Murcia, Valencia, Catalonia, and Arragon, — all contributed to form the third and most considerable of the Roman governments, which, from the name of its capital, was styled the province of Tarragona.[74] Of the native barbarians, the Celtiberians were the most powerful, as the Cantabrians and Asturians proved the most obstinate. Confident in the strength of their mountains, they were the last who submitted to the arms of Rome, and the first who threw off the yoke of the Arabs.

Ancient Gaul, as it contained the whole country between the Pyrenees, the Alps, the Rhine, and the Ocean, was of

[72] [This list of the provinces is incomplete. For full list see Appendix 6.]

[73] [Bætica was divided from Tarraconensis by the *saltus Castulonensis*.]

[74] See Strabo, l. ii. [Rather iii. p. 166.] It is natural enough to suppose, that Arragon is derived from Tarraconensis, and several moderns who have written in Latin use those words as synonymous. It is, however, certain, that the Arragon, a little stream which falls from the Pyrenees into the Ebro, first gave its name to a country, and gradually to a kingdom. See d'Anville, Géographie du Moyen Age, p. 181.

greater extent than modern France. To the dominions of that powerful monarchy, with its recent acquisitions of Alsace and Lorraine, we must add the duchy of Savoy, the cantons of Switzerland, the four electorates of the Rhine, and the territories of Liege, Luxemburg, Hainault, Flanders, and Brabant. When Augustus gave laws to the conquests of his father, he introduced a division of Gaul equally adapted to the progress of the legions, to the course of the rivers, and to the principal national distinctions, which had comprehended above an hundred independent states.[78] The sea-coast of the Mediterranean, Languedoc, Provence, and Dauphiné, received their provincial appellation from the colony of Narbonne. The government of Aquitaine was extended from the Pyrenees to the Loire. The country between the Loire and the Seine was styled the Celtic Gaul, and soon borrowed a new denomination from the celebrated colony of Lugdunum, or Lyons. The Belgic lay beyond the Seine, and in more ancient times had been bounded only by the Rhine; but a little before the age of Cæsar, the Germans, abusing their superiority of valour, had occupied a considerable portion of the Belgic territory. The Roman conquerors very eagerly embraced so flattering a circumstance, and the Gallic frontier of the Rhine, from Basil to Leyden, received the pompous names of the Upper and the Lower Germany.[79] Such, under the reign of the Antonines, were the six provinces of Gaul; the Narbonnese, Aquitaine, the Celtic, or Lyonnese, the Belgic, and the two Germanies.

We have already had occasion to mention the conquest of Britain, and to fix the boundary of the Roman province in this

[78] One hundred and fifteen *cities* appear in the Notitia of Gaul; and it is well known that this appellation was applied not only to the capital town, but to the whole territory of each state. But Plutarch and Appian increase the number of tribes to three or four hundred.

[79] D'Anville, Notice de l'Ancienne Gaule. [These frontier districts received their names when the true province of Germany, between Rhine and Elbe, which had been won by Drusus, was lost by the defeat of Varus in 9 A.D.]

island. It comprehended all England, Wales, and the Lowlands of Scotland, as far as the Friths of Dumbarton and Edinburgh. Before Britain lost her freedom, the country was irregularly divided between thirty tribes of barbarians, of whom the most considerable were the Belgæ in the West, the Brigantes in the North, the Silures in South Wales, and the Iceni in Norfolk and Suffolk.[77] As far as we can either trace or credit the resemblance of manners and language, Spain, Gaul, and Britain were peopled by the same hardy race of savages. Before they yielded to the Roman arms, they often disputed the field, and often renewed the contest. After their submission they constituted the western division of the European provinces, which extended from the columns of Hercules to the wall of Antoninus,[78] and from the mouth of the Tagus to the sources of the Rhine and Danube.

Before the Roman conquest, the country which is now called Lombardy was not considered as a part of Italy. It had been occupied by a powerful colony of Gauls, who, settling themselves along the banks of the Po, from Piedmont to Romagna, carried their arms and diffused their name from the Alps to the Apennine. The Ligurians dwelt on the rocky coast, which now forms the republic of Genoa.[79] Venice was yet unborn; but the territories of that state, which lie to the east of the Adige, were inhabited by the Venetians.[80] The middle part of the peninsula, that now composes the duchy of Tuscany and the ecclesiastical state, was the ancient seat of the Etruscans and Umbrians; to the

[77] Whitaker's History of Manchester, vol. i. c. 3.

[78] [A rampart from the Clyde to the Forth built in the reign of Antoninus Pius by the prefect Lollius Urbicus. For this wall see Stuart's Caledonia.]

[79] [We shall find late Greek historians calling the Genoese *Ligurians* (Λιγούριοι). It sounds odd, but serves to remind us that the great city of Liguria did not preserve the ancient name of the territory like her eastern rival, the great city of Venetia.]

[80] The Italian Veneti, though often confounded with the Gauls, were more probably of Illyrian origin. See M. Freret, Mémoires de l'Académie des Inscriptions, tom. xviii.

former of whom Italy was indebted for the first rudiments of a civilised life.[81] The Tiber rolled at the foot of the seven hills of Rome, and the country of the Sabines, the Latins, and the Volsci, from that river to the frontiers of Naples, was the theatre of her infant victories. On that celebrated ground the first consuls deserved triumphs, their successors adorned villas, and *their* posterity have erected convents.[82] Capua and Campania possessed the immediate territory of Naples; the rest of the kingdom was inhabited by many warlike nations, the Marsi, the Samnites, the Apulians, and the Lucanians; and the sea-coasts had been covered by the flourishing colonies of the Greeks. We may remark, that when Augustus divided Italy into eleven regions, the little province of Istria was annexed to that seat of Roman sovereignty.[83]

The European provinces of Rome were protected by the course of the Rhine and the Danube. The latter of those mighty streams, which rises at the distance of only thirty miles from the former, flows above thirteen hundred miles, for the most part to the south-east, collects the tribute of sixty navigable rivers, and is, at length, through six mouths, received into the Euxine, which appears scarcely equal to such an accession of waters.[84] The provinces of the Danube soon acquired the general appellation of Illyricum, or the Illyrian frontier,[85] and were esteemed the most warlike of the empire; but they deserve to be more particularly considered under the names of Rhætia, Noricum, Pannonia, Dalmatia, Dacia, Mæsia, Thrace, Macedonia, and Greece.

The province of Rhætia, which soon extinguished the name of the Vindelicians, extended from the summit of the Alps to

[81] See Maffei, Verona Illustrata.

[82] The first contrast was observed by the ancients. See Florus, l. 11. The second must strike every modern traveller.

[83] Pliny (Hist. Natur. l. iii. [6]) follows the division of Italy, by Augustus.

[84] Tournefort, Voyages en Grèce et Asie Mineure, lettre xviii.

[85] The name of Illyricum originally belonged to the sea-coast of the Adriatic, and was gradually extended by the Romans from the Alps to the Euxine Sea. See Severini Pannonia, l. i. c. 3.

the banks of the Danube; from its source, as far as its conflux with the Inn. The greatest part of the flat country is subject to the elector of Bavaria; the city of Augsburg is protected by the constitution of the German empire; the Grisons are safe in their mountains; and the country of Tyrol is ranked among the numerous provinces of the house of Austria.

The wide extent of territory which is included between the Inn, the Danube, and the Save, — Austria, Styria, Carinthia, Carniola, the Lower Hungary, and Sclavonia, — was known to the ancients under the names of Noricum and Pannonia. In their original state of independence their fierce inhabitants were intimately connected. Under the Roman government they were frequently united, and they still remain the patrimony of a single family. They now contain the residence of a German prince, who styles himself Emperor of the Romans, and form the centre, as well as strength, of the Austrian power. It may not be improper to observe, that, if we except Bohemia, Moravia, the northern skirts of Austria, and a part of Hungary, between the Theiss and the Danube, all the other dominions of the house of Austria were comprised within the limits of the Roman empire.

Dalmatia, to which the name of Illyricum more properly belonged, was a long, but narrow tract, between the Save and the Adriatic. The best part of the sea-coast, which still retains its ancient appellation, is a province of the Venetian state, and the seat of the little republic of Ragusa. The inland parts have assumed the Sclavonian names of Croatia and Bosnia; the former obeys an Austrian governor, the latter a Turkish pasha; but the whole country is still infested by tribes of barbarians, whose savage independence irregularly marks the doubtful limit of the Christian and Mahometan power.[88]

[88] A Venetian traveller, the Abbate Fortis, has lately given us some account of those very obscure countries. But the geography and antiquities of the western Illyricum can be expected only from the munificence of the emperor, its sovereign. [See Mr. Jackson's work entitled Dalmatia, the Quarnero, and Istria.]

After the Danube had received the waters of the Theiss and the Save, it acquired, at least among the Greeks, the name of Ister.[87] It formerly divided Mæsia and Dacia, the latter of which, as we have already seen, was a conquest of Trajan, and the only province beyond the river. If we inquire into the present state of those countries, we shall find that, on the left hand of the Danube, Temeswar and Transylvania have been annexed, after many revolutions, to the crown of Hungary; whilst the principalities of Moldavia and Walachia acknowledge the supremacy of the Ottoman Porte. On the right hand of the Danube, Mæsia, which during the middle ages was broken into the barbarian kingdoms of Servia and Bulgaria, is again united in Turkish slavery.

The appellation of Roumelia, which is still bestowed by the Turks on the extensive countries of Thrace, Macedonia, and Greece, preserves the memory of their ancient state under the Roman empire.[88] In the time of the Antonines, the martial regions of Thrace, from the mountains of Hæmus and Rhodope to the Bosphorus and the Hellespont, had assumed the form of a province. Notwithstanding the change of masters and of religion, the new city of Rome, founded by Constantine on the banks of the Bosphorus, has ever since remained the capital of a great monarchy. The kingdom of Macedonia, which, under the reign of Alexander, gave laws to Asia, derived more solid advantages from the policy of the two Philips; and, with its dependencies of Epirus and Thessaly, extended from the Ægean to the Ionian sea. When we reflect on the fame of Thebes and Argos, of Sparta and Athens, we can scarcely persuade ourselves that so many immortal

[87] The Save rises near the confines of *Istria*, and was considered by the more early Greeks as the principal stream of the Danube.

[88] [Thrace is Eastern Roumelia; Macedonia and Greece, Western Roumelia. Since Greece became independent, one bears less of Western Roumelia, but the name is still applicable to Macedonia; Greece has severed her connection with the usurped inheritance of New Rome. Only the Eastern Roumelia will as a rule be found marked on maps. See Appendix 7.]

republics of ancient Greece were lost in a single province of the Roman empire, which, from the superior influence of the Achæan league, was usually denominated the province of Achaia.

Such was the state of Europe under the Roman emperors. The provinces of Asia, without excepting the transient conquests of Trajan, are all comprehended within the limits of the Turkish power. But instead of following the arbitrary divisions of despotism and ignorance, it will be safer for us, as well as more agreeable, to observe the indelible characters of nature. The name of Asia Minor is attributed, with some propriety, to the peninsula which, confined between the Euxine and the Mediterranean, advances from the Euphrates towards Europe. The most extensive and flourishing district westward of Mount Taurus and the river Halys, was dignified by the Romans with the exclusive title of Asia. The jurisdiction of that province extended over the ancient monarchies of Troy, Lydia, and Phrygia, the maritime countries of the Pamphylians, Lycians, and Carians, and the Grecian colonies of Ionia, which equalled in arts, though not in arms, the glory of their parent. The kingdoms of Bithynia and Pontus possessed the northern side of the peninsula from Constantinople to Trebizond. On the opposite side the province of Cilicia was terminated by the mountains of Syria: the inland country, separated from the Roman Asia by the river Halys, and from Armenia by the Euphrates, had once formed the independent kingdom of Cappadocia. In this place we may observe that the northern shores of the Euxine, beyond Trebizond in Asia and beyond the Danube in Europe, acknowledged the sovereignty of the emperors, and received at their hands either tributary princes or Roman garrisons. Budzak, Crim Tartary, Circassia, and Mingrelia are the modern appellations of those savage countries.[89]

[89] See the Periplus of Arrian. He examined the coasts of the Euxine, when he was governor of Cappadocia.

Under the successors of Alexander, Syria was the seat of the Seleucidæ, who reigned over Upper Asia, till the successful revolt of the Parthians confined their dominions between the Euphrates and the Mediterranean. When Syria became subject to the Romans, it formed the eastern frontier of their empire; nor did that province, in its utmost latitude, know any other bounds than the mountains of Cappadocia to the north, and, towards the south, the confines of Egypt and the Red Sea. Phœnicia and Palestine were sometimes annexed to, and sometimes separated from, the jurisdiction of Syria. The former of these was a narrow and rocky coast; the latter was a territory scarcely superior to Wales, either in fertility or extent. Yet Phœnicia and Palestine will for ever live in the memory of mankind; since America, as well as Europe, has received letters from the one, and religion from the other.[90] A sandy desert, alike destitute of wood and water, skirts along the doubtful confine of Syria, from the Euphrates to the Red Sea. The wandering life of the Arabs was inseparably connected with their independence, and wherever, on some spots less barren than the rest, they ventured to form any settled habitations, they soon became subjects to the Roman empire.[91]

The geographers of antiquity have frequently hesitated to what portion of the globe they should ascribe Egypt.[92] By

[90] The progress of religion is well known. The use of letters was introduced among the savages of Europe about fifteen hundred years before Christ; and the Europeans carried them to America, about fifteen centuries after the Christian era. But in a period of three thousand years, the Phœnician alphabet received considerable alterations, as it passed through the hands of the Greeks and Romans. [The date here given for the introduction of the Phœnician alphabet to Europe, that is, among the Greeks, is much too early. The earliest date that can be plausibly maintained is the tenth century, the latest, the eighth. But there are traces of hieroglyphic writing at Mycenæ, and Mr. Arthur Evans's discoveries in Crete point to the use not only of hieroglyphics, but of a syllabary (like the Cyprian) centuries before the introduction of the Phœnician letters.]

[91] Dion Cassius, lxviii. p. 1131 [14].

[92] Ptolemy and Strabo, with the modern geographers, fix the Isthmus of Suez as the boundary of Asia and Africa. Dionysius, Mela, Pliny, Sallust, Hirtius, and Solinus have preferred for that purpose the western branch of

its situation that celebrated kingdom is included within the immense peninsula of Africa; but it is accessible only on the side of Asia, whose revolutions, in almost every period of history, Egypt has humbly obeyed. A Roman prefect was seated on the splendid throne of the Ptolemies; and the iron sceptre of the Mamelukes is now in the hands of a Turkish pasha. The Nile flows down the country, above five hundred miles from the tropic of Cancer to the Mediterranean, and marks, on either side, the extent of fertility by the measure of its inundations. Cyrene, situated towards the west and along the sea-coast, was first a Greek colony, afterwards a province of Egypt, and is now lost in the desert of Barca.

From Cyrene to the ocean, the coast of Africa extends above fifteen hundred miles; yet so closely is it pressed between the Mediterranean and the Sahara, or sandy desert, that its breadth seldom exceeds fourscore or an hundred miles. The eastern division was considered by the Romans as the more peculiar and proper province of Africa. Till the arrival of the Phœnician colonies, that fertile country was inhabited by the Libyans, the most savage of mankind. Under the immediate jurisdiction of Carthage it became the centre of commerce and empire; but the republic of Carthage is now degenerated into the feeble and disorderly states of Tripoli and Tunis. The military government of Algiers oppresses the wide extent of Numidia, as it was once united under Massinissa and Jugurtha: but in the time of Augustus the limits of Numidia were contracted; and at least two-thirds of the country acquiesced in the name of Mauritania, with the epithet of Cæsariensis.[89] The genuine Mauritania, or country of the Moors, which, from the ancient city of Tingi, or Tangier, was distinguished by the appellation of Tingitana, is represented by the modern

the Nile, or even the great Catabathmus, or descent, which last would assign to Asia not only Egypt, but part of Libya. [For Roman Egypt see Mr. J. G. Milne's History of Egypt under Roman Rule, 1898.]

[89] [The boundary between Maur. Cæs. and Maur. Ting. was the river Mulucha.]

kingdom of Fez. Sallè, on the Ocean, so infamous at present for its piratical depredations, was noticed by the Romans, as the extreme object of their power, and almost of their geography. A city of their foundation may still be discovered near Mequinez, the residence of the barbarian whom we condescend to style the Emperor of Morocco; but it does not appear that his more southern dominions, Morocco itself, and Segelmessa, were ever comprehended within the Roman province. The western parts of Africa are intersected by the branches of Mount Atlas, a name so idly celebrated by the fancy of poets;[84] but which is now diffused over the immense ocean that rolls between the ancient and the new continent.[85]

Having now finished the circuit of the Roman empire, we may observe that Africa is divided from Spain by a narrow strait of about twelve miles, through which the Atlantic flows into the Mediterranean. The columns of Hercules, so famous among the ancients, were two mountains which seemed to have been torn asunder by some convulsion of the elements; and at the foot of the European mountain the fortress of Gibraltar is now seated. The whole extent of the Mediterranean Sea, its coasts and its islands, were comprised within the Roman dominion. Of the larger islands, the two Baleares, which derive their names of Majorca and Minorca from their respective size, are subject at present, the former to Spain, the latter to Great Britain. It is easier to deplore the fate

[84] The long range, moderate height, and gentle declivity of Mount Atlas (see Shaw's Travels, p. 5) are very unlike a solitary mountain which rears its head into the clouds, and seems to support the heavens. The peak of Teneriff, on the contrary, rises a league and a half above the surface of the sea, and, as it was frequently visited by the Phœnicians, might engage the notice of the Greek poets. See Buffon, Histoire Naturelle, tom. i. p. 312. Histoire des Voyages, tom. ii.

[85] M. de Voltaire, tom. xiv. p. 297, unsupported by either fact or probability, has generously bestowed the Canary Islands on the Roman empire. [In recent years the history and geography of the Roman Africa have been explored by French scholars. Tissot, Géographie comparée de la province romaine d'Afrique, 1884-8; Fastes de la province d'Afrique, 1885; Cagnat, L'armée romaine d'Afrique, 1893; may be mentioned.]

than to describe the actual condition of Corsica. Two Italian sovereigns assume a regal title from Sardinia and Sicily. Crete, or Candia, with Cyprus, and most of the smaller islands of Greece and Asia, have been subdued by the Turkish arms; whilst the little rock of Malta defies their power, and has emerged, under the government of its military Order, into fame and opulence.

This long enumeration of provinces, whose broken fragments have formed so many powerful kingdoms, might almost induce us to forgive the vanity or ignorance of the ancients. Dazzled with the extensive sway, the irresistible strength, and the real or affected moderation of the emperors, they permitted themselves to despise, and sometimes to forget, the outlying countries which had been left in the enjoyment of a barbarous independence; and they gradually assumed the licence of confounding the Roman monarchy with the globe of the earth.[96] But the temper, as well as knowledge, of a modern historian require a more sober and accurate language. He may impress a juster image of the greatness of Rome by observing that the empire was above two thousand miles in breadth, from the wall of Antoninus and the northern limits of Dacia to Mount Atlas and the tropic of Cancer; that it extended in length more than three thousand miles, from the Western Ocean to the Euphrates; that it was situated in the finest part of the Temperate Zone, between the twenty-fourth and fifty-sixth degrees of northern latitude; and that it was supposed to contain above sixteen hundred thousand square miles, for the most part of fertile and well-cultivated land.[97]

[96] Bergier, Hist. des Grands Chemins, l. iii. c. 1, 2, 3, 4: a very useful collection.

[97] See Templeman's Survey of the Globe; but I distrust both the doctor's learning and his maps.

CHAPTER II

Of the Union and Internal Prosperity of the Roman Empire, in the Age of the Antonines

It is not alone by the rapidity or extent of conquest that we should estimate the greatness of Rome. The sovereign of the Russian deserts commands a larger portion of the globe. In the seventh summer after his passage of the Hellespont, Alexander erected the Macedonian trophies on the banks of the Hyphasis.[1] Within less than a century, the irresistible Zingis, and the Mogul princes of his race, spread their cruel devastations and transient empire from the sea of China to the confines of Egypt and Germany.[2] But the firm edifice of Roman power was raised and preserved by the wisdom of ages. The obedient provinces of Trajan and the Antonines were united by laws and adorned by arts. They might occasionally suffer from the partial abuse of delegated authority; but the general principle of government was wise, simple, and beneficent. They enjoyed the religion of their ancestors, whilst in civil honours and advantages they were exalted, by just degrees, to an equality with their conquerors.

I. The policy of the emperors and the senate, as far as it concerned religion, was happily seconded by the reflections of the enlightened, and by the habits of the superstitious, part of their subjects. The various modes of worship which pre-

[1] They were erected about the midway between Lahor and Delhi. The conquests of Alexander in Hindostan were confined to the Punjab, a country watered by the five great streams of the Indus. [Alexander reached the Hyphasis in the eighth summer (B.C. 326) after his passage of the Hellespont (B.C. 334).]

[2] See M. de Guignes, Histoire des Huns, l. xv. xvi. and xvii.

vailed in the Roman world were all considered by the people as equally true; by the philosopher as equally false; and by the magistrate as equally useful. And thus toleration produced not only mutual indulgence, but even religious concord.

The superstition of the people was not embittered by any mixture of theological rancour; nor was it confined by the chains of any speculative system. The devout polytheist, though fondly attached to his national rites, admitted with implicit faith the different religions of the earth.[8] Fear, gratitude, and curiosity, a dream or an omen, a singular disorder, or a distant journey, perpetually disposed him to multiply the articles of his belief, and to enlarge the list of his protectors. The thin texture of the pagan mythology was interwoven with various but not discordant materials. As soon as it was allowed that sages and heroes, who had lived or who had died for the benefit of their country, were exalted to a state of power and immortality, it was universally confessed that they deserved, if not the adoration, at least the reverence of all mankind. The deities of a thousand groves and a thousand streams possessed in peace their local and respective influence; nor could the Roman who deprecated the wrath of the Tiber deride the Egyptian who presented his offering to the beneficent genius of the Nile. The visible powers of Nature, the planets, and the elements, were the same throughout the universe. The invisible governors of the moral world were inevitably cast in a similar mould of fiction and allegory. Every virtue, and even vice, acquired its divine representative; every art and profession its patron, whose attributes in the most distant ages and countries were uni-

[8] There is not any writer who describes in so lively a manner as Herodotus, the true genius of Polytheism. The best commentary may be found in Mr. Hume's Natural History of Religion; and the best contrast in Bossuet's Universal History. Some obscure traces of an intolerant spirit appear in the conduct of the Egyptians (see Juvenal, Sat. xv.); and the Christians as well as Jews, who lived under the Roman empire, formed a very important exception; so important indeed, that the discussion will require a distinct chapter of this work.

formly derived from the character of their peculiar votaries. A republic of gods of such opposite tempers and interests required, in every system, the moderating hand of a supreme magistrate, who, by the progress of knowledge and of flattery, was gradually invested with the sublime perfections of an Eternal Parent and an Omnipotent Monarch.[4] Such was the mild spirit of antiquity, that the nations were less attentive to the difference than to the resemblance of their religious worship. The Greek, the Roman, and the Barbarian, as they met before their respective altars, easily persuaded themselves that, under various names and with various ceremonies, they adored the same deities. The elegant mythology of Homer gave a beautiful and almost a regular form to the polytheism of the ancient world.[5]

The philosophers of Greece deduced their morals from the nature of man rather than from that of God. They meditated, however, on the Divine Nature as a very curious and important speculation, and in the profound inquiry they displayed the strength and weakness of the human understanding.[6] Of the four most celebrated schools, the Stoics and the Platonists endeavoured to reconcile the jarring interests of reason and piety. They have left us the most sublime proofs of the existence and perfections of the first cause; but, as it was impossible for them to conceive the creation of matter, the workman in the Stoic philosophy was not sufficiently distinguished from the work; whilst, on the contrary, the spiritual God of Plato and his disciples

[4] The rights, power, and pretensions of the sovereign of Olympus are very clearly described in the xvth book of the Iliad: in the Greek original, I mean; for Mr. Pope, without perceiving it, has improved the theology of Homer.

[5] See for instance, Cæsar de Bell. Gall. vi. 17. Within a century or two the Gauls themselves applied to their gods the names of Mercury, Mars, Apollo, &c.

[6] The admirable work of Cicero, de Naturâ Deorum, is the best clue we have to guide us through the dark and profound abyss. He represents with candour, and confutes with subtlety, the opinions of the philosophers.

resembled an idea rather than a substance. The opinions of the Academics and Epicureans were of a less religious cast; but, whilst the modest science of the former induced them to doubt, the positive ignorance of the latter urged them to deny, the providence of a Supreme Ruler. The spirit of inquiry, prompted by emulation and supported by freedom, had divided the public teachers of philosophy into a variety of contending sects; but the ingenuous youth, who from every part resorted to Athens and the other seats of learning in the Roman empire, were alike instructed in every school to reject and to despise the religion of the multitude. How, indeed, was it possible that a philosopher should accept as divine truths the idle tales of the poets, and the incoherent traditions of antiquity; or that he should adore, as gods, those imperfect beings whom he must have despised, as men! Against such unworthy adversaries, Cicero condescended to employ the arms of reason and eloquence; but the satire of Lucian was a much more adequate as well as more efficacious weapon. We may be well assured that a writer conversant with the world would never have ventured to expose the gods of his country to public ridicule, had they not already been the objects of secret contempt among the polished and enlightened orders of society.[7]

Notwithstanding the fashionable irreligion which prevailed in the age of the Antonines, both the interests of the priests and the credulity of the people were sufficiently respected. In their writings and conversation the philosophers of antiquity asserted the independent dignity of reason; but they resigned their actions to the commands of law and of custom. Viewing with a smile of pity and indulgence the various errors of the vulgar, they diligently practised the ceremonies of their fathers, devoutly frequented the temples of the gods; and,

[7] I do not pretend to assert that, in this irreligious age, the natural terrors of superstition, dreams, omens, apparitions, &c., had lost their efficacy.

sometimes condescending to act a part on the theatre of superstition, they concealed the sentiments of an Atheist under the sacerdotal robes. Reasoners of such a temper were scarcely inclined to wrangle about their respective modes of faith or of worship. It was indifferent to them what shape the folly of the multitude might choose to assume; and they approached, with the same inward contempt and the same external reverence, the altars of the Libyan, the Olympian, or the Capitoline Jupiter.[8]

It is not easy to conceive from what motives a spirit of persecution could introduce itself into the Roman councils. The magistrates could not be actuated by a blind though honest bigotry, since the magistrates were themselves philosophers; and the schools of Athens had given laws to the senate. They could not be impelled by ambition or avarice, as the temporal and ecclesiastical powers were united in the same hands. The pontiffs were chosen among the most illustrious of the senators; and the office of Supreme Pontiff was constantly exercised by the emperors themselves. They knew and valued the advantages of religion, as it is connected with civil government. They encouraged the public festivals which humanize the manners of the people. They managed the arts of divination as a convenient instrument of policy; and they respected, as the firmest bond of society, the useful persuasion that, either in this or in a future life, the crime of perjury is most assuredly punished by the avenging gods.[9] But, whilst they acknowledged the general advantages of religion, they were convinced that the various modes of worship contributed alike to the same salutary purposes; and that, in

[8] Socrates, Epicurus, Cicero, and Plutarch, always inculcated a decent reverence for the religion of their own country, and of mankind. The devotion of Epicurus was assiduous and exemplary. Diogen. Laert. x. 10. [In this passage nothing is said of the devotion of Epicurus. τῆς μὲν γὰρ πρὸς θεοὺς ὁσιότητος . . . ἄλεκτος ἡ διάθεσις seems to have been mistranslated.]

[9] Polybius, l. vi. c. 56. Juvenal, Sat. xiii., laments that in his time this apprehension had lost much of its effect.

every country, the form of superstition which had received the sanction of time and experience was the best adapted to the climate and to its inhabitants. Avarice and taste very frequently despoiled the vanquished nations of the elegant statues of their gods and the rich ornaments of their temples;[10] but, in the exercise of the religion which they derived from their ancestors, they uniformly experienced the indulgence, and even protection, of the Roman conquerors. The province of Gaul seems, and indeed only seems, an exception to this universal toleration. Under the specious pretext of abolishing human sacrifices, the emperors Tiberius and Claudius suppressed the dangerous power of the Druids;[11] but the priests themselves, their gods, and their altars, subsisted in peaceful obscurity till the final destruction of Paganism.[12]

Rome, the capital of a great monarchy, was incessantly filled with subjects and strangers from every part of the world,[13] who all introduced and enjoyed the favourite superstitions of their native country.[14] Every city in the empire was justified in maintaining the purity of its ancient ceremonies; and the Roman senate, using the common privilege, sometimes interposed to check this inundation of foreign rites. The Egyptian superstition, of all the most contemptible and abject, was frequently prohibited; the temples of Serapis and Isis demolished, and their worshippers banished from Rome and Italy.[15] But the zeal of fanaticism prevailed over

[10] See the fate of Syracuse, Tarentum, Ambracia, Corinth, &c., the conduct of Verres, in Cicero (Actio ii. Orat. 4), and the usual practice of governors, in the viiith Satire of Juvenal.

[11] Sueton. in Claud. [25] — Plin. Hist. Nat. xxx. i.

[12] Pelloutier, Histoire des Celtes, tom. vi. p. 230–252.

[13] Seneca Consolat. ad Helviam, p. 74 [6]. Edit. Lips.

[14] Dionysius Halicarn. Antiquitat. Roman., l. ii. [i. p. 275, Reiske].

[15] In the year of Rome 701, the temple of Isis and Serapis was demolished by the order of the senate (Dion Cassius, l. xl. p. 252 [47]), and even by the hands of the consul (Valerius Maximus, 1, 3). [But this passage in Valerius refers to the first demolition in B.C. 219.] After the death of Cæsar, it was

the cold and feeble efforts of policy. The exiles returned, the proselytes multiplied, the temples were restored with increasing splendour, and Isis and Serapis at length assumed their place among the Roman deities.[16] Nor was this indulgence a departure from the old maxims of government. In the purest ages of the commonwealth, Cybele and Æsculapius had been invited by solemn embassies;[17] and it was customary to tempt the protectors of besieged cities by the promise of more distinguished honours than they possessed in their native country.[18] Rome gradually became the common temple of her subjects; and the freedom of the city was bestowed on all the gods of mankind.[19]

II. The narrow policy of preserving without any foreign mixture the pure blood of the ancient citizens, had checked the fortune, and hastened the ruin, of Athens and Sparta. The aspiring genius of Rome sacrificed vanity to ambition, and deemed it more prudent, as well as honourable, to adopt virtue and merit for her own wheresoever they were found, among slaves or strangers, enemies or barbarians.[20] During the most flourishing era of the Athenian commonwealth the number of citizens gradually decreased from about thirty[21]

restored at the public expense (Dion, l. xlvii. p. 501 [15]). When Augustus was in Egypt, he revered the majesty of Serapis (Dion, l. li. p. 647 [16]); but in the Pomærium of Rome, and a mile round it, he prohibited the worship of the Egyptian gods (Dion, l. liii. p. 697 [2], l. liv. p. 735 [6]). They remained, however, very fashionable under his reign (Ovid. de Art. Amand. l. i. [77]) and that of his successor, till the justice of Tiberius was provoked to some acts of severity. (See Tacit. Annal. ii. 85, Joseph. Antiquit. l. xviii. c. 3.)

[16] Tertullian in Apologetic. c. 6, p. 74. Edit. Havercamp. I am inclined to attribute their establishment to the devotion of the Flavian family.

[17] See Livy, l. xi. [12] and xxix. [11].

[18] Macrob. Saturnalia, l. iii. c. 9. He gives us a form of evocation.

[19] Minucius Felix in Octavio, p. 54. Arnobius, l. vi. p. 115.

[20] Tacit. Annal. xi. 24. The Orbis Romanus of the learned Spanheim is a complete history of the progressive admission of Latium, Italy, and the provinces to the freedom of Rome.

[21] Herodotus, v. 97. It should seem, however, that he followed a large and popular estimation.

to twenty-one thousand.[22] If, on the contrary, we study the growth of the Roman republic, we may discover that, notwithstanding the incessant demands of wars and colonies, the citizens, who, in the first census of Servius Tullius, amounted to no more than eighty-three thousand,[23] were multiplied, before the commencement of the social war, to the number of four hundred and sixty-three thousand men able to bear arms in the service of their country.[24] When the allies of Rome claimed an equal share of honours and privileges, the senate indeed preferred the chance of arms to an ignominous concession. The Samnites and the Lucanians paid the severe penalty of their rashness; but the rest of the Italian states, as they successively returned to their duty, were admitted into the bosom of the republic,[25] and soon contributed to the ruin of public freedom. Under a democratical government the citizens exercise the powers of sovereignty; and those powers will be first abused, and afterwards lost, if they are committed to an unwieldy multitude. But, when the popular assemblies had been suppressed by the administration of the emperors, the conquerors were distinguished from the vanquished nations only as the first and most honourable order of subjects; and their increase, however rapid, was no longer exposed to the same dangers. Yet the wisest princes who adopted the maxims of Augustus guarded with the strictest care the dignity of the Roman name, and diffused the freedom of the city with a prudent liberality.[26]

[22] Athenæus Deipnosophist. l. vi. p. 272, Edit. Casaubon. Meursius de Fortunâ Atticâ, c. 4. [For the population of Athens, see Clinton's Fasti Hellenici, vol. i. p. 381, and Boeckh's Staatshaushaltung der Athener. But new light has been thrown on the Athenian as on other ancient populations by Beloch. He estimates the population of Athens c. 431 B.C. at 35,000.]

[23] [Perhaps about 20,000. See Mommsen, Hist. of Rome, i. 436, Eng. Tr.]

[24] See a very accurate collection of the numbers of each Lustrum in M. de Beaufort, République Romaine, l. iv. c. 4.

[25] Appian de Bell. civil. l. i. [53]. Velleius Paterculus, l. ii. c. 15, 16, 17.

[26] Mæcenas had advised him to declare, by one edict, all his subjects citizens. But we may justly suspect that the Historian Dion was the author of a counsel, so much adapted to the practice of his own age and so little to that of Augustus.

Till the privileges of Romans had been progressively extended to all the inhabitants of the empire, an important distinction was preserved between Italy and the provinces. The former was esteemed the centre of public unity, and the firm basis of the constitution. Italy claimed the birth, or at least the residence, of the emperors and the senate.[27] The estates of the Italians were exempt from taxes, their persons from the arbitrary jurisdiction of governors. Their municipal corporations, formed after the perfect model of the capital,[28] were intrusted, under the immediate eye of the supreme power, with the execution of the laws. From the foot of the Alps to the extremity of Calabria, all the natives of Italy were born citizens of Rome. Their partial distinctions were obliterated, and they insensibly coalesced into one great nation, united by language, manners, and civil institutions, and equal to the weight of a powerful empire. The republic gloried in her generous policy, and was frequently rewarded by the merit and services of her adopted sons. Had she always confined the distinction of Romans to the ancient families within the walls of the city, that immortal name would have been deprived of some of its noblest ornaments. Virgil was a native of Mantua; Horace was inclined to doubt whether he should call himself an Apulian or a Lucanian; it was in Padua that an historian was found worthy to record the majestic series of Roman victories. The patriot family of the Catos emerged from Tusculum; and the little town of Arpinum claimed the double honour of producing Marius and Cicero, the former of whom deserved, after Romulus and Camillus, to be styled

[27] The senators were obliged to have one-third of their own landed property in Italy. See Plin. l. vi. ep. 19. The qualification was reduced by Marcus to one-fourth. Since the reign of Trajan, Italy had sunk nearer to the level of the provinces.

[28] [This statement is too strong. The municipal constitutions of the Italian towns were hardly created in a day. The old constitutions were modified by the new relation with Rome, but not abolished.]

the Third Founder of Rome; and the latter, after saving his country from the designs of Catiline, enabled her to contend with Athens for the palm of eloquence.[28]

The provinces of the empire (as they have been described in the preceding chapter) were destitute of any public force or constitutional freedom. In Etruria, in Greece,[30] and in Gaul,[31] it was the first care of the senate to dissolve those dangerous confederacies which taught mankind that, as the Roman arms prevailed by division, they might be resisted by union. Those princes whom the ostentation of gratitude or generosity permitted for a while to hold a precarious sceptre were dismissed from their thrones, as soon as they had performed their appointed task of fashioning to the yoke the vanquished nations. The free states and cities which had embraced the cause of Rome were rewarded with a nominal alliance, and insensibly sunk into real servitude. The public authority was everywhere exercised by the ministers of the senate and of the emperors, and that authority was absolute and without control. But the same salutary maxims of government, which had secured the peace and obedience of Italy, were extended to the most distant conquests. A nation of Romans was gradually formed in the provinces, by the double expedient of introducing colonies, and of admitting the most faithful and deserving of the provincials to the freedom of Rome.

"Wheresoever the Roman conquers, he inhabits," is a very just observation of Seneca,[32] confirmed by history and

[29] The first part of the Verona Illustrata of the Marquis Maffei gives the clearest and most comprehensive view of the state of Italy under the Cæsars.

[30] See Pausanias, l. vii. [16]. The Romans condescended to restore the names of those assemblies, when they could no longer be dangerous.

[31] They are frequently mentioned by Cæsar. The Abbé Dubos attempts, with very little success, to prove that the assemblies of Gaul were continued under the emperors. Histoire de l'Etablissement de la Monarchie Françoise, l. i. c. 4. [These assemblies did exist in Gaul as well as in other provinces. See E. Carette, Les assemblées provinciales de la Gaule romaine, 1895.]

[32] Seneca in Consolat. ad Helviam, c. 6.

experience. The natives of Italy, allured by pleasure or by interest, hastened to enjoy the advantages of victory; and we may remark that, about forty years after the reduction of Asia, eighty thousand Romans were massacred in one day by the cruel orders of Mithridates.[33] These voluntary exiles were engaged for the most part in the occupations of commerce, agriculture, and the farm of the revenue. But after the legions were rendered permanent by the emperors, the provinces were peopled by a race of soldiers; and the veterans, whether they received the reward of their service in land or in money, usually settled with their families in the country where they had honourably spent their youth. Throughout the empire, but more particularly in the western parts, the most fertile districts and the most convenient situations were reserved for the establishment of colonies; some of which were of a civil and others of a military nature. In their manners and internal policy, the colonies formed a perfect representation of their great parent; and [as] they were soon endeared to the natives by the ties of friendship and alliance, they effectually diffused a reverence for the Roman name, and a desire which was seldom disappointed of sharing, in due time, its honours and advantages.[34] The municipal cities insensibly equalled the rank and splendour of the colonies; and in the reign of Hadrian it was disputed which was the preferable condition, of those societies which had issued from, or those which

[33] Memnon apud Photium, c. 33 [c. 31; Müller, *F.H.G.*, iii. p. 542]. Valer. Maxim. ix. 2. Plutarch [Sulla, 24] and Dion Cassius [fr. 99; vol. i. p. 342, ed. Melber] swell the massacre to 150,000 citizens; but I should esteem the smaller number to be more than sufficient.

[34] Twenty-five colonies were settled in Spain (see Plin. Hist. Natur. iii. 3, 4, iv. 35): and nine in Britain, of which London, Colchester, Lincoln, Chester, Gloucester, and Bath, still remain considerable cities (see Richard of Cirencester, p. 36, and Whitaker's History of Manchester, l. i. c. 3). [The authority of Richard of Cirencester on Roman Britain is of no value. See Appendix 2.]

had been received into, the bosom of Rome.[85] The right of Latium, as it was called, conferred on the cities to which it had been granted a more partial favour. The magistrates only, at the expiration of their office, assumed the quality of Roman citizens; but as those offices were annual, in a few years they circulated round the principal families.[86] Those of the provincials who were permitted to bear arms in the legions;[87] those who exercised any civil employment; all, in a word, who performed any public service, or displayed any personal talents, were rewarded with a present, whose value was continually diminished by the increasing liberality of the emperors. Yet even in the age of the Antonines, when the freedom of the city had been bestowed on the greater number of their subjects, it was still accompanied with very solid advantages. The bulk of the people acquired, with that title, the benefit of the Roman laws, particularly in the interesting articles of marriage, testaments, and inheritances; and the road of fortune was open to those whose pretensions were seconded by favour or merit. The grandsons of the Gauls who had besieged Julius Cæsar in Alesia commanded legions, governed provinces, and were admitted into the senate of Rome.[88] Their ambition, instead of disturbing the tranquillity of the state, was intimately connected with its safety and greatness.

So sensible were the Romans of the influence of language over national manners, that it was their most serious care to extend, with the progress of their arms, the use of the Latin

[85] Aul. Gell. Noctes Atticæ, xvi. 13. The Emperor Hadrian expressed his surprise that the cities of Utica, Gades, and Italica, which already enjoyed the rights of *Municipia*, should solicit the title of *colonies*. Their example, however, became fashionable, and the empire was filled with honorary colonies. See Spanheim, de Usu Numismatum, Dissertat. xiii. [For colonies, municipal towns and the right of Latium, see Appendix 8.]

[86] Spanheim, Orbis Roman. c. 8. p. 62.

[87] Aristid. in Romæ Encomio, tom. i. p. 218. Edit. Jebb.

[88] Tacit. Annal. xi. 23, 24. Hist. iv. 74.

tongue.[39] The ancient dialects of Italy, the Sabine, the Etruscan, and the Venetian, sunk into oblivion; but in the provinces, the east was less docile than the west to the voice of its victorious preceptors. This obvious difference marked the two portions of the empire with a distinction of colours, which, though it was in some degree concealed during the meridian splendour of prosperity, became gradually more visible as the shades of night descended upon the Roman world. The western countries were civilized by the same hands which subdued them. As soon as the barbarians were reconciled to obedience, their minds were opened to any new impressions of knowledge and politeness. The language of Virgil and Cicero, though with some inevitable mixture of corruption, was so universally adopted in Africa, Spain, Gaul, Britain, and Pannonia,[40] that the faint traces of the Punic or Celtic idioms were preserved only in the mountains, or among the peasants.[41] Education and study insensibly inspired the natives of those countries with the sentiments of Romans; and Italy gave fashions, as well as laws, to her Latin provincials. They solicited with more ardour, and obtained with more facility, the freedom and honours of the state; supported the national dignity in letters[42] and in arms; and, at length, in the person of Trajan, pro-

[39] See Plin. Hist. Natur. iii. 5. Augustin. de Civitate Dei, xix. 7. Lipsius de pronunciatione Linguæ Latinæ, c. 3.

[40] Apuleius and Augustin will answer for Africa; Strabo for Spain and Gaul; Tacitus, in the life of Agricola, for Britain; and Velleius Paterculus, for Pannonia. To them we may add the language of the Inscriptions. [The statement in the text needs modification especially in regard to Britain.]

[41] The Celtic was preserved in the mountains of Wales, Cornwall, and Armorica. We may observe that Apuleius reproaches an African youth, who lived among the populace, with the use of the Punic; whilst he had almost forgot Greek, and neither could nor would speak Latin. (Apolog. p. 596.) The greater part of St. Austin's congregations were strangers to the Punic.

[42] Spain alone produced Columella, the Senecas, Lucan, Martial, and Quintilian [but *not*, as far as we know, Silius Italicus, who, if his name really connected him with Italica, must have been *Italicensis*].

duced an emperor whom the Scipios would not have disowned for their countryman. The situation of the Greeks was very different from that of the barbarians. The former had been long since civilized and corrupted. They had too much taste to relinquish their language, and too much vanity to adopt any foreign institutions. Still preserving the prejudices, after they had lost the virtues, of their ancestors, they affected to despise the unpolished manners of the Roman conquerors, whilst they were compelled to respect their superior wisdom and power.[43] Nor was the influence of the Grecian language and sentiments confined to the narrow limits of that once celebrated country. Their empire, by the progress of colonies and conquest, had been diffused from the Hadriatic to the Euphrates and the Nile. Asia was covered with Greek cities, and the long reign of the Macedonian kings had introduced a silent revolution into Syria and Egypt. In their pompous courts those princes united the elegance of Athens with the luxury of the East, and the example of the court was imitated, at an humble distance, by the higher ranks of their subjects. Such was the general division of the Roman empire into the Latin and Greek languages. To these we may add a third distinction for the body of the natives in Syria, and especially in Egypt. The use of their ancient dialects, by secluding them from the commerce of mankind, checked the improvement of those barbarians.[44] The slothful effeminacy of the former exposed them to the contempt, the sullen ferociousness of the latter excited the aversion, of the conquerors.[45] Those nations had submitted to the Roman power, but they

[43] There is not, I believe, from Dionysius to Libanius, a single Greek critic who mentions Virgil or Horace. They seem ignorant that the Romans had any good writers.

[44] The curious reader may see in Dupin (Bibliothèque Ecclésiastique, tom. xix. p. 1, c. 8) how much the use of the Syriac and Egyptian languages was still preserved.

[45] See Juvenal, Sat. iii. and xv. Ammian. Marcellin. xxii. 16.

seldom desired or deserved the freedom of the city; and it was remarked that more than two hundred and thirty years elapsed after the ruin of the Ptolemies, before an Egyptian was admitted into the senate of Rome.[46]

It is a just though trite observation, that victorious Rome was herself subdued by the arts of Greece. Those immortal writers who still command the admiration of modern Europe soon became the favourite object of study and imitation in Italy and the western provinces. But the elegant amusements of the Romans were not suffered to interfere with their sound maxims of policy. Whilst they acknowledged the charms of the Greek, they asserted the dignity of the Latin, tongue, and the exclusive use of the latter was inflexibly maintained in the administration of civil as well as military government.[47] The two languages exercised at the same time their separate jurisdiction throughout the empire: the former, as the natural idiom of science; the latter, as the legal dialect of public transactions. Those who united letters with business were equally conversant with both; and it was almost impossible, in any province, to find a Roman subject, of a liberal education, who was at once a stranger to the Greek and to the Latin language.

It was by such institutions that the nations of the empire insensibly melted away into the Roman name and people. But there still remained, in the centre of every province and of every family, an unhappy condition of men who endured the weight, without sharing the benefits, of society. In the free states of antiquity the domestic slaves were exposed to the wanton rigour of despotism. The perfect settlement of the Roman empire was preceded by ages of violence and rapine. The slaves consisted, for the most part, of barbarian

[46] Dion Cassius, l. lxxvi. p. 1275 [5]. The first instance happened under the reign of Septimius Severus.

[47] See Valerius Maximus, l. ii. c. 2, n. 2. The Emperor Claudius disfranchised an eminent Grecian for not understanding Latin. He was probably in some public office. Suetonius in Claud. c. 16.

captives, taken in thousands by the chance of war, purchased at a vile price,[48] accustomed to a life of independence, and impatient to break and to revenge their fetters. Against such internal enemies, whose desperate insurrections had more than once reduced the republic to the brink of destruction,[49] the most severe regulations[50] and the most cruel treatment seemed almost justified by the great law of self-preservation. But when the principal nations of Europe, Asia, and Africa were united under the laws of one sovereign, the source of foreign supplies flowed with much less abundance, and the Romans were reduced to the milder but more tedious method of propagation. In their numerous families, and particularly in their country estates, they encouraged the marriage of their slaves. The sentiments of nature, the habits of education, and the possession of a dependent species of property, contributed to alleviate the hardships of servitude.[51] The existence of a slave became an object of greater value, and though his happiness still depended on the temper and circumstances of the master, the humanity of the latter, instead of being restrained by fear, was encouraged by the sense of his own interest. The progress of manners was accelerated by the virtue or policy of the emperors; and by the edicts of Hadrian and the Antonines the protection of the laws was extended to the most abject part of mankind. The jurisdiction of life and death over the slaves, a power long exercised and often abused, was taken out of private hands, and reserved to the magistrates alone. The subterraneous prisons were abolished; and, upon a just complaint of intolerable treatment, the in-

[48] In the camp of Lucullus, an ox sold for a drachma, and a slave for four drachmæ, or about three shillings. Plutarch, in Lucull. p. 580 [14]. [Compare Dureau de la Malle, *Econ. Pol. des Romains*, i. 15.]

[49] Diodorus Siculus in Eclog. Hist. l. xxxiv. and xxxvi. Florus, iii. 19, 20.

[50] See a remarkable instance of severity, in Cicero in Verrem, v. 3.

[51] See in Gruter, and the other collectors, a great number of inscriptions addressed by slaves to their wives, children, fellow-servants, masters, &c. They are all most probably of the Imperial age.

jured slave obtained either his deliverance or a less cruel master.[52]

Hope, the best comfort of our imperfect condition, was not denied to the Roman slave; and, if he had any opportunity of making himself either useful or agreeable, he might very naturally expect that the diligence and fidelity of a few years would be rewarded with the inestimable gift of freedom. The benevolence of the master was so frequently prompted by the meaner suggestions of vanity and avarice, that the laws found it more necessary to restrain than to encourage a profuse and undistinguishing liberality, which might degenerate into a very dangerous abuse.[53] It was a maxim of ancient jurisprudence, that a slave had not any country of his own; he acquired with his liberty an admission into the political society of which his patron was a member. The consequences of this maxim would have prostituted the privileges of the Roman city to a mean and promiscuous multitude. Some seasonable exceptions were therefore provided; and the honourable distinction was confined to such slaves only as, for just causes, and with the approbation of the magistrate, should receive a solemn and legal manumission. Even these chosen freedmen obtained no more than the private rights of citizens, and were rigorously excluded from civil or military honours. Whatever might be the merit or fortune of their sons, *they* likewise were esteemed unworthy of a seat in the senate; nor were the traces of a servile origin allowed to be completely obliterated till the third or fourth generation.[54] Without destroying the distinction of ranks, a distant prospect of freedom and honours was presented, even to those whom pride and prejudice almost disdained to number among the human species.

[52] See the Augustan History [1, 18], and a dissertation of M. de Burigny, in the xxxvth volume of the Academy of Inscriptions, upon the Roman slaves.

[53] See another dissertation of M. de Burigny in the xxxviith volume, on the Roman freedmen.

[54] Spanheim, Orbis Roman. l. i. c. 16. p. 124, &c.

It was once proposed to discriminate the slaves by a peculiar habit, but it was justly apprehended that there might be some danger in acquainting them with their own numbers.[55] Without interpreting, in their utmost strictness, the liberal appellations of legions and myriads,[56] we may venture to pronounce that the proportion of slaves, who were valued as property, was more considerable than that of servants, who can be computed only as an expense.[57] The youths of a promising genius were instructed in the arts and sciences, and their price was ascertained by the degree of their skill and talents.[58] Almost every profession, either liberal[59] or mechanical, might be found in the household of an opulent senator. The ministers of pomp and sensuality were multiplied beyond the conception of modern luxury.[60] It was more for the interest of the merchant or manufacturer to purchase than to hire his workmen; and in the country slaves were employed as the cheapest and most laborious instruments of agriculture. To confirm the general observation, and to display the multitude of slaves, we might allege a variety of particular instances. It was discovered, on a very melancholy occasion, that four hundred slaves were maintained in a single palace of Rome.[61] The same number

[55] Seneca de Clementiâ, l. i. c. 24. The original is much stronger, "Quantum periculum immineret si servi nostri numerare nos cœpissent."

[56] See Pliny (Hist. Natur. l. xxxiii.) and Athenæus (Deipnosophist, l. vi. p. 272). The latter boldly asserts that he knew very many (πάμπολλοι) Romans who possessed, not for use, but ostentation, ten and even twenty thousand slaves.

[57] In Paris there are not more than 43,700 domestics of every sort, and not a twelfth part of the inhabitants. Messange, Recherches sur la Population, p. 186.

[58] A learned slave sold for many hundred pounds sterling; Atticus always bred and taught them himself. Cornel. Nepos in Vit. c. 13.

[59] Many of the Roman physicians were slaves. See Dr. Middleton's Dissertation and Defence. [On the state of Physicians among the Old Romans, 1734.]

[60] Their ranks and offices are very copiously enumerated by Pignorius de Servis. [For whole subject cp. Wallon, Hist. de l'Esclavage.]

[61] Tacit. Annal. xiv. 43. They all were executed for not preventing their master's murder.

of four hundred belonged to an estate, which an African widow, of a very private condition, resigned to her son, whilst she reserved for herself a much larger share of her property.[62] A freedman, under the reign of Augustus, though his fortune had suffered great losses in the civil wars, left behind him three thousand six hundred yoke of oxen, two hundred and fifty thousand head of smaller cattle, and, what was almost included in the description of cattle, four thousand one hundred and sixteen slaves.[63]

The number of subjects who acknowledged the laws of Rome, of citizens, of provincials, and of slaves, cannot now be fixed with such a degree of accuracy as the importance of the object would deserve.[64] We are informed that, when the emperor Claudius exercised the office of censor, he took an account of six millions nine hundred and forty-five thousand Roman citizens, who, with the proportion of women and children, must have amounted to about twenty millions of souls. The multitude of subjects of an inferior rank was uncertain and fluctuating. But, after weighing with attention every circumstance which could influence the balance, it seems probable that there existed, in the time of Claudius, about twice as many provincials as there were citizens, of either sex and of every age; and that the slaves were at least equal in number to the free inhabitants of the Roman world. The total amount of this imperfect calculation would rise to about one hundred and twenty millions of persons: a degree of population which possibly exceeds that of

[62] Apuleius in Apolog. p. 548. Edit. Delphin.

[63] Plin. Hist. Natur. l. xxxiii. 47.

[64] [The subject of the population of the Roman empire has been discussed in detail in Dureau de la Malle's Economie Politique, on which work Merivale's investigation is based (History of the Romans under the Empire, chap. 39). Merivale reckons the entire population under Augustus, "including both sexes, all ages and every class of inhabitants," at eighty-five millions, of which forty fall to the European, forty-five to the Asiatic provinces. In the present day the total population of these European lands is two and a half times as great. Gibbon's calculation is, on any theory, far too large.]

modern Europe,[a] and forms the most numerous society that has ever been united under the same system of government.

Domestic peace and union were the natural consequences of the moderate and comprehensive policy embraced by the Romans. If we turn our eyes towards the monarchies of Asia, we shall behold despotism in the centre and weakness in the extremities; the collection of the revenue, or the administration of justice, enforced by the presence of an army; hostile barbarians, established in the heart of the country, hereditary satraps usurping the dominion of the provinces and subjects, inclined to rebellion, though incapable of freedom. But the obedience of the Roman world was uniform, voluntary, and permanent. The vanquished nations, blended into one great people, resigned the hope, nay even the wish, of resuming their independence, and scarcely considered their own existence as distinct from the existence of Rome. The established authority of the emperors pervaded without an effort the wide extent of their dominions, and was exercised with the same facility on the banks of the Thames, or of the Nile, as on those of the Tiber. The legions were destined to serve against the public enemy, and the civil magistrate seldom required the aid of a military force.[b] In this state of general security, the leisure as well as opulence both of the prince and people were devoted to improve and to adorn the Roman empire.

Among the innumerable monuments of architecture con-

[a] Compute twenty millions in France, twenty-two in Germany, four in Hungary, ten in Italy with its islands, eight in Great Britain and Ireland, eight in Spain and Portugal, ten or twelve in the European Russia, six in Poland, six in Greece and Turkey, four in Sweden, three in Denmark and Norway, four in the Low Countries. The whole would amount to one hundred and five or one hundred and seven millions. See Voltaire, de l'Histoire Générale. [The present population of Europe is somewhat about three hundred and fifty millions.]

[b] Joseph. de Bell. Judaico, l. ii. c. 16. The oration of Agrippa, or rather of the historian, is a fine picture of the Roman empire.

structed by the Romans, how many have escaped the notice of history, how few have resisted the ravages of time and barbarism! And yet even the majestic ruins that are still scattered over Italy and the provinces would be sufficient to prove that those countries were once the seat of a polite and powerful empire. Their greatness alone, or their beauty, might deserve our attention; but they are rendered more interesting by two important circumstances, which connect the agreeable history of the arts with the more useful history of human manners. Many of those works were erected at private expense, and almost all were intended for public benefit.

It is natural to suppose that the greatest number, as well as the most considerable of the Roman edifices, were raised by the emperors, who possessed so unbounded a command both of men and money. Augustus was accustomed to boast that he had found his capital of brick, and that he had left it of marble.[87] The strict economy of Vespasian was the source of his magnificence. The works of Trajan bear the stamp of his genius. The public monuments with which Hadrian adorned every province of the empire were executed not only by his orders, but under his immediate inspection. He was himself an artist; and he loved the arts, as they conduced to the glory of the monarch. They were encouraged by the Antonines, as they contributed to the happiness of the people. But if the emperors were the first, they were not the only architects of their dominions. Their example was universally imitated by their principal subjects, who were not afraid of declaring that they had spirit to con-

[87] Sueton. in August. c. 28. Augustus built in Rome the temple and forum of Mars the Avenger; the Temple of Jupiter Tonans in the capitol; that of Apollo Palatine, with public libraries; the portico and basilica of Caius and Lucius; the porticos of Livia and Octavia, and the theatre of Marcellus. The example of the sovereign was imitated by his ministers and generals; and his friend Agrippa left behind him the immortal monument of the Pantheon.

ceive, and wealth to accomplish, the noblest undertakings. Scarcely had the proud structure of the Coliseum been dedicated at Rome, before the edifices of a smaller scale indeed, but of the same design and materials, were erected for the use, and at the expense, of the cities of Capua and Verona.[88] The inscription of the stupendous bridge of Alcantara attests that it was thrown over the Tagus by the contribution of a few Lusitanian communities. When Pliny was intrusted with the government of Bithynia and Pontus, provinces by no means the richest or most considerable of the empire, he found the cities within his jurisdiction striving with each other in every useful and ornamental work that might deserve the curiosity of strangers or the gratitude of their citizens. It was the duty of the Proconsul to supply their deficiencies, to direct their taste, and sometimes to moderate their emulation.[89] The opulent senators of Rome and the provinces esteemed it an honour, and almost an obligation, to adorn the splendour of their age and country; and the influence of fashion very frequently supplied the want of taste or generosity. Among a crowd of these private benefactors, we may select Herodes Atticus, an Athenian citizen, who lived in the age of the Antonines. Whatever might be the motive of his conduct, his magnificence would have been worthy of the greatest kings.

The family of Herod, at least after it had been favoured by fortune, was lineally descended from Cimon and Miltiades, Theseus and Cecrops, Æacus and Jupiter. But the posterity of so many gods and heroes was fallen into the most abject state. His grandfather had suffered by the hands

[88] See Maffei, Verona illustrata, l. iv. p. 68.

[89] See the xth book of Pliny's Epistles. He mentions the following works, carried on at the expense of the cities. At Nicomedia, a new forum, an aqueduct, and a canal, left unfinished by a king; at Nice, a Gymnasium and a theatre, which had already cost near ninety thousand pounds; baths at Prusa and Claudiopolis; and an aqueduct of sixteen miles in length for the use of Sinope.

of justice, and Julius Atticus, his father, must have ended his life in poverty and contempt, had he not discovered an immense treasure buried under an old house, the last remains of his patrimony. According to the rigour of law, the emperor might have asserted his claim; and the prudent Atticus prevented, by a frank confession, the officiousness of informers. But the equitable Nerva, who then filled the throne, refused to accept any part of it, and commanded him to use, without scruple, the present of fortune. The cautious Athenian still insisted that the treasure was too considerable for a subject, and that he knew not how to *use it*. *Abuse it then*, replied the monarch, with a good-natured peevishness; for it is your own.[70] Many will be of opinion that Atticus literally obeyed the emperor's last instructions, since he expended the greatest part of his fortune, which was much increased by an advantageous marriage, in the service of the Public. He had obtained for his son Herod the prefecture of the free cities of Asia; and the young magistrate, observing that the town of Troas was indifferently supplied with water, obtained from the munificence of Hadrian three hundred myriads of drachms (about a hundred thousand pounds) for the construction of a new aqueduct. But in the execution of the work the charge amounted to more than double the estimate, and the officers of the revenue began to murmur, till the generous Atticus silenced their complaints by requesting that he might be permitted to take upon himself the whole additional expense.[71]

The ablest preceptors of Greece and Asia had been invited by liberal rewards to direct the education of young Herod. Their pupil soon became a celebrated orator in

[70] Hadrian afterwards made a very equitable regulation, which divided all treasure trove between the right of property and that of discovery. Hist. August. p. 9 [i. 18].

[71] Philostrat. in Vit. Sophist. l. ii. p. 548. [We cannot implicitly trust the statements of Philostratus, the biographer of Herodes, for he was also the biographer of Apollonius of Tyana.]

the useless rhetoric of that age, which, confining itself to the schools, disdained to visit either the Forum or the Senate. He was honoured with the consulship at Rome; but the greatest part of his life was spent in a philosophic retirement at Athens, and his adjacent villas; perpetually surrounded by sophists, who acknowledged, without reluctance, the superiority of a rich and generous rival.[72] The monuments of his genius have perished; some remains still preserve the fame of his taste and munificence: modern travellers have measured the remains of the stadium which he constructed at Athens. It was six hundred feet in length, built entirely of white marble, capable of admitting the whole body of the people, and finished in four years, whilst Herod was president of the Athenian games. To the memory of his wife Regilla he dedicated a theatre, scarcely to be paralleled in the empire: no wood except cedar very curiously carved, was employed in any part of the building. The Odeum, designed by Pericles for musical performances and the rehearsal of new tragedies, had been a trophy of the victory of the arts over Barbaric greatness; as the timbers employed in the construction consisted chiefly of the masts of the Persian vessels. Notwithstanding the repairs bestowed on that ancient edifice by a king of Cappadocia, it was again fallen to decay. Herod restored its ancient beauty and magnificence.[73] Nor was the liberality of that illustrious citizen confined to the walls of Athens. The most splendid ornaments bestowed on the temple of Neptune in the Isthmus, a theatre at Corinth, a stadium at Delphi, a bath at Thermopylæ, and an aqueduct at Canusium in Italy, were in-

[72] Aulus Gellius, in Noct. Attic. i. 2, ix. 2, xviii. 10, xix. 12. Philostrat. p. 564 [ii. 14].

[73] [The Odeum of Herodes is here wrongly distinguished from his theatre and confounded with the Odeum of Pericles. The latter, which has disappeared, was close to the Theatre of Dionysus, but on the east side; that of Herodes, of which there are still ample remains, was on the west (S. W. of the Acropolis).]

sufficient to exhaust his treasures. The people of Epirus, Thessaly, Eubœa, Bœotia, and Peloponnesus, experienced his favours; and many inscriptions of the cities of Greece and Asia gratefully style Herodes Atticus their patron and benefactor.[74]

In the commonwealths of Athens and Rome, the modest simplicity of private houses announced the equal condition of freedom; whilst the sovereignty of the people was represented in the majestic edifices destined to the public use:[75] nor was this republican spirit totally extinguished by the introduction of wealth and monarchy. It was in works of national honour and benefit that the most virtuous of the emperors affected to display their magnificence. The golden palace of Nero excited a just indignation, but the vast extent of ground which had been usurped by his selfish luxury was more nobly filled under the succeeding reigns by the Coliseum, the baths of Titus, the Claudian portico, and the temples dedicated to the goddess of Peace and to the genius of Rome.[76] These monuments of architecture, the property of the Roman people, were adorned with the most beautiful productions of Grecian painting and sculpture; and in the temple of Peace a very curious library was open to the curiosity of the learned. At a small distance from thence was situated the Forum of Trajan. It was surrounded with a lofty portico in the form of a quadrangle, into which four triumphal arches opened a noble and spacious entrance:

[74] See Philostrat. l. ii. p. 548, 560 [3 *sqq.*]. Pausanias l. i. [19] and vii. 20. The life of Herodes, in the xxxth volume of the Memoirs of the Academy of Inscriptions.

[75] It is particularly remarked of Athens by Dicæarchus, de Statu Græciæ, p. 8, inter Geographos Minores, edit. Hudson.

[76] Donatus de Roma Vetere, l. iii. c. 4, 5, 6, Nardini Roma Antica, l. iii. 11, 12, 13, and a MS. description of ancient Rome, by Bernardus Oricellarius, or Rucellas, of which I obtained a copy from the library of the Canon Ricardi at Florence. Two celebrated pictures of Timanthes and of Protogenes are mentioned by Pliny [xxxv. 36] as in the Temple of Peace; and the Laocoon was found in the Baths of Titus. [The Temple of Peace was erected by Vespasian.]

in the centre arose a column of marble, whose height of one hundred and ten feet denoted the elevation of the hill that had been cut away. This column, which still subsists in its ancient beauty, exhibited an exact representation of the Dacian victories of its founder. The veteran soldier contemplated the story of his own campaigns, and, by an easy illusion of national vanity, the peaceful citizen associated himself to the honours of the triumph. All the other quarters of the capital, and all the provinces of the empire, were embellished by the same liberal spirit of public magnificence, and were filled with amphitheatres, theatres, temples, porticos, triumphal arches, baths, and aqueducts, all variously conducive to the health, the devotion, and the pleasures of the meanest citizen. The last mentioned of those edifices deserve our peculiar attention. The boldness of the enterprise, the solidity of the execution, and the uses to which they were subservient, rank the aqueducts among the noblest monuments of Roman genius and power. The aqueducts of the capital claim a just pre-eminence; but the curious traveller, who, without the light of history, should examine those of Spoleto, of Metz, or of Segovia, would very naturally conclude that those provincial towns had formerly been the residence of some potent monarch. The solitudes of Asia and Africa were once covered with flourishing cities, whose populousness, and even whose existence, was derived from such artificial supplies of a perennial stream of fresh water.[77]

We have computed the inhabitants, and contemplated the public works, of the Roman empire. The observation of the number and greatness of its cities will serve to confirm the former and to multiply the latter. It may not be unpleasing to collect a few scattered instances relative to that subject,

[77] Montfaucon, l'Antiquité Expliquée, tom. iv. p. 2. l. i. c. 9. Fabretti has composed a very learned treatise on the aqueducts of Rome. [The chief work on the aqueducts now is Lanciani's Le acque egli acquedotti di Roma antica, 1890. There is a good account in Hodgkin's Italy and her Invaders, vol. iv. bk. v. c. vi.]

without forgetting, however, that, from the vanity of nations and the poverty of language, the vague appellation of city has been indifferently bestowed on Rome and upon Laurentum. I. *Ancient* Italy is said to have contained eleven hundred and ninety-seven cities; and, for whatsoever era of antiquity the expression might be intended,[78] there is not any reason to believe the country less populous in the age of the Antonines, than in that of Romulus. The petty states of Latium were contained within the metropolis of the empire, by whose superior influence they had been attracted. Those parts of Italy which have so long languished under the lazy tyranny of priests and viceroys had been afflicted only by the more tolerable calamities of war; and the first symptoms of decay which *they* experienced were amply compensated by the rapid improvements of the Cisalpine Gaul. The splendour of Verona may be traced in its remains: yet Verona was less celebrated than Aquileia or Padua, Milan or Ravenna. II. The spirit of improvement had passed the Alps, and been felt even in the woods of Britain, which were gradually cleared away to open a free space for convenient and elegant habitations. York was the seat of government; London was already enriched by commerce; and Bath was celebrated for the salutary effects of its medicinal waters. Gaul could boast of her twelve hundred cities;[79] and, though, in the northern parts, many of them, without excepting Paris itself, were little more than the rude and imperfect townships of a rising people, the southern provinces imitated the wealth and elegance of Italy.[80] Many were the cities of Gaul, Marseilles, Arles, Nismes, Narbonne, Toulouse, Bordeaux, Autun, Vienne, Lyons, Langres, and Treves, whose ancient condition might sustain an equal,

[78] Ælian Hist. Var. l. ix. c. 16. He lived in the time of Alexander Severus. See Fabricius, Biblioth. Græca, l. iv. c. 21.

[79] Joseph. de Bell. Jud. ii. 16. The number, however, is mentioned and should be received with a degree of latitude.

[80] Plin. Hist. Natur. iii. 5.

and perhaps advantageous, comparison with their present state. With regard to Spain, that country flourished as a province, and has declined as a kingdom. Exhausted by the abuse of her strength, by America, and by superstition, her pride might possibly be confounded, if we required such a list of three hundred and sixty cities as Pliny has exhibited under the reign of Vespasian.[81] III. Three hundred African cities had once acknowledged the authority of Carthage,[82] nor is it likely that their numbers diminished under the administration of the emperors: Carthage itself rose with new splendour from its ashes; and that capital, as well as Capua and Corinth, soon recovered all the advantages which can be separated from independent sovereignty. IV. The provinces of the East present the contrast of Roman magnificence with Turkish barbarism. The ruins of antiquity, scattered over uncultivated fields, and ascribed by ignorance to the power of magic, scarcely afford a shelter to the oppressed peasant or wandering Arab. Under the reign of the Cæsars, the proper Asia alone contained five hundred populous cities,[83] enriched with all the gifts of nature, and adorned with all the refinements of art. Eleven cities of Asia had once disputed the honour of dedicating a temple to Tiberius, and their respective merits were examined by the senate.[84]

[81] Plin. Hist. Natur. iii. 3, 4. iv. 35. The list seems authentic and accurate: the division of the provinces and the different condition of the cities are minutely distinguished.

[82] Strabon. Geograph. l. xvii. p. 1189.

[83] Joseph. de Bell. Jud. ii. 16. Philostrat. in Vit. Sophist. l. ii. p. 548. Edit. Olear. [Life of Herodes, 3.]

[84] Tacit. Annal. iv. 55. I have taken some pains in consulting and comparing modern travellers, with regard to the fate of those eleven cities of Asia; seven or eight are totally destroyed, Hypæpe, Tralles, Laodicea, Ilium, Halicarnassus, Miletus, Ephesus, and we may add Sardis. Of the remaining three, Pergamus is a straggling village of two or three thousand inhabitants; Magnesia, under the name of Guzel-hissar, a town of some consequence; and Smyrna, a great city, peopled by a hundred thousand souls. But even at Smyrna, while the Franks have maintained commerce, the Turks have ruined the arts.

Four of them were immediately rejected as unequal to the burden; and among these was Laodicea, whose splendour is still displayed in its ruins.[85] Laodicea collected a very considerable revenue from its flocks of sheep, celebrated for the fineness of their wool, and had received, a little before the contest, a legacy of above four hundred thousand pounds by the testament of a generous citizen.[86] If such was the poverty of Laodicea, what must have been the wealth of those cities, whose claim appeared preferable, and particularly of Pergamus, of Smyrna, and of Ephesus, who so long disputed with each other the titular primacy of Asia?[87] The capitals of Syria and Egypt held a still superior rank in the empire: Antioch and Alexandria looked down with disdain on a crowd of dependent cities,[88] and yielded with reluctance to the majesty of Rome itself.

All these cities were connected with each other, and with the capital, by the public highways, which, issuing from the Forum of Rome, traversed Italy, pervaded the provinces, and were terminated only by the frontiers of the empire. If we carefully trace the distance from the wall of Antoninus to Rome, and from thence to Jerusalem, it will be found that the great chain of communication, from the north-west to the south-east point of the empire, was drawn out to the length of four thousand and eighty Roman miles.[89] The public

[85] See a very exact and pleasing description of the ruins of Laodicea, in Chandler's Travels through Asia Minor, p. 225, &c.

[86] Strabo, l. xii. p. 866. He had studied at Tralles.

[87] See a dissertation of M. de Bose, Mem. de l'Académie, tom. xviii. Aristides pronounced an oration which is still extant, to recommend concord to the rival cities.

[88] The inhabitants of Egypt, exclusive of Alexandria, amounted to seven millions and a half (Joseph. de Bell. Jud. ii. 16). Under the military government of the Mamelukes, Syria was supposed to contain sixty thousand villages (Histoire de Timur Bec, l. v. c. 20).

[89] The following Itinerary may serve to convey some idea of the direction of the road, and of the distance between the principal towns. I. From the wall of Antoninus to York, 222 Roman miles. II. London 227. III. Rhutupiæ or Sandwich 67. IV. The navigation to Boulogne 45. V. Rheims

roads were accurately divided by milestones, and ran in a direct line from one city to another, with very little respect for the obstacles either of nature or private property. Mountains were perforated, and bold arches thrown over the broadest and most rapid streams.[60] The middle part of the road was raised into a terrace which commanded the adjacent country, consisted of several strata of sand, gravel, and cement and was paved with large stones, or, in some places near the capital, with granite.[61] Such was the solid construction of the Roman highways, whose firmness has not entirely yielded to the effort of fifteen centuries. They united the subjects of the most distant provinces by an easy and familiar intercourse; but their primary object had been to facilitate the marches of the legions; nor was any country considered as completely subdued, till it had been rendered, in all its parts, pervious to the arms and authority of the conqueror. The advantage of receiving the earliest intelligence, and of conveying their orders with celerity, induced the emperors to establish, throughout their extensive dominions, the regular institution of posts.[62] Houses were everywhere erected at the distance only of five or six miles; each of them was constantly provided with forty horses, and, by the help of these relays, it was easy to travel an hundred miles in a day along the Roman roads.[63] The use of the posts was allowed to

174. VI. Lyons 330. VII. Milan 324. VIII. Rome 426. IX. Brundusium 360. X. The navigation to Dyrrachium 40. XI. Byzantium 711. XII. Ancyra 283. XIII. Tarsus 301. XIV. Antioch 141. XV. Tyre 252. XVI. Jerusalem 168. In all 4080 Roman, or 3740 English miles. See the Itineraries published by Wesseling, his annotations; Gale and Stukeley for Britain, and M. d'Anville for Gaul and Italy.

[60] Montfaucon (l'Antiquité Expliquée, tom. iv. p. 2. l. i. c. 5) has described the bridges of Narni, Alcantara, Nismes, &c.

[61] Bergier. Histoire des grands Chemins de l'Empire Romain, l. ii. c. 1–28.

[62] Procopius in Hist. Arcanâ, c. 30. Bergier, Hist. des grands Chemins, l. iv. Codex Theodosian, l. viii. tit. v. vol. ii. p. 506–563, with Godefroy's learned commentary.

[63] In the time of Theodosius, Cæsarius, a magistrate of high rank, went

those who claimed it by an Imperial mandate; but, though originally intended for the public service, it was sometimes indulged to the business or conveniency of private citizens.[84] Nor was the communication of the Roman empire less free and open by sea than it was by land. The provinces surrounded and enclosed the Mediterranean; and Italy, in the shape of an immense promontory, advanced into the midst of that great lake. The coasts of Italy are, in general, destitute of safe harbours; but human industry had corrected the deficiencies of nature; and the artificial port of Ostia, in particular, situate at the mouth of the Tiber, and formed by the Emperor Claudius, was an useful monument of Roman greatness.[85] From this port, which was only sixteen miles from the capital, a favourable breeze frequently carried vessels in seven days to the columns of Hercules, and in nine or ten to Alexandria in Egypt.[86]

Whatever evils either reason or declamation have imputed to extensive empire, the power of Rome was attended with some beneficial consequences to mankind; and the same freedom of intercourse which extended the vices, diffused likewise the improvements, of social life. In the more remote ages of antiquity, the world was unequally divided. The East was in the immemorial possession of arts and luxury; whilst the West was inhabited by rude and warlike barbarians, who either disdained agriculture, or to whom it was totally unknown. Under the protection of an established govern-

post from Antioch to Constantinople. He began his journey at night, was in Cappadocia (165 miles from Antioch) the ensuing evening, and arrived at Constantinople the sixth day about noon. The whole distance was 725 Roman, or 665 English miles. See Libanius Orat. xxii. and the Itineraria, p. 572–581. [For the post-system or *cursus publicus* see the article under this title in Smith's Dict. of Antiquities; and Hudemann's Gesch. des röm. Postwesens.]

[84] Pliny, though a favourite and a minister, made an apology for granting post horses to his wife on the most urgent business, Epist. x. 121, 122.

[85] Bergier, Hist. des grands Chemins, l. iv. c. 49.

[86] Plin. Hist. Natur. xix. 1. [From Puteoli, Pliny says.]

ment, the productions of happier climates and the industry of more civilised nations were gradually introduced into the western countries of Europe; and the natives were encouraged, by an open and profitable commerce, to multiply the former as well as to improve the latter. It would be almost impossible to enumerate all the articles, either of the animal or the vegetable reign, which were successively imported into Europe from Asia and Egypt;[97] but it will not be unworthy of the dignity, and much less of the utility, of an historical work, slightly to touch on a few of the principal heads. 1. Almost all the flowers, the herbs, and the fruits that grow in our European gardens are of foreign extraction, which, in many cases, is betrayed even by their names: the apple was a native of Italy, and, when the Romans had tasted the richer flavour of the apricot, the peach, the pomegranate, the citron, and the orange, they contented themselves with applying to all these new fruits the common denomination of apple, discriminating them from each other by the additional epithet of their country. 2. In the time of Homer, the vine grew wild in the island of Sicily and most probably in the adjacent continent; but it was not improved by the skill, nor did it afford a liquor grateful to the taste, of the savage inhabitants.[98] A thousand years afterwards, Italy could boast that, of the fourscore most generous and celebrated wines, more than two-thirds were produced from her soil.[99] The blessing was soon communicated to the Narbonnese province of Gaul; but so intense was the cold to the north of the Cevennes, that, in the time of Strabo, it was thought impossible to ripen the grapes in those parts of Gaul.[100] This difficulty, however,

[97] It is not improbable that the Greeks and Phœnicians introduced some new arts and productions into the neighbourhood of Marseilles and Gades.

[98] See Homer, Odyss. l. ix. v. 358.

[99] Plin. Hist. Natur. l. xiv. [11].

[100] Strab. Geograph. l. iv. p. 223. The intense cold of a Gallic winter was almost proverbial among the ancients. [Compare Cicero, de Rep., iii. 9.]

was gradually vanquished; and there is some reason to believe that the vineyards of Burgundy are as old as the age of the Antonines.[101] 3. The olive, in the western world, followed the progress of peace, of which it was considered as the symbol. Two centuries after the foundation of Rome, both Italy and Africa were strangers to that useful plant; it was naturalised in those countries; and at length carried into the heart of Spain and Gaul. The timid errors of the ancients, that it required a certain degree of heat, and could only flourish in the neighbourhood of the sea, were insensibly exploded by industry and experience.[102] 4. The cultivation of flax was transported from Egypt to Gaul, and enriched the whole country, however it might impoverish the particular lands on which it was sown.[103] 5. The use of artificial grasses became familiar to the farmers both of Italy and the provinces, particularly the Lucerne, which derived its name and origin from Media.[104] The assured supply of wholesome and plentiful food for the cattle during winter multiplied the number of the flocks and herds, which in their turn contributed to the fertility of the soil. To all these improvements may be added an assiduous attention to mines and fisheries, which, by employing a multitude of laborious hands, serve to increase the pleasures of the rich and the subsistence of the poor. The elegant treatise of Columella describes the advanced state of the Spanish husbandry, under the reign of Tiberius; and it may be observed that those famines which so frequently afflicted the infant republic were seldom or never experienced

[101] In the beginning of the ivth century, the orator Eumenius (Panegyric. Veter. viii. 6. edit. Delphin. [Incerti, Grat. Actio Constantino Aug., viii. 6 ed. Bährens]) speaks of the vines in the territory of Autun, which were decayed through age, and the first plantation of which was totally unknown. The Pagus Arebrignus is supposed by M. d'Anville to be the district of Beaune, celebrated, even at present, for one of the first growths of Burgundy.

[102] Plin. Hist. Natur. l. xv. [1].

[103] *Ibid.* l. xix. [1, 2].

[104] See the agreeable Essays on Agriculture by Mr. Harte, in which he has collected all that the ancients and moderns have said of lucerne.

by the extensive empire of Rome. The accidental scarcity, in any single province, was immediately relieved by the plenty of its more fortunate neighbours.

Agriculture is the foundation of manufactures; since the productions of nature are the materials of art. Under the Roman empire, the labour of an industrious and ingenious people was variously, but incessantly, employed in the service of the rich. In their dress, their table, their houses, and their furniture, the favourites of fortune united every refinement of conveniency, of elegance, and of splendour, whatever could soothe their pride or gratify their sensuality. Such refinements, under the odious name of luxury, have been severely arraigned by the moralists of every age; and it might perhaps be more conducive to the virtue, as well as happiness, of mankind, if all possessed the necessaries, and none the superfluities, of life. But in the present imperfect condition of society, luxury, though it may proceed from vice or folly, seems to be the only means that can correct the unequal distribution of property. The diligent mechanic, and the skilful artist, who have obtained no share in the division of the earth, receive a voluntary tax from the possessors of land; and the latter are prompted, by a sense of interest, to improve those estates, with whose produce they may purchase additional pleasures. This operation, the particular effects of which are felt in every society, acted with much more diffusive energy in the Roman world. The provinces would soon have been exhausted of their wealth, if the manufactures and commerce of luxury had not insensibly restored to the industrious subjects the sums which were exacted from them by the arms and authority of Rome. As long as the circulation was confined within the bounds of the empire, it impressed the political machine with a new degree of activity, and its consequences, sometimes beneficial, could never become pernicious.

But it is no easy task to confine luxury within the limits of an empire. The most remote countries of the ancient world were ransacked to supply the pomp and delicacy of Rome. The forest of Scythia afforded some valuable furs. Amber was brought overland from the shores of the Baltic to the Danube; and the barbarians were astonished at the price which they received in exchange for so useless a commodity.[105] There was a considerable demand for Babylonian carpets, and other manufactures of the East; but the most important and unpopular branch of foreign trade was carried on with Arabia and India. Every year, about the time of the summer solstice, a fleet of an hundred and twenty vessels sailed from Myos-hormos, a port of Egypt, on the Red Sea. By the periodical assistance of the monsoons, they traversed the ocean in about forty days. The coast of Malabar, or the island of Ceylon,[106] was the usual term of their navigation, and it was in those markets that the merchants from the more remote countries of Asia expected their arrival. The return of the fleet of Egypt was fixed to the months of December or January; and as soon as their rich cargo had been transported on the backs of camels from the Red Sea to the Nile, and had descended that river as far as Alexandria, it was poured, without delay, into the capital of the empire.[107] The objects of oriental traffic were splendid and trifling: silk, a pound of which was esteemed not inferior in value to a pound of gold;[108] precious stones, among which the pearl claimed the first rank after the diamond;[109] and a variety of aro-

[105] Tacit. Germania, c. 45. Plin. Hist. Natur. xxxvii. 11 [7]. The latter observed, with some humour, that even fashion had not yet found out the use of amber. Nero sent a Roman knight to purchase great quantities on the spot, where it was produced, the coast of modern Prussia.

[106] Called Taprobana by the Romans, and Serendib by the Arabs. It was discovered under the reign of Claudius, and gradually became the principal mart of the East.

[107] Plin. Hist. Natur. l. vi. [23]. Strabo, l. xvii. [p. 798].

[108] Hist. August. p. 224 [xxvi. 45]. A silk garment was considered as an ornament to a woman, but as a disgrace to a man.

[109] The two great pearl fisheries were the same as at present, Ormuz and Cape Comorin. As well as we can compare ancient with modern geography, Rome was supplied with diamonds from the mine of Sumelpur, in

matics, that were consumed in religious worship and the pomp of funerals.[110] The labour and risk of the voyage was rewarded with almost incredible profit; but the profit was made upon Roman subjects, and a few individuals were enriched at the expense of the Public. As the natives of Arabia and India were contented with the productions and manufactures of their own country, silver, on the side of the Romans, was the principal, if not the only, instrument of commerce. It was a complaint worthy of the gravity of the senate, that, in the purchase of female ornaments, the wealth of the state was irrecoverably given away to foreign and hostile nations.[111] The annual loss is computed, by a writer of an inquisitive but censorious temper, at upwards of eight hundred thousand pounds sterling.[112] Such was the style of discontent, brooding over the dark prospect of approaching poverty. And yet, if we compare the proportion between gold and silver, as it stood in the time of Pliny, and as it was fixed in the reign of

Bengal, which is described in the Voyages de Tavernier, tom. ii. p. 281. [See Appendix 9.]

[110] [But the use of aromatic spices among the Romans was by no means confined to these purposes.]

[111] Tacit. Annal. iii. 53. In a speech of Tiberius. [The statement in the text is an exaggeration and must be considerably modified, as also the subsequent remark about the plentifulness of the precious metals. Silver was not the only, though it seems to have been the chief, commodity sent to the East; and there was certainly, as Merivale admits, a distinct though gradual diminution in the amount of gold and silver in circulation in the second century. Yet in regard to the first question, Gibbon had grasped facts; the spirit of his observation is right. "Two texts of Pliny assert the constant drain of specie to the East; and the assertion is confirmed by the circumstances of the case, for the Indians and the nations beyond India, who transmitted to the West their silks and spices, cared little for the wines and oils of Europe, still less for the manufactures in wool and leather which formed the staples of commerce in the Mediterranean. . . . The difficulty of maintaining the yield of the precious metals is marked in the severe regulations of the late emperors, and is further attested by the progressive debasement of the currency." (Merivale, Hist. of the Romans, cap. 68, vol. viii. p. 352.) Cp. Finley, History of Greece, i. 49, 50.]

[112] Plin. Hist. Natur. xii. 18. In another place he computes half that sum, Quingenties HS., for India exclusive of Arabia.

Constantine, we shall discover within that period a very considerable increase.[113] There is not the least reason to suppose that gold was become more scarce; it is therefore evident that silver was grown more common; that whatever might be the amount of the Indian and Arabian exports, they were far from exhausting the wealth of the Roman world; and that the produce of the mines abundantly supplied the demands of commerce.

Notwithstanding the propensity of mankind to exalt the past, and to depreciate the present, the tranquil and prosperous state of the empire was warmly felt, and honestly confessed, by the provincials as well as Romans. "They acknowledged that the true principles of social life, laws, agriculture, and science, which had been first invented by the wisdom of Athens, were now firmly established by the power of Rome, under whose auspicious influence the fiercest barbarians were united by an equal government and common language. They affirm that, with the improvement of arts, the human species was visibly multiplied. They celebrate the increasing splendour of the cities, the beautiful face of the country, cultivated and adorned like an immense garden; and the long festival of peace, which was enjoyed by so many nations, forgetful of their ancient animosities, and delivered from the apprehension of future danger." [114] Whatever suspicions may be suggested by the air of rhetoric and declamation which seems to prevail in these passages, the substance of them is perfectly agreeable to historic truth.

It was scarcely possible that the eyes of contemporaries should discover in the public felicity the latent causes of decay and corruption. This long peace, and the uniform government of the Romans, introduced a slow and secret poison into the vitals of the empire. The minds of men were

[113] The proportion which was 1 to 10, and 12½, rose to 14⅖, the legal regulation of Constantine. See Arbuthnot's Table of ancient Coins, c. v.

[114] Among many other passages, see Pliny (Hist. Natur. iii. 5), Aristides (de Urbe Româ) and Tertullian (de Animâ, c. 30).

gradually reduced to the same level, the fire of genius was extinguished, and even the military spirit evaporated. The natives of Europe were brave and robust. Spain, Gaul, Britain, and Illyricum supplied the legions with excellent soldiers, and constituted the real strength of the monarchy. Their personal valour remained, but they no longer possessed that public courage which is nourished by the love of independence, the sense of national honour, the presence of danger, and the habit of command. They received laws and governors from the will of their sovereign, and trusted for their defence to a mercenary army. The posterity of their boldest leaders was contented with the rank of citizens and subjects. The most aspiring spirits resorted to the court or standard of the emperors; and the deserted provinces, deprived of political strength or union, insensibly sunk into the languid indifference of private life.

The love of letters, almost inseparable from peace and refinement, was fashionable among the subjects of Hadrian and the Antonines, who were themselves men of learning and curiosity. It was diffused over the whole extent of their empire; the most northern tribes of Britons had acquired a taste for rhetoric; Homer as well as Virgil were transcribed and studied on the banks of the Rhine and Danube; and the most liberal rewards sought out the faintest glimmerings of literary merit.[115] The sciences of physic and astronomy were successfully cultivated by the Greeks; the observations of

[115] Herodes Atticus gave the sophist Polemo above eight thousand pounds for three declamations. See Philostrat. l. i. p. 558 [Life of Herodes, 7]. The Antonines founded a school at Athens, in which professors of grammar, rhetoric, politics, and the four great sects of philosophy were maintained at the public expense for the instruction of youth. The salary of a philosopher was ten thousand drachmæ, between three and four hundred pounds a year. Similar establishments were formed in the other great cities of the empire. See Lucian in Eunuch. tom. ii. p. 353. edit. Reitz. Philostrat. l. ii. p. 566. Hist. August. p. 21 [iii., 11]. Dion Cassius, l. lxxxi. p. 1195 [31]. Juvenal himself, in a morose satire, which in every line betrays his own disappointment and envy, is obliged, however, to say — O Juvenes,

Ptolemy and the writings of Galen are studied by those who have improved their discoveries and corrected their errors; but, if we except the inimitable Lucian, this age of indolence passed away without having produced a single writer of original genius or who excelled in the arts of elegant composition. The authority of Plato and Aristotle, of Zeno and Epicurus, still reigned in the schools, and their systems, transmitted with blind deference from one generation of disciples to another, precluded every generous attempt to exercise the powers, or enlarge the limits, of the human mind. The beauties of the poets and orators, instead of kindling a fire like their own, inspired only cold and servile imitations: or, if any ventured to deviate from those models, they deviated at the same time from good sense and propriety. On the revival of letters, the youthful vigour of the imagination after a long repose, national emulation, a new religion, new languages, and a new world, called forth the genius of Europe. But the provincials of Rome, trained by a uniform artificial foreign education, were engaged in a very unequal competition with those bold ancients, who, by expressing their genuine feelings in their native tongue, had already occupied every place of honour. The name of Poet was almost forgotten; that of Orator was usurped by the sophists. A cloud of critics, of compilers, of commentators, darkened the face of learning, and the decline of genius was soon followed by the corruption of taste.

The sublime Longinus, who in somewhat a later period, and in the court of a Syrian queen, preserved the spirit of ancient Athens, observes and laments this degeneracy of his contemporaries, which debased their sentiments, enervated their courage, and depressed their talents. "In the same manner," says he, "as some children always remain pigmies,

circumspicit et agitat [*leg.* stimulat] vos, Materiamque sibi Ducis indulgentia quaerit. — Satir. vii. 20. [Vespasian was the first to appoint salaried professors in Rome; Suetonius, in Vespas. 18.]

whose infant limbs have been too closely confined; thus our tender minds, fettered by the prejudices and habits of a just servitude, are unable to expand themselves, or to attain that well-proportioned greatness which we admire in the ancients, who, living under a popular government, wrote with the same freedom as they acted." [116] This diminutive stature of mankind, if we pursue the metaphor, was daily sinking below the old standard, and the Roman world was indeed peopled by a race of pigmies, when the fierce giants of the North broke in and mended the puny breed. They restored a manly spirit of freedom; and, after the revolution of ten centuries, freedom became the happy parent of taste and science.

[116] Longin. de Sublim. c. 43, p. 229 edit. Toll. Here too we may say of Longinus, "his own example strengthens all his laws." Instead of proposing his sentiments with a manly boldness, he insinuates them with the most guarded caution, puts them into the mouth of a friend, and, as far as we can collect from a corrupted text, makes a show of refuting them himself. [The author calls him "sublime" in allusion to the work On Sublimity, περὶ ὕψους. But the authorship of this able and striking treatise is very doubtful; it is certain that it was not written by Zenobia's Longinus.]

CHAPTER III

Of the Constitution of the Roman Empire, in the Age of the Antonines

THE obvious definition of a monarchy seems to be that of a state, in which a single person, by whatsoever name he may be distinguished, is entrusted with the execution of the laws, the management of the revenue, and the command of the army. But unless public liberty is protected by intrepid and vigilant guardians, the authority of so formidable a magistrate will soon degenerate into despotism. The influence of the clergy, in an age of superstition, might be usefully employed to assert the rights of mankind; but so intimate is the connection between the throne and the altar, that the banner of the church has very seldom been seen on the side of the people. A martial nobility and stubborn commons, possessed of arms, tenacious of property, and collected into constitutional assemblies, form the only balance capable of preserving a free constitution against enterprises of an aspiring prince.

Every barrier of the Roman constitution had been levelled by the vast ambition of the dictator; every fence had been extirpated by the cruel hand of the triumvir. After the victory of Actium, the fate of the Roman world depended on the will of Octavianus, surnamed Cæsar by his uncle's adoption, and afterwards Augustus, by the flattery of the senate.[1] The conqueror was at the head of forty-four veteran legions,[2] con-

[1] [His original name was C. Octavius, hence Merivale usually (incorrectly) speaks of him as Octavius. For he ceased to be an Octavius, and became a Julius, by his uncle's adoption; his full name in 44 B.C. was C. Julius Cæsar Octavianus. The title *Augustus* was conferred Jan. 16, 27 B.C.]

[2] Orosius, vi. 18.

scious of their own strength and of the weakness of the constitution, habituated during twenty years' civil war to every act of blood and violence, and passionately devoted to the house of Cæsar, from whence alone they had received and expected the most lavish rewards. The provinces, long oppressed by the ministers of the republic, sighed for the government of a single person, who would be the master, not the accomplice, of those petty tyrants. The people of Rome, viewing with a secret pleasure the humiliation of the aristocracy, demanded only bread and public shows, and were supplied with both by the liberal hand of Augustus. The rich and polite Italians, who had almost universally embraced the philosophy of Epicurus, enjoyed the present blessings of ease and tranquillity, and suffered not the pleasing dream to be interrupted by the memory of their old tumultuous freedom. With its power, the senate had lost its dignity; many of the most noble families were extinct. The republicans of spirit and ability had perished in the field of battle, or in the proscription. The door of the assembly had been designedly left open for a mixed multitude of more than a thousand persons, who reflected disgrace upon their rank, instead of deriving honour from it.[3]

The reformation of the senate was one of the first steps in which Augustus laid aside the tyrant and professed himself the father of his country. He was elected censor; and, in concert with his faithful Agrippa, he examined the list of the senators, expelled a few members,[4] whose vices or whose obstinacy required a public example, persuaded near two hundred to prevent the shame of an expulsion by a voluntary retreat, raised the qualification of a senator to about ten thousand pounds, created a sufficient number of patrician families,

[3] Julius Cæsar introduced soldiers, strangers and half-barbarians, into the senate. (Sueton. in Cæsar. c. 80.) The abuse became still more scandalous after his death.

[4] [But Dion, as Milman pointed out, says that he erased no senator's name from the list; see next note.]

and accepted for himself the honourable title of Prince of the Senate, which had always been bestowed by the censors on the citizen the most eminent for his honours and services.[5] But, whilst he thus restored the dignity, he destroyed the independence of the senate. The principles of a free constitution are irrecoverably lost, when the legislative power is nominated by the executive.

Before an assembly thus modelled and prepared, Augustus pronounced a studied oration, which displayed his patriotism, and disguised his ambition. "He lamented, yet excused, his past conduct. Filial piety had required at his hands the revenge of his father's murder; the humanity of his own nature had sometimes given way to the stern laws of necessity, and to a forced connection with two unworthy colleagues: as long as Antony lived, the republic forbade him to abandon her to a degenerate Roman and a barbarian queen. He was now at liberty to satisfy his duty and his inclination. He solemnly restored the senate and people to all their ancient rights; and wished only to mingle with the crowd of his fellow-citizens, and to share the blessings which he had obtained for his country."[6]

It would require the pen of Tacitus (if Tacitus had assisted at this assembly) to describe the various emotions of the senate; those that were suppressed, and those that were effected. It was dangerous to trust the sincerity of Augustus; to seem to distrust it was still more dangerous. The respective advantages of monarchy and a republic have often divided speculative inquirers; the present greatness of the Roman state, the corruption of manners, and the licence of the soldiers, supplied new arguments to the advocates of monarchy; and these general views of government were again warped by

[5] Dion Cassius, l. iii. p. 693 [42], Suetonius in August. c. 35. [But see Appendix 10.]

[6] Dion, l. liii. p. 6983 [3], gives us a prolix and bombastic speech on this great occasion. I have borrowed from Suetonius and Tacitus the general language of Augustus.

the hopes and fears of each individual. Amidst this confusion of sentiments, the answer of the senate was unanimous and decisive. They refused to accept the resignation of Augustus; they conjured him not to desert the republic which he had saved. After a decent resistance the crafty tyrant submitted to the orders of the senate; and consented to receive the government of the provinces, and the general command of the Roman armies, under the well-known names of PROCONSUL and IMPERATOR.[7] But he would receive them only for ten years. Even before the expiration of that period, he hoped that the wounds of civil discord would be completely healed, and that the republic, restored to its pristine health and vigour, would no longer require the dangerous interposition of so extraordinary a magistrate. The memory of this comedy, repeated several times during the life of Augustus, was preserved to the last ages of the empire by the peculiar pomp with which the perpetual monarchs of Rome always solemnised the tenth years of their reign.[8]

Without any violation of the principles of the constitution, the general of the Roman armies might receive and exercise an authority almost despotic over the soldiers, the enemies, and the subjects of the republic. With regard to the soldiers, the jealousy of freedom had, even from the earliest ages of Rome, given way to the hopes of conquest, and a just sense of military discipline. The dictator, or consul, had a right to command the service of the Roman youth, and to punish an obstinate or cowardly disobedience by the most severe and

[7] *Imperator* (from which we have derived emperor) signified under the republic no more than *general*, and was emphatically bestowed by the soldiers, when on the field of battle they proclaimed their victorious leader worthy of that title. When the Roman *emperors* assumed it in that sense, they placed it after their name, and marked how often they had taken it. [Thus, as an imperial title *imperator* preceded the emperor's name, but *Imp. iii.* after his name meant that he was saluted Imperator by his troops for the third time, on the occasion of his second victory after his accession.]

[8] Dion, l. liii. p. 703, etc. [11, cp. 16].

ignominious penalties, by striking the offender out of the list of citizens, by confiscating his property, and by selling his person into slavery.[9] The most sacred rights of freedom, confirmed by the Porcian and Sempronian laws, were suspended by the military engagement. In his camp the general exercised an absolute power of life and death; his jurisdiction was not confined by any forms of trial or rules of proceeding, and the execution of the sentence was immediate and without appeal.[10] The choice of the enemies of Rome was regularly decided by the legislative authority. The most important resolutions of peace and war were seriously debated in the senate, and solemnly ratified by the people. But when the arms of the legions were carried to a great distance from Italy, the generals assumed the liberty of directing them against whatever people, and in whatever manner, they judged most advantageous for the public service. It was from the success, not from the justice, of their enterprises, that they expected the honours of a triumph. In the use of victory, especially after they were no longer controlled by the commissioners of the senate, they exercised the most unbounded despotism. When Pompey commanded in the East, he rewarded his soldiers and allies, dethroned princes, divided kingdoms, founded colonies, and distributed the treasures of Mithridates. On his return to Rome he obtained, by a single act of the senate and people, the universal ratification of all his proceedings.[11] Such was the power over the soldiers, and

[9] Liv. Epitom. l. xiv. Valer. Maxim. vi. 3.

[10] See in the viiith book of Livy, the conduct of Manlius Torquatus and Papirius Cursor. They violated the laws of nature and humanity, but they asserted those of military discipline; and the people, who abhorred the action, were obliged to respect the principle.

[11] By the lavish but unconstrained suffrages of the people, Pompey had obtained a military command scarcely inferior to that of Augustus. Among the extraordinary acts of power executed by the former, we may remark the foundation of twenty-nine cities, and the distribution of three or four millions sterling to his troops. The ratification of his acts met with some opposition and delays in the senate. See Plutarch, Appian, Dion Cassius, and the first book of the epistles to Atticus.

over the enemies of Rome, which was either granted to, or assumed by, the generals of the republic. They were, at the same time, the governors, or rather monarchs, of the conquered provinces, united the civil with the military character, administered justice as well as the finances, and exercised both the executive and legislative power of the state.

From what has been already observed in the first chapter of this work, some notion may be formed of the armies and provinces thus entrusted to the ruling hand of Augustus. But, as it was impossible that he could personally command the legions of so many distant frontiers, he was indulged by the senate, as Pompey had already been, in the permission of devolving the execution of his great office on a sufficient number of lieutenants. In rank and authority these officers seemed not inferior to the ancient proconsuls; but their station was dependent and precarious. They received and held their commissions at the will of a superior, to whose *auspicious* influence the merit of their action was legally attributed.[12] They were the representatives of the emperor. The emperor alone was the general of the republic, and his jurisdiction, civil as well as military, extended over all the conquests of Rome. It was some satisfaction, however, to the senate that he always delegated his power to the members of their body. The imperial lieutenants were of consular or prætorian dignity; the legions were commanded by senators, and the prefecture of Egypt was the only important trust committed to a Roman knight.

Within six days after Augustus had been compelled to accept so very liberal a grant, he resolved to gratify the pride

[12] Under the commonwealth, a triumph could only be claimed by the general, who was authorised to take the Auspices in the name of the people. By an exact consequence, drawn from this principle of policy and religion, the triumph was reserved to the emperor, and his most successful lieutenants were satisfied with some marks of distinction, which, under the name of triumphal honours, were invented in their favour. [On the provincial governors see Appendix 10.]

of the senate by an easy sacrifice. He represented to them that they had enlarged his powers, even beyond that degree which might be required by the melancholy condition of the times. They had not permitted him to refuse the laborious command of the armies and the frontiers; but he must insist on being allowed to restore the more peaceful and secure provinces to the mild administration of the civil magistrate. In the division of the provinces Augustus provided for his own power and for the dignity of the republic. The proconsuls of the senate, particularly those of Asia, Greece, and Africa, enjoyed a more honourable character than the lieutenants of the emperor, who commanded in Gaul or Syria. The former were attended by lictors, the latter by soldiers. A law was passed that, wherever the emperor was present, his extraordinary commission should supersede the ordinary jurisdiction of the governor; a custom was introduced, that the new conquests belonged to the imperial portion; and it was soon discovered that the authority of the *Prince*, the favourite epithet of Augustus, was the same in every part of the empire.

In return for this imaginary concession, Augustus obtained an important privilege, which rendered him master of Rome and Italy. By a dangerous exception to the ancient maxims, he was authorised to preserve his military command, supported by a numerous body of guards, even in time of peace, and in the heart of the capital.[18] His command, indeed, was confined to those citizens who were engaged in the service by the military oath; but such was the propensity of the Romans to servitude, that the oath was voluntarily taken by the magistrates, the senators, and the equestrian order, till the homage of flattery was insensibly converted into an annual and solemn protestation of fidelity.

Although Augustus considered a military force as the firmest

[18] [The prætorian guards and the fleets (at Ravenna and Misenum) were the two exceptions to the principle that Italy was outside the jurisdiction of the *Imperator*.]

foundation, he wisely rejected it as a very odious instrument, of government. It was more agreeable to his temper, as well as to his policy, to reign under the venerable names of ancient magistracy, and artfully to collect in his own person all the scattered rays of civil jurisdiction. With this view, he permitted the senate to confer upon him, for his life, the powers of the consular [14] and tribunitian offices,[15] which were, in the same manner, continued to all his successors. The consuls had succeeded to the kings of Rome, and represented the dignity of the state. They superintended the ceremonies of religion, levied and commanded the legions, gave audience to foreign ambassadors, and presided in the assemblies both of the senate and people. The general control of the finances was entrusted to their care; and, though they seldom had leisure to administer justice in person, they were considered as the supreme guardians of law, equity, and the public peace. Such was their ordinary jurisdiction; but, whenever the senate empowered the first magistrate to consult the safety of the commonwealth, he was raised by that degree above the laws, and exercised, in the defence of liberty, a temporary despotism.[16] The character of the tribunes was, in every respect, different from that of the consuls. The appearance of the former was modest and humble; but their persons were

[14] Cicero (de Legibus, iii. 3) gives the consular office the name of *Regia potestas:* and Polybius (l. vi. c. 3) observes three powers in the Roman constitution. The monarchical was represented and exercised by the consuls. [But see Appendix 10.]

[15] As the tribunitian power (distinct from the annual office) was first invented for the dictator Cæsar (Dion, l. xliv. p. 384 [5]), we may easily conceive that it was given as a reward for having so nobly asserted, by arms, the sacred rights of the tribunes and people. See his own commentaries, de Bell. Civil. l. i.

[16] Augustus exercised nine annual consulships without interruption. He then most artfully refused that magistracy as well as the dictatorship, absented himself from Rome, and waited till the fatal effects of tumult and faction forced the senate to invest him with a perpetual consulship. Augustus, as well as his successors, affected, however, to conceal so invidious a title. [See Appendix 10, p. 318.]

sacred and inviolable. Their force was suited rather for opposition than for action. They were instituted to defend the oppressed, to pardon offences, to arraign the enemies of the people, and, when they judged it necessary, to stop, by a single word, the whole machine of government. As long as the republic subsisted, the dangerous influence which either the consul or the tribune might derive from their respective jurisdiction was diminished by several important restrictions. Their authority expired with the year in which they were elected; the former office was divided between two, the latter among ten persons; and, as both in their private and public interest they were adverse to each other, their mutual conflicts contributed, for the most part, to strengthen rather than to destroy the balance of the constitution. But when the consular and tribunitian powers were united,[17] when they were vested for life in a single person, when the general of the army was, at the same time, the minister of the senate and the representative of the Roman people, it was impossible to resist the exercise, nor was it easy to define the limits, of his imperial prerogative.

To these accumulated honours the policy of Augustus soon added the splendid as well as important dignities of supreme pontiff, and of censor.[18] By the former he acquired the management of the religion, and by the latter a legal inspection over the manners and fortunes, of the Roman people. If so many distinct and independent powers did not exactly unite with each other, the complaisance of the senate was prepared to supply every deficiency by the most ample and extraordinary concessions. The emperors, as the first ministers of the republic, were exempted from the obligation and penalty of many inconvenient laws: they were authorised to convoke the senate, to make several motions in the same day,

[17] [But observe that the tribunate (as the author afterwards points out) was not discontinued, though, overshadowed by the *tribunicia potestas* of the emperor, it lost all political significance.]

[18] [See Appendix 10.]

to recommend candidates for the honours of the state, to enlarge the bounds of the city, to employ the revenue at their discretion, to declare peace and war, to ratify treaties; and by a most comprehensive clause, they were empowered to execute whatsoever they should judge advantageous to the empire, and agreeable to the majesty of things private or public, human or divine.[19]

When all the various powers of executive government were committed to the *Imperial magistrate*, the ordinary magistrates of the commonwealth languished in obscurity, without vigour, and almost without business. The names and forms of the ancient administration were preserved by Augustus with the most anxious care. The usual number of consuls, prætors, and tribunes[20] were annually invested with their respective ensigns of office, and continued to discharge some of their least important functions. Those honours still attracted the vain ambition of the Romans; and the emperors themselves, though invested for life with the powers of the consulship,[21] frequently aspired to the title of that annual dignity, which they condescended to share with the most illustrious of their fellow-citizens.[22] In the election of these magistrates, the

[19] See a fragment of a Decree of the Senate, conferring on the Emperor Vespasian all the powers granted to his predecessors, Augustus, Tiberius, and Claudius. This curious and important monument is published in Gruter's Inscriptions, No. ccxlii. [Corp. Insc. Lat. vi. 930. This document is known as the *lex de imperio Vespasiani*.]

[20] Two consuls were created on the Calends of January; but in the course of the year others were substituted in their places, till the annual number seems to have amounted to no less than twelve. The prætors were usually sixteen or eighteen (Lipsius in Excurs. D. ad. Tacit. Annal. l. i.). I have not mentioned the Ædiles or Quæstors. Officers of the police or revenue easily adapt themselves to any form of government. In the time of Nero the tribunes legally possessed the right of intercession, though it might be dangerous to exercise it (Tacit. Annal. xvi. 26). In the time of Trajan, it was doubtful whether the tribuneship was an office or a name (Plin. Epist. 123). [But it still existed in the 5th century, being mentioned in the Theodosian Code.]

[21] [See above, note 11.]

[22] The tyrants themselves were ambitious of the consulship. The vir-

people, during the reign of Augustus, were permitted to expose all the inconveniences of a wild democracy. That artful prince, instead of discovering the least symptom of impatience, humbly solicited their suffrages for himself or his friends, and scrupulously practised all the duties of an ordinary candidate.[33] But we may venture to ascribe to his councils the first measure of the succeeding reign, by which the elections were transferred to the senate.[34] The assemblies of the people were for ever abolished, and the emperors were delivered from a dangerous multitude, who, without restoring liberty, might have disturbed, and perhaps endangered, the established government.

By declaring themselves the protectors of the people, Marius and Cæsar had subverted the constitution of their country. But as soon as the senate had been humbled and disarmed, such an assembly, consisting of five or six hundred persons, was found a much more tractable and useful instrument of dominion. It was on the dignity of the senate that Augustus and his successors founded their new empire; and they affected, on every occasion, to adopt the language and principles of Patricians. In the administration of their own powers, they frequently consulted the great national council, and *seemed* to refer to its decision the most important concerns of peace and war. Rome, Italy, and the internal provinces were subject to the immediate jurisdiction of the senate.

tuous princes were moderate in the pursuit, and exact in the discharge, of it. Trajan revived the ancient oath, and swore before the consul's tribunal that he would observe the laws (Plin. Panegyric. c. 64).

[33] Quoties Magistratuum Comitiis interesset, tribus cum candidatis suis circuibat; supplicabatque more solemni. Ferebat et ipse suffragium in tribubus, ut unus e populo. Suetonius in August. c. 56.

[34] Tum primum Comitia e campo ad patres translata sunt. Tacit. Annal. i. 15. The word *primum* seems to allude to some faint and unsuccessful efforts, which were made towards restoring them to the people. [One formality was still left to the popular assembly — the *renuntiatio* of the elected candidates. Gibbon's inference from *primum* is hardly tenable; but he is right in so far that Augustus had prepared the way for the change of Tiberius.]

With regard to civil objects, it was the supreme court of appeal; with regard to criminal matters, a tribunal, constituted for the trial of all offences that were committed by men in any public station, or that affected the peace and majesty of the Roman people. The exercise of the judicial power became the most frequent and serious occupation of the senate; and the important causes that were pleaded before them afforded a last refuge to the spirit of ancient eloquence. As a council of state, and as a court of justice, the senate possessed very considerable prerogatives; but in its legislative capacity, in which it was supposed virtually to represent the people, the rights of sovereignty were acknowledged to reside in that assembly. Every power was derived from their authority, every law was ratified by their sanction. Their regular meetings were held on three stated days in every month, the Calends, the Nones, and the Ides. The debates were conducted with decent freedom; and the emperors themselves, who gloried in the name of senators, sat, voted, and divided with their equals.

To resume, in a few words, the system of the Imperial government, as it was instituted by Augustus, and maintained by those princes who understood their own interest and that of the people, it may be defined an absolute monarchy disguised by the forms of a commonwealth. The masters of the Roman world surrounded their throne with darkness, concealed their irresistible strength, and humbly professed themselves the accountable ministers of the senate, whose supreme decrees they dictated and obeyed.[35]

[35] Dion Cassius (l. liii. p. 703–714 [12–18]) has given a very loose and partial sketch of the Imperial system. To illustrate and often to correct him, I have mentioned Tacitus, examined Suetonius, and consulted the following moderns: the Abbé de la Bléterie in the Mémoires de l'Académie des Inscriptions, tom. xix. xxi. xxiv. xxv. xxvii. Beaufort, République Romaine, tom. i. p. 255–275. The dissertations of Noodt and Gronovius, *de lege Regia:* printed at Leyden, in the year 1731. Gravina de Imperio Romano, p. 479–544 of his Opuscula. Maffei, Verona Illustrata, i. p. 245, &c.

The face of the court corresponded with the forms of the administration. The emperors, if we except those tyrants whose capricious folly violated every law of nature and decency, disdained that pomp and ceremony which might offend their countrymen, but could add nothing to their real power. In all the offices of life, they affected to confound themselves with their subjects, and maintained with them an equal intercourse of visits and entertainments. Their habit, their palace, their table, were suited only to the rank of an opulent senator. Their family, however numerous or splendid, was composed entirely of their domestic slaves and freedmen.[36] Augustus or Trajan would have blushed at employing the meanest of the Romans in those menial offices which, in the household and bedchamber of a limited monarch, are so eagerly solicited by the proudest nobles of Britain.

The deification of the emperors [37] is the only instance in which they departed from their accustomed prudence and modesty. The Asiatic Greeks were the first inventors, the successors of Alexander [38] the first objects, of this servile and impious mode of adulation. It was easily transferred from the kings to the governors of Asia; and the Roman magistrates very frequently were adored as provincial deities, with the pomp of altars and temples, of festivals and sacrifices.[39] It was natural that the emperors should not refuse what the proconsuls had accepted; and the divine honours which both

[36] A weak prince will always be governed by his domestics. The power of slaves aggravated the shame of the Romans; and the senate paid court to a Pallas or a Narcissus. There is a chance that a modern favourite may be a gentleman.

[37] See a treatise of Van Dale de Consecratione Principum. It would be easier for me to copy, than it has been to verify, the quotations of that learned Dutchman.

[38] [And Alexander himself.]

[39] See a dissertation of the Abbé Mongault in the first volume of the Academy of Inscriptions. [For the whole subject see the admirable article of Mr. Purser on *Apotheosis*, in the new edit. of Smith's Dictionary of Greek and Roman Antiquities.]

the one and the other received from the provinces attested rather the despotism than the servitude of Rome. But the conquerors soon imitated the vanquished nations in the arts of flattery; and the imperious spirit of the first Cæsar too easily consented to assume, during his lifetime, a place among the tutelar deities of Rome. The milder temper of his successor declined so dangerous an ambition, which was never afterwards revived, except by the madness of Caligula and Domitian. Augustus permitted indeed some of the provincial cities to erect temples to his honour, on condition that they should associate the worship of Rome with that of the sovereign; he tolerated private superstition, of which he might be the object;[80] but he contented himself with being revered by the senate and people in his human character, and wisely left to his successor the care of his public deification. A regular custom was introduced, that, on the decease of every emperor who had neither lived nor died like a tyrant, the senate by a solemn decree should place him in the number of the gods: and the ceremonies of his apotheosis were blended with those of his funeral. This legal, and, as it should seem, injudicious profanation, so abhorrent to our stricter principles, was received with a very faint murmur[81] by the easy nature of Polytheism; but it was received as an institution, not of religion, but of policy. We should disgrace the virtues of the Antonines by comparing them with the vices of Hercules or Jupiter. Even the characters of Cæsar or Augustus were far superior to those of the popular deities. But it was the misfortune of the former to live in an enlightened age, and their actions were too faithfully recorded to admit of such a mixture of fable and mystery as the devotion of the vulgar requires. As soon as their divinity was established by law,

[80] Jurandasque tuum per nomen ponimus *aras*, says Horace to the emperor himself, and Horace was well acquainted with the court of Augustus.

[81] See Cicero in Philippic, i. 6. Julian in Cæsaribus, Inque Deûm templis jurabit Roma per umbras, is the indignant expression of Lucan; but it is a patriotic rather than a devout indignation.

it sunk into oblivion, without contributing either to their own fame or to the dignity of succeeding princes.

In the consideration of the Imperial government, we have frequently mentioned the artful founder, under his well-known title of Augustus, which was not however conferred upon him till the edifice was almost completed. The obscure name of Octavianus he derived from a mean family in the little town of Aricia. It was stained with the blood of the proscriptions; and he was desirous, had it been possible, to erase all memory of his former life. The illustrious surname of Cæsar he had assumed, as the adopted son of the dictator; but he had too much good sense either to hope to be confounded, or to wish to be compared, with that extraordinary man. It was proposed in the senate to dignify their minister with a new appellation; and after a very serious discussion, that of Augustus was chosen, among several others, as being the most expressive of the character of peace and sanctity which he uniformly affected.[88] *Augustus* was therefore a personal, *Cæsar* a family distinction. The former should naturally have expired with the prince on whom it was bestowed; and however the latter was diffused by adoption and female alliance, Nero was the last prince who could allege any hereditary claim to the honours of the Julian line. But, at the time of his death, the practice of a century had inseparably connected those appellations with the Imperial dignity, and they have been preserved by a long succession of emperors, — Romans, Greeks, Franks, and Germans, — from the fall of the republic to the present time. A distinction was, however, soon introduced. The sacred title of Augustus was always reserved for the monarch, whilst the name of Cæsar was more freely communicated to his relations; and, from the reign of Hadrian at least, was appro-

[88] Dion Cassius, l. liii. p. 710 [16] with the curious Annotations of Reimar. [*Augustus*, rendered in Greek by Σεβαστός, cast a certain religious halo over the head of the emperor; cp. Dion *loc. cit.*]

priated to the second person in the state, who was considered as the presumptive heir of the empire.

The tender respect of Augustus for a free constitution which he had destroyed can only be explained by an attentive consideration of the character of that subtle tyrant. A cool head, an unfeeling heart, and a cowardly disposition, prompted him at the age of nineteen to assume the mask of hypocrisy, which he never afterwards laid aside. With the same hand, and probably with the same temper, he signed the proscription of Cicero and the pardon of Cinna. His virtues, and even his vices, were artificial; and according to the various dictates of his interest, he was at first the enemy, and at last the father, of the Roman world.[33] When he framed the artful system of the Imperial authority, his moderation was inspired by his fears. He wished to deceive the people by an image of civil liberty, and the armies by an image of civil government.

I. The death of Cæsar was ever before his eyes. He had lavished wealth and honours on his adherents; but the most favoured friends of his uncle were in the number of the conspirators. The fidelity of the legions might defend his authority against open rebellion, but their vigilance could not secure his person from the dagger of a determined republican; and the Romans, who revered the memory of Brutus,[34] would applaud the imitation of his virtue. Cæsar had provoked his fate as much by the ostentation of his power as by his power itself. The consul or the tribune might have reigned in peace. The title of king had armed the Romans against his

[33] As Octavianus advanced to the banquet of the Cæsars, his colour changed like that of the chameleon; pale at first, then red, afterwards black, he at last assumed the mild livery of Venus and the Graces (Cæsars, p. 309). This image, employed by Julian in his ingenious fiction, is just and elegant; but, when he considers this change of character as real, and ascribes it to the power of philosophy, he does too much honour to philosophy and to Octavianus.

[34] Two centuries after the establishment of monarchy, the emperor Marcus Antoninus recommends the character of Brutus as a perfect model of Roman virtue.

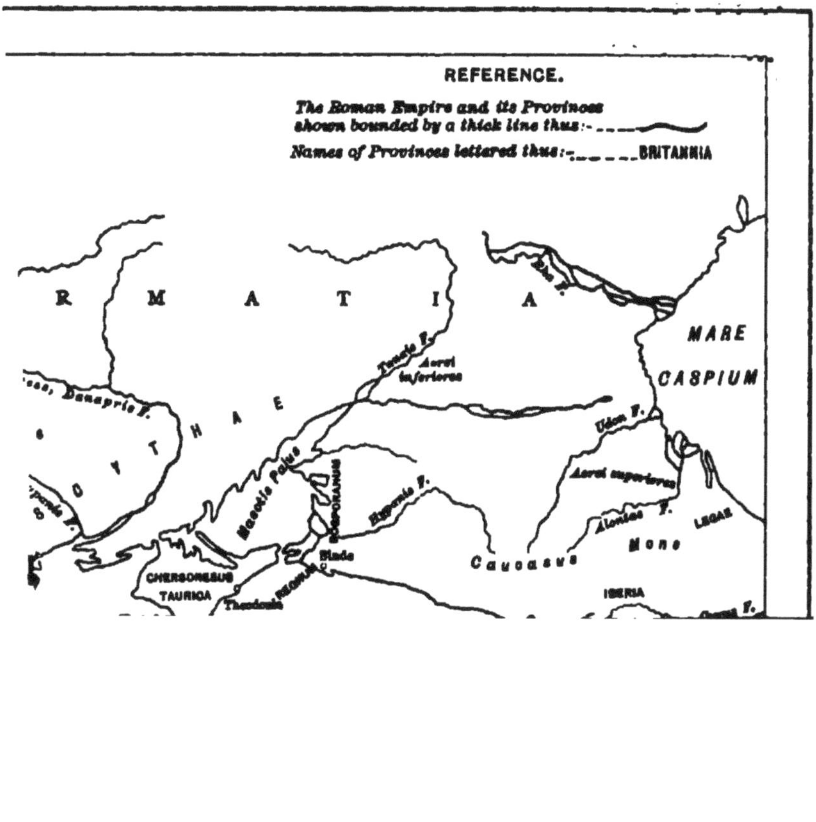
REFERENCE.
The Roman Empire and its Provinces shown bounded by a thick line thus:-
Names of Provinces lettered thus:- BRITANNIA
R M A T I A
MARE CASPIUM
Tanais F.
Aorsi inferiores
Danapris F.
S C Y T H A E
Maeotis Palus
BOSPORANUS
Hypanis F.
Sinde
CHERSONESUS TAURICA
Theodosia
Caucasus
Mons
Udon F.
Aorsi superiores
LEGAE
IBERIA

life. Augustus was sensible that mankind is governed by names; nor was he deceived in his expectation that the senate and people would submit to slavery, provided they were respectfully assured that they still enjoyed their ancient freedom. A feeble senate and enervated people cheerfully acquiesced in the pleasing illusion, as long as it was supported by the virtue, or by even the prudence, of the successors of Augustus. It was a motive of self-preservation, not a principle of liberty, that animated the conspirators against Caligula, Nero, and Domitian. They attacked the person of the tyrant, without aiming their blow at the authority of the emperor.

There appears, indeed, *one* memorable occasion, in which the senate, after seventy years of patience, made an ineffectual attempt to reassume its long-forgotten rights. When the throne was vacant by the murder of Caligula, the consuls convoked that assembly in the Capitol, condemned the memory of the Cæsars, gave the watchword *liberty* to the few cohorts who faintly adhered to their standard, and during eight and forty hours acted as the independent chiefs of a free commonwealth. But while they deliberated, the prætorian guards had resolved. The stupid Claudius, brother of Germanicus, was already in their camp, invested with the Imperial purple, and prepared to support his election by arms. The dream of liberty was at an end; and the senate awoke to all the horrors of inevitable servitude. Deserted by the people, and threatened by a military force, that feeble assembly was compelled to ratify the choice of the prætorians, and to embrace the benefit of an amnesty, which Claudius had the prudence to offer, and the generosity to observe.[38]

II. The insolence of the armies inspired Augustus with fears of a still more alarming nature. The despair of the

[38] It is much to be regretted that we have lost the part of Tacitus which treated of that transaction. We are forced to content ourselves with the popular rumours of Josephus, and the imperfect hints of Dion and Suetonius.

citizens could only attempt what the power of the soldiers was, at any time, able to execute. How precarious was his own authority over men whom he had taught to violate every social duty! He had heard their seditious clamours; he dreaded their calmer moments of reflection. One revolution had been purchased by immense rewards; but a second revolution might double those rewards. The troops professed the fondest attachment to the house of Cæsar; but the attachments of the multitude are capricious and inconstant. Augustus summoned to his aid whatever remained in those fierce minds of Roman prejudices; enforced the rigour of discipline by the sanction of law; and, interposing the majesty of the senate between the emperor and the army, boldly claimed their allegiance as the first magistrate of the republic.[36]

During a long period of two hundred and twenty years, from the establishment of this artful system to the death of Commodus, the dangers inherent to a military government were, in a great measure, suspended. The soldiers were seldom roused to that fatal sense of their own strength, and of the weakness of the civil authority, which was, before and afterwards, productive of such dreadful calamities. Caligula and Domitian were assassinated in their palace by their own domestics:[37] the convulsions which agitated Rome on the death of the former were confined to the walls of the city. But Nero involved the whole empire in his ruin. In the space of eighteen months four princes perished by the sword; and the Roman world was shaken by the fury of the contending armies. Excepting only this short, though violent, eruption of military licence, the two centuries from Augustus to Commodus passed away, unstained with civil blood, and undisturbed by revolutions. The emperor was elected by

[36] Augustus restored the ancient severity of discipline. After the civil wars, he dropped the endearing name of Fellow-Soldiers, and called them only Soldiers (Sueton. in August. c. 25). See the use Tiberius made of the senate in the mutiny of the Pannonian legions (Tacit. Annal. i. [25]).

[37] [Caligula was slain by officers of the prætorian guards.]

the *authority of the senate* and *the consent of the soldiers*.[38] The legions respected their oath of fidelity; and it requires a minute inspection of the Roman annals to discover three inconsiderable rebellions, which were all suppressed in a few months, and without even the hazard of a battle.[39]

In elective monarchies, the vacancy of the throne is a moment big with danger and mischief. The Roman emperors, desirous to spare the legions that interval of suspense, and the temptation of an irregular choice, invested their designed successor with so large a share of present power, as should enable him, after their decease, to assume the remainder without suffering the empire to perceive the change of masters. Thus Augustus, after all his fairer prospects had been snatched from him by untimely deaths, rested his last hopes on Tiberius, obtained for his adopted son the censorial and tribunitian powers, and dictated a law, by which the future prince was invested with an authority equal to his own over the provinces and the armies.[40] Thus Vespasian subdued the generous mind of his eldest son. Titus was adored by the eastern legions, which, under his command, had recently achieved the conquest of Judea. His power was dreaded, and, as his virtues were clouded by the intemperance of youth, his designs were suspected. Instead of listening to such unworthy suspicions, the prudent monarch associated Titus to the full powers of the Imperial dignity; and the grateful son ever approved him-

[38] These words seem to have been the constitutional language. See Tacit. Annal. xiii. 4.

[39] The first was Camillus Scribonianus, who took up arms in Dalmatia against Claudius, and was deserted by his own troops in five days; the second, L. Antonius, in Germany, who rebelled against Domitian; and the third, Avidius Cassius, in the reign of M. Antoninus. The two last reigned but a few months and were cut off by their own adherents. We may observe, that both Camillus and Cassius coloured their ambition with the design of restoring the republic, a task, said Cassius, peculiarly reserved for his name and family.

[40] Velleius Paterculus, lii. c. 121. Sueton. in Tiber. c. 20.

self the humble and faithful minister of so indulgent a father.[41]

The good sense of Vespasian engaged him indeed to embrace every measure that might confirm his recent and precarious elevation. The military oath, and the fidelity of the troops, had been consecrated, by the habits of an hundred years, to the name and family of the Cæsars; and, although that family had been continued only by the fictitious rite of adoption, the Romans still revered, in the person of Nero, the grandson of Germanicus, and the lineal successor of Augustus. It was not without reluctance and remorse that the prætorian guards had been persuaded to abandon the cause of the tyrant.[42] The rapid downfall of Galba, Otho, and Vitellius taught the armies to consider the emperors as the creatures of *their* will, and the instruments of *their* licence. The birth of Vespasian was mean; his grandfather had been a private soldier, his father a petty officer of the revenue,[43] his own merit had raised him, in an advanced age, to the empire; but his merit was rather useful than shining, and his virtues were disgraced by a strict and even sordid parsimony. Such a prince consulted his true interest by the association of a son whose more splendid and amiable character might turn the public attention from the obscure origin to the future glories of the Flavian house. Under the mild administration of Titus, the Roman world enjoyed a transient felicity, and his beloved memory served to protect, above fifteen years, the vices of his brother Domitian.

Nerva had scarcely accepted the purple from the assassins of Domitian before he discovered that his feeble age was

[41] Sueton. in Tit. c. 6. Plin. in Præfat. Hist. Natur.

[42] This idea is frequently and strongly inculcated by Tacitus. See Hist. i. 5. 16. ii. 76.

[43] The emperor Vespasian, with his usual good sense, laughed at the Genealogists, who deduced his family from Flavius, the founder of Reate (his native country), and one of the companions of Hercules. Sueton. in Vespasian. i. 12.

unable to stem the torrent of public disorders which had multiplied under the long tyranny of his predecessor. His mild disposition was respected by the good; but the degenerate Romans required a more vigorous character, whose justice should strike terror into the guilty. Though he had several relations, he fixed his choice on a stranger. He adopted Trajan, then about forty years of age, and who commanded a powerful army in the Lower Germany; and immediately, by a decree of the senate, declared him his colleague and successor in the empire.[44] It is sincerely to be lamented, that, whilst we are fatigued with the disgustful relation of Nero's crimes and follies, we are reduced to collect the actions of Trajan from the glimmerings of an abridgment, or the doubtful light of a panegyric. There remains, however, one panegyric far removed beyond the suspicion of flattery. Above two hundred and fifty years after the death of Trajan, the senate, in pouring out the customary acclamations on the accession of a new emperor, wished that he might surpass the felicity of Augustus, and the virtue of Trajan.[45]

We may readily believe that the father of his country hesitated whether he ought to entrust the various and doubtful character of his kinsman Hadrian with sovereign power. In his last moments, the arts of the empress Plotina either fixed the irresolution of Trajan, or boldly supposed a fictitious adoption,[46] the truth of which could not be safely disputed; and Hadrian was peaceably acknowledged as his lawful successor. Under his reign, as has been already mentioned,

[44] Dio. l. lxviii. p. 1121 [3]. Plin. Secund. in Panegyric. [7].

[45] Felicior Augusto, MELIOR TRAJANO. Eutrop. viii. 5.

[46] Dion (l. lxix. p. 1249 [1]) affirms the whole to have been a fiction, on the authority of his father, who, being governor of the province where Trajan died, had very good opportunities of sifting this mysterious transaction. Yet Dodwell (Prælect. Camden. xvii.) has maintained, that Hadrian was called to the certain hope of the empire during the lifetime of Trajan.

the empire flourished in peace and prosperity. He encouraged the arts, reformed the laws, asserted military discipline, and visited all his provinces in person. His vast and active genius was equally suited to the most enlarged views and the minute details of civil policy. But the ruling passions of his soul were curiosity and vanity. As they prevailed, and as they were attracted by different objects, Hadrian was, by turns, an excellent prince, a ridiculous sophist, and a jealous tyrant. The general tenor of his conduct deserved praise for its equity and moderation. Yet, in the first days of his reign, he put to death four consular senators, his personal enemies, and men who had been judged worthy of empire; and the tediousness of a painful illness rendered him, at last, peevish and cruel. The senate doubted whether they should pronounce him a god or a tyrant; and the honours decreed to his memory were granted to the prayers of the pious Antoninus.[47]

The caprice of Hadrian influenced his choice of a successor. After revolving in his mind several men of distinguished merit, whom he esteemed and hated, he adopted Ælius Verus, a gay and voluptuous nobleman, recommended by uncommon beauty to the lover of Antinous.[48] But whilst Hadrian was delighting himself with his own applause, and the acclamations of the soldiers, whose consent had been secured by an immense donative, the new Cæsar[49] was ravished from his embraces by an untimely death. He left only one son. Hadrian commended the boy to the gratitude of the Antonines. He was adopted by Pius; and, on the accession of Marcus, was invested with an equal share of sovereign

[47] Dion, l. lxx. p. 1171 [1]. Aurel. Victor [13].

[48] The deification of Antinous, his medals, statues, temples, city, oracles, and constellation, are well known, and still dishonour the memory of Hadrian. Yet we may remark, that of the first fifteen emperors Claudius was the only one whose taste in love was entirely correct. For the honours of Antinous, see Spanheim, Commentaires sur les Cæsars de Julien, p. 80.

[49] Hist. August. p. 13 [ii. 1]. Aurelius Victor in Epitom. [9].

power. Among the many vices of this younger Verus, he possessed one virtue — a dutiful reverence for his wiser colleague, to whom he willingly abandoned the ruder cares of empire. The philosophic emperor dissembled his follies, lamented his early death, and cast a decent veil over his memory.

As soon as Hadrian's passion was either gratified or disappointed, he resolved to deserve the thanks of posterity by placing the most exalted merit on the Roman throne. His discerning eye easily discovered a senator about fifty years of age, blameless in all the offices of life; and a youth of about seventeen, whose riper years opened the fair prospect of every virtue: the elder of these was declared the son and successor of Hadrian, on condition, however, that he himself should immediately adopt the younger. The two Antonines (for it is of them that we are now speaking) governed the Roman world forty-two years with the same invariable spirit of wisdom and virtue. Although Pius had two sons,[80] he preferred the welfare of Rome to the interest of his family, gave his daughter Faustina in marriage to young Marcus, obtained from the senate the tribunitian and proconsular powers, and, with a noble disdain, or rather ignorance, of jealousy, associated him to all the labours of government. Marcus, on the other hand, revered the character of his benefactor, loved him as a parent, obeyed him as his sovereign,[81] and, after he was no more, regulated his own administration by the example and maxims of his predecessor. Their united reigns are possibly the only period of history in which the happiness of a great people was the sole object of government.

[80] Without the help of medals and inscriptions, we should be ignorant of this fact, so honourable to the memory of Pius. [But see Hist. Aug. iii. i. 7. We have their names from coins.]

[81] During the twenty-three years of Pius's reign, Marcus was only two nights absent from the palace, and even those were at different times. Hist. August. p. 25 [iv. 7].

Titus Antoninus Pius had been justly denominated a second Numa. The same love of religion, justice, and peace was the distinguishing characteristic of both princes. But the situation of the latter opened a much larger field for the exercise of those virtues. Numa could only prevent a few neighbouring villages from plundering each other's harvests. Antoninus diffused order and tranquillity over the greatest part of the earth. His reign is marked by the rare advantage of furnishing very few materials for history; which is, indeed, little more than the register of the crimes, follies, and misfortunes of mankind. In private life he was an amiable as well as a good man. The native simplicity of his virtue was a stranger to vanity or affectation. He enjoyed with moderation the conveniences of his fortune, and the innocent pleasures of society;[82] and the benevolence of his soul displayed itself in a cheerful serenity of temper.

The virtue of Marcus Aurelius Antoninus was of a severer and more laborious kind.[83] It was the well-earned harvest of many a learned conference, of many a patient lecture, and many a midnight lucubration. At the age of twelve years he embraced the rigid system of the Stoics, which taught him to submit his body to his mind, his passions to his reason; to consider virtue as the only good, vice as the only evil, all things external as things indifferent.[84] His

[82] He was fond of the theatre and not insensible to the charms of the fair sex. Marcus Antoninus, i. 16. Hist. August. p. 20. 21 [iii. 8 and 11]. Julian in Cæsar.

[83] The enemies of Marcus charged him with hypocrisy and with a want of that simplicity which distinguished Pius and even Verus (Hist. Aug. p. 34 [iii. 29]). This suspicion, unjust as it was, may serve to account for the superior applause bestowed upon personal qualifications, in preference to the social virtues. Even Marcus Antoninus has been called a hypocrite; but the wildest scepticism never insinuated that Cæsar might possibly be a coward, or Tully a fool. Wit and valour are qualifications more easily ascertained than humanity or the love of justice.

[84] Tacitus has characterised, in a few words, the principles of the Portico: Doctores sapientiæ secutus est, qui sola bona quæ honesta, mala tantum quæ turpia; potentiam, nobilitatem, cæteraque extra animum, neque bonis neque malis adnumerant. Tacit. Hist. iv. 5.

Meditations, composed in the tumult of a camp, are still extant; and he even condescended to give lessons on philosophy, in a more public manner than was perhaps consistent with the modesty of a sage or the dignity of an emperor.[55] But his life was the noblest commentary on the precepts of Zeno. He was severe to himself, indulgent to the imperfection of others, just and beneficent to all mankind. He regretted that Avidius Cassius, who excited a rebellion in Syria, had disappointed him, by a voluntary death, of the pleasure of converting an enemy into a friend; and he justified the sincerity of that sentiment, by moderating the zeal of the senate against the adherents of the traitor.[56] War he detested, as the disgrace and calamity of human nature; but when the necessity of a just defence called upon him to take up arms, he readily exposed his person to eight winter campaigns on the frozen banks of the Danube, the severity of which was at last fatal to the weakness of his constitution. His memory was revered by a grateful posterity, and above a century after his death many persons preserved the image of Marcus Antoninus among those of their household gods.[57]

If a man were called to fix the period in the history of the world during which the condition of the human race was most happy and prosperous, he would, without hesitation, name that which elapsed from the death of Domitian to the accession of Commodus. The vast extent of the Roman empire was governed by absolute power, under the guidance of virtue and wisdom. The armies were restrained by the firm but gentle hand of four successive emperors, whose characters and authority commanded involuntary respect.

[55] Before he went on the second expedition against the Germans, he read lectures of philosophy to the Roman people, during three days. He had already done the same in the cities of Greece and Asia. Hist. August. p. 41, in Cassio, c. 3.

[56] Dio. l. lxxi. p. 1190 [23]. Hist. August. in Avid. Cassio [8].

[57] Hist. August. in Marc. Antonin. c. 18.

The forms of the civil administration were carefully preserved by Nerva, Trajan, Hadrian, and the Antonines, who delighted in the image of liberty, and were pleased with considering themselves as the accountable ministers of the laws. Such princes deserved the honour of restoring the republic, had the Romans of their days been capable of enjoying a rational freedom.

The labours of these monarchs were over-paid by the immense reward that inseparably waited on their success; by the honest pride of virtue, and by the exquisite delight of beholding the general happiness of which they were the authors. A just but melancholy reflection embittered, however, the noblest of human enjoyments. They must often have recollected the instability of a happiness which depended on the character of a single man. The fatal moment was perhaps approaching, when some licentious youth, or some jealous tyrant, would abuse, to the destruction, that absolute power which they had exerted for the benefit of their people. The ideal restraints of the senate and the laws might serve to display the virtues, but could never correct the vices, of the emperor. The military force was a blind and irresistible instrument of oppression; and the corruption of Roman manners would always supply flatterers eager to applaud, and ministers prepared to serve, the fear or the avarice, the lust or the cruelty, of their masters.

These gloomy apprehensions had been already justified by the experience of the Romans. The annals of the emperors exhibit a strong and various picture of human nature, which we should vainly seek among the mixed and doubtful characters of modern history. In the conduct of those monarchs we may trace the utmost lines of vice and virtue; the most exalted perfection and the meanest degeneracy of our own species. The golden age of Trajan and the Antonines had been preceded by an age of iron. It is almost superfluous to enumerate the unworthy successors of Augustus. Their unparalleled vices, and the splendid theatre on which they were acted, have saved them from oblivion. The dark unrelenting Tiberius, the furious Caligula, the stupid Claudius, the profligate and cruel Nero, the beastly Vitellius,[88] and the timid inhuman Domitian are condemned to everlasting infamy. During fourscore years (excepting only the short and doubtful respite of Vespasian's reign),[89] Rome groaned beneath an unremitting tyranny, which exterminated the ancient families of the republic, and was fatal to almost every virtue and every talent that arose in that unhappy period.

Under the reign of these monsters[90] the slavery of the Romans was accompanied with two peculiar circumstances, the one occasioned by their former liberty, the other by their extensive conquests, which rendered their condition more wretched than that of the victims of tyranny in any other age or country. From these causes were derived, 1. The exquisite sensibility of the sufferers; and 2. The impossibility of escaping from the hand of the oppressor.

I. When Persia was governed by the descendants of Sefi, a race of princes whose wanton cruelty often stained their divan, their table, and their bed with the blood of their favourites, there is a saying recorded of a young nobleman, that he never departed from the sultan's presence without satisfying himself whether his head was still on his shoulders. The experience of every day might almost justify the scepti-

[88] Vitellius consumed in mere eating at least six millions of our money, in about seven months. It is not easy to express his vices with dignity, or even decency. Tacitus fairly calls him a hog; but it is by substituting for a coarse word a very fine image. "At Vitellius, umbraculis hortorum abditus, ut *ignava animalia*, quibus si cibum suggeras jacent torpentque, praeterita, instantia, futura, pari oblivione dimiserat. Atque illum nemore Aricino desidem et marcentem," &c. Tacit. Hist. iii. 36, ii. 95. Sueton. in Vitell. c. 13. Dio. Cassius, l. lxv. p. 1062 [3].

[89] The execution of Helvidius Priscus and of the virtuous Eponina disgraced the reign of Vespasian.

[90] [But there is another side to this picture, which may be seen by studying Mommsen's volume on the provinces.]

cism of Rustan.[61] Yet the fatal sword, suspended above him by a single thread, seems not to have disturbed the slumbers, or interrupted the tranquillity, of the Persian. The monarch's frown, he well knew, could level him with the dust; but the stroke of lightning or apoplexy might be equally fatal; and it was the part of a wise man to forget the inevitable calamities of human life in the enjoyment of the fleeting hour. He was dignified with the appellation of the king's slave; had, perhaps, been purchased from obscure parents, in a country which he had never known; and was trained up from his infancy in the severe discipline of the seraglio.[62] His name, his wealth, his honours, were the gift of a master, who might, without injustice, resume what he had bestowed. Rustan's knowledge, if he possessed any, could only serve to confirm his habits by prejudices. His language afforded not words for any form of government, except absolute monarchy. The history of the East informed him that such had ever been the condition of mankind.[63] The Koran, and the interpreters of that divine book, inculcated to him that the sultan was the descendant of the prophet, and the vicegerent of heaven; that patience was the first virtue of a Mussulman, and unlimited obedience the great duty of a subject.

The minds of the Romans were very differently prepared for slavery. Oppressed beneath the weight of their own corruption and of military violence, they for a long while preserved the sentiments, or at least the ideas, of their free-born ancestors. The education of Helvidius and Thrasea, of Tacitus and Pliny, was the same as that of Cato and Cicero.

[61] Voyage de Chardin en Perse, vol. iii. p. 293.

[62] The practice of raising slaves to the great offices of state is still more common among the Turks than among the Persians. The miserable countries of Georgia and Circassia supply rulers to the greatest part of the East.

[63] Chardin says that European travellers have diffused among the Persians some ideas of the freedom and mildness of our governments. They have done them a very ill office.

From Grecian philosophy they had imbibed the justest and most liberal notions of the dignity of human nature and the origin of civil society. The history of their own country had taught them to revere a free, a virtuous, and a victorious commonwealth; to abhor the successful crimes of Cæsar and Augustus; and inwardly to despise those tyrants whom they adored with the most abject flattery. As magistrates and senators, they were admitted into the great council which had once dictated laws to the earth, whose name gave still a sanction to the acts of the monarch, and whose authority was so often prostituted to the vilest purposes of tyranny. Tiberius, and those emperors who adopted his maxims, attempted to disguise their murders by the formalities of justice, and perhaps enjoyed a secret pleasure in rendering the senate their accomplice as well as their victim. By this assembly the last of the Romans were condemned for imaginary crimes and real virtues. Their infamous accusers assumed the language of independent patriots, who arraigned a dangerous citizen before the tribunal of his country; and the public service was rewarded by riches and honours.[64] The servile judges professed to assert the majesty of the commonwealth, violated in the person of its first magistrate,[65] whose clemency they most applauded when they trembled the most at his inexorable and impending cruelty.[66] The tyrant beheld their baseness

[64] They alleged the example of Scipio and Cato (Tacit. Annal. iii. 66). Marcellus Eprius and Crispius Vibius had acquired two millions and a half under Nero. Their wealth, which aggravated their crimes, protected them under Vespasian. See Tacit. Hist. iv. 43. Dialog. de Orator. c. 8. For one accusation, Regulus, the just object of Pliny's satire, received from the senate the consular ornaments, and a present of sixty thousand pounds.

[65] The crime of *majesty* was formerly a treasonable offence against the Roman people. As tribunes of the people, Augustus and Tiberius applied it to their own persons, and extended it to an infinite latitude.

[66] After the virtuous and unfortunate widow of Germanicus had been put to death, Tiberius received the thanks of the senate for his clemency. She had not been publicly strangled; nor was the body drawn with a hook to the Gemoniæ, where those of common malefactors were exposed. See Tacit. Annal. vi. 25. Sueton. in Tiberio. c. 53.

with just contempt, and encountered their secret sentiments of detestation with sincere and avowed hatred for the whole body of the senate.

II. The division of Europe into a number of independent states, connected, however, with each other, by the general resemblance of religion, language, and manners, is productive of the most beneficial consequences to the liberty of mankind. A modern tyrant, who should find no resistance either in his own breast or in his people, would soon experience a gentle restraint from the example of his equals, the dread of present censure, the advice of his allies, and the apprehension of his enemies. The object of his displeasure, escaping from the narrow limits of his dominions, would easily obtain, in a happier climate, a secure refuge, a new fortune adequate to his merit, the freedom of complaint, and perhaps the means of revenge. But the empire of the Romans filled the world, and, when that empire fell into the hands of a single person, the world became a safe and dreary prison for his enemies. The slave of Imperial despotism, whether he was condemned to drag his gilded chain in Rome and the senate, or to wear out a life of exile on the barren rock of Seriphus, or the frozen banks of the Danube, expected his fate in silent despair.[87] To resist was fatal, and it was impossible to fly. On every side he was encompassed with a vast extent of sea and land, which he could never hope to traverse without being discovered, seized, and restored to his irritated master. Beyond the frontiers, his anxious view could discover nothing, except the ocean, inhospitable deserts, hostile tribes of barbarians, of fierce manners and unknown language, or dependent kings, who would gladly purchase the emperor's protection

[87] Seriphus was a small rocky island in the Ægean Sea, the inhabitants of which were despised for their ignorance and obscurity. The place of Ovid's exile is well known by his just but unmanly lamentations. It should seem that he only received an order to leave Rome in so many days, and to transport himself to Tomi. Guards and gaolers were unnecessary.

by the sacrifice of an obnoxious fugitive.[58] "Wherever you are," said Cicero to the exiled Marcellus, "remember that you are equally within the power of the conqueror."[59]

[58] Under Tiberius, a Roman knight attempted to fly to the Parthians. He was stopt in the straits of Sicily; but so little danger did there appear in the example, that the most jealous of tyrants disdained to punish it. Tacit. Annal. vi. 14.

[59] Cicero ad Familiares, iv. 7.

CHAPTER IV

The cruelty, follies, and murder of Commodus — Election of Pertinax — his attempts to reform the State — his assassination by the Prætorian Guards

THE mildness of Marcus, which the rigid discipline of the Stoics was unable to eradicate, formed, at the same time, the most amiable, and the only defective, part of his character. His excellent understanding was often deceived by the unsuspecting goodness of his heart. Artful men, who study the passions of princes and conceal their own, approached his person in the disguise of philosophic sanctity, and acquired riches and honours by affecting to despise them.[1] His excessive indulgence to his brother,[2] his wife, and his son, exceeded the bounds of private virtue, and became a public injury, by the example and consequences of their vices.

Faustina, the daughter of Pius and the wife of Marcus, has been as much celebrated for her gallantries as for her beauty. The grave simplicity of the philosopher was ill calculated to engage her wanton levity, or to fix that unbounded passion for variety which often discovered personal merit in the meanest of mankind.[3] The Cupid of the ancients was, in general, a very sensual deity; and the amours of an empress, as they

[1] See the complaints of Avidius Cassius. Hist. August. p. 45 [vi. 14]. These are, it is true, the complaints of faction; but even faction exaggerates, rather than invents.

[2] [L. Verus, his brother by adoption.]

[3] [Siquidem] Faustinam satis constat [constet] apud Cayetam, *conditiones* sibi et nauticas et gladiatorias elegisse. Hist. August. p. 30 [iv. 19]. Lampridius explains the sort of merit which Faustina chose, and the *conditions* which she exacted. Hist. August. p. 102 [xvii. 5]. [There is no trustworthy evidence for the truth of these charges.]

exact on her side the plainest advances, are seldom susceptible of much sentimental delicacy. Marcus was the only man in the empire who seemed ignorant or insensible of the irregularities of Faustina; which, according to the prejudices of every age, reflected some disgrace on the injured husband. He promoted several of her lovers to posts of honour and profit,[4] and, during a connection of thirty years, invariably gave her proofs of the most tender confidence, and of a respect which ended not with her life. In his Meditations he thanks the gods, who had bestowed on him a wife so faithful, so gentle, and of such a wonderful simplicity of manners.[5] The obsequious senate, at his earnest request, declared her a goddess. She was represented in her temples, with the attributes of Juno, Venus, and Ceres; and it was decreed that, on the day of their nuptials, the youth of either sex should pay their vows before the altar of their chaste patroness.[6]

The monstrous vices of the son have cast a shade on the purity of the father's virtues. It has been objected to Marcus, that he sacrificed the happiness of millions to a fond partiality for a worthless boy; and that he chose a successor in his own family rather than in the republic. Nothing, however, was neglected by the anxious father, and by the men of virtue and learning whom he summoned to his assistance, to expand the narrow mind of young Commodus, to correct his growing vices, and to render him worthy of the throne for which he was designed. But the power of instruction is seldom of much efficacy, except in those happy dispositions where it is almost superfluous. The distasteful lesson of a grave philosopher was, in a moment, obliterated by the whisper

[4] Hist. August. p. 34 [iv. 29].

[5] Meditat. l. i. [17]. The world has laughed at the credulity of Marcus; but Madame Dacier assures us (and we may credit a lady) that the husband will always be deceived, if the wife condescends to dissemble.

[6] Dio. Cassius, l. lxxi. p. 1195 [31]. Hist. August. p. 33 [iv. 26]. Commentaire de Spanheim sur les Cæsars de Julien, p. 289. The deification of Faustina is the only defect which Julian's criticism is able to discover in the all-accomplished character of Marcus.

of a profligate favourite; and Marcus himself blasted the fruits of this laboured education, by admitting his son, at the age of fourteen or fifteen, to a full participation of the Imperial power. He lived but four years afterwards; but he lived long enough to repent a rash measure, which raised the impetuous youth above the restraint of reason and authority.

Most of the crimes which disturb the internal peace of society are produced by the restraints which the necessary, but unequal, laws of property have imposed on the appetites of mankind, by confining to a few the possession of those objects that are coveted by many. Of all our passions and appetites, the love of power is of the most imperious and unsociable nature, since the pride of one man requires the submission of the multitude. In the tumult of civil discord the laws of society lose their force, and their place is seldom supplied by those of humanity. The ardour of contention, the pride of victory, the despair of success, the memory of past injuries, and the fear of future dangers, all contribute to inflame the mind, and to silence the voice of pity. From such motives almost every page of history has been stained with civil blood; but these motives will not account for the unprovoked cruelties of Commodus, who had nothing to wish, and everything to enjoy. The beloved son of Marcus succeeded to his father, amidst the acclamations of the senate and armies;[7] and when he ascended the throne, the happy youth saw round him neither competitor to remove, nor enemies to punish. In this calm elevated station it was surely natural that he should prefer the love of mankind to

[7] Commodus was the first *Porphyrogenitus* (born since his father's accession to the throne). By a new strain of flattery, the Egyptian medals date by the years of his life; as if they were synonymous to those of his reign. Tillemont. Hist. des Empereurs, tom. ii. p. 752. [The claim of Commodus to be *nobilissimus omnium principum* (Corp. Insc. Lat. v. 4867) was well grounded. He could point to five emperors as his ancestors. His imperial name was M. Aurelius Commodus Antoninus. He had been made a Cæsar in 166, and Imperator in 176 A.D. at the age of 15.]

their detestation, the mild glories of his five predecessors to the ignominious fate of Nero and Domitian.

Yet Commodus was not, as he has been represented, a tiger born with an insatiate thirst of human blood, and capable, from his infancy, of the most inhuman actions.[8] Nature had formed him of a weak, rather than a wicked, disposition. His simplicity and timidity rendered him the slave of his attendants, who gradually corrupted his mind. His cruelty, which at first obeyed the dictates of others, degenerated into habit, and at length became the ruling passion of his soul.[9]

Upon the death of his father Commodus found himself embarrassed with the command of a great army, and the conduct of a difficult war against the Quadi and Marcomanni.[10] The servile and profligate youths whom Marcus had banished soon regained their station and influence about the new emperor. They exaggerated the hardships and dangers of a campaign in the wild countries beyond the Danube; and they assured the indolent prince that the terror of his name and the arms of his lieutenants would be sufficient to complete the conquest of the dismayed barbarians, or to impose such conditions as were more advantageous than any conquest. By a dexterous application to his sensual appetites, they compared the tranquillity, the splendour, the refined pleasures of Rome with the tumult of a Pannonian camp, which afforded neither leisure nor materials for luxury.[11] Commodus listened to the pleasing advice; but whilst he hesitated between his own inclination and the awe which he still retained for his father's counsellors, the summer

[8] Hist. August. p. 46 [vii. 1].

[9] Dion Cassius, l. lxxii. p. 1203 [1].

[10] According to Tertullian (Apolog. c. 25) he died at Sirmium. But the situation of Vindobona, or Vienna, where both the Victors place his death, is better adapted to the operations of the war against the Marcomanni and Quadi. [Date 17th March, 180 A.D.]

[11] Herodian, l. i. p. 12 [6].

insensibly elapsed, and his triumphal entry into the capital was deferred till the autumn. His graceful person,[12] popular address, and imagined virtues attracted the public favour; the honourable peace which he had recently granted to the barbarians diffused an universal joy;[13] his impatience to revisit Rome was fondly ascribed to the love of his country; and his dissolute course of amusements was faintly condemned in a prince of nineteen years of age.

During the three first years of his reign, the forms, and even the spirit, of the old administration were maintained by those faithful counsellors to whom Marcus had recommended his son, and for whose wisdom and integrity Commodus still entertained a reluctant esteem. The young prince and his profligate favourites revelled in all the licence of sovereign power; but his hands were yet unstained with blood; and he had even displayed a generosity of sentiment, which might perhaps have ripened into solid virtue.[14] A fatal incident decided his fluctuating character.

One evening, as the emperor was returning to the palace through a dark and narrow portico in the amphitheatre,[15] an assassin, who waited his passage, rushed upon him with a drawn sword, loudly exclaiming, *The senate sends you this*. The menace prevented the deed; the assassin was seized by the guards, and immediately revealed the authors

[12] Herodian, l. i. p. 16 [7].

[13] This universal joy is well described (from the medals as well as historians) by Mr. Wotton, Hist. of Rome, p. 192, 193. [The terms of the peace were that the Marcomanni and Quadi should not approach nearer than 150 Roman miles to the Danube, should pay a tribute of corn, and furnish a contingent of recruits, and should not make war on the Vandals, Buri, and Jazyges, who were *Roman subjects*. The treaty was a good one if Commodus had been strong enough to insist on its execution. Its articles were not carried out, yet the peace was not disturbed.]

[14] Manilius, the confidential secretary of Avidius Cassius, was discovered after he had lain concealed for several years. The emperor nobly relieved the public anxiety by refusing to see him, and burning his papers without opening them. Dion Cassius, l. lxxii. p. 1209.

[15] See Maffei degli Amphitheatri, p. 126.

of the conspiracy. It had been formed, not in the state, but within the walls of the palace. Lucilla, the emperor's sister, and widow of Lucius Verus, impatient of the second rank, and jealous of the reigning empress, had armed the murderer against her brother's life. She had not ventured to communicate the black design to her second husband, Claudius Pompeianus, a senator of distinguished merit and unshaken loyalty; but among the crowd of her lovers (for she imitated the manners of Faustina) she found men of desperate fortunes and wild ambition, who were prepared to serve her more violent as well as her tender passions. The conspirators experienced the rigour of justice, and the abandoned princess was punished, first with exile, and afterwards with death.[16]

But the words of the assassin sunk deep into the mind of Commodus, and left an indelible impression of fear and hatred against the whole body of the senate. Those whom he had dreaded as importunate ministers, he now suspected as secret enemies. The Delators, a race of men discouraged, and almost extinguished, under the former reigns, again became formidable as soon as they discovered that the emperor was desirous of finding disaffection and treason in the senate. That assembly, whom Marcus had ever considered as the great council of the nation, was composed of the most distinguished of the Romans; and distinction of every kind soon became criminal. The possession of wealth stimulated the diligence of the informers; rigid virtue implied a tacit censure of the irregularities of Commodus; important services implied a dangerous superiority of merit, and the friendship of the father always insured the aversion of the son. Suspicion was equivalent to proof; trial to condemnation. The execution of a considerable senator was attended with the death of all who might lament

[16] Dio. l. lxxii. p. 1205 [4]. Herodian, l. i. p. 16 [8]. Hist. August. p. 46 [vii. 4]. [The would-be assassin was Claudius Pompeianus Quintianus, Lucilla's stepson.]

or revenge his fate; and when Commodus had once tasted human blood, he became incapable of pity or remorse.

Of these innocent victims of tyranny, none died more lamented than the two brothers of the Quintilian family, Maximus and Condianus, whose fraternal love has saved their names from oblivion, and endeared their memory to posterity. Their studies and their occupations, their pursuits and their pleasures, were still the same. In the enjoyment of a great estate, they never admitted the idea of a separate interest: some fragments are now extant of a treatise[17] which they composed in common; and in every action of life it was observed that their two bodies were animated by one soul. The Antonines, who valued their virtues and delighted in their union, raised them, in the same year, to the consulship; and Marcus afterwards entrusted to their joint care the civil administration of Greece, and a great military command, in which they obtained a signal victory over the Germans. The kind cruelty of Commodus united them in death.[18]

The tyrant's rage, after having shed the noblest blood of the senate, at length recoiled on the principal instrument of his cruelty. Whilst Commodus was immersed in blood and luxury, he devolved the detail of the public business on Perennis; a servile and ambitious minister, who had obtained his post by the murder of his predecessor, but who possessed a considerable share of vigour and ability. By acts of extortion, and the forfeited estates of the nobles sacrificed to his avarice, he had accumulated an immense treasure. The Prætorian guards were under his immediate command; and his son, who already discovered a military genius, was at the head of the Illyrian legions. Perennis aspired to the empire; or what, in the eyes of Commodus, amounted

[17] [On agriculture.]

[18] In a note upon the Augustan History, Casaubon has collected a number of particulars concerning these celebrated brothers. See p. 94 of his learned commentary.

to the same crime, he was capable of aspiring to it, had he not been prevented, surprised, and put to death. The fall of a minister is a very trifling incident in the general history of the empire; but it was hastened by an extraordinary circumstance, which proved how much the nerves of discipline were already relaxed. The legions of Britain, discontented with the administration of Perennis, formed a deputation of fifteen hundred select men, with instructions to march to Rome and lay their complaints before the emperor. These military petitioners, by their own determined behaviour, by inflaming the divisions of the guards, by exaggerating the strength of the British army, and by alarming the fears of Commodus, exacted and obtained the minister's death, as the only redress of their grievances.[10] This presumption of a distant army, and their discovery of the weakness of government, was a sure presage of the most dreadful convulsions.

The negligence of the public administration was betrayed soon afterwards by a new disorder, which arose from the smallest beginnings. A spirit of desertion began to prevail among the troops, and the deserters, instead of seeking their safety in flight or concealment, infested the highways. Maternus, a private soldier, of a daring boldness above his station, collected these bands of robbers into a little army, set open the prisons, invited the slaves to assert their freedom, and plundered with impunity the rich and defenceless cities of Gaul and Spain. The governors of the provinces, who had long been the spectators, and perhaps the partners, of his depredations, were, at length, roused from their supine indolence

[10] Dio. l. lxxii. p. 1210 [9]. Herodian, l. i. p. 22 [9]. Hist. August. p. 48 [vii. 6. 1–5]. Dion gives a much less odious character of Perennis, than the other historians. His moderation is almost a pledge of his veracity. [The policy of Perennis, which caused his fall, aimed at ousting the senators from military appointments and substituting men of the Equestrian order. The intervention of the Britannic legions rests on Dion. Date 185, cp. Müller, Hermes, 18, p. 623 *sqq.*]

by the threatening commands of the emperor. Maternus found that he was encompassed, and foresaw that he must be overpowered. A great effort of despair was his last resource. He ordered his followers to disperse, to pass the Alps in small parties and various disguises, and to assemble at Rome, during the licentious tumult of the festival of Cybele.[20] To murder Commodus, and to ascend the vacant throne, was the ambition of no vulgar robber. His measures were so ably concerted that his concealed troops already filled the streets of Rome. The envy of an accomplice discovered and ruined this singular enterprise in the moment when it was ripe for execution.[21]

Suspicious princes often promote the last of mankind, from a vain persuasion that those who have no dependence except on their favour will have no attachment except to the person of their benefactor. Cleander, the successor of Perennis, was a Phrygian by birth; of a nation, over whose stubborn but servile temper blows only could prevail.[22] He had been sent from his native country to Rome in the capacity of a slave. As a slave he entered the imperial palace, rendered himself useful to his master's passions, and rapidly ascended to the most exalted station which a subject could enjoy. His influence over the mind of Commodus was much greater than that of his predecessor; for Cleander was devoid of any ability or virtue which could inspire the emperor with envy or distrust. Avarice was the reigning passion of his soul, and the great principle of his administration. The rank of consul, of Patrician, of senator, was exposed to public sale; and it would have been considered as disaffection if

[20] During the second Punic war, the Romans imported from Asia the worship of the mother of the gods. Her festival, the *Megalesia*, began on the fourth of April, and lasted six days. The streets were crowded with mad processions, the theatres with spectators, and the public tables with unbidden guests. Order and police were suspended, and pleasure was the only serious business of the city. See Ovid de Fastis, l. iv. 189, &c.

[21] Herodian, l. i. p. 23, 28 [10].

[22] Cicero pro Flacco, c. 27.

any one had refused to purchase these empty and disgraceful honours with the greatest part of his fortune.[23] In the lucrative provincial employments the minister shared with the governor the spoils of the people. The execution of the laws was venal and arbitrary. A wealthy criminal might obtain not only the reversal of the sentence by which he was justly condemned; but might likewise inflict whatever punishment he pleased on the accuser, the witnesses, and the judge.

By these means Cleander, in the space of three years, had accumulated more wealth than had ever yet been possessed by any freedman.[24] Commodus was perfectly satisfied with the magnificent presents which the artful courtier laid at his feet in the most seasonable moments. To divert the public envy, Cleander, under the emperor's name, erected baths, porticos, and places of exercise, for the use of the people.[25] He flattered himself that the Romans, dazzled and amused by this apparent liberality, would be less affected by the bloody scenes which were daily exhibited; that they would forget the death of Byrrhus, a senator to whose superior merit the late emperor had granted one of his daughters; and that they would forgive the execution of Arrius Antoninus, the last representative of the name and virtues of the Antonines. The former, with more integrity than prudence, had attempted to disclose to his brother-in-law the true character of Cleander. An equitable sentence pronounced by the latter, when proconsul of Asia, against a worthless creature of the favourite, proved fatal to him.[26] After the fall of Perennis

[23] One of these dear-bought promotions occasioned a current bon mot, that Julius Solon was *banished* into the senate. [In one year there were no less than twenty-five consuls.]

[24] Dion (l. lxxii. p. 1213 [12]) observes that no freedman had possessed riches equal to those of Cleander. The fortune of Pallas amounted, however, to upwards of five and twenty hundred thousand pounds — *ter millies*.

[25] Dion, l. lxxii. p. 1213 [12]. Herodian, l. i. p. 29 [12]. Hist. August. p. 52 [vii. 17]. These baths were situated near the *Porta Capena*. See Nardini Roma Antica, p. 79.

[26] Hist. August. p. 48.

the terrors of Commodus had, for a short time, assumed the appearance of a return to virtue. He repealed the most odious of his acts, loaded his memory with the public execration, and ascribed to the pernicious counsels of that wicked minister all the errors of his inexperienced youth. But his repentance lasted only thirty days; and, under Cleander's tyranny, the administration of Perennis was often regretted.

Pestilence and famine contributed to fill up the measure of the calamities of Rome.[27] The first could only be imputed to the just indignation of the gods; but a monopoly of corn, supported by the riches and power of the minister, was considered as the immediate cause of the second. The popular discontent, after it had long circulated in whispers, broke out in the assembled circus. The people quitted their favourite amusements for the more delicious pleasure of revenge, rushed in crowds towards a palace in the suburbs, one of the emperor's retirements, and demanded, with angry clamours, the head of the public enemy. Cleander, who commanded the Pretorian guards,[28] ordered a body of cavalry to sally forth and disperse the seditious multitude. The multitude fled with precipitation towards the city; several were slain, and many more were trampled to death; but, when the cavalry entered the streets their pursuit was checked by a shower of stones and darts from the roofs and windows of the houses. The foot guards,[29] who had been long jealous of the prerogatives and insolence of the Prætorian

[27] Herodian, l. i. p. 28 [12]. Dion, l. lxxii. p. 1215 [14]. The latter says, that two thousand persons died every day at Rome, during a considerable length of time. [The pestilence was probably a new outbreak of the same plague which had ravaged the Empire under Marcus.]

[28] Tuncque primum tres præfecti prætorio fuere: inter quos libertinus. From some remains of modesty, Cleander declined the title, whilst he assumed the powers, of Prætorian Prefect. As the other freedmen were styled, from their several departments, *a rationibus*, *ab epistolis*, Cleander called himself *a pugione*, as entrusted with the defence of his master's person. Salmasius and Casaubon seem to have talked very idly upon this passage.

[29] Οἱ τῆς πόλεως πεζοὶ στρατιῶται. Herodian, l. i. p. 31 [12]. It is doubtful whether he means the Prætorian infantry, or the cohortes urbanæ, a body of six

cavalry, embraced the party of the people. The tumult became a regular engagement, and threatened a general massacre. The Prætorians at length gave way, oppressed with numbers; and the tide of popular fury returned with redoubled violence against the gates of the palace, where Commodus lay dissolved in luxury, and alone unconscious of the civil war. It was death to approach his person with the unwelcome news. He would have perished in this supine security had not two women, his eldest sister Fadilla, and Marcia the most favoured of his concubines, ventured to break into his presence. Bathed in tears, and with dishevelled hair, they threw themselves at his feet, and, with all the pressing eloquence of fear, discovered to the affrighted emperor the crimes of the minister, the rage of the people, and the impending ruin which in a few minutes would burst over his palace and person. Commodus started from his dream of pleasure, and commanded that the head of Cleander should be thrown out to the people. The desired spectacle instantly appeased the tumult; and the son of Marcus might even yet have regained the affection and confidence of his subjects.[80]

But every sentiment of virtue and humanity was extinct in the mind of Commodus. Whilst he thus abandoned the reins of empire to these unworthy favourites, he valued nothing in sovereign power except the unbounded licence of indulging his sensual appetites. His hours were spent in a seraglio of three hundred beautiful women and as many boys, of every rank and of every province; and, wherever the arts of seduction proved ineffectual, the brutal lover had recourse to violence. The ancient historians[81] have

thousand men, but whose rank and discipline were not equal to their numbers. Neither Tillemont nor Wotton choose to decide this question. [Doubtless the *cohortes urbanæ*.]

[80] Dion Cassius, l. lxxii. p. 1215 [13]. Herodian, l. i. p. 32 [13]. Hist. August. p. 48 [vii. 7].

[81] Sororibus suis constupratis. Ipsas concubinas suas sub oculis suis

expatiated on these abandoned scenes of prostitution, which scorned every restraint of nature or modesty; but it would not be easy to translate their too faithful descriptions into the decency of modern language. The intervals of lust were filled up with the basest amusements. The influence of a polite age and the labour of an attentive education had never been able to infuse into his rude and brutish mind the least tincture of learning; and he was the first of the Roman emperors totally devoid of taste for the pleasures of the understanding. Nero himself excelled, or affected to excel, in the elegant arts of music and poetry; nor should we despise his pursuits, had he not converted the pleasing relaxation of a leisure hour into the serious business and ambition of his life. But Commodus, from his earliest infancy, discovered an aversion to whatever was rational or liberal, and a fond attachment to the amusements of the populace, — the sports of the circus and amphitheatre, the combats of gladiators, and the hunting of wild beasts. The masters in every branch of learning, whom Marcus provided for his son, were heard with inattention and disgust; whilst the Moors and Parthians, who taught him to dart the javelin and to shoot with the bow, found a disciple who delighted in his application, and soon equalled the most skilful of his instructors in the steadiness of the eye and the dexterity of the hand.

The servile crowd, whose fortune depended on their master's vices, applauded these ignoble pursuits. The perfidious voice of flattery reminded him that, by exploits of the same nature, by the defeat of the Nemean lion, and the slaughter of the wild boar of Erymanthus, the Grecian Hercules had acquired a place among the gods, and an immortal memory among men. They only forgot to observe

stuprari jubebat. Nec irruentium in se juvenum carebat infamiâ, omni parte corporis atque ore in sexum utrumque pollutus. Hist. August. p. 47 [vii. 5].

that, in the first ages of society, when the fiercer animals often dispute with man the possession of an unsettled country, a successful war against those savages is one of the most innocent and beneficial labours of heroism. In the civilised state of the Roman empire the wild beasts had long since retired from the face of man and the neighbourhood of populous cities. To surprise them in their solitary haunts, and to transport them to Rome, that they might be slain in pomp by the hand of an emperor, was an enterprise equally ridiculous for the prince and oppressive for the people.[32] Ignorant of these distinctions, Commodus eagerly embraced the glorious resemblance, and styled himself (as we still read on his medals)[33] the *Roman Hercules*. The club and the lion's hide were placed by the side of the throne amongst the ensigns of sovereignty; and statues were erected, in which Commodus was represented in the character and with the attributes of the God whose valour and dexterity he endeavoured to emulate in the daily course of his ferocious amusements.[34]

Elated with these praises, which gradually extinguished the innate sense of shame, Commodus resolved to exhibit, before the eyes of the Roman people, those exercises which till then he had decently confined within the walls of his palace and to the presence of a few favourites. On the appointed day the various motives of flattery, fear, and curiosity attracted to the amphitheatre an innumerable multitude of spectators; and some degree of applause was deservedly

[32] The African lions, when pressed by hunger, infested the open villages and cultivated country; and they infested them with impunity. The royal beast was reserved for the pleasures of the emperor and the capital; and the unfortunate peasant who killed one of them, though in his own defence, incurred a very heavy penalty. This extraordinary *game law* was mitigated by Honorius, and finally repealed by Justinian. Codex Theodos. tom. v. p. 92, et Comment. Gothofred.

[33] Spanheim de Numismat. Dissertat. xii. tom. ii. 493. [*Herc. Comm.*, and on Alexandrine coins Ῥωμαῖον Ἡρακλέα].

[34] Dion, l. lxxii. p. 1216 [15]. Hist. August. p. 49 [vii. 8].

bestowed on the uncommon skill of the Imperial performer. Whether he aimed at the head or heart of the animal, the wound was alike certain and mortal. With arrows, whose point was shaped into the form of a crescent, Commodus often intercepted the rapid career and cut asunder the long bony neck of the ostrich.[85] A panther was let loose; and the archer waited till he had leaped upon a trembling malefactor. In the same instant the shaft flew, the beast dropt dead, and the man remained unhurt. The dens of the amphitheatre disgorged at once a hundred lions; a hundred darts from the unerring hand of Commodus laid them dead as they ran raging round the *Arena*. Neither the huge bulk of the elephant nor the scaly hide of the rhinoceros could defend them from his stroke. Æthiopia and India yielded their most extraordinary productions; and several animals were slain in the amphitheatre which had been seen only in the representations of art, or perhaps of fancy.[86] In all these exhibitions, the surest precautions were used to protect the person of the Roman Hercules from the desperate spring of any savage who might possibly disregard the dignity of the emperor and the sanctity of the god.[87]

But the meanest of the populace were affected with shame and indignation, when they beheld their sovereign enter the lists as a gladiator, and glory in a profession which the laws and manners of the Romans had branded with the justest note of infamy.[88] He chose the habit and arms of the

[85] The ostrich's neck is three feet long, and composed of seventeen vertebræ. See Buffon, Hist. Naturelle.

[86] Commodus killed a camelopardalis or giraffe (Dion, l. lxxii. p. 1211 [10]), the tallest, the most gentle, and the most useless of the large quadrupeds. This singular animal, a native only of the interior parts of Africa, has not been seen in Europe since the revival of letters, and though M. de Buffon (Hist. Naturelle, tom. xiii.) has endeavoured to describe, he has not ventured to delineate, the giraffe.

[87] Herodian, l. i. p. 37 [15]. Hist. August. p. 50 [vii. 11].

[88] The virtuous, and even the wise, princes forbade the senators and knights to embrace this scandalous profession, under pain of infamy, or

Secutor, whose combat with the *Retiarius* formed one of the most lively scenes in the bloody sports of the amphitheatre. The *Secutor* was armed with an helmet, sword, and buckler; his naked antagonist had only a large net and a trident; with the one he endeavoured to entangle, with the other to despatch, his enemy. If he missed the first throw he was obliged to fly from the pursuit of the *Secutor* till he had prepared his net for a second cast.[39] The emperor fought in this character seven hundred and thirty-five several times. These glorious achievements were carefully recorded in the public acts of the empire; and, that he might omit no circumstance of infamy, he received from the common fund of gladiators a stipend so exorbitant that it became a new and most ignominious tax upon the Roman people.[40] It may be easily supposed that in these engagements the master of the world was always successful: in the amphitheatre his victories were not often sanguinary; but when he exercised his skill in the school of gladiators, or his own palace, his wretched antagonists were frequently honoured with a mortal wound from the hand of Commodus, and obliged to seal their flattery with their blood.[41] He now disdained the appellation of Hercules. The name of Paulus, a celebrated Secutor, was the only one which delighted his ear. It was inscribed on his colossal statues, and repeated in the redoubled acclamations[42] of the mournful and applaud-

what was more dreaded by those profligate wretches, of exile. The tyrants allured them to dishonour by threats and rewards. Nero once produced, in the arena, forty senators and sixty knights. See Lipsius, Saturnalia, l. ii. c. 2. He has happily corrected a passage of Suetonius, in Nerone, c. 12.

[39] Lipsius, l. ii. c. 7, 8. Juvenal in the eighth satire gives a picturesque description of this combat.

[40] Hist. August. p. 50 [vii. 11]. Dion, l. lxxii. p. 1220 [19]. He received, for each time, *decies*, about £8000 sterling.

[41] Victor tells us that Commodus only allowed his antagonists a leaden weapon, dreading most probably the consequences of their despair. [*Cæsar*. 4.]

[42] They were obliged to repeat six hundred and twenty-six times, *Paulus, first of the Secutors*, &c.

ing senate.[43] Claudius Pompeianus, the virtuous husband of Lucilla, was the only senator who asserted the honour of his rank. As a father he permitted his sons to consult their safety by attending the amphitheatre. As a Roman he declared that his own life was in the emperor's hands, but that he would never behold the son of Marcus prostituting his person and dignity. Notwithstanding his manly resolution, Pompeianus escaped the resentment of the tyrant, and, with his honour, had the good fortune to preserve his life.[44]

Commodus had now attained the summit of vice and infamy. Amidst the acclamations of a flattering court, he was unable to disguise from himself that he had deserved the contempt and hatred of every man of sense and virtue in his empire. His ferocious spirit was irritated by the consciousness of that hatred, by the envy of every kind of merit, by the just apprehension of danger, and by the habit of slaughter which he contracted in his daily amusements. History has preserved a long list of consular senators sacrificed to his wanton suspicion, which sought out, with peculiar anxiety, those unfortunate persons connected, however remotely, with the family of the Antonines, without sparing even the ministers of his crimes or pleasures.[45] His cruelty proved at last fatal to himself. He had shed with impunity the noblest blood of Rome: he perished as soon as he was dreaded by his own domestics. Marcia, his favourite concubine, Eclectus, his chamberlain, and Lætus, his Prætorian

[43] Dion, l. lxxii. p. 1221 [20]. He speaks of his own baseness and danger.

[44] He mixed however some prudence with his courage, and passed the greatest part of his time in a country retirement; alleging his advanced age, and the weakness of his eyes. "I never saw him in the senate," says Dion, "except during the short reign of Pertinax." All his infirmities had suddenly left him, and they returned as suddenly upon the murder of that excellent prince. Dion, l. lxxiii. p. 1227 [3].

[45] The prefects were changed almost hourly or daily; and the caprice of Commodus was often fatal to his most favoured chamberlains. Hist. August. 46, 51 [vii. 14 and 15].

prefect, alarmed by the fate of their companions and predecessors, resolved to prevent the destruction which every hour hung over their heads, either from the mad caprice of the tyrant, or the sudden indignation of the people. Marcia seized the occasion of presenting a draught of wine to her lover, after he had fatigued himself with hunting some wild beasts. Commodus retired to sleep; but whilst he was labouring with the effects of poison and drunkenness, a robust youth, by profession a wrestler, entered his chamber, and strangled him without resistance. The body was secretly conveyed out of the palace, before the least suspicion was entertained in the city, or even in the court, of the emperor's death. Such was the fate of the son of Marcus, and so easy was it to destroy a hated tyrant, who, by the artificial powers of government, had oppressed, during thirteen years, so many millions of subjects, every one of whom was equal to their master in personal strength and personal abilities.[48]

The measures of the conspirators were conducted with the deliberate coolness and celerity which the greatness of the occasion required. They resolved instantly to fill the vacant throne with an emperor whose character would justify and maintain the action that had been committed. They fixed on Pertinax, prefect of the city, an ancient senator of consular rank, whose conspicuous merit had broken through the obscurity of his birth, and raised him to the first honours of the state. He had successively governed most of the provinces of the empire; and in all his great employments, military as well as civil, he had uniformly distinguished himself, by the firmness, the prudence, and the integrity

[48] Dion, l. lxxii. p. 1222 [22]. Herodian, l. i. p. 43. Hist. August. p. 52 [vii. 17]. [The situation on the death of Commodus has been well compared with the situation on the death of Nero. The general joy at deliverance from tyranny, the measures taken by the senate in branding the memory of the fallen tyrant, were alike; and Pertinax, the successor of Commodus, closely resembled Galba, the successor of Nero, in age, respectability, good intentions, and unfitness for the imperial power (Schiller, i. 668).]

of his conduct.[47] He now remained almost alone of the friends and ministers of Marcus; and, when, at a late hour of the night, he was awakened with the news that the chamberlain and the prefect were at his door, he received them with intrepid resignation, and desired they would execute their master's orders. Instead of death, they offered him the throne of the Roman world. During some moments he distrusted their intentions and assurances. Convinced at length of the death of Commodus, he accepted the purple with a sincere reluctance, the natural effect of his knowledge both of the duties and of the dangers of the supreme rank.[48]

Lætus conducted without delay his new emperor to the camp of the Prætorians, diffusing at the same time through the city a seasonable report that Commodus died suddenly of an apoplexy; and that the virtuous Pertinax had *already* succeeded to the throne. The guards were rather surprised than pleased with the suspicious death of a prince whose

[47] Pertinax was a native of Alba Pompeia, in Piedmont, and son of a timber merchant. The order of his employments (it is marked by Capitolinus) well deserves to be set down as expressive of the form of government and manners of the age. 1. He was a centurion. 2. Prefect of a cohort in Syria, in the Parthian war, and in Britain. 3. He obtained an *Ala*, or squadron of horse, in Mæsia. 4. He was commissary of provisions on the Æmilian way. [This refers to the distribution of alimentary state charity. Alimentary institutions had been founded by Nerva and Trajan. See Desjardins, De tabulis alimentariis, 1854; Hirschfeld, Römische Verwaltungsgeschichte, 113 *sqq.*] 5. He commanded the fleet upon the Rhine. 6. He was procurator of Dacia, with a salary of about 1600*l.* a year. 7. He commanded the Veterans of a legion. 8. He obtained the rank of senator. 9. Of prætor. 10. With the command of the first legion in Rhætia and Noricum. 11. He was consul about the year 175. 12. He attended Marcus into the East. 13. He commanded an army on the Danube. 14. He was consular legate of Mæsia. 15. Of Dacia. 16. Of Syria. 17. Of Britain. 18. He had the care of the public provisions at Rome. 19. He was proconsul of Africa. 20. Prefect of the city. Herodian (l. i. p. 48 [ii. 1]) does justice to his disinterested spirit; but Capitolinus, who collected every popular rumour, charges him with a great fortune acquired by bribery and corruption. [He is a favourite with the historian Dion Cassius. His full name was P. Helvius Pertinax, and he was born in 126 A.D.]

[48] Julian, in the Cæsars, taxes him with being accessory to the death of Commodus.

indulgence and liberality they alone had experienced; but the emergency of the occasion, the authority of their prefect, the reputation of Pertinax, and the clamours of the people obliged them to stifle their secret discontents, to accept the donative promised by the new emperor, to swear allegiance to him, and, with joyful acclamations and laurels in their hands, to conduct him to the senate-house, that the military consent might be ratified by the civil authority.

This important night was now far spent; with the dawn of day, and the commencement of the new year, the senators expected a summons to attend an ignominious ceremony. In spite of all remonstrances, even of those of his creatures who yet preserved any regard for prudence or decency, Commodus had resolved to pass the night in the gladiators' school, and from thence to take possession of the consulship, in the habit and with the attendance of that infamous crew. On a sudden, before the break of day, the senate was called together in the temple of Concord, to meet the guards, and to ratify the election of a new emperor. For a few minutes they sat in silent suspense, doubtful of their unexpected deliverance, and suspicious of the cruel artifices of Commodus: but, when at length they were assured that the tyrant was no more, they resigned themselves to all the transports of joy and indignation. Pertinax, who modestly represented the meanness of his extraction, and pointed out several noble senators more deserving than himself of the empire, was constrained by their dutiful violence to ascend the throne, and received all the titles of Imperial power, confirmed by the most sincere vows of fidelity. The memory of Commodus was branded with eternal infamy. The names of tyrant, of gladiator, of public enemy, resounded in every corner of the house. They decreed in tumultuous[40] votes, that his

[40] [By this epithet Gibbon alludes to the rhythmical acclamations which were the usage in the proceedings of the senate. In the *adclamationes graves* recorded here by Lampridius, the words *hostis* and *parricida* recur as a sort of refrain.]

honours should be reversed, his titles erased from the public monuments, his statues thrown down, his body dragged with a hook into the stripping-room of the gladiators, to satiate the public fury; and they expressed some indignation against those officious servants who had already presumed to screen his remains from the justice of the senate. But Pertinax could not refuse those last rites to the memory of Marcus and the tears of his first protector Claudius Pompeianus, who lamented the cruel fate of his brother-in-law, and lamented still more that he had deserved it.[50]

These effusions of impotent rage against a dead emperor, whom the senate had flattered when alive with the most abject servility, betrayed a just but ungenerous spirit of revenge. The legality of these decrees was, however, supported by the principles of the Imperial constitution. To censure, to depose, or to punish with death, the first magistrate of the republic who had abused his delegated trust, was the ancient and undoubted prerogative of the Roman senate;[51] but that feeble assembly was obliged to content itself with inflicting on a fallen tyrant that public justice from which, during his life and reign, he had been shielded by the strong arm of military despotism.

Pertinax found a nobler way of condemning his predecessor's memory, — by the contrast of his own virtues with the vices of Commodus. On the day of his accession he resigned over to his wife and son his whole private fortune;[52]

[50] Capitolinus gives us the particulars of these tumultuary votes, which were moved by one senator, and repeated, or rather chaunted, by the whole body. Hist. August. p. 52 [vii. 18].

[51] The senate condemned Nero to be put to death *more majorum*. Sueton. c. 49.

[52] [This act has considerable significance in the history of the exchequer of the Roman empire. Antoninus Pius had already acted in the same way, making over his private property to his daughter Faustina. The principle involved was the separation of the Emperor's private purse from the *fiscus*, or public money which came to him as Emperor. This separation was systematically carried out by Septimius Severus.]

that they might have no pretence to solicit favours at the expense of the state. He refused to flatter the vanity of the former with the title of Augusta, or to corrupt the inexperienced youth of the latter by the rank of Cæsar. Accurately distinguishing between the duties of a parent and those of a sovereign, he educated his son with a severe simplicity, which, while it gave him no assured prospect of the throne, might in time have rendered him worthy of it. In public the behaviour of Pertinax was grave and affable. He lived with the virtuous part of the senate[83] (and, in a private station, he had been acquainted with the true character of each individual), without either pride or jealousy; considered them as friends and companions, with whom he had shared the dangers of the tyranny, and with whom he wished to enjoy the security of the present time. He very frequently invited them to familiar entertainments, the frugality of which was ridiculed by those who remembered and regretted the luxurious prodigality of Commodus.[84]

To heal, as far as it was possible, the wounds inflicted by the hand of tyranny, was the pleasing, but melancholy, task of Pertinax. The innocent victims who yet survived were recalled from exile, released from prison, and restored to the full possession of their honours and fortunes. The unburied bodies of murdered senators (for the cruelty of Commodus endeavoured to extend itself beyond death) were deposited in the sepulchres of their ancestors; their memory was justified; and every consolation was bestowed on their ruined and afflicted families. Among these consolations, one of the most grateful was the punishment

[83] [The note of the policy of Pertinax was the restoration of the authority of the senate, which, during the preceding century, had been gradually becoming less and less. He assumed the title *princeps senatus*, and things looked like a return of the system of Augustus.]

[84] Dion (l. lxxiii. p. 122 [3]) speaks of these entertainments, as a senator who had supped with the emperor; Capitolinus (Hist. August. p. 58 [viii. 12]) like a slave who had received his intelligence from one of the scullions.

of the Delators, the common enemies of their master, of virtue, and of their country. Yet, even in the inquisition of these legal assassins, Pertinax proceeded with a steady temper, which gave everything to justice, and nothing to popular prejudice and resentment.

The finances of the state demanded the most vigilant care of the emperor. Though every measure of injustice and extortion had been adopted which could collect the property of the subject into the coffers of the prince, the rapaciousness of Commodus had been so very inadequate to his extravagance that, upon his death, no more than eight thousand pounds were found in the exhausted treasury,[88] to defray the current expenses of government, and to discharge the pressing demand of a liberal donative, which the new emperor had been obliged to promise to the Prætorian guards. Yet, under these distressed circumstances, Pertinax had the generous firmness to remit all the oppressive taxes invented by Commodus, and to cancel all the unjust claims of the treasury; declaring, in a decree of the senate, "that he was better satisfied to administer a poor republic with innocence, than to acquire riches by the ways of tyranny and dishonour." Economy and industry he considered as the pure and genuine sources of wealth; and from them he soon derived a copious supply for the public necessities. The expense of the household was immediately reduced to one half. All the instruments of luxury Pertinax exposed to public auction,[89] gold and silver plate, chariots of a singular construction, a superfluous wardrobe of silk and embroidery, and a great number of beautiful slaves of both sexes; excepting only, with attentive humanity, those who were born in a state of

[88] *Decies.* The blameless economy of Pius left his successors a treasure of *vicies septies millies*, above two and twenty millions sterling. Dion, l. lxxiii. p. 1231 [8].

[89] Besides the design of converting these useless ornaments into money, Dion (l. lxxiii. p. 1229 [5]) assigns two secret motives of Pertinax. He wished to expose the vices of Commodus, and to discover by the purchasers those who most resembled him.

freedom, and had been ravished from the arms of their weeping parents. At the same time that he obliged the worthless favourites of the tyrant to resign a part of their ill-gotten wealth, he satisfied the just creditors of the state, and unexpectedly discharged the long arrears of honest services. He removed the oppressive restrictions which had been laid upon commerce, and granted all the uncultivated lands in Italy and the provinces to those who would improve them; with an exemption from tribute during the term of ten years.[87]

Such an uniform conduct had already secured to Pertinax the noblest reward of a sovereign, the love and esteem of his people. Those who remembered the virtues of Marcus were happy to contemplate in their new emperor the features of that bright original, and flattered themselves that they should long enjoy the benign influence of his administration. A hasty zeal to reform the corrupted state, accompanied with less prudence than might have been expected from the years and experience of Pertinax, proved fatal to himself and to his country. His honest indiscretion united against him the servile crowd, who found their private benefit in the public disorders, and who preferred the favour of a tyrant to the inexorable equality of the laws.[88]

Amidst the general joy the sullen and angry countenance of the Prætorian guards betrayed their inward dissatisfaction. They had reluctantly submitted to Pertinax; they dreaded the strictness of the ancient discipline, which he was preparing to restore; and they regretted the licence of the former reign. Their discontents were secretly fomented by Lætus, their prefect, who found, when it was too late, that his new emperor would reward a servant, but would not be ruled by a favourite. On the third day of his reign, the soldiers seized on a noble senator, with a design to carry him to the camp,

[87] Though Capitolinus has picked up many idle tales of the private life of Pertinax, he joins with Dion and Herodian in admiring his public conduct [viii. 13].

[88] Leges, rem surdam, inexorabilem esse. T. Liv. ii. 3.

and to invest him with the imperial purple. Instead of being dazzled by the dangerous honour, the affrighted victim escaped from their violence, and took refuge at the feet of Pertinax. A short time afterwards Sosius Falco, one of the consuls of the year, a rash youth,[60] but of an ancient and opulent family, listened to the voice of ambition; and a conspiracy was formed during a short absence of Pertinax, which was crushed by his sudden return to Rome and his resolute behaviour. Falco was on the point of being justly condemned to death as a public enemy, had he not been saved by the earnest and sincere entreaties of the injured emperor; who conjured the senate that the purity of his reign might not be stained by the blood even of a guilty senator.

These disappointments served only to irritate the rage of the Prætorian guards. On the twenty-eighth of March, eighty-six days only after the death of Commodus, a general sedition broke out in the camp, which the officers wanted either power or inclination to suppress. Two or three hundred of the most desperate soldiers marched at noon-day, with arms in their hands and fury in their looks, towards the Imperial palace. The gates were thrown open by their companions upon guard; and by the domestics of the old court, who had already formed a secret conspiracy against the life of the too virtuous emperor. On the news of their approach, Pertinax, disdaining either flight or concealment, advanced to meet his assassins; and recalled to their minds his own innocence, and the sanctity of their recent oath. For a few moments they stood in silent suspense, ashamed of their atrocious design, and awed by the venerable aspect and majestic firmness of their sovereign, till at length, the despair of pardon reviving their fury, a barbarian of the country of

[60] If we credit Capitolinus (which is rather difficult) Falco behaved with the most petulant indecency to Pertinax on the day of his accession. The wise emperor only admonished him of his youth and inexperience. Hist. August. p. 55 [viii. 5].

Tongres[60] levelled the first blow against Pertinax, who was instantly despatched with a multitude of wounds. His head, separated from his body, and placed on a lance, was carried in triumph to the Prætorian camp, in the sight of a mournful and indignant people, who lamented the unworthy fate of that excellent prince, and the transient blessings of a reign, the memory of which could serve only to aggravate their approaching misfortunes.[61]

[60] The modern bishopric of Liege. This soldier probably belonged to the Batavian horse-guards, who were mostly raised in the Duchy of Gueldres and the neighbourhood, and were distinguished by their valour, and by the boldness with which they swam their horses across the broadest and most rapid rivers. Tacit. Hist. iv. 12. Dion, l. lv. p. 797 [24]. Lipsius de magnitudine Romanâ, l. i. c. 4.

[61] Dion, l. lxxiii. p. 1232 [10]. Herodian, l. ii. p. 60 [5]. Hist. August. p. 58 [viii. 11]. Victor in Epitom., and in Cæsarib. Eutropius, viii. 16.

CHAPTER V

Public sale of the empire to Didius Julianus by the Prætorian Guards — Clodius Albinus in Britain, Pescennius Niger in Syria, and Septimius Severus in Pannonia, declare against the murderers of Pertinax — Civil wars, and victory of Severus over his three rivals — Relaxation of discipline — New maxims of government

THE power of the sword is more sensibly felt in an extensive monarchy than in a small community. It has been calculated by the ablest politicians that no state, without being soon exhausted, can maintain above the hundredth part of its members in arms and idleness. But, although this relative proportion may be uniform, its influence over the rest of the society will vary according to the degree of its positive strength. The advantages of military science and discipline cannot be exerted, unless a proper number of soldiers are united into one body, and actuated by one soul. With a handful of men, such an union would be ineffectual; with an unwieldy host, it would be impracticable; and the powers of the machine would be alike destroyed by the extreme minuteness, or the excessive weight, of its springs. To illustrate this observation we need only reflect that there is no superiority of natural strength, artificial weapons, or acquired skill, which could enable one man to keep in constant subjection one hundred of his fellow-creatures: the tyrant of a single town, or a small district, would soon discover that an hundred armed followers were a weak defence against ten thousand peasants or citizens; but an hundred thousand well-disciplined soldiers will command, with despotic sway, ten millions of subjects; and a body of ten or fifteen thousand guards will strike terror into the most numerous populace that ever crowded the streets of an immense capital.

The Prætorian bands, whose licentious fury was the first symptom and cause of the decline of the Roman empire, scarcely amounted to the last mentioned number.[1] They derived their institution from Augustus. That crafty tyrant, sensible that laws might colour, but that arms alone could maintain, his usurped dominion, had gradually formed this powerful body of guards, in constant readiness to protect his person, to awe the senate, and either to prevent or to crush the first motions of rebellion. He distinguished these favoured troops by a double pay, and superior privileges; but, as their formidable aspect would at once have alarmed and irritated the Roman people, three cohorts only were stationed in the capital; whilst the remainder was dispersed in the adjacent towns of Italy.[2] But after fifty years of peace and servitude, Tiberius ventured on a decisive measure, which for ever riveted the fetters of his country. Under the fair pretences of relieving Italy from the heavy burden

[1]* They were originally nine or ten thousand men (for Tacitus and Dion are not agreed upon the subject), divided into as many cohorts. Vitellius increased them to sixteen thousand, and, as far as we can learn from inscriptions, they never afterwards sunk much below that number. See Lipsius de magnitudine Romanâ, i. 4. [The last statement must be modified. The Prætorian guard was a reorganisation of the bodyguard of the generals of the republic. Augustus fixed the Prætorium in Rome, and determined, as the number of the guard, nine cohorts, each cohort consisting of a thousand men. A tenth cohort was subsequently added, but the exact date of this addition is not clear. Vitellius, as Gibbon says (Tacitus, Hist. ii. 93), increased the number to sixteen; but Vespasian restored the original nine (Aurelius Victor, Cæs. 40, 24, cp. Zosimus ii. 17). There is some evidence in inscriptions suggesting that there were twelve cohorts between the reign of Gaius and that of Vitellius. For number of prefects, see Appendix 11.]

[2] Sueton. in August. c. 49.

* Since this note was written, the work of Borghesi on the history of the Prætorian Prefects has been completed (mainly by E. Cuq) and published as vol. x. of his collected works, in two parts, 1897. It contains a list of the prefects, both before and after Constantine, with the evidence set out in full.

of military quarters, and of introducing a stricter discipline among the guards, he assembled them at Rome, in a permanent camp,[3] which was fortified with skilful care,[4] and placed on a commanding situation.[5]

Such formidable servants are always necessary, but often fatal, to the throne of despotism. By thus introducing the Prætorian guards, as it were, into the palace and the senate, the emperors taught them to perceive their own strength, and the weakness of the civil government; to view the vices of their masters with familiar contempt, and to lay aside that reverential awe which distance only, and mystery, can preserve towards an imaginary power. In the luxurious idleness of an opulent city, their pride was nourished by the sense of their irresistible weight; nor was it possible to conceal from them that the person of the sovereign, the authority of the senate, the public treasure, and the seat of empire, were all in their hands. To divert the Prætorian bands from these dangerous reflections the firmest and best established princes were obliged to mix blandishments with commands, rewards with punishments, to flatter their pride, indulge their pleasures, connive at their irregularities, and to purchase their precarious faith by a liberal donative; which, since the elevation of Claudius, was exacted as a legal claim on the accession of every new emperor.[6]

[3] Tacit. Annal. iv. 2. Suet. in Tiber. c. 37. Dion Cassius, l. lvii. p. 867 [19].

[4] In the civil war between Vitellius and Vespasian, the Prætorian camp was attacked and defended with all the machines used in the siege of the best-fortified cities. Tacit. Hist. iii. 84.

[5] Close to the walls of the city, on the broad summit of the Quirinal and Viminal hills. See Nardini, Roma Antica, p. 174. Donatus de Româ Antiquâ, p. 46. [Not on the hills, but to the east of them.]

[6] Claudius, raised by the soldiers to the empire, was the first who gave a donative. He gave *quina dena*, 120*l.* (Sueton. in Claud. c. 10): when Marcus, with his colleague Lucius Verus, took quiet possession of the throne, he gave *vicena*, 160*l.*, to each of the guards. Hist. August. p. 25 [iv. 7]. (Dion, lxxiii. p. 1231 [8].) We may form some idea of the amount of these sums, by Hadrian's complaint, that the promotion of a Cæsar had cost him *ter millies*, two millions and a half sterling.

The advocates of the guards endeavoured to justify by arguments the power which they asserted by arms; and to maintain that, according to the purest principles of the constitution, *their* consent was essentially necessary in the appointment of an emperor. The election of consuls, of generals, and of magistrates, however it had been recently usurped by the senate, was the ancient and undoubted right of the Roman people.[7] But where was the Roman people to be found? Not surely amongst the mixed multitude of slaves and strangers that filled the streets of Rome; a servile populace, as devoid of spirit as destitute of property. The defenders of the state, selected from the flower of Italian youth,[8] and trained in the exercise of arms and virtue, were the genuine representatives of the people, and the best entitled to elect the military chief of the republic. These assertions, however defective in reason, became unanswerable, when the fierce Prætorians increased their weight, by throwing, like the barbarian conqueror of Rome, their swords into the scale.[9]

The Prætorians had violated the sanctity of the throne, by the atrocious murder of Pertinax; they dishonoured the majesty of it, by their subsequent conduct. The camp was without a leader, for even the prefect Lætus, who had excited the tempest, prudently declined the public indignation. Amidst the wild disorder, Sulpicianus, the emperor's father-in-law, and governor of the city, who had been sent to the camp on the first alarm of mutiny, was endeavouring to calm the fury of the multitude, when he was silenced by the clamorous return of the murderers, bearing on a lance the

[7] Cicero de Legibus, iii. 3. The first book of Livy, and the second of Dionysius of Halicarnassus, show the authority of the people, even in the election of the kings.

[8] They were originally recruited in Latium, Etruria, and the old colonies (Tacit. Annal. iv. 5). The emperor Otho compliments their vanity, with the flattering titles of Italiæ Alumni, Romana vere juventus. Tacit. Hist. i. 84.

[9] In the siege of Rome by the Gauls. See Livy, v. 48. Plutarch. in Camill. p. 143 [29].

head of Pertinax. Though history has accustomed us to observe every principle and every passion yielding to the imperious dictates of ambition, it is scarcely credible that, in these moments of horror, Sulpicianus should have aspired to ascend a throne polluted with the recent blood of so near a relation, and so excellent a prince. He had already begun to use the only effectual argument, and to treat for the Imperial dignity; but the more prudent of the Prætorians, apprehensive that, in this private contract, they should not obtain a just price for so valuable a commodity, ran out upon the ramparts; and, with a loud voice, proclaimed that the Roman world was to be disposed of to the best bidder by public auction.[10]

This infamous offer, the most insolent excess of military licence, diffused an universal grief, shame, and indignation throughout the city. It reached at length the ears of Didius Julianus, a wealthy senator, who, regardless of the public calamities, was indulging himself in the luxury of the table.[11] His wife and his daughter, his freedmen and his parasites, easily convinced him that he deserved the throne, and earnestly conjured him to embrace so fortunate an opportunity. The vain old man hastened to the Prætorian camp, where Sulpicianus was still in treaty with the guards; and began to bid against him from the foot of the rampart. The unworthy negotiation was transacted by faithful emissaries, who passed alternately from one candidate to the other, and acquainted each of them with the offers of his rival. Sulpicianus had already promised a donative of five thousand drachms (above one hundred and sixty pounds) to each soldier; when Julian, eager for the prize, rose at once to the sum of six thousand two hundred and fifty drachms, or upwards

[10] Dion, l. lxxiii. p. 1234 [11]. Herodian, l. ii. p. 63 [6]. Hist. August. p. 60 [ix. 2]. Though the three historians agree that it was in fact an auction, Herodian alone affirms that it was proclaimed as such by the soldiers.

[11] Spartianus softens the most odious parts of the character and elevation of Julian.

of two hundred pounds sterling. The gates of the camp were instantly thrown open to the purchaser; he was declared emperor, and received an oath of allegiance from the soldiers, who retained humanity enough to stipulate that he should pardon and forget the competition of Sulpicianus.

It was now incumbent on the Prætorians to fulfil the conditions of the sale. They placed their new sovereign, whom they served and despised, in the centre of their ranks, surrounded him on every side with their shields, and conducted him in close order of battle through the deserted streets of the city. The senate was commanded to assemble, and those who had been the distinguished friends of Pertinax, or the personal enemies of Julian, found it necessary to affect a more than common share of satisfaction at this happy revolution.[12] After Julian had filled the senate house with armed soldiers, he expatiated on the freedom of his election, his own eminent virtues, and his full assurance of the affections of the senate. The obsequious assembly congratulated their own and the public felicity; engaged their allegiance, and conferred on him all the several branches of the Imperial power.[13] From the senate Julian was conducted by the same military procession, to take possession of the palace. The first objects which struck his eyes were the abandoned trunk of Pertinax, and the frugal entertainment prepared for his supper. The one he viewed with indifference; the other with contempt. A magnificent feast was prepared by his order, and he amused himself till a very late hour, with dice, and the performances of Pylades, a celebrated dancer. Yet it was observed that, after the crowd of flatterers dispersed,

[12] Dion Cassius, at that time prætor, had been a personal enemy to Julian, l. lxxiii. p. 1235 [12].

[13] Hist. August. p. 61 [ix. 3, 3]. We learn from thence one curious circumstance, that the new emperor, whatever had been his birth, was immediately aggregated to the number of Patrician families. [His imperial name was M. Didius Severus Julianus. His wife, Malfa Scantilla, and his daughter, Didia Clara, received the title of Augusta (Hist. Aug. ix. 3). Pertinax had declined that honour for his consort.]

and left him to darkness, solitude, and terrible reflection, he passed a sleepless night; revolving most probably in his mind his own rash folly, the fate of his virtuous predecessor, and the doubtful and dangerous tenure of an empire, which had not been acquired by merit, but purchased by money.[14]

He had reason to tremble. On the throne of the world he found himself without a friend, and even without an adherent. The guards themselves were ashamed of the prince whom their avarice had persuaded them to accept; nor was there a citizen who did not consider his elevation with horror, as the last insult on the Roman name. The nobility, whose conspicuous station and ample possessions exacted the strictest caution, dissembled their sentiments, and met the affected civility of the emperor with smiles of complacency and professions of duty. But the people, secure in their numbers and obscurity, gave a free vent to their passions. The streets and public places of Rome resounded with clamours and imprecations. The enraged multitude affronted the person of Julian, rejected his liberality, and, conscious of the impotence of their own resentment, they called aloud on the legions of the frontiers to assert the violated majesty of the Roman empire.

The public discontent was soon diffused from the centre to the frontiers of the empire. The armies of Britain, of Syria, and of Illyricum, lamented the death of Pertinax, in whose company, or under whose command, they had so often fought and conquered. They received with surprise, with indignation, and perhaps with envy, the extraordinary intelligence that the Prætorians had disposed of the empire by public auction; and they sternly refused to ratify the ignominious bargain. Their immediate and unanimous revolt was fatal to Julian, but it was fatal at the same time

[14] Dion, l. lxxiii. p. 1235 [13]. Hist. August. p. 61 [ix. 3, 10]. I have endeavoured to blend into one consistent story, the seeming contradictions of the two writers.

to the public peace; as the generals of the respective armies, Clodius Albinus, Pescennius Niger, and Septimius Severus, were still more anxious to succeed than to revenge the murdered Pertinax. Their forces were exactly balanced. Each of them was at the head of three legions,[15] with a numerous train of auxiliaries; and, however different in their characters, they were all soldiers of experience and capacity.

Clodius Albinus,[16] governor of Britain, surpassed both his competitors in the nobility of his extraction, which he derived from some of the most illustrious names of the old republic.[17] But the branch, from whence he claimed his descent, was sunk into mean circumstances, and transplanted into a remote province. It is difficult to form a just idea of his true character. Under the philosophic cloak of austerity, he stands accused of concealing most of the vices which degrade human nature.[18] But his accusers are those venal writers who adored the fortune of Severus, and trampled on the ashes of an unsuccessful rival. Virtue, or the appearances of virtue, recommended Albinus to the confidence and good opinion of Marcus; and his preserving with the son the same interest which he had acquired with the father is a proof at least that he was possessed of a very flexible disposition. The favour of a tyrant does not always suppose a want of merit in the object of it; he may, without intending it, reward a man of worth and ability, or he may find such a man useful to his own service. It does not appear that Albinus served the son of Marcus, either as the minister of his cruelties, or even as the associate of his pleasures. He was employed in a distant honourable command, when he

[15] Dion, l. lxxiii. p. 1235 [14].

[16] [D. Clodius Septimus Albinus.]

[17] The Postumian and the Cejonian; the former of whom was raised to the consulship in the fifth year after its institution.

[18] Spartianus in his undigested collections, mixes up all the virtues and all the vices that enter into the human composition, and bestows them on the same object. Such, indeed, are many of the characters in the Augustan history.

received a confidential letter from the emperor, acquainting him of the treasonable designs of some discontented generals, and authorising him to declare himself the guardian and successor of the throne, by assuming the title and ensigns of Cæsar.[19] The governor of Britain wisely declined the dangerous honour, which would have marked him for the jealousy, or involved him in the approaching ruin, of Commodus. He courted power by nobler, or, at least, by more specious, arts. On a premature report of the death of the emperor, he assembled his troops; and, in an eloquent discourse, deplored the inevitable mischiefs of despotism, described the happiness and glory which their ancestors had enjoyed under the consular government, and declared his firm resolution to reinstate the senate and people in their legal authority. This popular harangue was answered by the loud acclamations of the British legions, and received at Rome with a secret murmur of applause. Safe in the possession of his little world, and in the command of an army less distinguished indeed for discipline than for numbers and valour,[20] Albinus braved the menaces of Commodus, maintained towards Pertinax a stately ambiguous reserve, and instantly declared against the usurpation of Julian. The convulsions of the capital added new weight to his sentiments, or rather to his professions, of patriotism. A regard to decency induced him to decline the lofty titles of Augustus and Emperor, and he imitated perhaps the example of Galba, who, on a similar occasion, had styled himself the Lieutenant of the senate and people.[21]

Personal merit alone had raised Pescennius Niger[22] from an obscure birth and station to the government of Syria; a

[19] Hist. August. p. 80, 84 [xii. 2, and 6, 4, 5].

[20] Pertinax, who governed Britain a few years before, had been left for dead in a mutiny of the soldiers. Hist. August. p. 54 [viii. 3]. Yet they loved and regretted him; admirantibus eam virtutem cui irascebantur.

[21] Sueton. in Galb. c. 10. [Legatum se senatus ac pop. R. professus est.]

[22] [C. Pescennius Niger Justus.]

lucrative and important command, which in times of civil confusion gave him a near prospect of the throne. Yet his parts seem to have been better suited to the second than to the first rank; he was an unequal rival, though he might have approved himself an excellent lieutenant, to Severus, who afterwards displayed the greatness of his mind by adopting several useful institutions from a vanquished enemy.[23] In his government, Niger acquired the esteem of the soldiers and the love of the provincials. His rigid discipline fortified the valour and confirmed the obedience of the former, whilst the voluptuous Syrians were less delighted with the mild firmness of his administration than with the affability of his manners and the apparent pleasure with which he attended their frequent and pompous festivals.[24] As soon as the intelligence of the atrocious murder of Pertinax had reached Antioch, the wishes of Asia invited Niger to assume the Imperial purple and revenge his death. The legions of the eastern frontier embraced his cause; the opulent but unarmed provinces, from the frontiers of Æthiopia[25] to the Hadriatic, cheerfully submitted to his power; and the kings beyond the Tigris and the Euphrates congratulated his election, and offered him their homage and services. The mind of Niger was not capable of receiving this sudden tide of fortune; he flattered himself that his accession would be undisturbed by competition, and unstained by civil blood; and whilst he enjoyed the vain pomp of triumph, he neglected to secure the means of victory. Instead of entering into an effectual negotiation with the powerful armies of the West, whose resolution might decide, or at least must balance,

[23] Hist. August. p. 76 [xi. 7].

[24] Herod. l. ii. p. 68 [7]. The Chronicle of John Malala, of Antioch, shows the zealous attachment of his countrymen to these festivals, which at once gratified their superstition, and their love of pleasure.

[25] A king of Thebes, in Egypt, is mentioned in the Augustan History, as an ally, and, indeed, as a personal friend of Niger. If Spartianus is not, as I strongly suspect, mistaken, he has brought to light a dynasty of tributary princes totally unknown to history.

the mighty contest; instead of advancing without delay towards Rome and Italy, where his presence was impatiently expected,[26] Niger trifled away in the luxury of Antioch those irretrievable moments which were diligently improved by the decisive activity of Severus.[27]

The country of Pannonia and Dalmatia, which occupied the space between the Danube and the Hadriatic, was one of the last and most difficult conquests of the Romans. In the defence of national freedom, two hundred thousand of these barbarians had once appeared in the field, alarmed the declining age of Augustus, and exercised the vigilant prudence of Tiberius at the head of the collected force of the empire.[28] The Pannonians yielded at length to the arms and institutions of Rome. Their recent subjection, however, the neighbourhood, and even the mixture of the unconquered tribes, and perhaps the climate, adapted, as it has been observed, to the production of great bodies and slow minds,[29] all contributed to preserve some remains of their original ferocity, and, under the tame resemblance of Roman provincials, the hardy features of the natives were still to be discerned. Their warlike youth afforded an inexhaustible supply of recruits to the legions stationed on the banks of the Danube, and which, from a perpetual warfare against the Germans and Sarmatians, were deservedly esteemed the best troops in the service.

The Pannonian army was at this time commanded by

[26] Dion, l. lxxiii. p. 1238 [15]. Herod, l. ii. p. 67 [7]. A verse in every-one's mouth at that time, seems to express the general opinion of the three rivals; Optimus est *Niger*, bonus *Afer*. pessimus *Albus*. Hist. August. p. 75 [xi. 8]. [The verse was originally in Greek, but the Latin of Spartianus was innocent of the false quantity which Gibbon ascribes to it. It ran *optimus est Fuscus*, &c.]

[27] Herodian, l. ii. p. 71 [8].

[28] See an account of that memorable war in Velleius Paterculus, ii. 119, &c., who served in the army of Tiberius.

[29] Such is the reflection of Herodian, l. ii. p. 74 [9]. Will the modern Austrians allow the influence?

Septimius Severus, a native of Africa, who, in the gradual ascent of private honours, had concealed his daring ambition, which was never diverted from its steady course by the allurements of pleasure, the apprehension of danger, or the feelings of humanity.[20] On the first news of the murder of Pertinax, he assembled his troops, painted in the most lively colours the crime, the insolence, and the weakness of the Prætorian guards, and animated the legions to arms and to revenge. He concluded (and the peroration was thought extremely eloquent) with promising every soldier about four hundred pounds; an honourable donative, double in value to the infamous bribe with which Julian had purchased the empire.[21] The acclamations of the army immediately saluted Severus with the names of Augustus, Pertinax, and Emperor; and he thus attained the lofty station to which he was invited by conscious merit and a long train of dreams and omens, the fruitful offspring either of his superstition or policy.[22]

The new candidate for empire saw and improved the peculiar advantage of his situation. His province extended to the Julian Alps, which gave an easy access into Italy; and he remembered the saying of Augustus, That a Panno-

[20] In the letter to Albinus, already mentioned, Commodus accuses Severus as one of the ambitious generals who censured his conduct, and wished to occupy his place. Hist. August. p. 80 [xii. 2].

[21] Pannonia was too poor to supply such a sum. It was probably promised in the camp, and paid at Rome, after the victory. In fixing the sum, I have adopted the conjecture of Casaubon. See Hist. August. p. 65 [x. 5]. Comment. p. 115.

[22] Herodian, l. ii. p. 78 [11]. Severus was declared emperor on the banks of the Danube, either at Carnuntum, according to Spartianus (Hist. August. p. 65 [x. 5]) or else at Sabaria, according to Victor [Cæs. xx. 1]. Mr. Hume, in supposing that the birth and dignity of Severus were too much inferior to the Imperial crown, and that he marched into Italy as general only, has not considered this transaction with his usual accuracy. (Essay on the original contract.) [The date in Hist. Aug. is *idibus Augustis*, but Baronius (followed by Pagi, Gibbon, Clinton, and De Ceuleneer) amended *idibus April.*, 13th April.]

nian army might in ten days appear in sight of Rome.[33] By a celerity proportioned to the greatness of the occasion, he might reasonably hope to revenge Pertinax, punish Julian, and receive the homage of the senate and people, as their lawful emperor, before his competitors, separated from Italy by an immense tract of sea and land, were apprised of his success, or even of his election. During the whole expedition, he scarcely allowed himself any moments for sleep or food; marching on foot, and in complete armour, at the head of his columns, he insinuated himself into the confidence and affection of his troops, pressed their diligence, revived their spirits, animated their hopes, and was well satisfied to share the hardships of the meanest soldier, whilst he kept in view the infinite superiority of his reward.

The wretched Julian had expected, and thought himself prepared, to dispute the empire with the governor of Syria; but in the invincible and rapid approach of the Pannonian legions, he saw his inevitable ruin.[34] The hasty arrival of every messenger increased his just apprehensions. He was successively informed that Severus had passed the Alps; that the Italian cities, unwilling or unable to oppose his progress, had received him with the warmest professions of joy and duty; that the important place of Ravenna had surrendered without resistance, and that the Hadriatic fleet was in the hands of the conqueror. The enemy was now within two hundred and fifty miles of Rome; and every moment diminished the narrow span of life and empire allotted to Julian.

He attempted, however, to prevent, or at least to protract,

[33] Velleius Paterculus, l. ii. c. 111. We must reckon the march from the nearest verge of Pannonia, and extend the sight of the city, as far as two hundred miles.

[34] [Schiller remarks that the events which attended the elevation of Vespasian repeat themselves in that of Severus. His march recalls the march of Antonius Primus with the Pannonian legions. Julianus neglected to occupy the Alpine passes.]

his ruin. He implored the venal faith of the Prætorians, filled the city with unavailing preparations for war, drew lines round the suburbs, and even strengthened the fortifications of the palace; as if those last intrenchments could be defended, without hope of relief, against a victorious invader. Fear and shame prevented the guards from deserting his standard; but they trembled at the name of the Pannonian legions, commanded by an experienced general, and accustomed to vanquish the barbarians on the frozen Danube.[28] They quitted, with a sigh, the pleasures of the baths and theatres, to put on arms, whose use they had almost forgotten, and beneath the weight of which they were oppressed. The unpractised elephants, whose uncouth appearance, it was hoped, would strike terror into the army of the North, threw their unskilful riders; and the awkward evolutions of the marines, drawn from the fleet of Misenum, were an object of ridicule to the populace; whilst the senate enjoyed, with secret pleasure, the distress and weakness of the usurper.[29]

Every motion of Julian betrayed his trembling perplexity. He insisted that Severus should be declared a public enemy by the senate. He entreated that the Pannonian general might be associated to the empire. He sent public ambassadors of consular rank to negotiate with his rival; he despatched private assassins to take away his life. He designed that the Vestal virgins, and all the colleges of priests, in their sacerdotal habits, and bearing before them the sacred pledges of the Roman religion, should advance, in solemn procession, to meet the Pannonian legions; and, at the same time, he

[28] This is not a puerile figure of rhetoric, but an allusion to a real fact recorded by Dion, l. lxxi. p. 1181 [7]. It probably happened more than once.

[29] Dion, l. lxxiii. p. 1238 [16]. Herodian, l. ii. p. 81 [11]. There is no surer proof of the military skill of the Romans, than their first surmounting the idle terror, and afterwards disdaining the dangerous use, of elephants in war.

vainly tried to interrogate, or to appease, the fates, by magic ceremonies, and unlawful sacrifices.[87]

Severus, who dreaded neither his arms nor his enchantments, guarded himself from the only danger of secret conspiracy by the faithful attendance of six hundred chosen men, who never quitted his person or their cuirasses, either by night or by day, during the whole march. Advancing with a steady and rapid course, he passed, without difficulty, the defiles of the Apennine, received into his party the troops and ambassadors sent to retard his progress, and made a short halt at Interamna, about seventy miles from Rome. His victory was already secure; but the despair of the Prætorians might have rendered it bloody; and Severus had the laudable ambition of ascending the throne without drawing the sword.[88] His emissaries, dispersed in the capital, assured the guards that, provided they would abandon their worthless prince, and the perpetrators of the murder of Pertinax, to the justice of the conqueror, he would no longer consider that melancholy event as the act of the whole body. The faithless Prætorians, whose resistance was supported only by sullen obstinacy, gladly complied with the easy conditions, seized the greatest part of the assassins, and signified to the senate that they no longer defended the cause of Julian. That assembly, convoked by the consul, unanimously acknowledged Severus as lawful emperor, decreed divine honours to Pertinax, and pronounced a sentence of deposition and death against his unfortunate successor. Julian was conducted into a private apartment of the baths of the palace, and beheaded as a common criminal, after having purchased, with an immense treasure, an anxious and precarious reign of only sixty-six days.[89] The almost incredible

[87] Hist. August. p. 62, 63 [ix. 5, 6].

[88] Victor [Cæs. 19] and Eutropius, viii. 17, mention a combat near the Milvian Bridge, the Ponte Molle, unknown to the better and more ancient writers.

[89] Dion, l. lxxiii. p. 1240 [17]. Herodian, l. ii. p. 83 [12]. Hist. August. p. 63 [ix. 9].

expedition of Severus, who, in so short a space of time, conducted a numerous army from the banks of the Danube to those of the Tiber, proves at once the plenty of provisions produced by agriculture and commerce, the goodness of the roads, the discipline of the legions, and the indolent subdued temper of the provinces.[40]

The first cares of Severus were bestowed on two measures, the one dictated by policy, the other by decency; the revenge, and the honours due to the memory of Pertinax. Before the new emperor entered Rome, he issued his commands to the Prætorian guards, directing them to wait his arrival on a large plain near the city, without arms, but in the habits of ceremony in which they were accustomed to attend their sovereign. He was obeyed by those haughty troops, whose contrition was the effect of their just terrors. A chosen part of the Illyrian army encompassed them with levelled spears. Incapable of flight or resistance, they expected their fate in silent consternation. Severus mounted the tribunal, sternly reproached them with perfidy and cowardice, dismissed them with ignominy from the trust which they had betrayed, despoiled them of their splendid ornaments, and banished them, on pain of death, to the distance of an hundred miles from the capital. During the transaction, another detachment had been sent to seize their arms, occupy their camp, and prevent the hasty consequences of their despair.[41]

The funeral and consecration of Pertinax was next solem-

[40] From these sixty-six days, we must first deduct sixteen, as Pertinax was murdered on the 28th of March, and Severus most probably elected on the 13th of April. (See Hist. August. p. 65, and Tillemont Hist. des Empereurs, tom. iii. p. 393, note 7.) We cannot allow less than ten days after his election, to put a numerous army in motion. Forty days remain for this rapid march, and, as we may compute about eight hundred miles from Rome to the neighbourhood of Vienna, the army of Severus marched twenty miles every day, without halt or intermission.

[41] Dion, l. lxxiv. p. 1241 [1]. Herodian, l. ii. p. 84 [13].

nised with every circumstance of sad magnificence.[42] The senate, with a melancholy pleasure, performed the last rites to that excellent prince, whom they had loved and still regretted. The concern of his successor was probably less sincere. He esteemed the virtues of Pertinax, but those virtues would for ever have confined his ambition to a private station. Severus pronounced his funeral oration with studied eloquence, inward satisfaction, and well-acted sorrow; and by this pious regard to his memory, convinced the credulous multitude that *he alone* was worthy to supply his place. Sensible, however, that arms, not ceremonies, must assert his claim to the empire, he left Rome at the end of thirty days, and, without suffering himself to be elated by this easy victory, prepared to encounter his more formidable rivals.

The uncommon abilities and fortune of Severus have induced an elegant historian to compare him with the first and greatest of the Cæsars.[43] The parallel is, at least, imperfect. Where shall we find, in the character of Severus, the commanding superiority of soul, the generous clemency, and the various genius, which could reconcile and unite the love of pleasure, the thirst of knowledge, and the fire of ambition?[44] In one instance only, they may be compared, with some degree of propriety, in the celerity of their motion, and their civil victories. In less than four years,[45] Severus subdued the riches of the East, and the valour of the West. He vanquished two competitors of reputation and ability,

[42] Dion, l. lxxiv. p. 1244 [4], who assisted at the ceremony as a senator gives a most pompous description of it.

[43] Herodian, l. iii. p. 112 [7, 7].

[44] Though it is not, most assuredly, the intention of Lucan to exalt the character of Cæsar, yet the idea he gives of that hero, in the tenth book of the Pharsalia, where he describes him, at the same time, making love to Cleopatra, sustaining a siege against the power of Egypt, and conversing with the sages of the country, is, in reality, the noblest panegyric.

[45] Reckoning from his election, April 13, 193, to the death of Albinus, February 19, 197. See Tillemont's Chronology.

and defeated numerous armies, provided with weapons and discipline equal to his own. In that age, the art of fortification and the principles of tactics, were well understood by all the Roman generals; and the constant superiority of Severus was that of an artist, who uses the same instruments with more skill and industry than his rivals. I shall not, however, enter into a minute narrative of these military operations; but as the two civil wars against Niger and against Albinus, were almost the same in their conduct, event, and consequences, I shall collect into one point of view the most striking circumstances, tending to develop the character of the conqueror, and the state of the empire.

Falsehood and insincerity, unsuitable as they seem to the dignity of public transactions, offend us with a less degrading idea of meanness than when they are found in the intercourse of private life. In the latter, they discover a want of courage; in the other, only a defect of power; and, as it is impossible for the most able statesmen to subdue millions of followers and enemies by their own personal strength, the world, under the name of policy, seems to have granted them a very liberal indulgence of craft and dissimulation. Yet the arts of Severus cannot be justified by the most ample privileges of state-reason. He promised only to betray, he flattered only to ruin; and however he might occasionally bind himself by oaths and treaties, his conscience, obsequious to his interest, always released him from the inconvenient obligation.[48]

If his two competitors, reconciled by their common danger, had advanced upon him without delay, perhaps Severus would have sunk under their united effort. Had they even attacked him at the same time, with separate views and separate armies, the contest might have been long and doubtful. But they fell, singly and successively, an easy prey to the arts as well as arms of their subtle enemy, lulled into

[48] Herodian, l. ii. p. 85 [13].

security by the moderation of his professions, and overwhelmed by the rapidity of his action. He first marched against Niger, whose reputation and power he the most dreaded: but he declined any hostile declarations, suppressed the name of his antagonist, and only signified to the senate and people his intention of regulating the eastern provinces. In private he spoke of Niger, his old friend and intended successor,[47] with the most affectionate regard, and highly applauded his generous design of revenging the murder of Pertinax. To punish the vile usurper of the throne was the duty of every Roman general. To persevere in arms, and to resist a lawful emperor, acknowledged by the senate, would alone render him criminal.[48] The sons of Niger had fallen into his hands among the children of the provincial governors, detained at Rome as pledges for the loyalty of their parents.[49] As long as the power of Niger inspired terror, or even respect, they were educated with the most tender care, with the children of Severus himself; but they were soon involved in their father's ruin, and removed, first by exile, and afterwards by death, from the eye of public compassion.[50]

Whilst Severus was engaged in his eastern war, he had reason to apprehend that the governor of Britain might pass the sea and the Alps, occupy the vacant seat of empire, and oppose his return with the authority of the senate and the forces of the West. The ambiguous conduct of Albinus,

[47] Whilst Severus was very dangerously ill, it was industriously given out that he intended to appoint Niger and Albinus his successors. As he could not be sincere with respect to both, he might not be so with regard to either. Yet Severus carried his hypocrisy so far as to profess that intention in the memoirs of his own life.

[48] Hist. August. p. 65 [x. 8, 7; and cp. 6].

[49] This practice, invented by Commodus, proved very useful to Severus. He found, at Rome, the children of many of the principal adherents of his rivals; and he employed them more than once to intimidate, or seduce, the parents.

[50] Herodian, l. iii. p. 96. Hist. August. p. 67, 68 [x. 8, 9].

in not assuming the Imperial title, left room for negotiation. Forgetting at once his professions of patriotism and the jealousy of sovereign power, he accepted the precarious rank of Cæsar, as a reward for his fatal neutrality. Till the first contest was decided, Severus treated the man whom he had doomed to destruction with every mark of esteem and regard. Even in the letter in which he announced his victory over Niger he styles Albinus the brother of his soul and empire, sends him the affectionate salutations of his wife Julia, and his young family, and entreats him to preserve the armies and the republic faithful to their common interest. The messengers charged with this letter were instructed to accost the Cæsar with respect, to desire a private audience, and to plunge their daggers into his heart.[81] The conspiracy was discovered, and the too credulous Albinus at length passed over to the continent, and prepared for an unequal contest with his rival, who rushed upon him at the head of a veteran and victorious army.

The military labours of Severus seem inadequate to the importance of his conquests. Two engagements, the one near the Hellespont, the other in the narrow defiles of Cilicia, decided the fate of his Syrian competitor; and the troops of Europe asserted their usual ascendant over the effeminate natives of Asia.[82] The battle of Lyons, where one hundred and fifty thousand Romans[83] were engaged, was equally fatal to Albinus. The valour of the British army maintained, indeed, a sharp and doubtful contest with the hardy discipline of the Illyrian legions. The fame and person of Severus appeared, during a few moments, irrecoverably lost, till that warlike prince rallied his fainting troops, and led them on

[81] Hist. August. p. 81 [xii. 7]. Spartianus has inserted this curious letter at full length.

[82] Consult the third book of Herodian, and the seventy-fourth book of Dion Cassius.

[83] Dion, l. lxxv. p. 1260 [6].

to a decisive victory.[84] The war was finished by that memorable day.

The civil wars of modern Europe have been distinguished, not only by the fierce animosity, but likewise by the obstinate perseverance, of the contending factions. They have generally been justified by some principle, or, at least, coloured by some pretext, of religion, freedom, or loyalty. The leaders were nobles of independent property and hereditary influence. The troops fought like men interested in the decision of the quarrel; and as military spirit and party zeal were strongly diffused throughout the whole community, a vanquished chief was immediately supplied with new adherents, eager to shed their blood in the same cause. But the Romans, after the fall of the republic, combated only for the choice of masters. Under the standard of a popular candidate for empire, a few enlisted from affection, some from fear, many from interest, none from principle. The legions, uninflamed by party zeal, were allured into civil war by liberal donatives, and still more liberal promises. A defeat, by disabling the chief from the performance of his engagements, dissolved the mercenary allegiance of his followers, and left them to consult their own safety by a timely desertion of an unsuccessful cause. It was of little moment to the provinces under whose name they were oppressed or governed; they were driven by the impulsion of the present power, and as soon as that power yielded to a superior force, they hastened to implore the clemency of the conqueror, who, as he had an immense debt to discharge, was obliged to sacrifice the most guilty countries to the avarice of his soldiers. In the vast extent of the Roman empire there were few fortified cities capable of protecting a routed army; nor was there any person, or family, or

[84] Dion, l. lxxv. p. 1261 [6]. Herodian, l. iii. p. 110 [7]. Hist. August. p. 68 [x. 11]. The battle was fought in the plain of Trevoux, three or four leagues from Lyons. See Tillemont, tom. iii. p. 406, note 18.

order of men, whose natural interest, unsupported by the powers of government, was capable of restoring the cause of a sinking party.[55]

Yet, in the contest between Niger and Severus, a single city deserves an honourable exception. As Byzantium was one of the greatest passages from Europe into Asia, it had been provided with a strong garrison, and a fleet of five hundred vessels was anchored in the harbour.[56] The impetuosity of Severus disappointed this prudent scheme of defence; he left to his generals the siege of Byzantium, forced the less guarded passage of the Hellespont, and, impatient of a meaner enemy, pressed forward to encounter his rival. Byzantium, attacked by a numerous and increasing army, and afterwards by the whole naval power of the empire, sustained a siege of three years, and remained faithful to the name and memory of Niger. The citizens and soldiers (we know not from what cause) were animated with equal fury; several of the principal officers of Niger, who despaired of, or who disdained a pardon, had thrown themselves into this last refuge; the fortifications were esteemed impregnable, and, in the defence of the place, a celebrated engineer displayed all the mechanic powers known to the ancients.[57] Byzantium, at length, surrendered to famine. The magistrates and soldiers were put to the sword, the walls demolished, the privileges suppressed, and the destined capital of the East subsisted only as an open village, subject to the insulting jurisdiction of Perinthus. The historian Dion, who had admired the flourishing, and lamented the desolate, state of Byzantium, accused the revenge of

[55] Montesquieu, Considérations sur la Grandeur et la Décadence des Romains, c. xii.

[56] Most of these, as may be supposed, were small open vessels; some, however, were galleys of two, and a few of three, ranks of oars.

[57] The engineer's name was Priscus. His skill saved his life, and he was taken into the service of the conqueror. For the particular facts of the siege consult Dion Cassius (l. lxx[i]v. p. 1251 [11–13]) and Herodian (l. iii. p. 95 [6]): for the theory of it, the fanciful Chevalier de Folard may be looked into. See Polybe, tom. i. p. 76.

Severus for depriving the Roman people of the strongest bulwark against the barbarians of Pontus and Asia.[58] The truth of this observation was but too well justified in the succeeding age, when the Gothic fleets covered the Euxine, and passed through the undefended Bosphorus into the centre of the Mediterranean.

Both Niger and Albinus were discovered and put to death in their flight from the field of battle. Their fate excited neither surprise nor compassion. They had staked their lives against the chance of empire, and suffered what they would have inflicted; nor did Severus claim the arrogant superiority of suffering his rivals to live in a private station. But his unforgiving temper, stimulated by avarice, indulged a spirit of revenge, where there was no room for apprehension. The most considerable of the provincials, who, without any dislike to the fortunate candidate, had obeyed the governor under whose authority they were accidentally placed, were punished by death, exile, and especially by the confiscation of their estates. Many cities of the East were stript of their ancient honours, and obliged to pay, into the treasury of Severus, four times the amount of the sums contributed by them for the service of Niger.[59]

Till the final decision of the war, the cruelty of Severus was, in some measure, restrained by the uncertainty of the event and his pretended reverence for the senate. The head of Albinus, accompanied with a menacing letter, announced to the Romans that he was resolved to spare none of the adherents of his unfortunate competitors. He was irritated by the just suspicion that he had never possessed the affec-

[58] Notwithstanding the authority of Spartianus and some modern Greeks, we may be assured, from Dion and Herodian, that Byzantium, many years after the death of Severus, lay in ruins. [But the statement of Spartianus (xiii. 1), that Severus repented of his harshness, owing (ostensibly?) to the intercession of Caracalla, is confirmed by the legend ἀντωνείνια Σεβαστά, on Byzantine coins; Eckhel, ii. 32 (cp. Schiller, i. 713). Not Byzantium, but its fortifications, were demolished.]

[59] Dion, l. lxxiv. p. 1250 [8].

tions of the senate, and he concealed his old malevolence under the recent discovery of some treasonable correspondencies. Thirty-five senators, however, accused of having favoured the party of Albinus, he freely pardoned; and, by his subsequent behaviour, endeavoured to convince them that he had forgotten, as well as forgiven, their supposed offences. But, at the same time, he condemned forty-one [60] other senators, whose names history has recorded; their wives, children, and clients, attended them in death, and the noblest provincials of Spain and Gaul were involved in the same ruin. Such rigid justice, for so he termed it, was, in the opinion of Severus, the only conduct capable of ensuring peace to the people, or stability to the prince; and he condescended slightly to lament that, to be mild, it was necessary that he should first be cruel.[61]

The true interest of an absolute monarch generally coincides with that of his people. Their numbers, their wealth, their order, and their security, are the best and only foundations of his real greatness; and, were he totally devoid of virtue, prudence might supply its place, and would dictate the same rule of conduct. Severus considered the Roman empire as his property, and had no sooner secured the possession, than he bestowed his care on the cultivation and improvement of so valuable an acquisition. Salutary laws, executed with inflexible firmness, soon corrected most of the abuses with which, since the death of Marcus, every part of the government had been infected. In the administration of justice, the judgments of the emperor were characterised by attention, discernment, and impartiality; and, whenever he deviated from the strict line of equity, it was generally in

[60] Dion (l. lxxv. p. 1262 [8]), only twenty-nine senators are mentioned by him, but forty-one are named in the Augustan History, p. 69 [x. 13], among whom were six of the name of Pescennius. Herodian (l. iii. p. 115 [8]) speaks in general of the cruelties of Severus. [It is safer here to follow Dion.]

[61] Aurelius Victor [Cæs. 20, 13].

favour of the poor and oppressed; not so much indeed from any sense of humanity, as from the natural propensity of a despot to humble the pride of greatness, and to sink all his subjects to the same common level of absolute dependence. His expensive taste for building, magnificent shows, and, above all, a constant and liberal distribution of corn and provisions, were the surest means of captivating the affection of the Roman people.[62] The misfortunes of civil discord were obliterated. The calm of peace and prosperity was once more experienced in the provinces, and many cities, restored by the munificence of Severus, assumed the title of his colonies, and attested by public monuments their gratitude and felicity.[63] The fame of the Roman arms was revived by that warlike and successful emperor,[64] and he boasted, with a just pride, that, having received the empire oppressed with foreign and domestic wars, he left it established in profound, universal, and honourable peace.[65]

Although the wounds of civil war appeared completely healed, its mortal poison still lurked in the vitals of the constitution. Severus possessed a considerable share of vigour and ability; but the daring soul of the first Cæsar, or the deep policy of Augustus, were scarcely equal to the task of curbing

[62] Dion, l. lxxvi. p. 1272 [1]. Hist. August. p. 67 [x. 8]. Severus celebrated the secular games with extraordinary magnificence, and he left in the public granaries a provision of corn for seven years, at the rate of 75,000 modii, or about 2500 quarters per day. I am persuaded that the granaries of Severus were supplied for a long term, but I am not less persuaded that policy on one hand, and admiration on the other, magnified the hoard far beyond its true contents.

[63] See Spanheim's treatise of ancient medals, the inscriptions, and our learned travellers Spon and Wheeler, Shaw, Pocock, &c., who, in Africa, Greece, and Asia, have found more monuments of Severus, than of any other Roman emperor whatsoever.

[64] He carried his victorious arms to Seleucia and Ctesiphon, the capitals of the Parthian monarchy. I shall have occasion to mention this war in its proper place.

[65] *Etiam in Britannis*, was his own just and emphatic expression. Hist. August. 73 [x. 23].

the insolence of the victorious legions. By gratitude, by misguided policy, by seeming necessity, Severus was induced to relax the nerves of discipline.[66] The vanity of his soldiers was flattered with the honour of wearing gold rings; their ease was indulged in the permission of living with their wives in the idleness of quarters. He increased their pay beyond the example of former times, and taught them to expect, and soon to claim, extraordinary donatives on every public occasion of danger or festivity. Elated by success, enervated by luxury, and raised above the level of subjects by their dangerous privileges,[67] they soon became incapable of military fatigue, oppressive to the country, and impatient of a just subordination. Their officers asserted the superiority of rank by a more profuse and elegant luxury. There is still extant a letter of Severus, lamenting the licentious state of the army, and exhorting one of his generals to begin the necessary reformation from the tribunes themselves; since, as he justly observes, the officer who has forfeited the esteem, will never command the obedience, of his soldiers.[68] Had the emperor pursued the train of reflection, he would have discovered that the primary cause of this general corruption might be ascribed, not indeed to the example, but to the pernicious indulgence, however, of the commander-in-chief.

The Prætorians, who murdered their emperor and sold the empire, had received the just punishment of their treason; but the necessary, though dangerous, institution of guards

[66] Herodian, l. iii. p. 115 [8]. Hist. August. p. 68 [x. 12]. [The popularity of Severus and his son Caracalla with the soldiers is illustrated by the vast number of inscriptions in their honour. It is true that discipline was in some respects relaxed; but in other respects the efficacy of the army was improved.]

[67] Upon the insolence and privileges of the soldiers [prætorian guards], the 16th satire, falsely ascribed to Juvenal, may be consulted; the style and circumstances of it would induce me to believe that it was composed under the reign of Severus or that of his son. [The opinion of modern scholars inclines to regard it as genuine.]

[68] Hist. August. p. 75 [xi. 3].

was soon restored on a new model by Severus, and increased to four times the ancient number.[69] Formerly these troops had been recruited in Italy; and, as the adjacent provinces gradually imbibed the softer manners of Rome, the levies were extended to Macedonia, Noricum, and Spain. In the room of these elegant troops, better adapted to the pomp of courts than to the uses of war, it was established by Severus, that, from all the legions of the frontiers, the soldiers most distinguished for strength, valour, and fidelity, should be occasionally draughted, and promoted, as an honour and reward, into the more eligible service of the guards.[70] By this new institution, the Italian youth were diverted from the exercise of arms, and the capital was terrified by the strange aspect and manners of a multitude of barbarians. But Severus flattered himself that the legions would consider these chosen Prætorians as the representatives of the whole military order; and that the present aid of fifty thousand men, superior in arms and appointments to any force that could be brought into the field against them, would for ever crush the hopes of rebellion, and secure the empire to himself and his posterity.

The command of these favoured and formidable troops soon became the first office of the empire. As the government degenerated into military despotism, the Prætorian prefect, who in his origin had been a simple captain of the guards, was placed, not only at the head of the army, but of the finances, and even of the law. In every department of administration, he represented the person, and exercised the authority, of the emperor. The first prefect who enjoyed and abused this immense power was Plautianus, the favourite minister of Severus. His reign lasted above ten years, till the marriage of his daughter with the eldest son of the emperor, which

[69] Herodian, l. iii. p. 131 [13].

[70] Dion, l. lxxiv. p. 1243 [2]. [It was the policy of Severus (the *African*) to level the distinctions which had subsisted between Italy and the provinces. Some acts of Hadrian had already pointed in the same direction. See Appendix 11. Caracalla, as we shall see, carried the policy to its logical end.]

seemed to assure his fortune, proved the occasion of his ruin.[71] The animosities of the palace, by irritating the ambition and alarming the fears of Plautianus, threatened to produce a revolution, and obliged the emperor, who still loved him, to consent with reluctance to his death.[72] After the fall of Plautianus, an eminent lawyer, the celebrated Papinian, was appointed to execute the motley office of Prætorian prefect.[73]

Till the reign of Severus, the virtue, and even the good sense of the emperors had been distinguished by their zeal or affected reverence for the senate, and by a tender regard to the nice frame of civil policy instituted by Augustus. But the youth of Severus had been trained in the implicit obedience of camps, and his riper years spent in the despotism of military command. His haughty and inflexible spirit could not discover, or would not acknowledge, the advantage of preserving an intermediate power, however imaginary, between the emperor and the army. He disdained to profess himself the servant of an assembly that detested his person and trembled at his frown; he issued his commands, where his request would have proved as effectual; assumed the conduct and style of a sovereign and a conqueror, and exercised, without disguise, the whole legislative as well as the executive power.

The victory over the senate was easy and inglorious. Every eye and every passion were directed to the supreme magistrate, who possessed the arms and treasure of the state; whilst the senate, neither elected by the people, nor guarded

[71] One of his most daring and wanton acts of power was the castration of a hundred free Romans, some of them married men, and even fathers of families; merely that his daughter, on her marriage with the young emperor, might be attended by a train of eunuchs worthy of an Eastern queen. Dion, l. lxxvi. p. 1271 [1]. [The daughter's name was Fulvia Plautilla. Caracalla hated her.]

[72] Dion, l. lxxvi. p. 1274 [4]. Herodian, l. iii. p. 122, 129 [12]. The grammarian of Alexandria seems, as it is not unusual, much better acquainted with this mysterious transaction; and more assured of the guilt of Plautianus than the Roman senator ventures to be. [Date 205 A.D.]

[73] [But not alone. He shared the office with Mæcius Lætus.]

by the military force, nor animated by public spirit, rested its declining authority on the frail and crumbling basis of ancient opinion. The fine theory of a republic insensibly vanished, and made way for the more natural and substantial feelings of monarchy. As the freedom and honours of Rome were successfully communicated to the provinces, in which the old government had been either unknown, or was remembered with abhorrence, the tradition of republican maxims was gradually obliterated. The Greek historians of the age of the Antonines [74] observe, with a malicious pleasure, that, although the sovereign of Rome, in compliance with an obsolete prejudice, abstained from the name of king, he possessed the full measure of regal power. In the reign of Severus, the senate was filled with polished and eloquent slaves from the eastern provinces, who justified personal flattery by speculative principles of servitude. These new advocates of prerogative were heard with pleasure by the court, and with patience by the people, when they inculcated the duty of passive obedience, and descanted on the inevitable mischiefs of freedom. The lawyers and the historians concurred in teaching that the Imperial authority was held, not by the delegated commission, but by the irrevocable resignation, of the senate; that the emperor was freed from the restraint of civil laws, could command by his arbitrary will the lives and fortunes of his subjects, and might dispose of the empire as of his private patrimony.[75] The most eminent of the civil lawyers, and particularly Papinian, Paulus, and Ulpian, flourished under the house of Severus; and the Roman jurisprudence, having closely united itself with the system of monarchy, was supposed to have attained its full maturity and perfection.

[74] Appian in Procem. [6].

[75] Dion Cassius seems to have written with no other view, than to form these opinions into an historical system. The Pandects will show how assiduously the lawyers, on their side, laboured in the cause of prerogative.

The contemporaries of Severus, in the enjoyment of the peace and glory of his reign, forgave the cruelties by which it had been introduced. Posterity, who experienced the fatal effect of his maxims and example, justly considered him as the principal author of the decline of the Roman empire.[78]

[78] [Cp. Appendix 11.]

CHAPTER VI

The death of Severus — Tyranny of Caracalla — Usurpation of Macrinus — Follies of Elagabalus — Virtues of Alexander Severus — Licentiousness of the army — General state of the Roman Finances

THE ascent to greatness, however steep and dangerous, may entertain an active spirit with the consciousness and exercise of its own powers: but the possession of a throne could never yet afford a lasting satisfaction to an ambitious mind. This melancholy truth was felt and acknowledged by Severus. Fortune and merit had, from an humble station, elevated him to the first place among mankind. He had been "all things," as he said himself, "and all was of little value."[1] Distracted with the care, not of acquiring, but of preserving, an empire, oppressed with age and infirmities, careless of fame,[2] and satiated with power, all his prospects of life were closed. The desire of perpetuating the greatness of his family was the only remaining wish of his ambition and paternal tenderness.

Like most of the Africans, Severus was passionately addicted to the vain studies of magic and divination, deeply versed in the interpretation of dreams and omens, and perfectly acquainted with the science of judicial astrology; which, in almost every age except the present, has maintained its dominion over the mind of man. He had lost his first wife whilst he was governor of the Lyonnese Gaul.[3] In the choice of a second, he sought only to connect himself with

[1] Hist. August. p. 71 [x. 18]. "Omnia fui, et nihil expedit."

[2] Dion Cassius, l. lxxvi. p. 1284 [16].

[3] About the year 186. M. de Tillemont is miserably embarrassed with a passage of Dion, in which the Empress Faustina, who died in the year 175,

some favourite of fortune; and, as soon as he had discovered that a young lady of Emesa in Syria had *a royal nativity*, he solicited and obtained her hand.[4] Julia Domna (for that was her name) deserved all that the stars could promise her. She possessed, even in an advanced age, the attractions of beauty,[5] and united to a lively imagination a firmness of mind, and strength of judgment, seldom bestowed on her sex. Her amiable qualities never made any deep impression on the dark and jealous temper of her husband; but, in her son's reign, she administered the principal affairs of the empire with a prudence that supported his authority; and with a moderation that sometimes corrected his wild extravagancies.[6] Julia applied herself to letters and philosophy with some success, and with the most splendid reputation. She was the patroness of every art, and the friend of every man of genius.[7] The grateful flattery of the learned has celebrated her virtues; but, if we may credit the scandal of ancient history, chastity was very far from being the most conspicuous virtue of the Empress Julia.[8]

Two sons, Caracalla[9] and Geta, were the fruit of this mar-

is introduced as having contributed to the marriage of Severus and Julia (l. lxxiv. p. 1243 [3]). The learned compiler forgot that Dion is relating, not a real fact, but a dream of Severus; and dreams are circumscribed to no limits of time or space. Did M. de Tillemont imagine that marriages were *consummated* in the Temple of Venus at Rome? Hist. des Empereurs, tom. iii. p. 389. Note 6.

[4] Hist. August. p. 65 [x. 3].

[5] Ibid. p. 85 [xiii. 10].

[6] Dion Cassius, l. lxxvii. p. 1304, 1312 [18 and lxxviii. 4].

[7] See a Dissertation of Menage, at the end of his edition of Diogenes Laertius, de Fœminis Philosophis.

[8] Dion, l. lxxvi. p. 1285 [16]. Aurelius Victor [Cæsar, xx. 23].

[9] Bassianus was his first name, as it had been that of his maternal grandfather. During his reign he assumed the appellation of Antoninus, which is employed by lawyers and ancient historians. [But see next note.] After his death, the public indignation loaded him with the nick-names of Tarantus and Caracalla. The first was borrowed from a celebrated Gladiator, the second from a long Gallic gown which he distributed to the people of Rome. [Hist. Aug. x. 11.]

riage, and the destined heirs of the empire. The fond hopes of the father, and of the Roman world, were soon disappointed by these vain youths, who displayed the indolent security of hereditary princes, and a presumption that fortune would supply the place of merit and application. Without any emulation of virtue or talents, they discovered, almost from their infancy, a fixed and implacable antipathy for each other.

Their aversion, confirmed by years, and fomented by the arts of their interested favourites, broke out in childish, and gradually in more serious, competitions; and at length divided the theatre, the circus, and the court, into two factions, actuated by the hopes and fears of their respective leaders. The prudent emperor endeavoured, by every expedient of advice and authority, to allay this growing animosity. The unhappy discord of his sons clouded all his prospects, and threatened to overturn a throne raised with so much labour, cemented with so much blood, and guarded with every defence of arms and treasure. With an impartial hand he maintained between them an exact balance of favour, conferred on both the rank of Augustus, with the revered name of Antoninus; and for the first time the Roman world beheld three emperors.[10] Yet even this equal conduct served only to inflame the contest,

[10] The elevation of Caracalla is fixed by the accurate M. de Tillemont to the year 198; the association of Geta, to the year 208. [Caracalla (the proper form is Caracallus) was made Cæsar in 196 at Viminacium, imperator under the name M. Aurelius Antoninus in 197, and finally Augustus with "tribunician power" in 198 (in the tenth year of his age). It is to be observed that on his first elevation Severus associated his name with the memory of Pertinax, and he appears on inscriptions as L. Septimius Severus Pertinax Augustus. But afterwards he resolved to affiliate his family to the more august house of the Antonines. In Imperial style he was the son of Marcus and brother of Commodus; both he and his sons were Antonines. He even thought of perpetuating *Antoninus* (like *Augustus*) as a synonym of the Imperial title. See Spartianus, Geta, ii. 2, *in animo habuit Severus ut omnes deinceps principes quemadmodum Augusti, ita etiam Antonini dicerentur idque amore Marci*, &c. As for the association of Geta as Augustus, it must be placed in Sept. or Oct. 209 A.D.; cp. Corp. Ins. Att. iii. p. 9.]

whilst the fierce Caracalla asserted the right of primogeniture, and the milder Geta courted the affections of the people and the soldiers. In the anguish of a disappointed father, Severus foretold that the weaker of his sons would fall a sacrifice to the stronger; who, in his turn, would be ruined by his own vices.[11]

In these circumstances the intelligence of a war in Britain, and of an invasion of the province by the barbarians of the North, was received with pleasure by Severus. Though the vigilance of his lieutenants might have been sufficient to repel the distant enemy, he resolved to embrace the honourable pretext of withdrawing his sons from the luxury of Rome, which enervated their minds and irritated their passions, and of inuring their youth to the toils of war and government. Notwithstanding his advanced age (for he was above threescore), and his gout, which obliged him to be carried in a litter, he transported himself in person into that remote island, attended by his two sons, his whole court, and a formidable army. He immediately passed the walls of Hadrian and Antoninus, and entered the enemy's country, with the design of completing the long-attempted conquest of Britain. He penetrated to the northern extremity of the island without meeting an enemy. But the concealed ambuscades of the Caledonians, who hung unseen on the rear and flanks of his army, the coldness of the climate, and the severity of a winter march across the hills and morasses of Scotland, are reported to have cost the Romans above fifty thousand men.[12] The Caledonians at length yielded to the powerful and obstinate attack, sued for peace, and surrendered a part of their arms, and a large tract of territory.[13] But their apparent submission lasted no longer than the present terror. As soon

[11] Herodian, l. iii. p. 130 [13]. The lives of Caracalla and Geta, in the Augustan History.

[12] [An exaggeration of Dion Cassius, lxxvi. 13. That some battles of importance were fought is proved by an inscription discovered some years ago (*Ephem. Epig.* iv. p. 327).]

[13] [The wall of Antoninus Pius had been abandoned; but Severus seems

as the Roman legions had retired, they resumed their hostile independence. Their restless spirit provoked Severus to send a new army into Caledonia, with the most bloody orders, not to subdue, but to extirpate the natives. They were saved by the death of their haughty enemy.[14]

This Caledonian war, neither marked by decisive events, nor attended with any important consequences, would ill deserve our attention; but it is supposed, not without a considerable degree of probability, that the invasion of Severus is connected with the most shining period of the British history of fable. Fingal, whose fame, with that of his heroes and bards, has been revived in our language by a recent publication, is said to have commanded the Caledonians in that memorable juncture, to have eluded the power of Severus, and to have obtained a signal victory on the banks of the Carun, in which the son of *the King of the World*, Caracul, fled from his arms along the fields of his pride.[15] Something of a doubtful mist still hangs over these Highland traditions; nor can it be entirely dispelled by the most ingenious researches of modern criticism:[16] but if we could, with safety, indulge the pleasing supposition that Fingal lived, and that Ossian sung, the striking contrast of the situation and manners of the contending nations might amuse a philosophic

to have renewed the wall of Hadrian from Tunnocelum to Segedunum. Hist. Aug. x. 18, 2. Muro per transversam insulam ducto utrinque ad finem oceani munivit. Whence he got the name *Britannicus Maximus*.]

[14] Dion, l. lxxvi. p. 1280, &c. [12]. Herodian, l. iii. p. 132, &c. [14].

[15] Ossian's Poems, vol. i. p. 175.

[16] That the Caracul of Ossian is the Caracalla of the Roman history, is, perhaps, the only point of British antiquity in which Mr. Macpherson and Mr. Whitaker are of the same opinion; and yet the opinion is not without difficulty. In the Caledonian war, the son of Severus was known only by the appellation of Antoninus; and it may seem strange that the Highland bard should describe him by a nickname, invented four years afterwards, scarcely used by the Romans till after the death of that emperor, and seldom employed by the most ancient historians. See Dion, l. lxxviii. p. 1317 [9]. Hist. August. p. 89 [xiii. 9]. Aurel. Victor [epit. 21]. Euseb. in Chron. ad ann. 214.

mind. The parallel would be little to the advantage of the more civilised people, if we compared the unrelenting revenge of Severus with the generous clemency of Fingal; the timid and brutal cruelty of Caracalla, with the bravery, the tenderness, the elegant genius of Ossian; the mercenary chiefs who, from motives of fear or interest, served under the Imperial standard, with the freeborn warriors who started to arms at the voice of the King of Morven; if, in a word, we contemplated the untutored Caledonians, glowing with the warm virtues of nature, and the degenerate Romans, polluted with the mean vices of wealth and slavery.

The declining health and last illness of Severus inflamed the wild ambition and black passions of Caracalla's soul. Impatient of any delay or division of empire, he attempted, more than once, to shorten the small remainder of his father's days, and endeavoured, but without success, to excite a mutiny among the troops.[17] The old emperor had often censured the misguided lenity of Marcus, who, by a single act of justice, might have saved the Romans from the tyranny of his worthless son. Placed in the same situation, he experienced how easily the rigour of a judge dissolves away in the tenderness of a parent. He deliberated, he threatened, but he could not punish; and this last and only instance of mercy was more fatal to the empire than a long series of cruelty.[18] The disorder of his mind irritated the pains of his body; he wished impatiently for death, and hastened the instant of it by his impatience. He expired at York in the sixty-fifth year of his life, and in the eighteenth of a glorious and successful reign. In his last moments he recommended concord to his sons, and his sons to the army. The salutary advice never reached the heart, or even the understanding, of the impetuous youths; but the more obedient troops, mindful of their oath of allegiance, and of the authority of their deceased master, resisted

[17] Dion, l. lxxvi. p. 1282 [14]. Hist. August. p. 72 [x. 20]. Aurel. Victor.
[18] Dion, l. lxxvi. p. 1283 [14]. Hist. August. p. 89 [xiii. 11, 3].

the solicitations of Caracalla, and proclaimed both brothers emperors of Rome. The new princes soon left the Caledonians in peace, returned to the capital, celebrated their father's funeral with divine honours, and were cheerfully acknowledged as lawful sovereigns by the senate, the people, and the provinces. Some pre-eminence of rank seems to have been allowed to the elder brother; but they both administered the empire with equal and independent power.[19]

Such a divided form of government would have proved a source of discord between the most affectionate brothers. It was impossible that it could long subsist between two implacable enemies, who neither desired nor could trust a reconciliation. It was visible that one only could reign, and that the other must fall; and each of them, judging of his rival's designs by his own, guarded his life with the most jealous vigilance from the repeated attacks of poison or the sword. Their rapid journey through Gaul and Italy, during which they never ate at the same table, or slept in the same house, displayed to the provinces the odious spectacle of fraternal discord. On their arrival at Rome, they immediately divided the vast extent of the Imperial palace.[20] No communication was allowed between their apartments; the

[19] Dion, l. lxxvi. p. 1284 [15]. Herodian, l. iii. p. 135 [15]. [The title *Pont. Max.* seems to have been reserved for the elder brother; Geta is only *Pont.* on coins and inscriptions. Eckhel, vii. 230.]

[20] Mr. Hume is justly surprised at a passage of Herodian (l. iv. p. 139 [1]), who, on this occasion, represents the Imperial palace as equal in extent to [greater than] the rest of Rome. The whole region of the Palatine Mount on which it was built occupied, at most, a circumference of eleven or twelve thousand feet. (See the Notitia and Victor, in Nardini's Roma Antica.) But we should recollect that the opulent senators had almost surrounded the city with their extensive gardens and suburb palaces, the greatest part of which had been gradually confiscated by the emperors. If Geta resided in the gardens that bore his name on the Janiculum and if Caracalla inhabited the gardens of Mæcenas on the Esquiline, the rival brothers were separated from each other by the distance of several miles; and yet the intermediate space was filled by the Imperial gardens of Sallust, of Lucullus, of Agrippa, of Domitian, of Caius, &c., all skirting round the city, and all connected with each other, and with the palace, by bridges thrown over the Tiber and

doors and passages were diligently fortified, and guards posted and relieved with the same strictness as in a besieged place. The emperors met only in public, in the presence of their afflicted mother; and each surrounded by a numerous train of armed followers. Even on these occasions of ceremony, the dissimulation of courts could ill disguise the rancour of their hearts.[21]

This latent civil war already distracted the whole government, when a scheme was suggested that seemed of mutual benefit to the hostile brothers. It was proposed, that, since it was impossible to reconcile their minds, they should separate their interest, and divide the empire between them. The conditions of the treaty were already drawn with some accuracy. It was agreed, that Caracalla, as the elder brother, should remain in possession of Europe and the western Africa; and that he should relinquish the sovereignty of Asia and Egypt to Geta, who might fix his residence at Alexandria or Antioch, cities little inferior to Rome itself in wealth and greatness; that numerous armies should be constantly encamped on either side of the Thracian Bosphorus, to guard the frontiers of the rival monarchies; and that the senators of European extraction should acknowledge the sovereign of Rome, whilst the natives of Asia followed the emperor of the East. The tears of the empress Julia interrupted the negotiation, the first idea of which had filled every Roman breast with surprise and indignation. The mighty mass of conquest was so intimately connected by the hand of time and policy, that it required the most forcible violence to rend it asunder. The Romans had reason to dread that the disjointed members would soon be reduced by a civil war under the dominion of one master; but, if the separation was permanent, the division of the provinces must terminate in the

the streets. But this explanation of Herodian would require, though it ill deserves, a particular dissertation, illustrated by a map of ancient Rome. [See Hume, Essay on Populousness of Ancient Nations. — Milman.]

[21] Herodian, l. iv. p. 139 [1].

dissolution of an empire whose unity had hitherto remained inviolate.[32]

Had the treaty been carried into execution, the sovereign of Europe might soon have been the conqueror of Asia; but Caracalla obtained an easier though a more guilty victory. He artfully listened to his mother's entreaties, and consented to meet his brother in her apartment, on terms of peace and reconciliation. In the midst of their conversation, some centurions, who had contrived to conceal themselves, rushed with drawn swords upon the unfortunate Geta. His distracted mother strove to protect him in her arms; but in the unavailing struggle, she was wounded in the hand, and covered with the blood of her younger son, while she saw the elder animating and assisting[33] the fury of the assassins. As soon as the deed was perpetrated, Caracalla, with hasty steps and horror in his countenance, ran towards the Prætorian camp, as his only refuge, and threw himself on the ground before the statues of the tutelar deities.[34] The soldiers attempted to raise and comfort him. In broken and disordered words he informed them of his imminent danger and fortunate escape: insinuating that he had prevented the designs of his

[32] Herodian, l. iv. p. 144 [4]. [Yet, in this proposal, we can see foreshadowed the geographical division of the empire among two or more emperors, which was made a principle of government by Diocletian. The tendency to disruption between the eastern and western groups of provinces had been already seen in the revolt of Avidius Cassius, and the "tyranny" of Pescennius Niger. In fact, at the elevation of Severus, the four sovereignties of Diocletian, — the four Prefectures of Constantine — are shadowed forth. (1) Albinus in Gaul; (2) Julianus in Italy; (3) Severus in the Illyrian Peninsula; (4) Niger in Asia, are, in a sense, forerunners of Constantine, Maximian, Galerius, and Diocletian respectively.]

[33] Caracalla consecrated, in the temple of Serapis, the sword with which, as he boasted, he had slain his brother Geta. Dion, l. lxxvii. p. 1307 [23].

[34] Herodian, l. iv. p. 147 [4]. In every Roman camp there was a small chapel near the headquarters, in which the statues of the tutelar deities were preserved and adored; and we may remark that the eagles, and other military ensigns, were in the first rank of these deities; an excellent institution, which confirmed discipline by the sanction of religion. See Lipsius de Militiâ Romanâ, iv. 5, v. 2.

enemy, and declaring his resolution to live and die with his faithful troops. Geta had been the favourite of the soldiers; but complaint was useless, revenge was dangerous, and they still reverenced the son of Severus. Their discontent died away in idle murmurs, and Caracalla soon convinced them of the justice of his cause, by distributing in one lavish donative the accumulated treasures of his father's reign.[25] The real *sentiments* of the soldiers alone were of importance to his power or safety. Their declaration in his favour commanded the dutiful *professions* of the senate. The obsequious assembly was always prepared to ratify the decision of fortune; but as Caracalla wished to assuage the first emotions of public indignation, the name of Geta was mentioned with decency, and he received the funeral honours of a Roman emperor.[26] Posterity, in pity to his misfortune, has cast a veil over his vices. We consider that young prince as the innocent victim of his brother's ambition, without recollecting that he himself wanted power, rather than inclination, to consummate the same attempts of revenge and murder.

The crime went not unpunished. Neither business, nor pleasure, nor flattery, could defend Caracalla from the stings of a guilty conscience; and he confessed, in the anguish of a tortured mind, that his disordered fancy often beheld the angry forms of his father and his brother rising into life, to threaten and upbraid him.[27] The consciousness of his crime should have induced him to convince mankind, by the virtues of his reign, that the bloody deed had been the involuntary effect of fatal necessity. But the repentance of Caracalla only prompted him to remove from the world whatever could remind him of his guilt, or recall the memory of his murdered brother. On his return from the senate to the palace, he

[25] Herodian, l. iv. p. 148 [4]. Dion, l. lxxvii. p. 1289 [3].

[26] Geta was placed among the gods. Sit *divus*, dum non sit *vivus*, said his brother. Hist. August. p. 91 [xiv. 2, 8]. Some marks of Geta's consecration are still found upon medals.

[27] Dion, l. lxxvii. p. 1301 [15].

found his mother in the company of several noble matrons, weeping over the untimely fate of her younger son. The jealous emperor threatened them with instant death: the sentence was executed against Fadilla, the last remaining daughter of the emperor Marcus; and even the afflicted Julia was obliged to silence her lamentations, to suppress her sighs, and to receive the assassin with smiles of joy and approbation. It was computed that, under the vague appellation of the friends of Geta, above twenty thousand persons of both sexes suffered death. His guards and freedmen, the ministers of his serious business, and the companions of his looser hours, those who by his interest had been promoted to any commands in the army or provinces, with the long connected chain of their dependants, were included in the proscription; which endeavoured to reach every one who had maintained the smallest correspondence with Geta, who lamented his death, or who even mentioned his name.[28] Helvius Pertinax, son to the prince of that name, lost his life by an unseasonable witticism.[29] It was a sufficient crime of Thrasea Priscus to be descended from a family in which the love of liberty seemed an hereditary quality.[30] The particular causes of calumny and suspicion were at length exhausted; and when a senator was accused of being a secret enemy to the government, the emperor was satisfied with the general proof that he was a man of property and virtue. From this well-grounded principle, he frequently drew the most bloody inferences.

[28] Dion, l. lxxvii. p. 1290 [4]. Herodian, l. iv. p. 150 [6]. Dion (p. 1298 [lxxvii. 12]) says that the comic poets no longer durst employ the name of Geta in their plays, and that the estates of those who mentioned it in their testaments were confiscated.

[29] Caracalla had assumed the names of several conquered nations; Pertinax observed, that the name of *Geticus* (he had obtained some advantage over the Goths or Getæ) would be a proper addition to Parthicus, Alemannicus, &c. Hist. August. p. 89 [xiii. 10, 6].

[30] Dion, l. lxxvii. p. 1291 [5]. He was probably descended from Helvidius Priscus, and Thrasea Pætus, those patriots whose firm, but useless and unseasonable, virtue has been immortalised by Tacitus.

The execution of so many innocent citizens was bewailed by the secret tears of their friends and families. The death of Papinian, the Prætorian prefect,[31] was lamented as a public calamity. During the last seven years of Severus, he had exercised the most important offices of the state, and, by his salutary influence, guided the emperor's steps in the paths of justice and moderation. In full assurance of his virtue and abilities, Severus, on his deathbed, had conjured him to watch over the prosperity and union of the Imperial family.[32] The honest labours of Papinian served only to inflame the hatred which Caracalla had already conceived against his father's minister. After the murder of Geta, the prefect was commanded to exert the powers of his skill and eloquence in a studied apology for that atrocious deed. The philosophic Seneca had condescended to compose a similar epistle to the senate, in the name of the son and assassin of Agrippina.[33] "That it was easier to commit than to justify a parricide," was the glorious reply of Papinian,[34] who did not hesitate between the loss of life and that of honour. Such intrepid virtue, which had escaped pure and unsullied from the intrigues of courts, the habits of business, and the arts of his profession, reflects more lustre on the memory of Papinian than all his great employments, his numerous writings, and the superior reputation as a lawyer, which he has preserved through every age of the Roman jurisprudence.[35]

It had hitherto been the peculiar felicity of the Romans, and in the worst of times their consolation, that the virtue of the emperors was active, and their vice indolent. Augustus,

[31] [Dion says that Caracalla, on his accession, had deposed Papinian from this office; and Dion was in a position to know.]

[32] It is said that Papinian was himself a relation of the empress Julia.

[33] Tacit. Annal. xiv. 2.

[34] Hist. August. p. 88 [xiii. 8, 5].

[35] With regard to Papinian, see Heineccius's Historia Juris Romani, l. 330, &c. [The true cause of Papinian's execution was probably that he was highly unpopular with the soldiers, whose wishes Caracalla was always ready to humour.]

Trajan, Hadrian, and Marcus visited their extensive dominions in person, and their progress was marked by acts of wisdom and beneficence. The tyranny of Tiberius, Nero, and Domitian, who resided almost constantly at Rome, or in the adjacent villas, was confined to the senatorial and equestrian orders.[86] But Caracalla was the common enemy of mankind. He left the capital (and he never returned to it)[87] about a year after the murder of Geta. The rest of his reign was spent in the several provinces of the empire, particularly those of the East, and every province was, by turns, the scene of his rapine and cruelty. The senators, compelled by fear to attend his capricious motions, were obliged to provide daily entertainments at an immense expense, which he abandoned with contempt to his guards; and to erect, in every city, magnificent palaces and theatres, which he either disdained to visit, or ordered to be immediately thrown down. The most wealthy families were ruined by partial fines and confiscations, and the great body of his subjects oppressed by ingenious and aggravated taxes.[88] In the midst of peace, and upon the slightest provocation, he issued his commands, at Alexandria in Egypt, for a general massacre. From a secure post in the temple of Serapis, he viewed and directed the slaughter of many thousand citizens, as well as strangers, without distinguishing either the number or the crime of the sufferers; since, as he coolly informed the senate, *all* the Alexandrians, those who had perished and those who had escaped, were alike guilty.[89]

[86] Tiberius and Domitian never moved from the neighbourhood of Rome. Nero made a short journey into Greece. "Et laudatorum Principum usus ex æquo quamvis procul agentibus. Sævi proximis ingruunt." Tacit. Hist. iv. 75.

[87] [There is a coin, however, which suggests that Caracalla returned to Italy and Rome in 214 A.D., after his successful campaigns on the Rhine and Neckar. Eckhel, vii. 211.]

[88] Dion, l. lxxvii. p. 1294 [9].

[89] *Ibid.* p. 1307 [23]. Herodian, l. iv. p. 158 [9]. The former represents it as a cruel massacre, the latter as a perfidious one too. It seems

The wise instructions of Severus never made any lasting impression on the mind of his son, who, although not destitute of imagination and eloquence, was equally devoid of judgment and humanity.[40] One dangerous maxim, worthy of a tyrant, was remembered and abused by Caracalla, "To secure the affections of the army, and to esteem the rest of his subjects as of little moment." [41] But the liberality of the father had been restrained by prudence, and his indulgence to the troops was tempered by firmness and authority. The careless profusion of the son was the policy of one reign, and the inevitable ruin both of the army and of the empire. The vigour of the soldiers, instead of being confirmed by the severe discipline of camps, melted away in the luxury of cities. The excessive increase of their pay and donatives [42] exhausted

probable that the Alexandrians had irritated the tyrant by their railleries, and perhaps by their tumults. [The punishment of Alexandria, which was given over to the soldiers to plunder, was hardly such an act of caprice as Gibbon represents it. The harshness of Caracalla to that city was inherited from Severus; under both reigns Alexandrine coins are very rare. There seem to have been serious conspiracies in Egypt, which demanded summary dealing.]

[40] Dion, l. lxxvii. p. 1296 [11].

[41] *Ibid*, l. lxxvi. p. 1284 [15]. M. Wotton (Hist. of Rome, p. 330) suspects that this maxim was invented by Caracalla himself and attributed to his father.

[42] Dion (l. lxxviii. p. 1343 [36]) informs us that the extraordinary gifts of Caracalla to the army amounted annually to seventy millions of drachmæ (about two million three hundred and fifty thousand pounds). There is another passage in Dion, concerning the military pay, infinitely curious; were it not obscure, imperfect, and probably corrupt. The best sense seems to be, that the Pretorian guards received twelve hundred and fifty drachmæ (forty pounds) a year. (Dion, l. lxxvii. p. 1307 [24].) Under the reign of Augustus, they were paid at the rate of two drachmæ, or denarii, per day, 720 a year (Tacit. Annal. i. 17). Domitian, who increased the soldiers' pay one-fourth, must have raised the Pretorians to 960 drachmæ (Gronovius de Pecuniâ Veteri, l. iii. c. 2). These successive augmentations ruined the empire, for, with the soldiers' pay, their numbers too were increased. We have seen the Pretorians alone increased from 10,000 to 50,000 men. [It has been pointed out by Guizot that Gibbon misunderstood the passage of Dion, which refers not to the annual pay of soldiers, but to the recompense given at the end of their term of service. But, as Valois saw, the numbers

the state to enrich the military order, whose modesty in peace, and service in war, is best secured by an honourable poverty. The demeanour of Caracalla was haughty and full of pride; but with the troops he forgot even the proper dignity of his rank, encouraged their insolent familiarity, and, neglecting the essential duties of a general, affected to imitate the dress and manners of a common soldier.

It was impossible that such a character and such a conduct as that of Caracalla could inspire either love or esteem; but, as long as his vices were beneficial to the armies, he was secure from the danger of rebellion. A secret conspiracy, provoked by his own jealousy, was fatal to the tyrant. The Pretorian prefecture was divided between two ministers. The military department was entrusted to Adventus, an experienced rather than an able solider; and the civil affairs were transacted by Opilius Macrinus, who, by his dexterity in business, had raised himself, with a fair character, to that high office. But his favour varied with the caprice of the emperor, and his life might depend on the slightest suspicion, or the most casual circumstance. Malice or fanaticism had suggested to an African, deeply skilled in the knowledge of futurity, a very dangerous prediction, that Macrinus and his son were destined to reign over the empire. The report was soon diffused through the province; and, when the man was sent in chains to Rome, he still asserted, in the presence of the prefect of the city, the faith of his prophecy. That magistrate, who had received the most pressing instructions to inform himself of the *successors* of Caracalla, immediately communicated the examination of the African to the Imperial court, which at that time resided in Syria. But notwithstanding the diligence of the public messengers, a friend of Macrinus found means to apprise him of the approaching danger. The emperor received the letters from Rome; and,

seems to be transposed, for the prætorians received a larger sum than the legionaries.]

as he was then engaged in the conduct of a chariot race, he delivered them unopened to the Prætorian prefect, directing him to despatch the ordinary affairs, and to report the more important business that might be contained in them. Macrinus read his fate and resolved to prevent it. He inflamed the discontents of some inferior officers, and employed the hand of Martialis, a desperate soldier, who had been refused the rank of centurion. The devotion of Caracalla had prompted him to make a pilgrimage from Edessa to the celebrated temple of the Moon at Carrhæ. He was attended by a body of cavalry; but having stopped on the road for some necessary occasion, his guards preserved a respectful distance, and Martialis, approaching his person under a pretence of duty, stabbed him with a dagger.[43] The bold assassin was instantly killed by a Scythian archer of the Imperial guard. Such was the end of a monster whose life disgraced human nature, and whose reign accused the patience of the Romans.[44] The grateful soldiers forgot his vices, remembered only his partial liberality, and obliged the senate to prostitute their own dignity and that of religion by granting him a place among the gods. Whilst he was upon earth, Alexander the Great was the only hero whom this god deemed worthy his admiration. He assumed the name and ensigns of Alexander, formed a Macedonian phalanx of guards,[45] persecuted the disciples of Aristotle, and displayed with a puerile enthusiasm the only sentiment by which he discovered any regard for virtue or glory. We can easily conceive that, after the battle of Narva and the conquest of Poland, Charles the Twelfth (though he still wanted the more elegant accomplishments of the son of Philip) might boast of having rivalled his valour

[43] A.D. 217, 8th March [8th April; see Clinton ad ann.].

[44] Dion, l. lxxviii. p. 1312 [5, 4]. Herodian, l. iv. p. 168 [13]. [Gibbon does not give this emperor due credit for his ability as an administrator (carrying out his father's policy) and his important military works.]

[45] [Those who have studied the question say that Caracalla's development of the phalanx was, under the circumstances of the empire, a benefit and a necessity. Hadrian had already pointed the way to this tactical change.]

and magnanimity; but in no one action of his life did Caracalla express the faintest resemblance of the Macedonian hero, except in the murder of a great number of his own and of his father's friends.[46]

After the extinction of the house of Severus, the Roman world remained three days without a master. The choice of the army (for the authority of a distant and feeble senate was little regarded) hung in anxious suspense; as no candidate presented himself whose distinguished birth and merit could engage their attachment and unite their suffrages. The decisive weight of the Prætorian guards elevated the hopes of their prefects, and these powerful ministers began to assert their *legal* claim to fill the vacancy of the Imperial throne. Adventus, however, the senior prefect, conscious of his age and infirmities, of his small reputation and his smaller abilities, resigned the dangerous honour to the crafty ambition of his colleague Macrinus, whose well-dissembled grief removed all suspicion of his being accessory to his master's death.[47] The troops neither loved nor esteemed his character. They cast their eyes around in search of a competitor, and at last yielded with reluctance to his promises of unbounded liberality and indulgence. A short time after his accession he conferred on his son Diadumenianus, at the age of only ten years, the Imperial title and the popular name of Antoninus.[48] The beautiful figure of the youth, assisted by an additional donative, for which the ceremony furnished a pretext, might attract,

[46] The fondness of Caracalla for the name and ensigns of Alexander is still preserved on the medals of that emperor. See Spanheim de Usu Numismatum. Dissertat. xii. Herodian (l. iv. p. 154 [8]) had seen very ridiculous pictures, in which a figure was drawn with one side of the face like Alexander, and the other like Caracalla. [Admiration for Alexander as an ideal was a feature of the age. Sulla and Hannibal were also special favourites of Caracalla.]

[47] Herodian, l. iv. p. 169 [14]. Hist. August. p. 94 [xv. 4].

[48] [M. Opellius (Opilius in Hist. Aug.) Antoninus Diadumenianus nobiliss. Cæsar. Macrinus himself took the name of Severus.]

it was hoped, the favour of the army, and secure the doubtful throne of Macrinus.

The authority of the new sovereign had been ratified by the cheerful submission of the senate and provinces. They exulted in their unexpected deliverance from a hated tyrant, and it seemed of little consequence to examine into the virtues of the successor of Caracalla. But as soon as the first transports of joy and surprise had subsided, they began to scrutinise the merits of Macrinus with a critical severity, and to arraign the hasty choice of the army. It had hitherto been considered as a fundamental maxim of the constitution that the emperor must always be chosen in the senate, and the sovereign power, no longer exercised by the whole body, was always delegated to one of its members. But Macrinus was not a senator.[49] The sudden elevation of the Prætorian prefects betrayed the meanness of their origin; and the equestrian order was still in possession of that great office, which commanded with arbitrary sway the lives and fortunes of the senate. A murmur of indignation was heard, that a man, whose obscure [50] extraction had never been illustrated by any signal service, should dare to invest himself with the purple, instead of bestowing it on some distinguished senator, equal in birth and dignity to the splendour of the Imperial station. As soon as the character of Macrinus was surveyed by the

[49] Dion, l. lxxxix. p. 1350 [1]. Elagabalus reproached his predecessor with daring to seat himself on the throne; though, as Prætorian prefect, he could not have been admitted into the senate after the voice of the crier had cleared the house. The personal favour of Plautianus and Sejanus had broken through the established rule. They rose indeed from the equestrian order; but they preserved the prefecture with the rank of senator, and even with the consulship. [Macrinus was the first man of equestrian order who became emperor.]

[50] He was a native of Cæsarea, in Numidia, and began his fortune by serving in the household of Plautian, from whose ruin he narrowly escaped. His enemies asserted that he was born a slave, and had exercised, among other infamous professions, that of Gladiator. The fashion of aspersing the birth and condition of an adversary seems to have lasted from the time of the Greek orators to the learned grammarians of the last age.

sharp eye of discontent, some vices, and many defects, were easily discovered. The choice of his ministers was in several instances justly censured, and the dissatisfied people, with their usual candour, accused at once his indolent tameness and his excessive severity.[51]

His rash ambition had climbed a height where it was difficult to stand with firmness, and impossible to fall without instant destruction. Trained in the arts of courts and the forms of civil business, he trembled in the presence of the fierce and undisciplined multitude, over whom he had assumed the command: his military talents were despised, and his personal courage suspected: a whisper that circulated in the camp, disclosed the fatal secret of the conspiracy against the late emperor, aggravated the guilt of murder by the baseness of hypocrisy, and heightened contempt by detestation. To alienate the soldiers, and to provoke inevitable ruin, the character of a reformer only was wanting; and such was the peculiar hardship of his fate, that Macrinus was compelled to exercise that invidious office. The prodigality of Caracalla had left behind it a long train of ruin and disorder: and, if that worthless tyrant had been capable of reflecting on the sure consequences of his own conduct, he would perhaps have enjoyed the dark prospect of the distress and calamities which he bequeathed to his successors.

In the management of this necessary reformation, Macrinus proceeded with a cautious prudence which would have restored health and vigour to the Roman army in an easy and almost imperceptible manner. To the soldiers already engaged in the service, he was constrained to leave the dangerous privileges and extravagant pay given by Caracalla; but the new recruits were received on the more moderate, though liberal, establishment of Severus, and gradually formed to

[51] Both Dion and Herodian speak of the virtues and vices of Macrinus with candour and impartiality; but the author of his Life, in the Augustan History, seems to have implicitly copied some of the venal writers employed by Elagabalus to blacken the memory of his predecessor.

modesty and obedience.[53] One fatal error destroyed the salutary effects of this judicious plan. The numerous army, assembled in the East by the late emperor, instead of being immediately dispersed by Macrinus through the several provinces, was suffered to remain united in Syria during the winter that followed his elevation. In the luxurious idleness of their quarters, the troops viewed their strength and numbers, communicated their complaints, and revolved in their minds the advantages of another revolution. The veterans, instead of being flattered by the advantageous distinction, were alarmed by the first steps of the emperor, which they considered as the presage of his future intentions. The recruits, with sullen reluctance, entered on a service, whose labours were increased while its rewards were diminished by a covetous and unwarlike sovereign. The murmurs of the army swelled with impunity into seditious clamours; and the partial mutinies betrayed a spirit of discontent and disaffection, that waited only for the slightest occasion to break out on every side into a general rebellion. To minds thus disposed the occasion soon presented itself.

The empress Julia had experienced all the vicissitudes of fortune. From an humble station, she had been raised to greatness, only to taste the superior bitterness of an exalted rank. She was doomed to weep over the death of one of her sons, and over the life of the other. The cruel fate of Caracalla, though her good sense must have long taught her to expect it, awakened the feelings of a mother and of an empress. Notwithstanding the respectful civility expressed by the usurper towards the widow of Severus, she descended with a painful struggle into the condition of a subject, and soon withdrew herself by a voluntary death from the anxious and

[53] Dion, l. lxxviii. p. 1336 [28]. The sense of the author is as clear as the intention of the emperor; but M. Wotton has mistaken both, by understanding the distinction, not of veterans and recruits, but of old and new legions. History of Rome, p. 347.

humiliating dependence.[52] Julia Mæsa, her sister, was ordered to leave the court and Antioch. She retired to Emesa with an immense fortune, the fruit of twenty years' favour, accompanied by her two daughters, Soæmias and Mamæa, each of whom was a widow, and each had an only son. Bassianus, for that was the name of the son of Soæmias, was consecrated to the honourable ministry of high priest of the Sun; and this holy vocation, embraced either from prudence or superstition, contributed to raise the Syrian youth to the empire of Rome. A numerous body of troops were stationed at Emesa; and, as the severe discipline of Macrinus had constrained them to pass the winter encamped, they were eager to revenge the cruelty of such unaccustomed hardships. The soldiers, who resorted in crowds to the temple of the Sun, beheld with veneration and delight the elegant dress and figure of the young pontiff: they recognised, or thought that they recognised, the features of Caracalla, whose memory they now adored. The artful Mæsa saw and cherished their rising partiality, and, readily sacrificing her daughter's reputation to the fortune of her grandson, she insinuated that Bassianus was the natural son of their murdered sovereign. The sums distributed by her emissaries with a lavish hand[54] silenced every objection, and the profusion sufficiently proved the affinity, or at least the resemblance, of Bassianus with the great original. The young Antoninus (for he had assumed and polluted that respectable name) was declared emperor by the troops of Emesa, asserted his hereditary right, and called aloud on the armies to follow the standard of a young and liberal prince, who had taken up arms to revenge his father's death and the oppression of the military order.[53]

[52] Dion, l. lxxviii. p. 1330 [23]. The abridgment of Xiphilin, though less particular, is in this place clearer than the original.

[54] [The temple of the Sun was rich.]

[53] According to Lampridius (Hist. August. p. 135 [xviii. 60]) Alexander Severus lived twenty-nine years, three months, and seven days. As he was killed March 19, 235, he was born December 12, 205, and was consequently

Whilst a conspiracy of women and eunuchs was concerted with prudence, and conducted with rapid vigour, Macrinus, who by a decisive motion might have crushed his infant enemy, floated between the opposite extremes of terror and security, which alike fixed him inactive at Antioch. A spirit of rebellion diffused itself through all the camps and garrisons of Syria, successive detachments murdered their officers,[86] and joined the party of the rebels; and the tardy restitution of military pay and privileges was imputed to the acknowledged weakness of Macrinus. At length he marched out of Antioch, to meet the increasing and zealous army of the young pretender. His own troops seemed to take the field with faintness and reluctance; but, in the heat of battle,[87] the Prætorian guards, almost by an involuntary impulse, asserted the superiority of their valour and discipline. The rebel ranks were broken; when the mother and grandmother of the Syrian prince, who, according to their Eastern custom, had attended the army, threw themselves from their covered chariots, and, by exciting the compassion of the soldiers, endeavoured to animate their drooping courage. Antoninus himself, who in the rest of his life never acted like a man, in this important crisis of his fate approved himself a hero, mounted his horse, and, at the head of his rallied troops,

about this time thirteen years old, as his elder cousin might be about seventeen. This computation suits much better the history of the young princes than that of Herodian (l. v. p. 181 [3]), who represents them as three years younger; whilst, by an opposite error of chronology, he lengthens the reign of Elagabalus two years beyond its real duration. For the particulars of the conspiracy, see Dion, l. lxxviii. p. 1339 [31]. Herodian, l. v. p. 184 [3]. [The author's conclusion is probably mistaken. Alexander was born October 1, 208, and was thus thirteen and a half years old on his elevation in March, 222 (Aur. Victor, Cæs. 24, 1). The statement of Lampridius may well be a slip.]

[86] By a most dangerous proclamation of the pretended Antoninus, every soldier who brought in his officer's head became entitled to his private estate, as well as to his military commission.

[87] Dion, l. lxxviii. p. 1344 [37]. Herodian, l. v. p. 186 [4]. The battle was fought near the village of Immæ, about two and twenty miles from Antioch.

charged sword in hand among the thickest of the enemy; whilst the eunuch Gannys, whose occupation had been confined to female cares and the soft luxury of Asia, displayed the talents of an able and experienced general. The battle still raged with doubtful violence, and Macrinus might have obtained the victory, had he not betrayed his own cause by a shameful and precipitate flight. His cowardice served only to protract his life a few days, and to stamp deserved ignominy on his misfortunes. It is scarcely necessary to add that his son Diadumenianus was involved in the same fate. As soon as the stubborn Prætorians could be convinced that they fought for a prince who had basely deserted them, they surrendered to the conqueror; the contending parties of the Roman army, mingling tears of joy and tenderness, united under the banners of the imagined son of Caracalla, and the East [58] acknowledged with pleasure the first emperor of Asiatic extraction.

The letters of Macrinus had condescended to inform the senate of the slight disturbance occasioned by an impostor in Syria, and a decree immediately passed, declaring the rebel and his family public enemies; with a promise of pardon, however, to such of his deluded adherents as should merit it by an immediate return to their duty. During the twenty days that elapsed from the declaration to the victory of Antoninus (for in so short an interval was the fate of the Roman world decided), the capital and the provinces, more especially those of the East, were distracted with hopes and fears, agitated with tumult, and stained with a useless effusion of civil blood, since whosoever of the rivals prevailed in Syria must reign over the empire. The specious letters in which the young conqueror announced his victory to the obedient senate were filled with professions of virtue and moderation;

[58] [In this episode, the opposition between East and West was probably an important element.]

the shining examples of Marcus and Augustus he should ever consider as the great rule of his administration; and he affected to dwell with pride on the striking resemblance of his own age and fortunes with those of Augustus, who in the earliest youth had revenged by a successful war the murder of his father. By adopting the style of Marcus Aurelius Antoninus, son of Antoninus, and grandson of Severus, he tacitly asserted his hereditary claim to empire; but, by assuming the tribunitian and proconsular powers[59] before they had been conferred on him by a decree of the senate, he offended the delicacy of Roman prejudice. This new and injudicious violation of the constitution was probably dictated either by the ignorance of his Syrian courtiers, or the fierce disdain of his military followers.[60]

As the attention of the new emperor was diverted by the most trifling amusements, he wasted many months in his luxurious progress from Syria to Italy, passed at Nicomedia the first winter after his victory, and deferred till the ensuing summer his triumphal entry into the capital. A faithful picture, however, which preceded his arrival, and was placed by his immediate order over the altar of Victory in the senate-house, conveyed to the Romans the just but unworthy resemblance of his person and manners. He was drawn in his sacerdotal robes of silk and gold, after the loose-flowing fashion of the Medes and Phœnicians; his head was covered with a lofty tiara, his numerous collars and bracelets were adorned with gems of an inestimable value. His eyebrows were tinged with black, and his cheeks painted with an artificial red and white.[61] The grave senators confessed with a sigh, that, after having long experienced the stern tyranny of their own countrymen, Rome was at length humbled beneath the effeminate luxury of Oriental despotism.

[59] [*Pius felix proconsul trib. pot.* was the form stereotyped by Caracalla. The senate conferred the title *Augusta* on Julia Mæsa.]

[60] Dion, l. lxxix. p. 1353 [4].

[61] *Ibid.* p. 1363 [14]. Herodian, l. v. p. 189 [5].

The Sun was worshipped at Emesa under the name of Elagabalus,[62] and under the form of a black conical stone, which, as it was universally believed, had fallen from heaven on that sacred place. To this protecting deity, Antoninus, not without some reason, ascribed his elevation to the throne. The display of superstitious gratitude was the only serious business of his reign. The triumph of the god of Emesa over all the religions of the earth, was the great object of his zeal and vanity; and the appellation of Elagabalus (for he presumed as pontiff and favourite to adopt that sacred name) was dearer to him than all the titles of Imperial greatness.[63] In a solemn procession through the streets of Rome, the way was strewed with gold dust; the black stone, set in precious gems, was placed on a chariot drawn by six milk-white horses richly caparisoned. The pious emperor held the reins, and, supported by his ministers, moved slowly backwards, that he might perpetually enjoy the felicity of the divine presence. In a magnificent temple raised on the Palatine Mount, the sacrifices of the god Elagabalus were celebrated with every circumstance of cost and solemnity. The richest wines, the most extraordinary victims, and the rarest aromatics, were profusely consumed on his altar. Around the altar a chorus of Syrian damsels performed their lascivious dances to the sound of barbarian music, whilst the gravest personages of the state and army, clothed in long Phœnician tunics, officiated in the meanest functions, with affected zeal and secret indignation.[64]

To this temple, as to the common centre of religious worship, the Imperial fanatic attempted to remove the Ancilia,

[62] This name is derived by the learned, from two Syriac words, *Ela*, a god, and *Gabal*, to form, the forming, or plastic God; a proper, and even happy epithet for the Sun. Wotton's History of Rome, p. 378. [The newer derivation is *al gebal*, "the mountain." The Greeks made the name into *Helio*-gabalos by a tempting popular etymology.]

[63] [His imperial name was M. Aurelius Antoninus, that of his reputed father.]

[64] Herodian, l. v. 190 [5].

the Palladium,[65] and all the sacred pledges of the faith of Numa. A crowd of inferior deities attended in various stations the majesty of the god of Emesa; but his court was still imperfect, till a female of distinguished rank was admitted to his bed. Pallas had been first chosen for his consort; but, as it was dreaded that her warlike terrors might affright the soft delicacy of a Syrian deity, the Moon, adored by the Africans[66] under the name of Astarte, was deemed a more suitable companion for the Sun. Her image, with the rich offerings of her temple as a marriage portion, was transported with solemn pomp from Carthage to Rome, and the day of these mystic nuptials was a general festival in the capital and throughout the empire.[67]

A rational voluptuary adheres with invariable respect to the temperate dictates of nature, and improves the gratifications of sense by social intercourse, endearing connections, and the soft colouring of taste and imagination. But Elagabalus (I speak of the emperor of that name), corrupted by his youth, his country, and his fortune, abandoned himself to the grossest pleasures with ungoverned fury, and soon found disgust and satiety in the midst of his enjoyments. The inflammatory powers of art were summoned to his aid: the confused multitude of women, of wines, and of dishes, and the studied variety of attitudes and sauces, served to revive his languid appetites. New terms and new inventions in these sciences, the only ones cultivated and patronised

[65] He broke into the sanctuary of Vesta, and carried away a statue, which he supposed to be the Palladium; but the vestals boasted that, by a pious fraud, they had imposed a counterfeit image on the profane intruder. Hist. August. p. 103 [xvii. 6].

[66] [That is, the Phoenician settlers in Africa; for Astarte was a Syrian goddess.]

[67] Dion, l. lxxix. p. 1360 [12]. Herodian, l. v. p. 193 [6]. The subjects of the empire were obliged to make liberal presents to the newly-married couple; and whatever they had promised during the life of Elagabalus was carefully exacted under the administration of Mamæa.

by the monarch,[68] signalised his reign, and transmitted his infamy to succeeding times. A capricious prodigality supplied the want of taste and elegance; and, whilst Elagabalus lavished away the treasures of his people in the wildest extravagance, his own voice and that of his flatterers applauded a spirit and magnificence unknown to the tameness of his predecessors. To confound the order of seasons and climates,[69] to sport with the passions and prejudices of his subjects, and to subvert every law of nature and decency, were in the number of his most delicious amusements. A long train of concubines, and a rapid succession of wives, among whom was a vestal virgin, ravished by force from her sacred asylum,[70] were insufficient to satisfy the impotence of his passions. The master of the Roman world affected to copy the dress and manners of the female sex, preferred the distaff to the sceptre, and dishonoured the principal dignities of the empire by distributing them among his numerous lovers; one of whom was publicly invested with the title and authority of the emperor's, or, as he more properly styled himself, of the empress's husband.[71]

It may seem probable the vices and follies of Elagabalus

[68] The invention of a new sauce was liberally rewarded: but if it was not relished, the inventor was confined to eat of nothing else, till he had discovered another more agreeable to the Imperial palate. Hist. August. p. 111 [xvii. 29].

[69] He never would eat sea-fish except at a great distance from the sea; he then would distribute vast quantities of the rarest sorts, brought at an immense expense, to the peasants of the inland country. Hist. August. p. 109 [xvii. 23].

[70] Dion, l. lxxix. p. 1358 [9]. Herodian, l. v. p. 192 [6].

[71] Hierocles enjoyed that honour; but he would have been supplanted by one Zoticus, had he not contrived, by a potion, to enervate the powers of his rival, who, being found on trial unequal to his reputation, was driven with ignominy from the palace. Dion, l. lxxix. p. 1363, 1364 [15, 16]. A dancer was made prefect of the city, a charioteer prefect of the watch, a barber prefect of the provisions. These three ministers, with many inferior officers, were all recommended *enormitate membrorum*. Hist. August. p. 105 [xvii. 12].

have been adorned by fancy and blackened by prejudice.[72] Yet, confining ourselves to the public scenes displayed before the Roman people, and attested by grave and contemporary historians, their inexpressible infamy surpasses that of any other age or country. The licence of an Eastern monarch is secluded from the eye of curiosity by the inaccessible walls of the seraglio. The sentiments of honour and gallantry have introduced a refinement of pleasure, a regard for decency, and a respect for the public opinion, into the modern courts of Europe; but the corrupt and opulent nobles of Rome gratified every vice that could be collected from the mighty conflux of nations and manners. Secure of impunity, careless of censure, they lived without restraint in the patient and humble society of their slaves and parasites. The emperor, in his turn, viewing every rank of his subjects with the same contemptuous indifference, asserted without control his sovereign privilege of lust and luxury.

The most worthless of mankind are not afraid to condemn in others the same disorders which they allow in themselves; and can readily discover some nice difference of age, character, or station, to justify the partial distinction. The licentious soldiers, who had raised to the throne the dissolute son of Caracalla, blushed at their ignominious choice, and turned with disgust from that monster, to contemplate with pleasure the opening virtues of his cousin Alexander, the son of Mamæa. The crafty Mæsa, sensible that her grandson Elagabalus must inevitably destroy himself by his own vices, had provided another and surer support of her family. Embracing a favourable moment of fondness and devotion, she had persuaded the young emperor to adopt Alexander, and to invest him with the title of Cæsar, that his own divine occupations might be no longer interrupted by the care of the earth. In the second rank, that amiable prince soon acquired

[72] Even the credulous compiler of his Life, in the Augustan History (p. 111 [*ib.* 30]), is inclined to suspect that his vices may have been exaggerated.

the affections of the public, and excited the tyrant's jealousy, who resolved to terminate the dangerous competition either by corrupting the manners, or by taking away the life, of his rival. His arts proved unsuccessful; his vain designs were constantly discovered by his own loquacious folly, and disappointed by those virtuous and faithful servants whom the prudence of Mamæa had placed about the person of her son. In a hasty sally of passion, Elagabalus resolved to execute by force what he had been unable to compass by fraud, and by a despotic sentence degraded his cousin from the rank and honours of Cæsar. The message was received in the senate with silence, and in the camp with fury. The Prætorian guards swore to protect Alexander, and to revenge the dishonoured majesty of the throne. The tears and promises of the trembling Elagabalus, who only begged them to spare his life, and to leave him in the possession of his beloved Hierocles, diverted their just indignation; and they contented themselves with empowering their prefects to watch over the safety of Alexander and the conduct of the emperor.[72]

It was impossible that such a reconciliation should last, or that even the mean soul of Elagabalus could hold an empire on such humiliating terms of dependence. He soon attempted, by a dangerous experiment, to try the temper of the soldiers. The report of the death of Alexander, and the natural suspicion that he had been murdered, inflamed their passions into fury, and the tempest of the camp could be appeased only by the presence and authority of the popular youth. Provoked at this new instance of their affection for his cousin, and their contempt for his person, the emperor ventured to punish some of the leaders of the mutiny. His unseasonable severity proved instantly fatal

[72] Dion, l. lxxix. p. 1366 [19]. Herodian, l. v. p. 195–201 [8]. Hist. August. p. 105 [xvii. 13]. The last of the three historians [Lampridius] seems to have followed the best authors in his account of the revolution. [His chief authority was Marius Maximus.]

to his minions, his mother, and himself. Elagabalus was massacred by the indignant Prætorians, his mutilated corpse dragged through the streets of the city, and thrown into the Tiber. His memory was branded with eternal infamy by the senate; the justice of whose decree has been ratified by posterity.[74]

In the room of Elagabalus, his cousin Alexander was raised to the throne by the Prætorian guards. His relation to the family of Severus, whose name he assumed,[75] was the same as that of his predecessor; his virtue and his danger had already endeared him to the Romans, and the eager liberality of the senate conferred upon him, in one day, the various titles and powers of the Imperial dignity.[76] But, as Alexander was a modest and dutiful youth of only seventeen years of age, the reins of government were in the hands of two women, of his mother Mamæa, and of Mæsa, his grandmother. After the death of the latter, who survived but a short time the elevation of Alexander, Mamæa remained the sole regent of her son and of the empire.

In every age and country, the wiser, or at least the stronger,

[74] The era of the death of Elagabalus, and of the accession of Alexander, has employed the learning and ingenuity of Pagi, Tillemont, Valsecchi, Vignoli, and Torre, bishop of Adria. The question is most assuredly intricate; but I still adhere to the authority of Dion, the truth of whose calculations is undeniable, and the purity of whose text is justified by the agreement of Xiphilin, Zonaras, and Cedrenus. Elagabalus reigned three years, nine months, and four days, from his victory over Macrinus, and was killed March 10, 222. But what shall we reply to the medals, undoubtedly genuine, which reckon the fifth year of his tribunitian power? We shall reply, with the learned Valsecchi, that the usurpation of Macrinus was annihilated, and that the son of Caracalla dated his reign from his father's death. After resolving this great difficulty, the smaller knots of this question may be easily untied, or cut asunder. [Exact date uncertain, but probably falls in the first half of March, 222; cp., however, Clinton, Fasti Romani, i. 234, 236. Eckhel, 8, 430.]

[75] [M. Aurelius Severus Alexander.]

[76] Hist. August. p. 114 [xvii. 1]. By this unusual precipitation, the senate meant to confound the hopes of pretenders, and prevent the factions of the armies.

of the two sexes has usurped the powers of the state, and confined the other to the cares and pleasures of domestic life. In hereditary monarchies, however, and especially in those of modern Europe, the gallant spirit of chivalry, and the law of succession, have accustomed us to allow a singular exception; and a woman is often acknowledged the absolute sovereign of a great kingdom, in which she would be deemed incapable of exercising the smallest employment, civil or military. But as the Roman emperors were still considered as the generals and magistrates of the republic, their wives and mothers, although distinguished by the name of Augusta, were never associated to their personal honours; and a female reign would have appeared an inexpiable prodigy in the eyes of those primitive Romans, who married without love, or loved without delicacy and respect.[77] The haughty Agrippina aspired, indeed, to share the honours of the empire which she had conferred on her son; but her mad ambition, detested by every citizen who felt for the dignity of Rome, was disappointed by the artful firmness of Seneca and Burrhus.[78] The good sense, or the indifference, of succeeding princes restrained them from offending the prejudices of their subjects; and it was reserved for the profligate Elagabalus to disgrace the acts of the senate with the name of his mother Soæmias, who was placed by the side of the consuls, and subscribed, as a regular member, the decrees of the legislative assembly. Her more prudent sister, Mamæa, declined the useless and odious prerogative, and a solemn law was enacted, excluding women for ever from the senate, and devoting to the infernal gods the head of the wretch by whom this sanction should be violated.[79]

[77] Metellus Numidicus, the censor, acknowledged to the Roman people, in a public oration, that, had kind Nature allowed us to exist without the help of woman, we should be delivered from a very troublesome companion; and he could recommend matrimony only as the sacrifice of private pleasure to public duty. Aulus Gellius, i. 6.

[78] Tacit. Annal. xiii. 5. [After Agrippina, the title Augusta had no political significance.]

[79] Hist. August. p. 102, 107 [xvii. 4 and 18].

The substance, not the pageantry, of power was the object of Mamæa's manly ambition. She maintained an absolute and lasting empire over the mind of her son, and in his affection the mother could not brook a rival. Alexander, with her consent, married the daughter of a patrician;[80] but his respect for his father-in-law, and love for the empress, were inconsistent with the tenderness or interest of Mamæa. The patrician was executed on the ready accusation of treason, and the wife of Alexander driven with ignominy from the palace, and banished into Africa.[81]

Notwithstanding this act of jealous cruelty, as well as some instances of avarice, with which Mamæa is charged, the general tenor of her administration was equally for the benefit of her son and of the empire. With the approbation of the senate, she chose sixteen of the wisest and most virtuous senators, as a perpetual council of state, before whom every public business of moment was debated and determined. The celebrated Ulpian, equally distinguished by his knowledge of, and his respect for, the laws of Rome, was at their head; and the prudent firmness of this aristocracy restored order and authority to the government. As soon as they had purged the city from foreign superstition and luxury, the remains of the capricious tyranny of Elagabalus, they applied themselves to remove his worthless creatures from every department of public administration, and to supply their places with men of virtue and ability. Learning, and the love of justice, became the only recommendations for civil offices;

[80] [Sallustia Barbia Orbiana, daughter of Sallustius Macrinus, who conspired against the life of Alexander. Gibbon is too ready to assume that Mamæa was to blame.]

[81] Dion, l. lxxx. p. 1369 [2]. Herodian, l. vi. p. 206 [1]. Hist. August. p. 131 [xviii. 49]. Herodian represents the patrician as innocent. The Augustan History, on the authority of Dexippus, condemns him as guilty of a conspiracy against the life of Alexander. It is impossible to pronounce between them: but Dion is an irreproachable witness of the jealousy and cruelty of Mamæa towards the young empress, whose hard fate Alexander lamented, but durst not oppose.

valour, and the love of discipline, the only qualifications for military employments.[82]

But the most important care of Mamæa and her wise counsellors was to form the character of the young emperor, on whose personal qualities the happiness or misery of the Roman world must ultimately depend. The fortunate soil assisted, and even prevented, the hand of cultivation. An excellent understanding soon convinced Alexander of the advantages of virtue, the pleasure of knowledge, and the necessity of labour. A natural mildness and moderation of temper preserved him from the assaults of passion and the allurements of vice. His unalterable regard for his mother, and his esteem for the wise Ulpian, guarded his unexperienced youth from the poison of flattery.

The simple journal of his ordinary occupations exhibits a pleasing picture of an accomplished emperor,[83] and, with some allowance for the difference of manners, might well deserve the imitation of modern princes. Alexander rose early; the first moments of the day were consecrated to private devotion, and his domestic chapel was filled with the images of those heroes who, by improving or reforming human life, had deserved the grateful reverence of posterity. But, as he deemed the service of mankind the most acceptable worship of the gods, the greatest part of his morning hours was employed in his council, where he discussed public affairs, and determined private causes, with a patience and discretion above his years. The dryness of business was relieved by the charms of literature; and a portion of time was always set apart for his favourite studies of poetry, history, and philosophy. The works of Virgil and Horace, the republics

[82] Herodian, l. vi. p. 203 [1]. Hist. August. p. 119 [xviii. 15]. The latter insinuates that, when any law was to be passed, the council was assisted by a number of able lawyers and experienced senators, whose opinions were separately given and taken down in writing.

[83] See his life in the Augustan History. The undistinguishing compiler has buried these interesting anecdotes under a load of trivial and unmeaning circumstances.

of Plato and Cicero, formed his taste, enlarged his understanding, and gave him the noblest ideas of man and government. The exercises of the body succeeded to those of the mind; and Alexander, who was tall, active, and robust, surpassed most of his equals in the gymnastic arts. Refreshed by the use of the bath and a slight dinner, he resumed, with new vigour, the business of the day, and, till the hour of supper, the principal meal of the Romans, he was attended by his secretaries, with whom he read and answered the multitude of letters, memorials, and petitions, that must have been addressed to the master of the greatest part of the world. His table was served with the most frugal simplicity; and, whenever he was at liberty to consult his own inclination, the company consisted of a few select friends, men of learning and virtue, amongst whom Ulpian was constantly invited. Their conversation was familiar and instructive; and the pauses were occasionally enlivened by the recital of some pleasing composition, which supplied the place of the dancers, comedians, and even gladiators, so frequently summoned to the tables of the rich and luxurious Romans.[84] The dress of Alexander was plain and modest, his demeanour courteous and affable: at the proper hours his palace was open to all his subjects, but the voice of a crier was heard, as in the Eleusinian mysteries, pronouncing the same salutary admonition: "Let none enter these holy walls, unless he is conscious of a pure and innocent mind."[85]

Such an uniform tenor of life, which left not a moment for vice or folly, is a better proof of the wisdom and justice of Alexander's government than all the trifling details preserved in the compilation of Lampridius. Since the accession of Commodus the Roman world had experienced, during a term of forty years, the successive and various vices of four tyrants. From the death of Elagabalus it enjoyed an auspicious calm of thirteen years. The provinces, relieved from the

[84] See the 13th Satire of Juvenal.

[85] Hist. August. p. 119 [xviii. 18].

oppressive taxes invented by Caracalla and his pretended son, flourished in peace and prosperity under the administration of magistrates who were convinced by experience that to deserve the love of the subjects was their best and only method of obtaining the favour of their sovereign. While some gentle restraints were imposed on the innocent luxury of the Roman people, the price of provisions and the interest of money were reduced by the paternal care of Alexander, whose prudent liberality, without distressing the industrious, supplied the wants and amusements of the populace. The dignity, the freedom, the authority of the senate were restored; and every virtuous senator might approach the person of the emperor without a fear and without a blush.

The name of Antoninus, ennobled by the virtues of Pius and Marcus, had been communicated by adoption to the dissolute Verus, and by descent to the cruel Commodus. It became the honourable appellation of the sons of Severus, was bestowed on young Diadumenianus, and at length prostituted to the infamy of the high priest of Emesa. Alexander, though pressed by the studied, and perhaps sincere, importunity of the senate, nobly refused the borrowed lustre of a name; whilst in his whole conduct he laboured to restore the glories and felicity of the age of the genuine Antonines.[68]

In the civil administration of Alexander, wisdom was enforced by power, and the people, sensible of the public felicity, repaid their benefactor with their love and gratitude. There still remained a greater, a more necessary, but a more difficult enterprise: the reformation of the military order, whose interest and temper, confirmed by long impunity,

[68] See in the Hist. August. p. 116, 117 [xviii. 6–11], the whole contest between Alexander and the senate, extracted from the journals of that assembly. It happened on the sixth of March, probably of the year 223, when the Romans had enjoyed, almost a twelvemonth, the blessings of his reign. Before the appellation of Antoninus was offered him as a title of honour, the senate waited to see whether Alexander would not assume it as a family name.

rendered them impatient of the restraints of discipline, and careless of the blessings of public tranquillity. In the execution of his design the emperor affected to display his love, and to conceal his fear, of the army. The most rigid economy in every other branch of the administration supplied a fund of gold and silver for the ordinary pay and the extraordinary rewards of the troops. In their marches he relaxed the severe obligation of carrying seventeen days' provision on their shoulders. Ample magazines were formed along the public roads, and as soon as they entered the enemy's country, a numerous train of mules and camels waited on their haughty laziness. As Alexander despaired of correcting the luxury of his soldiers, he attempted, at least, to direct it to objects of martial pomp and ornament, fine horses, splendid armour, and shields enriched with silver and gold. He shared whatever fatigues he was obliged to impose, visited, in person, the sick and wounded, preserved an exact register of their services and his own gratitude, and expressed, on every occasion, the warmest regard for a body of men, whose welfare, as he affected to declare, was so closely connected with that of the state.[87] By the most gentle arts he laboured to inspire the fierce multitude with a sense of duty, and to restore at least a faint image of that discipline to which the Romans owed their empire over so many other nations, as warlike and more powerful than themselves. But his prudence was vain, his courage fatal, and the attempt towards a reformation served only to inflame the ills it was meant to cure.

The Prætorian guards were attached to the youth of Alexander. They loved him as a tender pupil, whom they had saved from a tyrant's fury, and placed on the Imperial throne. That amiable prince was sensible of the obligation;

[87] It was a favourite saying of the emperor's, Se milites magis servare, quam seipsum; quod salus publica in his esset. Hist. August. p. 130 [xviii. 47].

but, as his gratitude was restrained within the limits of reason and justice, they soon were more dissatisfied with the virtues of Alexander than they had ever been with the vices of Elagabalus. Their prefect, the wise Ulpian, was the friend of the laws and of the people; he was considered as the enemy of the soldiers, and to his pernicious counsels every scheme of reformation was imputed. Some trifling accident blew up their discontent into a furious mutiny; and a civil war raged, during three days, in Rome, whilst the life of that excellent minister was defended by the grateful people.[88] Terrified, at length, by the sight of some houses in flames, and by the threats of a general conflagration, the people yielded with a sigh, and left the virtuous but unfortunate Ulpian to his fate. He was pursued into the Imperial palace, and massacred at the feet of his master, who vainly strove to cover him with the purple, and to obtain his pardon from the inexorable soldiers. Such was the deplorable weakness of government that the emperor was unable to revenge his murdered friend and his insulted dignity, without stooping to the arts of patience and dissimulation. Epagathus, the principal leader of the mutiny, was removed from Rome by the honourable employment of prefect of Egypt; from that high rank he was gently degraded to the government of Crete; and when, at length, his popularity among the guards was effaced by time and absence, Alexander ventured to inflict the tardy, but deserved, punishment of his crimes.[89] Under the reign of a just and virtuous prince, the tyranny

[88] [Gibbon has fallen into error by confusing different occasions. There is no reason to suppose that Ulpian's life was in danger during the street battles between the populace and guards. They disobeyed his discipline then, but it was in a later mutiny, directed against himself, that he was slain. See Zonaras, xii. 15, and Dion, lxxx. 2.]

[89] Though the author of the life of Alexander (Hist. August. p. 132 [xviii. 51]), mentions the sedition raised against Ulpian by the soldiers, he conceals the catastrophe, as it might discover a weakness in the administration of his hero. From this designed omission, we may judge of the weight and candour of that author.

of the army threatened with instant death his most faithful ministers, who were suspected of an intention to correct their intolerable disorders. The historian Dion Cassius had commanded the Pannonian legions with the spirit of ancient discipline. Their brethren of Rome, embracing the common cause of military licence, demanded the head of the reformer. Alexander, however, instead of yielding to their seditious clamours, showed a just sense of his merit and services, by appointing him his colleague in the consulship, and defraying from his own treasury the expense of that vain dignity; but, as it was justly apprehended that if the soldiers beheld him with the ensigns of his office they would revenge the insult in his blood, the nominal first magistrate of the states retired, by the emperor's advice, from the city, and spent the greatest part of his consulship at his villas in Campania.[90]

The lenity of the emperor confirmed the insolence of the troops; the legions imitated the example of the guards, and defended their prerogative of licentiousness with the same furious obstinacy. The administration of Alexander was an unavailing struggle against the corruption of his age. In Illyricum, in Mauritania, in Armenia, in Mesopotamia, in Germany, fresh mutinies perpetually broke out; his officers were murdered, his authority was insulted, and his life at last sacrificed to the fierce discontents of the army.[91] One particular fact well deserves to be recorded, as it illustrates the manners of the troops, and exhibits a singular instance of their return to a sense of duty and obedience. Whilst the emperor lay at Antioch, in his Persian expedition, the particulars of which we shall hereafter relate, the punishment of some soldiers, who had been discovered in the baths of women, excited a sedition in the legion to which they belonged.

[90] For an account of Ulpian's fate and his own danger, see the mutilated conclusion of Dion's History, l. lxxx. p. 1371 [4].

[91] Annotat. Reimar. ad Dion Cassius, l. lxxx. p. 1369 [2].

Alexander ascended his tribunal, and with a modest firmness represented to the armed multitude the absolute necessity, as well as his inflexible resolution, of correcting the vices introduced by his impure predecessor, and of maintaining the discipline, which could not be relaxed without the ruin of the Roman name and empire. Their clamours interrupted his mild expostulation. "Reserve your shouts," said the undaunted emperor, "till you take the field against the Persians, the Germans, and the Sarmatians. Be silent in the presence of your sovereign and benefactor, who bestows upon you the corn, the clothing, and the money of the provinces. Be silent, or I shall no longer style you soldiers, but *citizens*,[95] if those indeed who disclaim the laws of Rome deserve to be ranked among the meanest of the people." His menaces inflamed the fury of the legion, and their brandished arms already threatened his person. "Your courage," resumed the intrepid Alexander, "would be more nobly displayed in the field of battle; *me* you may destroy, you cannot intimidate; and the severe justice of the republic would punish your crime and revenge my death." The legion still persisted in clamorous sedition, when the emperor pronounced, with a loud voice, the decisive sentence, "Citizens! lay down your arms, and depart in peace to your respective habitations." The tempest was instantly appeased; the soldiers, filled with grief and shame, silently confessed the justice of their punishment and the power of discipline, yielded up their arms and military ensigns, and retired in confusion, not to their camp, but to the several inns of the city. Alexander enjoyed, during thirty days, the edifying

[95] Julius Cæsar had appeased a sedition with the same word, *Quirites:* which, thus opposed to *Soldiers*, was used in a sense of contempt, and reduced the offenders to the less honourable condition of mere citizens. Tacit. Annal. i. 43. [The truth of this anecdote of Alexander's firmness has been suspected by recent historians, and Schiller suggests that it may have been due to the ambiguity of the name *Severus*. It is clear that, if the story is true, Alexander was consciously imitating Julius.]

spectacle of their repentance; nor did he restore them to their former rank in the army, till he had punished with death those tribunes whose connivance had occasioned the mutiny. The grateful legion served the emperor whilst living, and revenged him when dead.[83]

The resolutions of the multitude generally depend on a moment; and the caprice of passion might equally determine the seditious legion to lay down their arms at the emperor's feet, or to plunge them into his breast. Perhaps, if the singular transaction had been investigated by the penetration of a philosopher, we should discover the secret causes which on that occasion authorised the boldness of the prince and commanded the obedience of the troops; and perhaps, if it had been related by a judicious historian, we should find this action, worthy of Cæsar himself, reduced nearer to the level of probability and the common standard of the character of Alexander Severus. The abilities of that amiable prince seem to have been inadequate to the difficulties of his situation, the firmness of his conduct inferior to the purity of his intentions. His virtues, as well as the vices of Elagabalus, contracted a tincture of weakness and effeminacy from the soft climate of Syria, of which he was a native; though he blushed at his foreign origin, and listened with a vain complacency to the flattering genealogists, who derived his race from the ancient stock of Roman nobility.[84] The pride and avarice of his mother cast a shade on the glories of his reign; and by exacting from his riper years the same dutiful obedience which she had justly claimed from his unexperienced youth, Mamæa exposed to public ridicule both her son's character and her own.[85] The fatigues of the Persian war

[83] Hist. August. p. 132 [xviii. 54].

[84] From the Metelli. Hist. August. p. 129 [xviii. 44]. The choice was judicious. In one short period of twelve years, the Metelli could reckon seven consulships, and five triumphs. See Velleius Paterculus, ii. 11, and the Fasti.

[85] The life of Alexander, in the Augustan History, is the mere idea of a

irritated the military discontent; the unsuccessful event degraded the reputation of the emperor as a general, and even as a soldier. Every cause prepared, and every circumstance hastened, a revolution, which distracted the Roman empire with a long series of intestine calamities.

The dissolute tyranny of Commodus, the civil wars occasioned by his death, and the new maxims of policy introduced by the house of Severus, had all contributed to increase the dangerous power of the army, and to obliterate the faint image of laws and liberty that was still impressed on the minds of the Romans. This internal change, which undermined the foundations of the empire, we have endeavoured to explain with some degree of order and perspicuity. The personal characters of the emperors, their victories, laws, follies, and fortunes, can interest us no further than as they are connected with the general history of the Decline and Fall of the monarchy. Our constant attention to that great object will not suffer us to overlook a most important edict of Antoninus Caracalla, which communicated to all the free inhabitants of the empire the name and privileges of Roman citizens. His unbounded liberality flowed not, however, from the sentiments of a generous mind; it was the sordid result of avarice,[86] and will naturally be illustrated

perfect prince, an awkward imitation of the Cyropædia. The account of his reign, as given by Herodian, is rational and moderate, consistent with the general history of the age; and, in some of the most invidious particulars, confirmed by the decisive fragments of Dion. Yet from a very paltry prejudice, the greater number of our modern writers abuse Herodian, and copy the Augustan History. See Mess. de Tillemont and Wotton. From the opposite prejudice, the emperor Julian (in Cæsarib. p. 315) dwells with a visible satisfaction on the effeminate weakness of the *Syrian*, and the ridiculous avarice of his mother.

[86] [Schiller is possibly right in his view (I. 751) that military, not financial, considerations were the chief motive in determining Caracalla's edict. Italy was no longer able to recruit the legions, and the auxilia were gradually taking their place, while the Germans were stepping into the place of the auxilia. The extension of citizenship was also expedient, in face of the barbarians who were pressing into the empire.]

by some observations on the finances of that state, from the victorious ages of the commonwealth to the reign of Alexander Severus.

The siege of Veii in Tuscany, the first considerable enterprise of the Romans, was protracted to the tenth year, much less by the strength of the place than by the unskilfulness of the besiegers. The unaccustomed hardships of so many winter campaigns, at the distance of near twenty miles from home,[97] required more than common encouragements; and the senate wisely prevented the clamours of the people, by the institution of a regular pay for the soldiers, which was levied by a general tribute, assessed according to an equitable proportion on the property of the citizens.[98] During more than two hundred years after the conquest of Veii, the victories of the republic added less to the wealth than to the power of Rome. The states of Italy paid their tribute in military service only, and the vast force, both by sea and land, which was exerted in the Punic wars, was maintained at the expense of the Romans themselves. That high-spirited people (such is often the generous enthusiasm of freedom) cheerfully submitted to the most excessive but voluntary burdens, in the just confidence that they should speedily enjoy the rich harvest of their labours. Their expectations were not disappointed. In the course of a few years, the riches of Syracuse, of Carthage, of Macedonia, and of Asia were brought in triumph to Rome. The treasures of Perseus alone amounted to near two millions sterling, and the Roman people, the sovereign of so many nations, was

[97] According to the more accurate Dionysius, the city itself was only an hundred stadia, or twelve miles and a half, from Rome; though some outposts might be advanced farther on the side of Etruria. Nardini, in a professed treatise, has combated the popular opinion and the authority of two popes, and has removed Veii from Cività Castellana, to a little spot called Isola, in the midway between Rome and the lake Bracciano. [It is now known to be Isola Farnese.]

[98] See the 4th [c. 59] and 5th [c. 7] books of Livy. In the Roman census, property, power, and taxation were commensurate with each other.

for ever delivered from the weight of taxes.[99] The increasing revenue of the provinces was found sufficient to defray the ordinary establishment of war and government, and the superfluous mass of gold and silver was deposited in the temple of Saturn, and reserved for any unforeseen emergency of the state.[100]

History has never perhaps suffered a greater or more irreparable injury than in the loss of that curious register bequeathed by Augustus to the senate, in which that experienced prince so accurately balanced the revenues and expenses of the Roman empire.[101] Deprived of this clear and comprehensive estimate, we are reduced to collect a few imperfect hints from such of the ancients as have accidentally turned aside from the splendid to the more useful parts of history. We are informed that, by the conquests of Pompey, the tributes of Asia were raised from fifty to one hundred and thirty-five millions of drachms, or about four millions and a half sterling.[102] Under the last and most indolent of the Ptolemies, the revenue of Egypt is said to have amounted to twelve thousand five hundred talents; a sum equivalent to more than two millions and a half of our money, but which was afterwards considerably improved by the more exact economy of the Romans, and the increase of the trade of Ethiopia and India.[103] Gaul was enriched by rapine, as Egypt was by commerce, and the tributes of those two great provinces have been compared as nearly equal to each other in value.[104] The ten thousand Euboic or Phœ-

[99] Plin. Hist. Natur. l. xxxiii. c. 3. Cicero de Officiis, ii. 22. Plutarch. in P. Æmil. p. 275 [38].

[100] See a fine description of this accumulated wealth of ages, in Lucan's Phars. l. iii. v. 155, &c.

[101] Tacit. in Annal. i. 11. It seems to have existed in the time of Appian. [The Breviarium Imperii; cp. Dion, lvi. 33.]

[102] Plutarch. in Pompeio, p. 642 [45. There is little doubt that Plutarch means they were raised to eighty-five millions.]

[103] Strabo, l. xvii. p. 798.

[104] Velleius Paterculus, l. ii. c. 39. He seems to give the preference to the revenue of Gaul.

nician talents, about four millions sterling,[105] which vanquished Carthage was condemned to pay within the term of fifty years, were a slight acknowledgment of the superiority of Rome,[106] and cannot bear the least proportion with the taxes afterwards raised both on the lands and on the persons of the inhabitants, when the fertile coast of Africa was reduced into a province.[107]

Spain, by a very singular fatality, was the Peru and Mexico of the old world. The discovery of the rich western continent by the Phœnicians, and the oppression of the simple natives, who were compelled to labour in their own mines for the benefit of strangers, form an exact type of the more recent history of Spanish America.[108] The Phœnicians were acquainted only with the sea-coast of Spain; avarice as well as ambition carried the arms of Rome and Carthage into the heart of the country, and almost every part of the soil was found pregnant with copper, silver, and gold. Mention is made of a mine near Carthagena which yielded every day twenty-five thousand drachms of silver, or about three hundred thousand pounds a year.[109] Twenty thousand pounds weight of gold was annually received from the provinces of Asturia, Gallicia, and Lusitania.[110]

We want both leisure and materials to pursue this curious inquiry through the many potent states that were annihilated in the Roman empire. Some notion, however, may be formed of the revenue of the provinces where considerable

[105] The Euboic, the Phœnician, and Alexandrian talents were double in weight to the Attic. See Hooper on ancient weights and measures, p. iv. c. 5. It is very probable that the same talent was carried from Tyre to Carthage. [The ratio of the Euboic to the Attic talent after the time of Solon was about 4 to 3.]

[106] Polyb. l. xv. c. 2.

[107] Appian in Punicis, p. 84.

[108] Diodorus Siculus, l. v. [37]. Cadiz was built by the Phœnicians a little more than a thousand years before Christ. See Vell. Patercul. i. 2.

[109] Strabo, l. iii. p. 148.

[110] Plin. Hist. Natur. l. xxxiii. c. 3. He mentions likewise a silver mine in Dalmatia, that yielded every day fifty pounds to the state.

wealth had been deposited by nature, or collected by man, if we observe the severe attention that was directed to the abodes of solitude and sterility. Augustus once received a petition from the inhabitants of Gyarus, humbly praying that they might be relieved from one third of their excessive impositions. Their whole tax amounted indeed to no more than one hundred and fifty drachms, or about five pounds; but Gyarus was a little island, or rather a rock, of the Ægean Sea, destitute of fresh water and every necessary of life, and inhabited only by a few wretched fishermen.[111]

From the faint glimmerings of such doubtful and scattered lights, we should be inclined to believe, 1st, That (with every fair allowance for the difference of times and circumstances) the general income of the Roman provinces could seldom amount to less than fifteen or twenty millions of our money;[112] and, 2ndly, That so ample a revenue must have been fully adequate to all the expenses of the moderate government instituted by Augustus, whose court was the modest family of a private senator, and whose military establishment was calculated for the defence of the frontiers, without any aspiring views of conquest, or any serious apprehension of a foreign invasion.

Notwithstanding the seeming probability of both these conclusions, the latter of them at least is positively disowned by the language and conduct of Augustus. It is not easy to determine whether, on this occasion, he acted as the common father of the Roman world, or as the oppressor of liberty; whether he wished to relieve the provinces, or to impoverish the senate and the equestrian order. But no sooner had he

[111] Strabo, l. x. p. 485. Tacit. Annal. iii. 69, and iv. 30. See in Tournefort (Voyages au Levant, Lettre viii.) a very lively picture of the actual misery of Gyarus.

[112] Lipsius de magnitudine Romanâ (l. ii. c. iii.) computes the revenue at one hundred and fifty millions of gold crowns; but his whole book, though learned and ingenious, betrays a very heated imagination. [For the inquiry touching the revenue of the empire we have not sufficient data to make even an approximate estimate.]

assumed the reins of government than he frequently intimated the insufficiency of the tributes, and the necessity of throwing an equitable proportion of the public burden upon Rome and Italy. In the prosecution of this unpopular design, he advanced, however, by cautious and well-weighed steps. The introduction of customs was followed by the establishment of an excise, and the scheme of taxation was completed by an artful assessment on the real and personal property of the Roman citizens, who had been exempted from any kind of contribution above a century and a half.

I. In a great empire like that of Rome, a natural balance of money must have gradually established itself. It has been already observed that, as the wealth of the provinces was attracted to the capital by the strong hand of conquest and power, so a considerable part of it was restored to the industrious provinces by the gentle influence of commerce and arts. In the reign of Augustus and his successors,[113] duties were imposed on every kind of merchandise, which through a thousand channels flowed to the great centre of opulence and luxury; and in whatsoever manner the law was expressed, it was the Roman purchaser, and not the provincial merchant, who paid the tax.[114] The rate of the customs varied from the eighth to the fortieth part of the value of the commodity; and we have a right to suppose that the variation was directed by the unalterable maxims of policy: that a higher duty was fixed on the articles of luxury than on those of necessity, and that the productions raised or manufactured by the labour of the subjects of the empire were treated with more indulgence than was shown to the pernicious, or at least the unpopular, commerce of Arabia and India.[115] There is still

[113] [But also in force before.]

[114] Tacit. Annal. xiii. 31.

[115] See Pliny (Hist. Natur. l. vi. c. 28, l. xii. c. 18). His observation, that the Indian commodities were sold at Rome at a hundred times their original price, may give us some notion of the produce of the customs, since that original price amounted to more than eight hundred thousand pounds.

extant a long but imperfect catalogue of Eastern commodities, which about the time of Alexander Severus were subject to the payment of duties: cinnamon, myrrh, pepper, ginger, and the whole tribe of aromatics; a great variety of precious stones, among which the diamond was the most remarkable for its price, and the emerald for its beauty:[116] Parthian and Babylonian leather, cottons, silks, both raw and manufactured, ebony, ivory, and eunuchs.[117] We may observe that the use and value of those effeminate slaves gradually rose with the decline of the empire.

II. The excise, introduced by Augustus after the civil wars, was extremely moderate, but it was general.[118] It seldom exceeded one *per cent.;* but it comprehended whatever was sold in the markets or by public auction, from the most considerable purchases of land and houses to those minute objects which can only derive a value from their infinite multitude and daily consumption. Such a tax, as it affects the body of the people, has ever been the occasion of clamour and discontent. An emperor well acquainted with the wants and resources of the state was obliged to declare, by a public edict, that the support of the army depended in a great measure on the produce of the excise.[119]

III. When Augustus resolved to establish a permanent military force for the defence of his government against foreign and domestic enemies, he instituted a peculiar treasury for the pay of the soldiers, the rewards of the veterans, and the extraordinary expenses of war. The ample revenue of the excise, though peculiarly appropriated to those uses, was found

[116] The ancients were unacquainted with the art of cutting diamonds.

[117] M. Bouchaud, in his treatise de l'Impôt chez les Romains, has transcribed this catalogue from the Digest, and attempts to illustrate it by a very prolix commentary.

[118] [It was imposed in Rome and Italy, but cannot be proved for the provinces.]

[119] Tacit. Annal. i. 78. Two years afterwards, the reduction of the poor kingdom of Cappadocia gave Tiberius a pretence for diminishing the excise to one half; but the relief was of a very short duration.

inadequate. To supply the deficiency, the emperor suggested a new tax of five *per cent.* on all legacies and inheritances. But the nobles of Rome were more tenacious of property than of freedom. Their indignant murmurs were received by Augustus with his usual temper. He candidly referred the whole business to the senate, and exhorted them to provide for the public service by some other expedient of a less odious nature. They were divided and perplexed. He insinuated to them that their obstinacy would oblige him to *propose* a general land-tax and capitation. They acquiesced in silence.[120] The new imposition on legacies and inheritances was however mitigated by some restrictions. It did not take place unless the object was of a certain value, most probably of fifty or an hundred pieces of gold:[121] nor could it be exacted from the nearest of kin on the father's side.[122] When the rights of nature and property were thus secured, it seemed reasonable that a stranger, or a distant relation, who acquired an unexpected accession of fortune, should cheerfully resign a twentieth part of it for the benefit of the state.[123]

Such a tax, plentiful as it must prove in every wealthy community, was most happily suited to the situation of the Romans, who could frame their arbitrary wills, according to the dictates of reason or caprice, without any restraint from the modern fetters of entails and settlements. From various causes, the partiality of paternal affection often lost its influence over the stern patriots of the commonwealth and the dissolute nobles of the empire; and if the father bequeathed

[120] Dion Cassius, l. lv. p. 799 [25], l. lvi. p. 825 [28]. [This tax was introduced 6 A.D.]

[121] The sum is only fixed by conjecture.

[122] As the Roman law subsisted for many ages, the *Cognati*, or relations on the mother's side, were not called to the succession. This harsh institution was gradually undermined by humanity, and finally abolished by Justinian.

[123] Plin. Panegyric. c. 37. [The tax was known as *vicesima hereditatium*, =5 per cent.]

to his son the fourth part of his estate, he removed all ground of legal complaint.[124] But a rich childless old man was a domestic tyrant, and his power increased with his years and infirmities. A servile crowd, in which he frequently reckoned prætors and consuls, courted his smiles, pampered his avarice, applauded his follies, served his passions, and waited with impatience for his death. The arts of attendance and flattery were formed into a most lucrative science; those who professed it acquired a peculiar appellation; and the whole city, according to the lively descriptions of satire, was divided between two parties, the hunters and their game.[125] Yet while so many unjust and extravagant wills were every day dictated by cunning, and subscribed by folly, a few were the result of rational esteem and virtuous gratitude. Cicero, who had so often defended the lives and fortunes of his fellow-citizens, was rewarded with legacies to the amount of an hundred and seventy thousand pounds;[126] nor do the friends of the younger Pliny seem to have been less generous to that amiable orator.[127] Whatever was the motive of the testator, the treasury claimed, without distinction, the twentieth part of his estate; and in the course of two or three generations, the whole property of the subject must have gradually passed through the coffers of the state.

In the first and golden years of the reign of Nero, that prince, from a desire of popularity, and perhaps from a blind impulse of benevolence, conceived a wish of abolishing the oppression of the customs and excise. The wisest senators applauded his magnanimity: but they diverted him from the execution of a design which would have dissolved the strength and resources of the republic.[128] Had it indeed been possible

[124] See Heineccius in the Antiquit. Juris Romani, l. ii.

[125] Horat. l. ii. Sat. v. Petron. c. 116, &c. Plin. l. ii. Epist. 20.

[126] Cicero in Philipp. ii. c. 16.

[127] See his epistles. Every such will gave him an occasion of displaying his reverence to the dead, and his justice to the living. He reconciled both, in his behaviour to a son who had been disinherited by his mother (v. 1).

[128] Tacit. Annal. xiii. 50. Esprit des Loix, l. xii. c. 19.

to realise this dream of fancy, such princes as Trajan and the Antonines would surely have embraced with ardour the glorious opportunity of conferring so signal an obligation on mankind. Satisfied, however, with alleviating the public burden, they attempted not to remove it. The mildness and precision of their laws ascertained the rule and measure of taxation, and protected the subject of every rank against arbitrary interpretations, antiquated claims, and the insolent vexation of the farmers of the revenue.[129] For it is somewhat singular that, in every age, the best and wisest of the Roman governors persevered in this pernicious method of collecting the principal branches at least of the excise and customs.[130]

The sentiments, and indeed the situation, of Caracalla were very different from those of the Antonines. Inattentive, or rather averse, to the welfare of his people, he found himself under the necessity of gratifying the insatiate avarice which he had excited in the army. Of the several impositions introduced by Augustus, the twentieth on inheritances and legacies was the most fruitful as well as the most comprehensive. As its influence was not confined to Rome or Italy, the produce continually increased with the gradual extension of the ROMAN CITY. The new citizens, though charged on equal terms[131] with the payment of new taxes which had not affected them as subjects, derived an ample compensation from the rank they obtained, the privileges they acquired, and the fair prospect of honours and fortune that was thrown open to their ambition. But the favour which implied a distinction was lost in the prodigality of Caracalla, and the reluctant provincials were compelled to assume the vain title and the real obligations of Roman citizens. Nor was the rapacious son of

[129] See Pliny's Panegyric, the Augustan History, and Burman. de Vectigal. passim.

[130] The tributes (properly so called) were not farmed, since the good princes often remitted many millions of arrears.

[131] The situation of the new citizens is minutely described by Pliny (Panegyric. c. 37, 38, 39). Trajan published a law very much in their favour.

Severus contented with such a measure of taxation as had appeared sufficient to his moderate predecessors. Instead of a twentieth, he exacted a tenth of all legacies and inheritances; and during his reign (for the ancient proportion was restored after his death) he crushed alike every part of the empire under the weight of his iron sceptre.[121]

When all the provincials became liable to the peculiar impositions of Roman citizens, they seemed to acquire a legal exemption from the tributes which they had paid in their former condition of subjects. Such were not the maxims of government adopted by Caracalla and his pretended son. The old as well as the new taxes were, at the same time, levied in the provinces. It was reserved for the virtue of Alexander to relieve them in a great measure from this intolerable grievance, by reducing the tributes to a thirtieth part of the sum exacted at the time of his accession.[122] It is impossible to conjecture the motive that engaged him to spare so trifling a remnant of the public evil; but the noxious weed, which had not been totally eradicated, again sprang up with the most luxuriant growth, and in the succeeding age darkened the Roman world with its deadly shade. In the course of this history, we shall be too often summoned to explain the land-tax, the capitation, and the heavy contributions of corn, wine, oil, and meat, which were exacted from the provinces for the use of the court, the army, and the capital.

As long as Rome and Italy were respected as the centre of government, a national spirit was preserved by the ancient, and insensibly imbibed by the adopted, citizens. The principal commands of the army were filled by men who had received a liberal education, were well instructed in the advantages of

[121] Dion, l. lxxvii. p. 1295 [9]. [The tax was reduced again to 5 per cent. by Macrinus. By the sixth century it had altogether disappeared.]

[122] He who paid ten *aurei*, the usual tribute, was charged with no more than the third part of an aureus, and proportional pieces of gold were coined by Alexander's order. Hist. August. p. 127 [xviii. 39], with the commentary of Salmasius.

laws and letters, and who had risen by equal steps through the regular succession of civil and military honours.[184] To their influence and example we may partly ascribe the modest obedience of the legions during the two first centuries of the Imperial history.

But when the last enclosure of the Roman constitution was trampled down by Caracalla, the separation of possessions gradually succeeded to the distinction of ranks. The more polished citizens of the internal provinces were alone qualified to act as lawyers and magistrates. The rougher trade of arms was abandoned to the peasants and barbarians of the frontiers, who knew no country but their camp, no science but that of war, no civil laws, and scarcely those of military discipline. With bloody hands, savage manners, and desperate resolutions, they sometimes guarded, but much oftener subverted, the throne of the emperors.

[184] See the lives of Agricola, Vespasian, Trajan, Severus, and his three competitors; and indeed of all the eminent men of those times.

CHAPTER VII

The elevation, and tyranny, of Maximin — Rebellion in Africa and Italy, under the authority of the Senate — Civil Wars and Seditions — Violent Deaths of Maximin and his Son, of Maximus and Balbinus, and of the three Gordians — Usurpation and Secular Games of Philip

OF the various forms of government which have prevailed in the world, an hereditary monarchy seems to present the fairest scope for ridicule. Is it possible to relate without an indignant smile, that, on the father's decease, the property of a nation, like that of a drove of oxen, descends to his infant son, as yet unknown to mankind and to himself, and that the bravest warriors and the wisest statesmen, relinquishing their natural right to empire, approach the royal cradle with bended knees and protestations of inviolable fidelity? Satire and declamation may paint these obvious topics in the most dazzling colours, but our more serious thoughts will respect a useful prejudice, that establishes a rule of succession, independent of the passions of mankind; and we shall cheerfully acquiesce in any expedient which deprives the multitude of the dangerous, and indeed the ideal, power of giving themselves a master.

In the cool shade of retirement, we may easily devise imaginary forms of government, in which the sceptre shall be constantly bestowed on the most worthy by the free and incorrupt suffrage of the whole community. Experience overturns these airy fabrics, and teaches us that in a large society the election of a monarch can never devolve to the wisest or to the most numerous part of the people. The army is the only order of men sufficiently united to concur in the same sentiments, and powerful enough to impose them on the rest of their fellow-citizens; but the temper of soldiers, habituated at once to violence and to slavery, renders them very unfit guardians of a legal or even a civil constitution. Justice, humanity, or political wisdom, are qualities they are too little acquainted with in themselves to appreciate them in others. Valour will acquire their esteem, and liberality will purchase their suffrage; but the first of these merits is often lodged in the most savage breasts; the latter can only exert itself at the expense of the public; and both may be turned against the possessor of the throne by the ambition of a daring rival.

The superior prerogative of birth, when it has obtained the sanction of time and popular opinion, is the plainest and least invidious of all distinctions among mankind. The acknowledged right extinguishes the hopes of faction, and the conscious security disarms the cruelty of the monarch. To the firm establishment of this idea we owe the peaceful succession and mild administration of European monarchies. To the defect of it we must attribute the frequent civil wars, through which an Asiatic despot is obliged to cut his way to the throne of his fathers. Yet, even in the East, the sphere of contention is usually limited to the princes of the reigning house, and, as soon as the more fortunate competitor has removed his brethren, by the sword and the bow-string, he no longer entertains any jealousy of his meaner subjects. But the Roman empire, after the authority of the senate had sunk into contempt, was a vast scene of confusion. The royal, and even noble, families of the provinces had long since been led in triumph before the car of the haughty republicans. The ancient families of Rome had successively fallen beneath the tyranny of the Cæsars; and, whilst those princes were shackled by the forms of a commonwealth, and disappointed by the repeated failure of their posterity,[1] it was impossible

[1] There had been no example of three successive generations on the throne; only three instances of sons who succeeded their fathers. The marriages of Cæsars (notwithstanding the permission, and the frequent practice, of divorces) were generally unfruitful.

that any idea of hereditary succession should have taken root in the minds of their subjects. The right to the throne, which none could claim from birth, every one assumed from merit. The daring hopes of ambition were set loose from the salutary restraints of law and prejudice, and the meanest of mankind might, without folly, entertain a hope of being raised by valour and fortune to a rank in the army, in which a single crime would enable him to wrest the sceptre of the world from his feeble and unpopular master. After the murder of Alexander Severus and the elevation of Maximin, no emperor could think himself safe upon the throne, and every barbarian peasant of the frontier might aspire to that august but dangerous station.

About thirty-two years before that event, the emperor Severus, returning from an Eastern expedition, halted in Thrace, to celebrate, with military games, the birthday of his younger son, Geta. The country flocked in crowds to behold their sovereign, and a young barbarian of gigantic stature earnestly solicited, in his rude dialect, that he might be allowed to contend for the prize of wrestling. As the pride of discipline would have been disgraced in the overthrow of a Roman soldier by a Thracian peasant, he was matched with the stoutest followers of the camp, sixteen of whom he successively laid on the ground. His victory was rewarded by some trifling gifts, and a permission to enlist in the troops. The next day the happy barbarian was distinguished above a crowd of recruits, dancing and exulting after the fashion of his country. As soon as he perceived that he had attracted the emperor's notice, he instantly ran up to his horse, and followed him on foot, without the least appearance of fatigue, in a long and rapid career. "Thracian," said Severus, with astonishment, "art thou disposed to wrestle after thy race?" "Most willingly, sir," replied the unwearied youth, and, almost in a breath, overthrew seven of the strongest soldiers in the army. A gold collar was the prize of his matchless vigour and activity, and he was immediately appointed to serve in the horse-guards who always attended on the person of the sovereign.[2]

Maximin, for that was his name, though born on the territories of the empire, descended from a mixed race of barbarians. His father was a Goth, and his mother of the nation of the Alani.[3] He displayed on every occasion a valour equal to his strength; and his native fierceness was soon tempered or disguised by the knowledge of the world. Under the reign of Severus and his son, he obtained the rank of centurion, with the favour and esteem of both those princes, the former of whom was an excellent judge of merit. Gratitude forbade Maximin to serve under the assassin of Caracalla. Honour taught him to decline the effeminate insults of Elagabalus. On the accession of Alexander he returned to court, and was placed by that prince in a station useful to the service and honourable to himself. The fourth legion, to which he was appointed tribune, soon became, under his care, the best disciplined of the whole army. With the general applause of the soldiers, who bestowed on their favourite hero the names of Ajax and Hercules, he was successively promoted to the first military command,[4] and had not he still retained too much of his savage origin, the emperor might perhaps have given his own sister in marriage to the son of Maximin.[5]

Instead of securing his fidelity, these favours served only to inflame the ambition of the Thracian peasant, who deemed his fortune inadequate to his merit as long as he was constrained to acknowledge a superior. Though a stranger to real wisdom, he was not devoid of a selfish cunning, which

[2] Hist. August. p. 138 [xix. 1].

[3] [His father's name was Micca, his mother's Hababa.]

[4] Hist. August. p. 140 [xix. 6]. Herodian, l. vi. p. 223 [8]. Aurelius Victor. By comparing these authors, it should seem, that Maximin had the particular command of the Triballian horse, with the general commission of disciplining the recruits of the whole army. His biographer ought to have marked, with more care, his exploits, and the successive steps of his military promotions.

[5] See the original letter of Alexander Severus, Hist. August. p. 149 [xix. 29].

showed him that the emperor had lost the affection of the army, and taught him to improve their discontent to his own advantage. It is easy for faction and calumny to shed their poison on the administration of the best of princes, and to accuse even their virtues by artfully confounding them with those vices to which they bear the nearest affinity. The troops listened with pleasure to the emissaries of Maximin. They blushed at their own ignominious patience, which, during thirteen years, had supported the vexatious discipline imposed by an effeminate Syrian, the timid slave of his mother and of the senate. It was time, they cried, to cast away that useless phantom of the civil power, and to elect for their prince and general a real soldier, educated in camps, exercised in war, who would assert the glory and distribute among his companions the treasures of the empire. A great army was at that time assembled on the banks of the Rhine, under the command of the emperor himself, who, almost immediately after his return from the Persian war, had been obliged to march against the barbarians of Germany. The important care of training and reviewing the new levies was entrusted to Maximin. One day, as he entered the field of exercise, the troops either from a sudden impulse or a formed conspiracy, saluted him emperor, silenced by their loud acclamations his obstinate refusal, and hastened to consummate their rebellion by the murder of Alexander Severus.

The circumstances of his death are variously related. The writers who suppose that he died in ignorance of the ingratitude and ambition of Maximin affirm that, after taking a frugal repast in the sight of the army, he retired to sleep, and that about the seventh hour of the day a party of his own guards broke into the Imperial tent, and, with many wounds, assassinated their virtuous and unsuspecting prince.[6] If we

[6] Hist. August. p. 135 [xviii. 61]. I have softened some of the most improbable circumstances of this wretched biographer. From this ill-worded narration, it should seem that, the prince's buffoon having accidentally

credit another, and indeed a more probable, account, Maximin was invested with the purple by a numerous detachment, at the distance of several miles from the headquarters, and he trusted for success rather to the secret wishes than to the public declarations of the great army. Alexander had sufficient time to awaken a faint sense of loyalty among his troops; but their reluctant professions of fidelity quickly vanished on the appearance of Maximin, who declared himself the friend and advocate of the military order, and was unanimously acknowledged emperor of the Romans by the applauding legions. The son of Mamæa, betrayed and deserted, withdrew into his tent, desirous at least to conceal his approaching fate from the insults of the multitude. He was soon followed by a tribune and some centurions, the ministers of death; but instead of receiving with manly resolution the inevitable stroke, his unavailing cries and entreaties disgraced the last moments of his life, and converted into contempt some portion of the just pity which his innocence and misfortunes must inspire. His mother, Mamæa, whose pride and avarice he loudly accused as the cause of his ruin, perished with her son. The most faithful of his friends were sacrificed to the first fury of the soldiers. Others were reserved for the more deliberate cruelty of the usurper, and those who experienced mildest treatment were stripped of their employments and ignominiously driven from the court and army.[7]

The former tyrants Caligula and Nero, Commodus and

entered the tent, and awakened the slumbering monarch, the fear of punishment urged him to persuade the disaffected soldiers to commit the murder. [The place of the event was doubtless Mainz or its neighbourhood (so the Chronicle of Jerome, based on the Canon of Eusebius), but Lampridius, Hist. Aug. xviii. 59, and Aurelius Victor, Cæsar xxiv. 4, strangely place the assassination at Sicilia in Britain. I do not profess to understand either Britain or Sicilia. Schiller guesses a confusion with *Vicus Britannicus*, Bretzenheim near Mainz.]

[7] Herodian, l. vi. p. 223-227 [8 and 9. The date of Alexander's death is March (18, or 19 according to Borghesi) 235. Maximin was acknowledged by the senate on the 25th. J. Löhrer (de C. Julio Vero Maximino, 1883) has sought to fix the date as Feb. 10.].

Caracalla, were all dissolute and unexperienced youths,[8] educated in the purple, and corrupted by the pride of empire, the luxury of Rome, and the perfidious voice of flattery. The cruelty of Maximin[9] was derived from a different source, the fear of contempt. Though he depended on the attachment of the soldiers, who loved him for virtues like their own, he was conscious that his mean and barbarian origin, his savage appearance, and his total ignorance of the arts and institutions of civil life,[10] formed a very unfavourable contrast with the amiable manners of the unhappy Alexander. He remembered that, in his humbler fortune, he had often waited before the doors of the haughty nobles of Rome, and had been denied admittance by the insolence of their slaves. He recollected too the friendship of a few who had relieved his poverty, and assisted his rising hopes. But those who had spurned, and those who had protected, the Thracian, were guilty of the same crime, the knowledge of his original obscurity. For this crime many were put to death; and by the execution of several of his benefactors Maximin published, in characters of blood, the indelible history of his baseness and ingratitude.[11]

[8] Caligula, the eldest of the four, was only twenty-five years of age when he ascended the throne; Caracalla was twenty-three, Commodus nineteen, and Nero no more than seventeen.

[9] [His imperial name is C. Julius Verus Maximinus.]

[10] It appears that he was totally ignorant of the Greek language; which, from its universal use in conversation and letters, was an essential part of every liberal education. [His Latin was very imperfect.]

[11] Hist. August. p. 141 [xix. 8]. Herodian, l. vii. p. 237 [1]. The latter of these historians has been most unjustly censured for sparing the vices of Maximin. [Gibbon is unfair to Maximin (though afterwards indeed, p. 183, in the name of "the candid severity of history," he partially retracts his harsh judgment). Maximin was a rude soldier, but he was thoroughly well meaning and capable. He was equal to the emergencies of the empire, and able to cope with the dangers on the Rhine and the Danube, with which Alexander had not the strength to deal. Like Septimius Severus, he had no sympathy with the senate, with Italy, or with the populace of Rome. For him the army was the *populus Romanus*. The intense hatred, however, which the senate conceived for him was chiefly due to the somewhat tyrannical rule of his prætorian prefect, Vitalian, who governed at Rome while the em-

The dark and sanguinary soul of the tyrant was open to every suspicion against those among his subjects who were the most distinguished by their birth or merit. Whenever he was alarmed with the sound of treason, his cruelty was unbounded and unrelenting. A conspiracy against his life was either discovered or imagined, and Magnus, a consular senator, was named as the principal author of it. Without a witness, without a trial, and without an opportunity of defence, Magnus, with four thousand of his supposed accomplices, were put to death. Italy and the whole empire were infested with innumerable spies and informers. On the slightest accusation, the first of the Roman nobles, who had governed provinces, commanded armies, and been adorned with the consular and triumphal ornaments, were chained on the public carriages, and hurried away to the emperor's presence. Confiscation, exile, or simple death, were esteemed uncommon instances of his lenity. Some of the unfortunate sufferers he ordered to be sewed up in the hides of slaughtered animals, others to be exposed to wild beasts, others again to be beaten to death with clubs. During the three years of his reign he disdained to visit either Rome or Italy. His camp, occasionally removed from the banks of the Rhine to those of the Danube, was the seat of his stern despotism, which trampled on every principle of law and justice, and was supported by the avowed power of the sword.[13] No man of noble birth, elegant accomplishments, or knowledge of civil business, was suffered near his person; and the court of a Roman emperor revived the idea of those ancient chiefs of slaves and

peror defended the frontiers. Numerous inscriptions testify to Maximin's activity in every province in repairing and extending roads.]

[13] The wife of Maximin, by insinuating wise counsels with female gentleness, sometimes brought back the tyrant to the way of truth and humanity. See Ammianus Marcellinus, xiv. 1 [8], where he alludes to the fact which he had more fully related under the reign of the Gordians. We may collect from the medals, that Paullina was the name of this benevolent empress; and from the title of *Diva*, that she died before Maximin. (Valesius ad loc. cit. Ammian.) Spanheim de U. et P. N. tom. ii. p. 300.

gladiators, whose savage power had left a deep impression of terror and detestation.[13]

As long as the cruelty of Maximin was confined to the illustrious senators, or even to the bold adventurers who in the court or army expose themselves to the caprice of fortune, the body of the people viewed their sufferings with indifference, or perhaps with pleasure. But the tyrant's avarice, stimulated by the insatiate desires of the soldiers, at length attacked the public property.[14] Every city of the empire was possessed of an independent revenue, destined to purchase corn for the multitude, and to supply the expenses of the games and entertainments. By a single act of authority, the whole mass of wealth was at once confiscated for the use of the Imperial treasury. The temples were stripped of their most valuable offerings of gold and silver, and the statues of gods, heroes, and emperors were melted down and coined into money. These impious orders could not be executed without tumults and massacres, as in many places the people chose rather to die in the defence of their altars than to behold in the midst of peace their cities exposed to the rapine and cruelty of war. The soldiers themselves, among whom this sacrilegious plunder was distributed, received it with a blush; and, hardened as they were in acts of violence, they dreaded the just reproaches of their friends and relations. Throughout the Roman world a general cry of indignation was heard, imploring vengeance on the common enemy of human kind; and at length, by an act of private oppression, a peaceful and unarmed province was driven into rebellion against him.[15]

[13] He was compared to Sparticus and Athenio. Hist. August. p. 141 [xix. 9].

[14] [This is put rather unfairly. Money was wanted for the military operations on the frontiers; and one can feel little indignation that the amusements of the populace should have been postponed for the defence of the empire. Gibbon hardly seems to realise that Maximin's warfare was serious, and that his organisation of the frontier defences was of capital importance.]

[15] Herodian, l. vii. p. 238 [3]. Zosimus, l. i. p. 15 [13].

The procurator of Africa was a servant worthy of such a master, who considered the fines and confiscations of the rich as one of the most fruitful branches of the Imperial revenue. An iniquitous sentence had been pronounced against some opulent youths of that country, the execution of which would have stripped them of far the greater part of their patrimony. In this extremity, a resolution that must either complete or prevent their ruin was dictated by despair. A respite of three days, obtained with difficulty from the rapacious treasurer, was employed in collecting from their estates a great number of slaves and peasants blindly devoted to the commands of their lords, and armed with the rustic weapons of clubs and axes. The leaders of the conspiracy, as they were admitted to the audience of the procurator, stabbed him with the daggers concealed under their garments, and, by the assistance of their tumultuary train, seized on the little town of Thysdrus,[16] and erected the standard of rebellion against the sovereign of the Roman empire. They rested their hopes on the hatred of mankind against Maximin, and they judiciously resolved to oppose to that detested tyrant an emperor whose mild virtues had already acquired the love and esteem of the Romans, and whose authority over the province would give weight and stability to the enterprise. Gordianus,[17] their proconsul, and the object of their choice, refused, with unfeigned reluctance, the dangerous honour, and begged with tears that they should suffer him to terminate in peace a long and innocent life, without staining his feeble age with civil blood. Their menaces compelled him to accept the Imperial purple, his only refuge indeed against the jealous cruelty of

[16] In the fertile territory of Byzacium, one hundred and fifty miles to the south of Carthage. This city was decorated, probably by the Gordians, with the title of colony, and with a fine amphitheatre, which is still in a very perfect state. See Itinerar. Wesseling, p. 59, and Shaw's Travels, p. 117. [Thysdrus is now El-Djemm. This revolt took place in spring 238. Eckhel, vii. 293. The chronology of the events of this year is hopelessly perplexing and uncertain. See App. 12.]

[17] [M. Antonius Gordianus.]

Maximin; since, according to the reasoning of tyrants, those who had been esteemed worthy of the throne deserve death, and those who deliberate have already rebelled.[18]

The family of Gordianus was one of the most illustrious of the Roman senate. On the father's side he was descended from the Gracchi; on his mother's, from the emperor Trajan. A great estate enabled him to support the dignity of his birth, and in the enjoyment of it he displayed an elegant taste and beneficent disposition. The palace in Rome formerly inhabited by the great Pompey had been, during several generations, in the possession of Gordian's family.[19] It was distinguished by ancient trophies of naval victories, and decorated with the works of modern painting. His villa on the road to Præneste was celebrated for baths of singular beauty and extent, for three stately rooms of an hundred feet in length, and for a magnificent portico, supported by two hundred columns of the four most curious and costly sorts of marble.[20] The public shows exhibited at his expense, and in which the people were entertained with many hundreds of wild beasts and gladiators,[21] seem to surpass the fortune of a sub-

[18] Herodian, l. vii. p. 239 [4]. Hist. August. p. 153 [xx. 7].

[19] Hist. August. p. 152 [xx. 3]. The celebrated house of Pompey *in carinis* was usurped by Marc Antony, and consequently became, after the Triumvir's death, a part of the Imperial domain. The emperor Trajan allowed and even encouraged the rich senators to purchase those magnificent and useless palaces (Plin. Panegyric. c. 50); and it may seem probable, that on this occasion, Pompey's house came into the possession of Gordian's great-grandfather.

[20] The Claudian, the Numidian, the Carystian, and the Synnadian. The colours of Roman marbles have been faintly described and imperfectly distinguished. It appears, however, that the Carystian was a sea-green, and that the marble of Synnada was white mixed with oval spots of purple [rose-red]. See Salmasius ad Hist. August. p. 164 [xx. 32, 2]. [The Numidian was a yellow crocus.]

[21] Hist. August. p. 151, 152 [xx. 3 and 4]. He sometimes gave five hundred pair of gladiators, never less than one hundred and fifty. He once gave for the use of the Circus one hundred Sicilian, and as many Cappadocian horses. The animals designed for hunting were chiefly bears, boars, bulls, stags, elks, wild asses, &c. Elephants and lions seem to have been appropriated to Imperial magnificence.

ject; and, whilst the liberality of other magistrates was confined to a few solemn festivals in Rome, the magnificence of Gordian was repeated, when he was ædile, every month in the year, and extended, during his consulship, to the principal cities of Italy. He was twice elevated to the last-mentioned dignity, by Caracalla and by Alexander; for he possessed the uncommon talent of acquiring the esteem of virtuous princes, without alarming the jealousy of tyrants. His long life was innocently spent in the study of letters and the peaceful honours of Rome; and, till he was named proconsul of Africa by the voice of the senate and the approbation of Alexander,[28] he appears prudently to have declined the command of armies and the government of provinces. As long as that emperor lived, Africa was happy under the administration of his worthy representative; after the barbarous Maximin had usurped the throne, Gordianus alleviated the miseries which he was unable to prevent. When he reluctantly accepted the purple, he was above fourscore years old; a last and valuable remains of the happy age of the Antonines, whose virtues he revived in his own conduct, and celebrated in an elegant poem of thirty books. With the venerable proconsul, his son, who had accompanied him into Africa as his lieutenant, was likewise declared emperor. His manners were less pure, but his character was equally amiable with that of his father. Twenty-two acknowledged concubines, and a library of sixty-two thousand volumes, attested the variety of his inclinations; and from the productions which he left behind him, it appears that both the one and the other were designed for use rather than for ostentation.[29] The Roman people acknowledged in the features of the younger Gordian

[28] See the original letter, in the Augustan History, p. 152 [xx. 5], which at once shows Alexander's respect for the authority of the senate, and his esteem for the proconsul appointed by that assembly.

[29] By each of his concubines, the younger Gordian left three or four children. His literary productions, though less numerous, were by no means contemptible.

the resemblance of Scipio Africanus, recollected with pleasure that his mother was the grand-daughter of Antoninus Pius, and rested the public hope on those latent virtues which had hitherto, as they fondly imagined, lain concealed in the luxurious indolence of a private life.

As soon as the Gordians had appeased the first tumult of a popular election they removed their court to Carthage. They were received with the acclamations of the Africans, who honoured their virtues, and who, since the visit of Hadrian, had never beheld the majesty of a Roman emperor. But these vain acclamations neither strengthened nor confirmed the title of the Gordians. They were induced by principle, as well as interest, to solicit the approbation of the senate; and a deputation of the noblest provincials was sent, without delay, to Rome, to relate and justify the conduct of their countrymen, who, having long suffered with patience, were at length resolved to act with vigour. The letters of the new princes were modest and respectful, excusing the necessity which had obliged them to accept the Imperial title, but submitting their election and their fate to the supreme judgment of the senate.[34]

The inclinations of the senate were neither doubtful nor divided. The birth and noble alliances of the Gordians had intimately connected them with the most illustrious houses of Rome. Their fortune had created many dependants in that assembly, their merit had acquired many friends. Their mild administration opened the flattering prospect of the restoration, not only of the civil, but even of the republican government. The terror of military violence, which had first obliged the senate to forget the murder of Alexander, and to ratify the election of a barbarian peasant,[35] now produced a contrary effect, and provoked them to assert the injured rights of freedom and humanity. The hatred of Maximin towards the

[34] Herodian, l. vii. p. 243 [6]. Hist. August. p. 144 [xix. 14].

[35] Quod tamen patres, dum periculosum existimant inermes armato resistere, approbaverunt. *Aurelius Victor* [Cæsar. 25].

senate was declared and implacable; the tamest submission had not appeased his fury, the most cautious innocence would not remove his suspicions; and even the care of their own safety urged them to share the fortune of an enterprise, of which (if unsuccessful) they were sure to be the first victims. These considerations, and perhaps others of a more private nature, were debated in a previous conference of the consuls and the magistrates. As soon as their resolution was decided, they convoked in the temple of Castor the whole body of the senate, according to an ancient form of secrecy,[26] calculated to awaken their attention and to conceal their decrees. "Conscript fathers," said the consul Syllanus, "the two Gordians, both of consular dignity, the one your proconsul, and the other your lieutenant, have been declared emperors by the general consent of Africa. Let us return thanks," he boldly continued, "to the youth of Thysdrus; let us return thanks to the faithful people of Carthage, our generous deliverers from a horrid monster. — Why do you hear me thus coolly, thus timidly? Why do you cast these anxious looks on each other? why hesitate? Maximin is a public enemy! may his enmity soon expire with him,[27] and may we long enjoy the prudence and felicity of Gordian the father, the valour and constancy of Gordian the son!"[28] The noble ardour of the consul revived the languid spirit of the senate. By an unanimous decree the election of the Gordians was ratified; Maximin, his son, and his adherents were pronounced enemies of their country, and liberal rewards were offered to whomsoever had the courage and good fortune to destroy them.

During the emperor's absence a detachment of the Præ-

[26] Even the servants of the house, the scribes, &c., were excluded, and their office was filled by the senators themselves. We are obliged to the Augustan History, p. 157 [xx. 12], for preserving this curious example of the old discipline of the commonwealth.

[27] [The true text has a confident future; *di facient ut esse iam desinat*. Gibbon renders it *faciant*, which stood in the edition which he used.]

[28] This spirited speech, translated from the Augustan historian, p. 156 [xx. 11], seems transcribed by him from the original registers of the senate.

torian guards remained at Rome, to protect, or rather to command, the capital. The prefect Vitalianus had signalised his fidelity to Maximin by the alacrity with which he had obeyed, and even prevented, the cruel mandates of the tyrant. His death alone could rescue the authority of the senate, and the lives of the senators, from a state of danger and suspense. Before their resolves had transpired, a quæstor and some tribunes were commissioned to take his devoted life. They executed the order with equal boldness and success; and, with their bloody daggers in their hands, ran through the streets, proclaiming to the people and the soldiers the news of the happy revolution. The enthusiasm of liberty was seconded by the promise of a large donative in lands and money; the statues of Maximin were thrown down; the capital of the empire acknowledged, with transport, the authority of the two Gordians and the senate;[28] and the example of Rome was followed by the rest of Italy.

A new spirit had arisen in that assembly, whose long patience had been insulted by wanton despotism and military licence. The senate assumed the reins of government, and, with a calm intrepidity, prepared to vindicate by arms the cause of freedom. Among the consular senators recommended by their merit and services to the favour of the emperor Alexander, it was easy to select twenty, not unequal to the command of an army and the conduct of a war.[29] To these was the defence of Italy entrusted. Each was appointed to act in his respective department, authorised to enrol and discipline the Italian youth, and instructed to fortify the ports and highways against the impending invasion of Maximin. A number of deputies, chosen from the most illustrious of the senatorian and equestrian orders, were despatched at the same time to the governors of the several provinces, earnestly conjuring them to fly to the assistance of their country, and to

[28] Herodian, l. vii. p. 244 [6].

[29] [Compare Herodian, viii. 5, 5, with Zosimus, i. 14, and Hist. Aug. xxi. 10.]

remind the nations of their ancient ties of friendship with the Roman senate and people. The general respect with which these deputies were received, and the zeal of Italy and the provinces in favour of the senate, sufficiently prove that the subjects of Maximin were reduced to that uncommon distress, in which the body of the people has more to fear from oppression than from resistance. The consciousness of that melancholy truth inspires a degree of persevering fury seldom to be found in those civil wars which are artificially supported for the benefit of a few factious and designing leaders.[81]

For, while the cause of the Gordians was embraced with such diffusive ardour, the Gordians themselves were no more. The feeble court of Carthage was alarmed with the rapid approach of Capelianus, governor of Mauritania,[82] who, with a small band of veterans[83] and a fierce host of barbarians, attacked a faithful but unwarlike province. The younger Gordian sallied out to meet the enemy at the head of a few guards, and a numerous undisciplined multitude, educated in the peaceful luxury of Carthage. His useless valour served only to procure him an honourable death in the field of battle. His aged father, whose reign had not exceeded thirty-six days, put an end to his life on the first news of the defeat. Carthage, destitute of defence, opened her gates to the conqueror, and Africa was exposed to the rapacious cruelty of a slave, obliged to satisfy his unrelenting master with a large account of blood and treasure.[84]

[81] Herodian, l. vii. p. 247 [7], l. viii. p. 277 [6]. Hist. August. p. 156–158 [xx. 13 *sqq.*]. [See Corp. Insc. Lat. iii. 1422, 1423, 1456.]

[82] [Not of Mauritania, but of Numidia. See C. I. L. viii. 2170.]

[83] [The legion iii. Augusta.]

[84] Herodian, l. vii. p. 254 [9]. Hist. August. p. 158–160 [xx. 15 *sqq.*]. We may observe that one month and six days for the reign of Gordian is a just correction of Casaubon and Panvinius, instead of the absurd reading of one year and six months. See Commentar. p. 193. Zosimus relates, l. i. p. 17 [16], that the two Gordians perished by a tempest in the midst of their navigation. A strange ignorance of history, or a strange abuse of metaphors! [The date of the death of the Gordians is now known to be

The fate of the Gordians filled Rome with just, but unexpected, terror. The senate, convoked in the temple of Concord, affected to transact the common business of the day; and seemed to decline, with trembling anxiety, the consideration of their own, and the public, danger. A silent consternation prevailed on the assembly, till a senator, of the name and family of Trajan, awakened his brethren from their fatal lethargy. He represented to them that the choice of cautious dilatory measures had been long since out of their power; that Maximin, implacable by nature and exasperated by injuries, was advancing towards Italy, at the head of the military force of the empire; and that their only remaining alternative was either to meet him bravely in the field, or tamely to expect the tortures and ignominious death reserved for unsuccessful rebellion. "We have lost," continued he, "two excellent princes; but, unless we desert ourselves, the hopes of the republic have not perished with the Gordians. Many are the senators whose virtues have deserved, and whose abilities would sustain, the Imperial dignity. Let us elect two emperors, one of whom may conduct the war against the public enemy, whilst his colleague remains at Rome to direct the civil administration. I cheerfully expose myself to the danger and envy of the nomination, and give my vote in favour of Maximus and Balbinus. Ratify my choice, conscript fathers, or appoint, in their place, others more worthy of the empire." The general apprehension silenced the whispers of jealousy; the merit of the candidates was universally acknowledged; and the house resounded with the sincere acclamations of "Long life and victory to the Emperors Maximus and Balbinus. You are happy in the judg-

238, but the month is uncertain. See Appendix 12. The meeting of the senate is stated to have taken place on the 9th June or July (see next note). It is clear that this meeting followed quickly on the news from Africa; the words of Capitolinus are — *senatus* praetrepidus *in aedem Concordiae concurrit*. Thus the view of Eckhel and Clinton that the Gordians fell in April, or March, 238, implies the rejection of this date.]

ment of the senate; may the republic be happy under your administration!"[85]

The virtues and the reputation of the new emperors justified the most sanguine hopes of the Romans. The various nature of their talents seemed to appropriate to each his peculiar department of peace and war, without leaving room for jealous emulation. Balbinus was an admired orator, a poet of distinguished fame, and a wise magistrate, who had exercised with innocence and applause the civil jurisdiction in almost all the interior provinces of the empire. His birth was noble,[86] his fortune affluent, his manners liberal and affable. In him, the love of pleasure was corrected by a sense of dignity, nor had the habits of ease deprived him of a capacity for business. The mind of Maximus[87] was formed in a rougher mould. By his valour and abilities he had raised himself from the meanest origin to the first employments of the state and army. His victories over the Sarmatians and the Germans, the austerity of his life, and the rigid impartiality of his justice whilst he was prefect of the city, commanded the esteem of a people whose affections were engaged in favour of the more amiable Balbinus. The two colleagues had both been consul (Balbinus had twice enjoyed that honourable

[85] See the Augustan History, p. 166 [xxi. 1], from the registers of the senate; the date is confessedly faulty, but the coincidence of the Apollinarian games enables us to correct it. [Iunias in Hist. Aug. xxi. 1, is supposed to be a mere slip of the pen for Iulias.]

[86] He was descended from Cornelius Balbus, a noble Spaniard, and the adopted son of Theophanes the Greek historian. Balbus obtained the freedom of Rome by the favour of Pompey, and preserved it by the eloquence of Cicero (see Orat. pro Cornel. Balbo). The friendship of Cæsar (to whom he rendered the most important secret services in the civil war) raised him to the consulship and the pontificate, honours never yet possessed by a stranger. The nephew of this Balbus triumphed over the Garamantes. See Dictionnaire de Bayle, au mot *Balbus*, where he distinguishes the several persons of that name, and rectifies, with his usual accuracy, the mistakes of former writers concerning them. [The full name of Balbinus was D. Cælius Calvinus Balbinus.]

[87] [M. Clodius Pupienus Maximus (on coins Pupienus, in African inscriptions Pupienius).]

office), both had been named among the twenty lieutenants of the senate; and, since the one was sixty and the other seventy-four years old,[38] they had both attained the full maturity of age and experience.

After the senate had conferred on Maximus and Balbinus an equal portion of the consular and tribunitian powers, the title of Fathers of their country, and the joint office of Supreme Pontiff, they ascended to the Capitol to return thanks to the gods, protectors of Rome.[39] The solemn rites of sacrifice were disturbed by a sedition of the people. The licentious multitude neither loved the rigid Maximus, nor did they sufficiently fear the mild and humane Balbinus. Their increasing numbers surrounded the temple of Jupiter; with obstinate clamours they asserted their inherent right of consenting to the election of their sovereign: and demanded, with an apparent moderation, that, besides the two emperors chosen by the senate, a third should be added of the family of the Gordians, as a just return of gratitude to those princes who had sacrificed their lives for the republic. At the head of the city guards and the youth of the equestrian order, Maximus and Balbinus attempted to cut their way through the seditious multitude. The multitude, armed with sticks and stones, drove them back into the Capitol. It is prudent to yield, when the contest, whatever may be the issue of it, must be fatal to both parties. A boy, only thirteen years of age, the grandson of the elder and nephew of the younger Gordian, was produced to the people, invested with the ornaments and title of Cæsar.[40] The tumult was appeased by this

[38] Zonaras, l. xii. p. 622 [17]. But little dependence is to be had on the authority of a modern Greek, so grossly ignorant of the history of the third century that he creates several imaginary emperors, and confounds those who really existed.

[39] Herodian, l. vii. p. 256 [10], supposes that the senate was at first convoked in the Capitol, and is very eloquent on the occasion. The Augustan History, p. 166 [xxi. 3], seems much more authentic.

[40] [It is worthy of notice that he was not adopted as son by either of the Augusti, as was usual in such cases.]

easy condescension; and the two emperors, as soon as they had been peaceably acknowledged in Rome, prepared to defend Italy against the common enemy.

Whilst in Rome and Africa revolutions succeeded each other with such amazing rapidity, the mind of Maximin was agitated by the most furious passions. He is said to have received the news of the rebellion of the Gordians, and of the decree of the senate against him, not with the temper of a man, but the rage of a wild beast; which, as it could not discharge itself on the distant senate, threatened the life of his son, of his friends, and of all who ventured to approach his person. The grateful intelligence of the death of the Gordians was quickly followed by the assurance that the senate, laying aside all hopes of pardon or accommodation, had substituted in their room two emperors, with whose merit he could not be unacquainted. Revenge was the only consolation left to Maximin, and revenge could only be obtained by arms. The strength of the legions had been assembled by Alexander from all parts of the empire. Three successful campaigns against the Germans and the Sarmatians[41] had raised their fame, confirmed their discipline, and even increased their numbers, by filling the ranks with the flower of the barbarian youth. The life of Maximin had been spent in war, and the candid severity of history cannot refuse him the valour of a soldier, or even the abilities of an experienced general.[42] It might naturally be expected that a prince of such a character, instead of suffering the rebellion to gain stability by delay, should immediately have marched from the banks of the Danube to those of the Tiber, and that his victorious army,

[41] [On the Rhine against the Germans 235 and 236, on the Danube against Sarmatians and Dacians in 237. Hence the titles *Germanicus*, *Dacicus*, *Sarmaticus*, which his son also bore.]

[42] In Herodian, l. vii. p. 249 [8], and in the Augustan History [xix. 18; xx. 14] we have three several orations of Maximin to his army, on the rebellion of Africa and Rome: M. de Tillemont has very justly observed, that they neither agree with each other, nor with truth. Histoire des Empereurs, tom. iii. p. 799.

instigated by contempt for the senate, and eager to gather the spoils of Italy, should have burned with impatience to finish the easy and lucrative conquest. Yet, as far as we can trust to the obscure chronology of that period,[43] it appears that the operations of some foreign war deferred the Italian expedition till the ensuing spring. From the prudent conduct of Maximin, we may learn that the savage features of his character have been exaggerated by the pencil of party; that his passions, however impetuous, submitted to the force of reason; and that the barbarian possessed something of the generous spirit of Sylla, who subdued the enemies of Rome before he suffered himself to revenge his private injuries.[44]

When the troops of Maximin, advancing[45] in excellent order, arrived at the foot of the Julian Alps, they were terrified by the silence and desolation that reigned on the frontiers of Italy. The villages and open towns had been abandoned, on their approach, by the inhabitants, the cattle was driven away, the provisions removed or destroyed, the bridges broken down, nor was anything left which could afford either shelter or subsistence to an invader. Such had been the wise orders of the generals of the senate, whose design was to protract the war, to ruin the army of Maximin by the

[43] The carelessness of the writers of that age leaves us in a singular perplexity. 1. We know that Maximus and Balbinus were killed during the Capitoline games. Herodian, l. viii. p. 285 [8]. The authority of Censorinus (de Die Natali, c. 18) enables us to fix those games with certainty to the year 238, but leaves us in ignorance of the month or day. 2. The election of Gordian by the senate is fixed, with equal certainty, to the 27th of May; but we are at a loss to discover, whether it was in the same or the preceding year. Tillemont and Muratori, who maintain the two opposite opinions, bring into the field a desultory troop of authorities, conjectures, and probabilities. The one seems to draw out, the other to contract, the series of events, between those periods, more than can be well reconciled to reason and history. Yet it is necessary to choose between them. [See further Appendix 12.]

[44] Velleius Paterculus, l. ii. c. 24. The president de Montesquieu (in his dialogue between Sylla and Eucrates) expresses the sentiments of the dictator in a spirited and even sublime manner.

[45] [From Sirmium.]

slow operation of famine, and to consume his strength in the sieges of the principal cities of Italy, which they had plentifully stored with men and provisions from the deserted country. Aquileia received and withstood the first shock of the invasion. The streams that issue from the head of the Hadriatic gulf, swelled by the melting of the winter snows,[48] opposed an unexpected obstacle to the arms of Maximin. At length, on a singular bridge, constructed, with art and difficulty, of large hogsheads, he transported his army to the opposite bank, rooted up the beautiful vineyards in the neighbourhood of Aquileia, demolished the suburbs, and employed the timber of the buildings in the engines and towers with which on every side he attacked the city. The walls, fallen to decay during the security of a long peace, had been hastily repaired on this sudden emergency; but the firmest defence of Aquileia consisted in the constancy of the citizens; all ranks of whom, instead of being dismayed, were animated by the extreme danger, and their knowledge of the tyrant's unrelenting temper. Their courage was supported and directed by Crispinus and Menophilus, two of the twenty lieutenants of the senate, who, with a small body of regular troops, had thrown themselves into the besieged place. The army of Maximin was repulsed in repeated attacks, his machines destroyed by showers of artificial fire; and the generous enthusiasm of the Aquileians was exalted into a confidence of success, by the opinion that Belenus, their

[48] Muratori (Annali d'Italia, tom. ii. p. 294) thinks the melting of the snows suits better with the months of June or July, than with that of February. The opinion of a man who passed his life between the Alps and the Apennines is undoubtedly of great weight; yet I observe, 1. That the long winter, of which Muratori takes advantage, is to be found only in the Latin version, and not in the Greek text, of Herodian. 2. That the vicissitude of suns and rains, to which the soldiers of Maximin were exposed (Herodian, l. viii. p. 277 [5]), denotes the spring rather than the summer. We may observe likewise, that these several streams, as they melted into one, composed the Timavus, so poetically (in every sense of the word) described by Virgil. They are about twelve miles to the east of Aquileia. See Cluver. Italia Antiqua, tom. i. p. 189, &c.

tutelar deity, combated in person in the defence of his distressed worshippers.[47]

The emperor Maximus, who had advanced as far as Ravenna, to secure that important place and to hasten the military preparations, beheld the event of the war in the more faithful mirror of reason and policy. He was too sensible that a single town could not resist the persevering efforts of a great army; and he dreaded lest the enemy, tired with the obstinate resistance of Aquileia, should on a sudden relinquish the fruitless siege and march directly towards Rome. The fate of the empire and the cause of freedom must then be committed to the chance of a battle; and what arms could he oppose to the veteran legions of the Rhine and Danube? Some troops newly levied among the generous but enervated youth of Italy, and a body of German auxiliaries, on whose firmness, in the hour of trial, it was dangerous to depend. In the midst of these just alarms, the stroke of domestic conspiracy punished the crimes of Maximin and delivered Rome and the senate from the calamities that would surely have attended the victory of an enraged barbarian.

The people of Aquileia had scarcely experienced any of the common miseries of a siege; their magazines were plentifully supplied, and several fountains within the walls assured them of an inexhaustible resource of fresh water. The soldiers of Maximin were, on the contrary, exposed to the inclemency of the season, the contagion of disease, and the horrors of famine. The naked country was ruined, the rivers filled with the slain and polluted with blood. A spirit of despair and disaffection began to diffuse itself among the troops; and, as they were cut off from all intelligence, they easily believed that the whole empire had embraced the

[47] Herodian, l. viii. p. 272 [3]. The Celtic deity was supposed to be Apollo, and received under that name the thanks of the senate. A temple was likewise built to Venus the Bald, in honour of the women of Aquileia, who had given up their hair to make ropes for the military engines.

cause of the senate, and that they were left as devoted victims to perish under the impregnable walls of Aquileia. The fierce temper of the tyrant was exasperated by disappointments, which he imputed to the cowardice of his army; and his wanton and ill-timed cruelty, instead of striking terror, inspired hatred and a just desire of revenge. A party of Prætorian guards, who trembled for their wives and children in the camp of Alba, near Rome, executed the sentence of the senate. Maximin, abandoned by his guards, was slain in his tent, with his son (whom he had associated to the honours of the purple), Anulinus the prefect, and the principal ministers of his tyranny.[48] The sight of their heads, borne on the point of spears, convinced the citizens of Aquileia that the siege was at an end; the gates of the city were thrown open, a liberal market was provided for the hungry troops of Maximin, and the whole army joined in solemn protestations of fidelity to the senate and people of Rome, and to their lawful emperors Maximus and Balbinus. Such was the deserved fate of a brutal savage, destitute, as he has generally been represented, of every sentiment that distinguishes a civilised, or even a human, being. The body was suited to the soul. The stature of Maximin exceeded the measure of eight feet, and circumstances almost incredible are related of his matchless strength and appetite.[49] Had he lived in a less enlightened age, tradition and poetry might well have described him as one

[48] Herodian, l. viii. p. 279 [5]. Hist. August. p. 146 [xix. 23]. The duration of Maximin's reign has not been defined with much accuracy, except by Eutropius, who allows him three years and a few days (l. ix. 1); we may depend on the integrity of the text, as the Latin original is checked by the Greek version of Pænius (see Appendix 1).

[49] Eight Roman feet and one third, which are equal to above eight English feet, as the two measures are to each other in the proportion of 967 to 1000. See Graves's discourse on the Roman foot. We are told that Maximin could drink in a day an amphora (or about seven gallons) of wine and eat thirty or forty pounds of meat. He could move a loaded waggon, break a horse's leg with his fist, crumble stones in his hand, and tear up small trees by the roots. See his Life in the Augustan History.

of those monstrous giants, whose supernatural power was constantly exerted for the destruction of mankind.

It is easier to conceive than to describe the universal joy of the Roman world on the fall of the tyrant, the news of which is said to have been carried in four days from Aquileia to Rome. The return of Maximus was a triumphal procession; his colleague and young Gordian went out to meet him, and the three princes made their entry into the capital, attended by the ambassadors of almost all the cities of Italy, saluted with the splendid offerings of gratitude and superstition, and received with the unfeigned acclamations of the senate and people, who persuaded themselves that a golden age would succeed to an age of iron.[80] The conduct of the two emperors corresponded with these expectations. They administered justice in person; and the rigour of the one was tempered by the other's clemency. The oppressive taxes with which Maximin had loaded the rights of inheritance and succession were repealed, or at least moderated. Discipline was revived, and with the advice of the senate many wise laws were enacted by their Imperial ministers, who endeavoured to restore a civil constitution on the ruins of military tyranny. "What reward may we expect for delivering Rome from a monster?" was the question asked by Maximus, in a moment of freedom and confidence. Balbinus answered it without hesitation, "The love of the senate, of the people, and of all mankind." "Alas!" replied his more penetrating colleague, "Alas! I dread the hatred of the soldiers, and the fatal effects of their resentment."[81] His apprehensions were but too well justified by the event.

Whilst Maximus was preparing to defend Italy against the common foe, Balbinus, who remained at Rome, had been engaged in scenes of blood and intestine discord. Distrust

[80] See the congratulatory letter of Claudius Julianus the consul, to the two emperors, in the Augustan History [xxi. 17].

[81] Hist. August. p. 171 [xxi. 15].

and jealousy reigned in the senate; and even in the temples where they assembled every senator carried either open or concealed arms. In the midst of their deliberations, two veterans of the guards, actuated either by curiosity or a sinister motive, audaciously thrust themselves into the house, and advanced by degrees beyond the altar of Victory. Gallicanus, a consular, and Mæcenas, a prætorian senator, viewed with indignation their insolent intrusion: drawing their daggers, they laid the spies, for such they deemed them, dead at the foot of the altar, and then, advancing to the door of the senate, imprudently exhorted the multitude to massacre the Prætorians as the secret adherents of the tyrant. Those who escaped the first fury of the tumult took refuge in the camp, which they defended with superior advantage against the reiterated attacks of the people, assisted by the numerous bands of gladiators, the property of opulent nobles. The civil war lasted many days, with infinite loss and confusion on both sides. When the pipes were broken that supplied the camp with water, the Prætorians were reduced to intolerable distress; but, in their turn, they made desperate sallies into the city, set fire to a great number of houses, and filled the streets with the blood of the inhabitants. The emperor Balbinus attempted, by ineffectual edicts and precarious truces, to reconcile the factions of Rome. But their animosity, though smothered for a while, burnt with redoubled violence. The soldiers, detesting the senate and the people, despised the weakness of a prince who wanted either the spirit or the power to command the obedience of his subjects.[80]

After the tyrant's death his formidable army had acknowledged, from necessity rather than from choice, the authority of Maximus, who transported himself without delay to the camp before Aquileia. As soon as he had received their oath of fidelity he addressed them in terms full of mildness

[80] Herodian, l. viii. p. 258 [12].

and moderation; lamented rather than arraigned the wild disorders of the times, and assured the soldiers that, of all their past conduct, the senate would remember only their generous desertion of the tyrant and their voluntary return to their duty. Maximus enforced his exhortations by a liberal donative, purified the camp by a solemn sacrifice of expiation, and then dismissed the legions to their several provinces, impressed, as he hoped, with a lively sense of gratitude and obedience.[83] But nothing could reconcile the haughty spirit of the Prætorians. They attended the emperors on the memorable day of their public entry into Rome; but, amidst the general acclamations, the sullen dejected countenance of the guards sufficiently declared that they considered themselves as the object, rather than the partners, of the triumph. When the whole body was united in their camp, those who had served under Maximin, and those who had remained at Rome, insensibly communicated to each other their complaints and apprehensions. The emperors chosen by the army had perished with ignominy; those elected by the senate were seated on the throne.[84] The long discord between the civil and military powers was decided by a war in which the former had obtained a complete victory. The soldiers must now learn a new doctrine of submission to the senate; and, whatever clemency was affected by that politic assembly, they dreaded a slow revenge, coloured by the name of discipline, and justified by fair pretences of the public good. But their fate was still in their own hands; and, if they had courage to despise the vain terrors of an impotent republic, it was easy to convince the world that those who were masters of the arms were masters of the authority of the state.

When the senate elected two princes, it is probable that,

[83] Herodian, l. viii. p. 213 [7].

[84] The observation had been made imprudently enough in the acclamations of the senate, and with regard to the soldiers it carried the appearance of a wanton insult. Hist. August. p. 170 [xxi. 12].

besides the declared reason of providing for the various emergencies of peace and war, they were actuated by the secret desire of weakening by division the despotism of the supreme magistrate. Their policy was effectual, but it proved fatal both to their emperors and to themselves. The jealousy of power was soon exasperated by the difference of character. Maximus despised Balbinus as a luxurious noble, and was in his turn disdained by his colleague as an obscure soldier. Their silent discord was understood rather than seen;[88] but the mutual consciousness prevented them from uniting in any vigorous measures of defence against their common enemies of the Prætorian camp. The whole city was employed in the Capitoline games, and the emperors were left almost alone in the palace. On a sudden they were alarmed by the approach of a troop of desperate assassins. Ignorant of each other's situation or designs, for they already occupied very distant apartments, afraid to give or to receive assistance, they wasted the important moments in idle debates and fruitless recriminations. The arrival of the guards put an end to the vain strife. They seized on these emperors of the senate, for such they called them with malicious contempt, stripped them of their garments, and dragged them in insolent triumph through the streets of Rome, with a design of inflicting a slow and cruel death on these unfortunate princes. The fear of a rescue from the faithful Germans of the Imperial guards shortened their tortures; and their bodies, mangled with a thousand wounds, were left exposed to the insults or to the pity of the populace.[89]

In the space of a few months six princes had been cut off

[88] Discordiæ tacitæ et quæ intelligerentur potius quam viderentur. Hist. August. p. 170 [xxi. 14]. This well-chosen expression is probably stolen from some better writer. [On the coins, however, we see *amor mutuus*, *concordia Augg.*, &c. It was arranged that Balbinus should undertake the war on the Danube, Pupienus that on the Euphrates.]

[89] Herodian, l. viii. p. 287, 288 [8]. [The date is probably August; see Appendix 12. Gibbon accepted 15th July.]

by the sword. Gordian, who had already received the title of Cæsar, was the only person that occurred to the soldiers as proper to fill the vacant throne.[57] They carried him to the camp and unanimously saluted him Augustus and Emperor.[58] His name was dear to the senate and people; his tender age promised a long impunity of military licence; and the submission of Rome and the provinces to the choice of the Prætorian guards saved the republic, at the expense indeed of its freedom and dignity, from the horrors of a new civil war in the heart of the capital.[59]

As the third Gordian was only nineteen years of age at the time of his death, the history of his life, were it known to us with greater accuracy than it really is, would contain little more than the account of his education and the conduct of the ministers who by turns abused or guided the simplicity of his inexperienced youth. Immediately after his accession he fell into the hands of his mother's eunuchs, that pernicious vermin of the East, who, since the days of Elagabalus, had infested the Roman palace. By the artful conspiracy of these wretches an impenetrable veil was drawn between an innocent prince and his oppressed subjects, the virtuous disposition of Gordian was deceived, and the honours of the empire sold without his knowledge, though in a very public manner, to the most worthless of mankind. We are ignorant by what fortunate accident the emperor escaped from this igno-

[57] Quia non alius erat in præsenti, is the expression of the Augustan History [xxi. 14].

[58] [Before 29th August, as is proved by Alexandrine coins.]

[59] Quintus Curtius (l. x. c. 9) pays an elegant compliment to the emperor of the day, for having, by his happy accession, extinguished so many fire-brands, sheathed so many swords, and put an end to the evils of a divided government. After weighing with attention every word of the passage, I am of opinion that it suits better with the elevation of Gordian than with any other period of the Roman History. In that case, it may serve to decide the age of Quintus Curtius. Those who place him under the first Cæsars argue from the purity of his style, but are embarrassed by the silence of Quintilian in his accurate list of Roman historians. [It is now generally agreed to place Curtius in the reign of Nero; but of his life we know nothing.]

minious slavery, and devolved his confidence on a minister whose wise counsels had no object except the glory of the sovereign and the happiness of the people. It should seem that love and learning introduced Misitheus [60] to the favour of Gordian. The young prince married the daughter of his master of rhetoric, and promoted his father-in-law to the first offices of the empire. Two admirable letters that passed between them are still extant. The minister, with the conscious dignity of virtue, congratulates Gordian that he is delivered from the tyranny of the eunuchs,[61] and still more, that he is sensible of his deliverance. The emperor acknowledges, with an amiable confusion, the errors of his past conduct; and laments, with singular propriety, the misfortune of a monarch from whom a venal tribe of courtiers perpetually labour to conceal the truth.[62]

The life of Misitheus had been spent in the profession of letters, not of arms; yet such was the versatile genius of that great man that, when he was appointed Prætorian prefect, he discharged the military duties of his place with vigour and ability. The Persians had invaded Mesopotamia, and threatened Antioch. By the persuasion of his father-in-law, the young emperor quitted the luxury of Rome, opened, for the last time recorded in history, the temple of Janus, and marched in person into the East.[63] On his approach

[60] [The true name of this minister was C. Furius Sabinius Aquila Timesitheus. His name occurs on inscriptions. Gibbon calls him Misitheus after the Augustan History. The marriage of Gordian with his daughter, Tranquillina, is placed too early by Gibbon (240 A.D.). Alexandrine coins prove that it took place in the fourth tribunate of the emperor, between 30th August 241 and 29th August 242.]

[61] Hist. August. p. 161 [xx. 24 and 25]. From some hints in the two letters, I should expect that the eunuchs were not expelled the palace without some degree of gentle violence, and that young Gordian rather approved of, than consented to, their disgrace.

[62] Duxit uxorem filiam Misithei, quem causâ eloquentiæ dignum parentelâ suâ putavit; et præfectum statim fecit; post quod non puerile jam et contemptibile videbatur imperium [ib. 23].

[63] [The army of Gordian halted on its way and cleared Thrace of bar-

with a great army, the Persians withdrew their garrisons from the cities which they had already taken, and retired from the Euphrates to the Tigris.[64] Gordian enjoyed the pleasure of announcing to the senate the first success of his arms, which he ascribed with a becoming modesty and gratitude to the wisdom of his father and prefect. During the whole expedition, Misitheus watched over the safety and discipline of the army; whilst he prevented their dangerous murmurs by maintaining a regular plenty in the camp, and by establishing ample magazines of vinegar, bacon, straw, barley, and wheat, in all the cities of the frontier.[65] But the prosperity of Gordian expired with Misitheus, who died of a flux, not without very strong suspicions of poison. Philip, his successor in the prefecture, was an Arab by birth, and consequently, in the earlier part of his life, a robber by profession. His rise from so obscure a station to the first dignities of the empire seems to prove that he was a bold and able leader. But his boldness prompted him to aspire to the throne, and his abilities were employed to supplant, not to serve, his indulgent master. The minds of the soldiers were irritated by an artificial scarcity, created by his contrivance in the camp; and the distress of the army was attributed to the youth and incapacity of the prince. It is not in our power to trace the successive steps of the secret conspiracy and open sedition which were at length fatal to Gordian. A sepulchral monument was erected to

barian invaders, Alans, Goths, and Sarmatians. It has been conjectured that on this occasion Viminacium was made a colonia.]

[64] [The successes were due to the abilities of Timesitheus. Carrhae and Nisibis, which, along with Hatra, had been taken by Sapor in his invasion of 241 A.D., were recovered, and the Roman army, having defeated the Persians at Resaina, prepared to march on Ctesiphon.]

[65] Hist. August. p. 162 [xx. 27]. Aurelius Victor [Caesar. 27]. Porphyrius in Vit. Plotin. ap. Fabricium Biblioth. Graec. l. iv. c. 36 [c. 3, p. 103, ed. Westermann and Boissonade]. The philosopher Plotinus accompanied the army, prompted by the love of knowledge, and by the hope of penetrating as far as India.

his memory on the spot [66] where he was killed, near the conflux of the Euphrates with the little river Aboras.[67] The fortunate Philip, raised to the empire by the votes of the soldiers, found a ready obedience from the senate and the provinces.[68]

We cannot forbear transcribing the ingenious, though somewhat fanciful, description, which a celebrated writer of our own times has traced of the military government of the Roman empire. "What in that age was called the Roman empire was only an irregular republic, not unlike the aristocracy [69] of Algiers,[70] where the militia, possessed of the sovereignty, creates and deposes a magistrate, who is styled a Dey. Perhaps, indeed, it may be laid down as a general rule, that a military government is, in some respects, more republican than monarchical. Nor can it be said that the soldiers only partook of the government by their disobedience and rebellions. The speeches made to them by the emperors, were they not at length of the same nature as those formerly pronounced to the people by the consuls and the tribunes? And although the armies had no regular

[66] About twenty miles from the little town of Circesium, on the frontier of the two empires. [Eutropius, ix. 2, 3.]

[67] The inscription (which contained a very singular pun) was erased by the order of Licinius, who claimed some degree of relationship to Philip (Hist. August. p. 165 [xx. 34]); but the *tumulus* or mound of earth which formed the sepulchre, still subsisted in the time of Julian. See Ammian. Marcellin. xxiii. 5. [The pun to which Gibbon refers was on the name of Philip. Gordian is described as the conqueror of various peoples. "Victori Persarum, victori, &c. — sed non victori Philipporum." It seems that Gordian had suffered a reverse in some skirmish with the Alans near Philippi.]

[68] Aurelius Victor. Eutrop. ix. 2. Orosius, vii. 20. Ammianus Marcellinus, xxiii. 5. Zosimus, l. i. p. 19 [19]. Philip, who was a native of Bostra, was about forty years of age. [His name was M. Julius Philippus.]

[69] Can the epithet of *Aristocracy* be applied, with any propriety, to the government of Algiers? Every military government floats between the extremes of absolute monarchy and wild democracy.

[70] The military republic of the Mamelukes in Egypt would have afforded M. de Montesquieu (see Considérations sur la Grandeur et la Décadence des Romains, c. 16) a juster and more noble parallel.

place or forms of assembly, though their debates were short, their action sudden, and their resolves seldom the result of cool reflection, did they not dispose, with absolute sway, of the public fortune? What was the emperor, except the minister of a violent government, elected for the private benefit of the soldiers?

"When the army had elected Philip, who was Prætorian prefect to the third Gordian, the latter demanded that he might remain sole emperor; he was unable to obtain it. He requested that the power might be equally divided between them; the army would not listen to his speech. He consented to be degraded to the rank of Cæsar; the favour was refused him. He desired, at least, he might be appointed Prætorian prefect; his prayer was rejected. Finally, he pleaded for his life. The army, in these several judgments, exercised the supreme magistracy." According to the historian, whose doubtful narrative the president De Montesquieu has adopted, Philip, who, during the whole transaction, had preserved a sullen silence, was inclined to spare the innocent life of his benefactor; till, recollecting that his innocence might excite a dangerous compassion in the Roman world, he commanded, without regard to his suppliant cries, that he should be seized, stript, and led away to instant death. After a moment's pause the inhuman sentence was executed.[71]

On his return from the East to Rome, Philip, desirous of obliterating the memory of his crimes, and of captivating the affections of the people, solemnised the secular games with infinite pomp and magnificence. Since their institution

[71] The Augustan History (p. 163, 164 [xx. 30]) cannot, in this instance, be reconciled with itself or with probability. How could Philip condemn his predecessor, and yet consecrate his memory? How could he order his public execution, and yet, in his letters to the senate, exculpate himself from the guilt of his death? Philip, though an ambitious usurper, was by no means a mad tyrant. Some chronological difficulties have likewise been discovered by the nice eyes of Tillemont and Muratori, in this supposed association of Philip to the empire.

or revival by Augustus,[72] they had been celebrated by Claudius, by Domitian, and by Severus, and were now renewed, the fifth time, on the accomplishment of the full period of a thousand years from the foundation of Rome. Every circumstance of the secular games was skilfully adapted to inspire the superstitious mind with deep and solemn reverence. The long interval between them [73] exceeded the term of human life; and, as none of the spectators had already seen them, none could flatter themselves with the expectation of beholding them a second time. The mystic sacrifices were performed, during three nights, on the banks of the Tiber; and the Campus Martius resounded with music and dances, and was illuminated with innumerable lamps and torches. Slaves and strangers were excluded from any participation in these national ceremonies. A chorus of twenty-seven youths, and as many virgins, of noble families, and whose parents were both alive, implored the propitious gods in favour of the present, and for the hope of the rising generation; requesting, in religious hymns, that, according to the faith of their ancient oracles, they would still maintain the virtue, the felicity, and the empire of the Roman people.[74] The magnificence of Philip's shows and entertainments

[72] The account of the last supposed celebration, though in an enlightened period of history, was so very doubtful and obscure, that the alternative seems not doubtful. When the popish jubilees, the copy of the secular games, were invented by Boniface VIII., the crafty pope pretended that he only revived an ancient institution. See M. le Chais, Lettres sur les Jubilés. [The celebrations of the secular games under Augustus in B.C. 17, and under Severus in A.D. 204, are fully discussed by Mommsen in the Ephemeris Epigraphica, viii. p. 225 *sqq.*, 1899 (Commentaria ludreum saecularium quintorum et septimorum), on the basis of large fragments of the Acta of both these festivals, discovered in excavations in 1890.]

[73] Either of a hundred, or a hundred and ten years. Varro and Livy adopted the former opinion, but the infallible authority of the Sybil consecrated the latter (Censorinus de Die Natal. c. 17). The emperors Claudius and Philip, however, did not treat the oracle with implicit respect.

[74] The idea of the secular games is best understood from the poem of Horace, and the description of Zosimus, l. ii. p. 167 [5], &c. [Milliarium Saeculum is on the coins.]

dazzled the eyes of the multitude. The devout were employed in the rites of superstition, whilst the reflecting few revolved in their anxious minds the past history and the future fate of the empire.

Since Romulus, with a small band of shepherds and outlaws, fortified himself on the hills near the Tiber, ten centuries had already elapsed.[78] During the four first ages, the Romans, in the laborious school of poverty, had acquired the virtues of war and government: by the vigorous exertion of those virtues, and by the assistance of fortune, they had obtained, in the course of the three succeeding centuries, an absolute empire over many countries of Europe, Asia, and Africa. The last three hundred years had been consumed in apparent prosperity and internal decline. The nation of soldiers, magistrates, and legislators, who composed the thirty-five tribes of the Roman people, was dissolved into the common mass of mankind, and confounded with the millions of servile provincials, who had received the name, without adopting the spirit, of Romans. A mercenary army, levied among the subjects and barbarians of the frontier, was the only order of men who preserved and abused their independence. By their tumultuary election, a Syrian, a Goth, or an Arab, was exalted to the throne of Rome, and invested with despotic power over the conquests and over the country of the Scipios.

The limits of the Roman empire still extended from the Western Ocean to the Tigris, and from Mount Atlas to the Rhine and the Danube. To the undiscerning eye of the vulgar, Philip appeared a monarch no less powerful than Hadrian or Augustus had formerly been. The form was still the same, but the animating health and vigour were fled. The industry of the people was discouraged and exhausted

[78] The received calculation of Varro assigns to the foundation of Rome an era that corresponds with the 754th year before Christ. But so little is the chronology of Rome to be depended on in the more early ages, that Sir Isaac Newton has brought the same event as low as the year 627.

by a long series of oppression. The discipline of the legions, which alone, after the extinction of every other virtue, had propped the greatness of the state, was corrupted by the ambition, or relaxed by the weakness, of the emperors. The strength of the frontiers, which had always consisted in arms rather than in fortifications, was insensibly undermined; and the fairest provinces were left exposed to the rapaciousness or ambition of the barbarians, who soon discovered the decline of the Roman empire.

CHAPTER VIII

Of the State of Persia after the Restoration of the Monarchy by Artaxerxes[1]

WHENEVER Tacitus indulges himself in those beautiful episodes, in which he relates some domestic transaction of the Germans or of the Parthians, his principal object is to relieve the attention of the reader from a uniform scene of vice and misery. From the reign of Augustus to the time of Alexander Severus, the enemies of Rome were in her bosom — the tyrants, and the soldiers; and her prosperity had a very distant and feeble interest in the revolutions that might happen beyond the Rhine and the Euphrates. But, when the military order had levelled in wild anarchy the power of the prince, the laws of the senate, and even the discipline of the camp, the barbarians of the North and of the East, who had long hovered on the frontier, boldly attacked the provinces of a declining monarchy. Their vexatious inroads were changed into formidable irruptions, and, after a long vicissitude of mutual calamities, many tribes of the victorious invaders established themselves in the provinces of the Roman empire. To obtain a clearer knowledge of these great events we shall endeavour to form a previous idea of the character, forces, and designs of those nations who avenged the cause of Hannibal and Mithridates.

In the more early ages of the world, whilst the forest that covered Europe afforded a retreat to a few wandering savages, the inhabitants of Asia were already collected into populous cities, and reduced under extensive empires, the seat of the

[1] [On the sources for Eastern affairs see Appendix 13; on the Zendavesta and Persian religion, Appendix 14.]

arts, of luxury and of despotism. The Assyrians reigned over the East,[2] till the sceptre of Ninus and Semiramis dropt from the hands of their enervated successors. The Medes and the Babylonians divided their power, and were themselves swallowed up in the monarchy of the Persians, whose arms could not be confined within the narrow limits of Asia. Followed, as it is said, by two millions of *men*, Xerxes, the descendant of Cyrus, invaded Greece. Thirty thousand *soldiers*, under the command of Alexander, the son of Philip, who was entrusted by the Greeks with their glory and revenge, were sufficient to subdue Persia. The princes of the house of Seleucus usurped and lost the Macedonian command over the East. About the same time that, by an ignominious treaty, they resigned to the Romans the country on this side Mount Taurus, they were driven by the Parthians, an obscure horde of Scythian origin, from all the provinces of Upper Asia. The formidable power of the Parthians, which spread from India to the frontiers of Syria, was in its turn subverted by Ardshir,[3] or Artaxerxes; the founder of a new dynasty, which, under the name of Sassanides, governed Persia till the invasion of the Arabs. This great revolution, whose fatal influence was soon experienced by the Romans, happened in the fourth year of Alexander Severus, two hundred and twenty-six years after the Christian era.[4]

[2] An ancient chronologist quoted by Velleius Paterculus (l. i. c. 6) observes that the Assyrians, the Medes, the Persians, and the Macedonians, reigned over Asia one thousand nine hundred and ninety-five years, from the accession of Ninus to the defeat of Antiochus by the Romans. As the latter of these great events happened 189 years before Christ, the former may be placed 2184 years before the same era. The Astronomical Observations, found at Babylon by Alexander, went fifty years higher. [Babylonian history begins in the fourth chiliad B.C.; Assyrian barely in the 14th century. The second and greater Assyrian empire was founded by Assur-nâsir-pal and Salmanassar II., his son, in the ninth century.]

[3] [Ardeshîr is the approved transliteration.]

[4] In the five hundred and thirty-eighth year of the era of Seleucus. See Agathias, l. ii. p. 63 [27]. This great event (such is the carelessness of the

Artaxerxes had served with great reputation in the armies of Artaban, the last king of the Parthians, and it appears that he was driven into exile and rebellion by royal ingratitude, the customary reward for superior merit. His birth was obscure, and the obscurity equally gave room to the aspersions of his enemies, and the flattery of his adherents. If we credit the scandal of the former, Artaxerxes sprang from the illegitimate commerce of a tanner's wife with a common soldier.[5] The latter represents him as descended from a branch of the ancient kings of Persia, though time and misfortune had gradually reduced his ancestors to the humble station of private citizens.[6] As the lineal heir of the monarchy, he asserted his right to the throne, and challenged the noble task of delivering the Persians from the oppression under which they groaned above five centuries since the death of Darius. The Parthians were defeated in three great battles. In the last of these their king Artaban was slain, and the spirit of the nation was for ever broken.[7] The authority of Artaxerxes was solemnly acknowledged in a great assembly held at Balch in Khorasan. Two younger branches of the royal house of Arsaces were confounded among the prostrate satraps. A third, more mindful of ancient grandeur than of present necessity, attempted to retire with a numerous train of vassals, towards their kinsman, the king of Armenia;

Orientals) is placed by Eutychius as high as the tenth year of Commodus, and by Moses of Chorene as low as the reign of Philip. Ammianus Marcellinus has so servilely copied (xxiii. 6) his ancient materials, which are indeed very good, that he describes the family of the Arsacides as still seated on the Persian throne in the middle of the fourth century.

[5] The tanner's name was Babec; the soldier's, Sassan; from the former Artaxerxes obtained the surname of Babegan; from the latter all his descendants have been styled *Sassanides*. [Ardeshîr IV. was the son of Bâbag, the eleventh prince of Pars or Persis. Bâbagân means "son of Bâbag."]

[6] D'Herbelot, Bibliothèque Orientale, *Ardshir*.

[7] Dion Cassius, l. lxxx. [3]. Herodian, l. vi. p. 207 [2]. Abulpharagius Dynast. p. 80. [The battle was fought at Hormuz, between Behbehan and Schuschter. The approved spelling of Artaban is Ardevân. He was the fifth Parthian king of that name.]

but this little army of deserters was intercepted and cut off by the vigilance of the conqueror,[8] who boldly assumed the double diadem, and the title of King of Kings, which had been enjoyed by his predecessor.[9] But these pompous titles, instead of gratifying the vanity of the Persian, served only to admonish him of his duty, and to inflame in his soul the ambition of restoring, in their full splendour, the religion and empire of Cyrus.

I. During the long servitude of Persia under the Macedonian and the Parthian yoke, the nations of Europe and Asia had mutually adopted and corrupted each other's superstitions. The Arsacides, indeed, practised the worship of the Magi; but they disgraced and polluted it with a various mixture of foreign idolatry. The memory of Zoroaster, the ancient prophet and philosopher of the Persians,[10] was still revered in the East; but the obsolete and mysterious language in which the Zendavesta was composed,[11] opened a field of dispute to seventy sects, who variously explained

[8] See Moses Chorenensis, l. ii. c. 65-71.

[9] [Ardeshîr IV. of the small kingdom of Persis became, when he overthrew the Parthian monarchy, Ardeshîr I. of the great kingdom of Persia. His title was "King of Kings of Eran and Turan." The Parthians were not completely quelled, though they had lost their king, till 232 A.D.]

[10] Hyde and Prideaux, working up the Persian legends and their own conjectures into a very agreeable story, represent Zoroaster as a contemporary of Darius Hystaspis. But it is sufficient to observe that the Greek writers, who lived almost in the same age, agree in placing the era of Zoroaster many hundred, or even thousand, years before their own time. The judicious criticism of Mr. Moyle perceived, and maintained against his uncle Dr. Prideaux, the antiquity of the Persian prophet. See his work, vol. ii. [Of Zarathustra or Zoroaster himself we know nothing. All the stories about him are mere fables; and it cannot be determined whether he was a god made into a man, or a man who really lived.]

[11] That ancient idiom was called the *Zend*. The language of the commentary, the Pehlvi, though much more modern, has ceased many ages ago to be a living tongue. [It was spoken in the western regions of Iran, Zend in the eastern.] This fact alone (if it is allowed as authentic) sufficiently warrants the antiquity of those writings, which M. d'Anquetil has brought into Europe, and translated into French. [On the Zendavesta see Appendix 14.]

the fundamental doctrines of their religion, and were all equally derided by a crowd of infidels, who rejected the divine mission and miracles of the prophet. To suppress the idolaters, re-unite the schismatics, and confute the unbelievers by the infallible decision of a general council, the pious Artaxerxes summoned the Magi from all parts of his dominions. These priests, who had so long sighed in contempt and obscurity, obeyed the welcome summons; and on the appointed day appeared to the number of about eighty thousand. But as the debates of so tumultuous an assembly could not have been directed by the authority of reason, or influenced by the art of policy, the Persian synod was reduced, by successive operations, to forty thousand, to four thousand, to four hundred, to forty, and at last to seven Magi, the most respected for their learning and piety. One of these, Erdaviraph, a young but holy prelate, received from the hands of his brethren three cups of soporiferous wine. He drank them off, and instantly fell into a long and profound sleep. As soon as he waked, he related to the king and to the believing multitude his journey to Heaven, and his intimate conferences with the Deity. Every doubt was silenced by this supernatural evidence; and the articles of the faith of Zoroaster were fixed with equal authority and precision.[12] A short delineation of that celebrated system will be found useful, not only to display the character of the Persian nation, but to illustrate many of their most important transactions, both in peace and war, with the Roman empire.[13]

The great and fundamental article of the system was the

[12] Hyde de Religione veterum Pers. c. 21.

[13] I have principally drawn this account from the Zendavesta of M. d'Anquetil and the Sadder, subjoined to Dr. Hyde's treatise. It must, however, be confessed, that the studied obscurity of a prophet, the figurative style of the East, and the deceitful medium of a French or Latin version, may have betrayed us into error and heresy, in this abridgment of Persian theology. [Unfortunately the Sadder is a late compilation, — post-Mahometan.]

celebrated doctrine of the two principles; a bold and injudicious attempt of Eastern philosophy to reconcile the existence of moral and physical evil with the attributes of a beneficent Creator and Governor of the world. The first and original Being, in whom, or by whom, the universe exists, is denominated in the writings of Zoroaster, *Time without bounds;* but it must be confessed that this infinite substance seems rather a metaphysical abstraction of the mind than a real object endowed with self-consciousness, or possessed of moral perfections.[14] From either the blind or the intelligent operation of this infinite Time, which bears but too near an affinity with the Chaos of the Greeks, the two secondary but active principles of the universe were from all eternity produced, Ormusd and Ahriman, each of them possessed of the powers of creation, but each disposed, by his invariable nature, to exercise them with different designs.[15] The principle of good is eternally absorbed in light: the principle of evil eternally buried in darkness. The wise benevolence of Ormusd formed man capable of virtue, and abundantly provided his fair habitation with the materials of happiness. By his vigilant providence, the motion of the planets, the order of the seasons, and the temperate mixture of the elements are preserved. But the malice of Ahriman has long since pierced *Ormusd's egg;* or, in other words, has violated the harmony of his works. Since that fatal eruption, the most minute particles of good and evil are intimately intermingled and agitated together, the rankest poisons spring up amidst the most salutary plants; deluges, earthquakes, and conflagrations attest the conflict of Nature; and the little world of man is perpetually shaken by vice and misfortune. Whilst the rest of human kind are led

[14] [This doctrine is not Zoroastrian. Late systems endeavoured to overcome the dualism, and unify the two principles by assuming a higher principle — space, or time, or fate — from which both sprang.]

[15] [Ahura Mazda and Angra Mainya. The law was revealed by Ahura Mazda to Zarathustra (Zoroaster).]

away captives in the chains of their infernal enemy, the faithful Persian alone reserves his religious adoration for his friend and protector Ormusd, and fights under his banner of light, in the full confidence that he shall, in the last day, share the glory of his triumph. At that decisive period the enlightened wisdom of goodness will render the power of Ormusd superior to the furious malice of his rival. Ahriman and his followers, disarmed and subdued, will sink into their native darkness; and virtue will maintain the eternal peace and harmony of the universe.[16]

The theology of Zoroaster was darkly comprehended by foreigners, and even by the far greater number of his disciples; but the most careless observers were struck with the philosophic simplicity of the Persian worship. "That people," says Herodotus,[17] "rejects the use of temples, of altars, and of statues, and smiles at the folly of those nations, who imagine that the gods are sprung from, or bear any affinity with, the human nature. The tops of the highest mountains are the places chosen for sacrifices. Hymns and prayers are the principal worship; the Supreme God who fills the wide circle of heaven, is the object to whom they are addressed." Yet, at the same time, in the true spirit of a polytheist, he accuses them of adoring Earth, Water, Fire, the Winds, and the Sun and Moon. But the Persians of every age have denied the charge, and explained the equivocal conduct which might appear to give a colour to it. The elements, and more particularly Fire, Light, and the Sun, whom they called Mithra, were the objects of their religious reverence, because they considered them as the

[16] The modern Parsees (and in some degree the Sadder) exalt Ormusd into the first and omnipotent cause, whilst they degrade Ahriman into an inferior but rebellious spirit. Their desire of pleasing the Mahometans may have contributed to refine their theological system. [The doctrine of the future triumph of Ormusd is not in the Zendavesta.]

[17] Herodotus, l. i. c. 131. But Dr. Prideaux thinks, with reason, that the use of temples was afterwards permitted in the Magian religion.

purest symbols, the noblest productions, and the most powerful agents of the Divine Power and Nature.[18]

Every mode of religion, to make a deep and lasting impression on the human mind, must exercise our obedience by enjoining practices of devotion, for which we can assign no reason; and must acquire our esteem, by inculcating moral duties analogous to the dictates of our own hearts. The religion of Zoroaster was abundantly provided with the former, and possessed a sufficient portion of the latter. At the age of puberty the faithful Persian was invested with a mysterious girdle, the badge of the divine protection; and from that moment all the actions of his life, even the most indifferent or the most necessary, were sanctified by their peculiar prayers, ejaculations, or genuflexions; the omission of which, under any circumstances, was a grievous sin, not inferior in guilt to the violation of the moral duties. The moral duties, however, of justice, mercy, liberality, &c., were in their turn required of the disciple of Zoroaster, who wished to escape the persecution of Ahriman, and to live with Ormusd in a blissful eternity, where the degree of felicity will be exactly proportioned to the degree of virtue and piety.[19]

But there are some remarkable instances in which Zoroaster lays aside the prophet, assumes the legislator, and discovers a liberal concern for private and public happiness, seldom to be found among the grovelling or visionary schemes of superstition. Fasting and celibacy, the common means of purchasing the divine favour, he condemns with abhorrence, as a criminal rejection of the best gifts of providence. The saint,

[18] Hyde de Relig. Pers. c. 8. Notwithstanding all their distinctions and protestations, which seem sincere enough, their tyrants, the Mahometans, have constantly stigmatised them as idolatrous worshippers of the fire.

[19] See the Sadder, the smallest part of which consists of moral precepts. The ceremonies enjoined are infinite and trifling. Fifteen genuflexions, prayers, &c., were required whenever the devout Persian cut his nails or made water; or as often as he put on the sacred girdle. Sadder, Art. 14, 50, 60.

in the Magian religion, is obliged to beget children, to plant useful trees, to destroy noxious animals, to convey water to the dry lands of Persia, and to work out his salvation by pursuing all the labours of agriculture. We may quote from the Zend Avesta a wise and benevolent maxim, which compensates for many an absurdity. "He who sows the ground with care and diligence acquires a greater stock of religious merit than he could gain by the repetition of ten thousand prayers."[20] In the spring of every year a festival was celebrated, destined to represent the primitive equality, and the present connection, of mankind. The stately kings of Persia, exchanging their vain pomp for more genuine greatness, freely mingled with the humblest but most useful of their subjects. On that day the husbandmen were admitted, without distinction, to the table of the king and his satraps. The monarch accepted their petitions, inquired into their grievances, and conversed with them on the most equal terms. "From your labours," was he accustomed to say (and to say with truth, if not with sincerity), "from your labours we receive our subsistence; you derive your tranquillity from our vigilance; since, therefore, we are mutually necessary to each other, let us live together like brothers in concord and love."[21] Such a festival must indeed have degenerated, in a wealthy and despotic empire, into a theatrical representation; but it was at least a comedy well worthy of a royal audience, and which might sometimes imprint a salutary lesson on the mind of a young prince.

Had Zoroaster, in all his institutions, invariably supported this exalted character, his name would deserve a place with those of Numa and Confucius, and his system would be justly entitled to all the applause which it has pleased some of our divines, and even some of our philosophers, to bestow on it. But in that motley composition, dictated by reason and pas-

[20] Zendavesta, tom. i. p. 224, and Précis du Système de Zoroastre, tom. iii.

[21] Hyde de Religione Persarum, c. 19.

sion, by enthusiasm and by selfish motives, some useful and sublime truths were disgraced by a mixture of the most abject and dangerous superstition. The Magi, or sacerdotal order, were extremely numerous, since, as we have already seen, fourscore thousand of them were convened in a general council. Their forces were multiplied by discipline. A regular hierarchy was diffused through all the provinces of Persia; and the Archimagus, who resided at Balch, was respected as the visible head of the church, and the lawful successor of Zoroaster.[22] The property of the Magi was very considerable. Besides the less invidious possession of a large tract of the most fertile lands of Media,[23] they levied a general tax on the fortunes and the industry of the Persians.[24] "Though your good works," says the interested prophet, "exceed in number the leaves of the trees, the drops of rain, the stars in the heaven, or the sands on the sea-shore, they will all be unprofitable to you, unless they are accepted by the *destour*, or priest. To obtain the acceptation of this guide to salvation, you must faithfully pay him *tithes* of all you possess, of your goods, of your lands, and of your money. If the destour be satisfied, your soul will escape hell tortures; you will secure praise in this world and happiness in the next. For the destours are the teachers of religion; they know all things, and they deliver all men."[25]

These convenient maxims of reverence and implicit faith were doubtless imprinted with care on the tender minds of

[22] Id. c. 28. Both Hyde and Prideaux affect to apply to the Magian the terms consecrated to the Christian hierarchy.

[23] Ammian. Marcellin. xxiii. 6. He informs us (as far as we may credit him) of two curious particulars: 1, that the Magi derived some of their most secret doctrines from the Indian Brachmans; and, 2, that they were a tribe or family, as well as order.

[24] The divine institution of tithes exhibits a singular instance of conformity between the law of Zoroaster and that of Moses. Those who cannot otherwise account for it may suppose, if they please, that the Magi of the latter times inserted so useful an interpolation into the writings of their prophet.

[25] Sadder, Art. 8.

youth; since the Magi were the masters of education in Persia, and to their hands the children even of the royal family were entrusted.[26] The Persian priests, who were of a speculative genius, preserved and investigated the secrets of Oriental philosophy; and acquired, either by superior knowledge or superior art, the reputation of being well versed in some occult sciences, which have derived their appellation from the Magi.[27] Those of more active dispositions mixed with the world in courts and cities; and it is observed that the administration of Artaxerxes was in a great measure directed by the counsels of the sacerdotal order, whose dignity, either from policy or devotion, that prince restored to its ancient splendour.[28]

The first counsel of the Magi was agreeable to the unsociable genius of their faith,[29] to the practice of ancient kings,[30] and even to the example of their legislator, who had fallen a victim to a religious war excited by his own intolerant zeal.[31] By an edict of Artaxerxes, the exercise of every worship, except that of Zoroaster, was severely prohibited. The temples of the Parthians, and the statues of their deified monarchs, were thrown down with ignominy.[32] The sword of Aristotle (such was the name given by the Orientals to the polytheism and philosophy of the Greeks) was easily broken:[33] the flames of persecution soon reached the more

[26] Plato in Alcibiad [37].

[27] Pliny (Hist. Natur. l. xxx. c. 1) observes that magic held mankind by the triple chain of religion, of physic, and of astronomy.

[28] Agathias, l. iv. p. 134 [24. As nothing is said here of the Magi, it has been supposed by Sir Wm. Smith that Gibbon meant to refer to ii. 26.]

[29] Mr. Hume, in the Natural History of Religion, sagaciously remarks that the most refined and philosophic sects are constantly the most intolerant.

[30] Cicero de Legibus, ii. 10. Xerxes, by the advice of the Magi, destroyed the temples of Greece.

[31] Hyde de Rel. Persar. c. 23, 24. D'Herbelot, Bibliothèque Orientale, *Zerdusht*. Life of Zoroaster in tom. ii. of the Zendavesta.

[32] Compare Moses of Chorene, l. ii. c. 74, with Ammian. Marcellin. xxiii. 6. Hereafter I shall make use of these passages.

[33] Rabbi Abraham, in the Tarikh Schickard, p. 108, 109.

stubborn Jews and Christians;[24] nor did they spare the heretics of their own nation and religion. The majesty of Ormusd, who was jealous of a rival, was seconded by the despotism of Artaxerxes, who could not suffer a rebel; and the schismatics within his vast empire were soon reduced to the inconsiderable number of eighty thousand.[25] This spirit of persecution reflects dishonour on the religion of Zoroaster; but, as it was not productive of any civil commotion, it served to strengthen the new monarchy by uniting all the various inhabitants of Persia in the bands of religious zeal.

II. Artaxerxes, by his valour and conduct, had wrested the sceptre of the East from the ancient royal family of Parthia. There still remained the more difficult task of establishing, throughout the vast extent of Persia, a uniform and vigorous administration. The weak indulgence of the Arsacides had resigned to their sons and brothers the principal provinces and the greatest offices of the kingdom, in the nature of hereditary possessions. The *vitaxæ*, or eighteen most powerful satraps, were permitted to assume the regal title, and the vain pride of the monarch was delighted with a nominal dominion over so many vassal kings. Even tribes of barbarians in their mountains, and the Greek cities of Upper Asia,[26] within their walls, scarcely acknowledged, or seldom obeyed, any superior; and the Parthian empire exhibited, under other names, a lively image of the feudal system[27]

[24] Basnage, Histoire des Juifs, l. viii. c. 3. Sozomen, l. ii. c. 1 [*leg.* 9; this passage refers to the persecution of Sapor II.]. Manes, who suffered an ignominious death, may be deemed a Magian, as well as a Christian, heretic.

[25] Hyde de Religione Persar. c. 21.

[26] These colonies were extremely numerous. Seleucus Nicator founded thirty-nine cities, all named from himself, or some of his relations (see Appian in Syriac. p. 124 [57]). The era of Seleucus (still in use among the Eastern Christians) appears as late as the year 508, of Christ 196, on the medals of the Greek cities within the Parthian empire. See Moyle's works, vol. i. p. 273, &c., and M. Freret. Mém. de l'Académie, tom. xix.

[27] The modern Persians distinguish that period as the dynasty of the kings of the nations. See Plin. Hist. Nat. vi. 25.

which has since prevailed in Europe. But the active victor, at the head of a numerous and disciplined army, visited in person every province of Persia. The defeat of the boldest rebels and the reduction of the strongest fortifications[38] diffused the terror of his arms and prepared the way for the peaceful reception of his authority. An obstinate resistance was fatal to the chiefs; but their followers were treated with lenity.[39] A cheerful submission was rewarded with honours and riches; but the prudent Artaxerxes, suffering no person except himself to assume the title of king, abolished every intermediate power between the throne and the people. His kingdom, nearly equal in extent to modern Persia, was, on every side, bounded by the sea or by great rivers, — by the Euphrates, the Tigris, the Araxes, the Oxus, and the Indus; by the Caspian Sea and the Gulf of Persia.[40] That country was computed to contain, in the last century, five hundred and fifty-four cities, sixty thousand villages, and about forty millions of souls.[41] If we compare the administration of the

[38] Eutychius (tom. i. p. 367, 371, 375) relates the siege of the Island of Mesene in the Tigris, with some circumstances not unlike the story of Nisus and Scylla.

[39] Agathias, ii. p. 64 [26]. The princes of Segestan defended their independence during many years. As romances generally transport to an ancient period the events of their own time, it is not impossible that the fabulous exploits of Rustan Prince of Segestan may have been grafted on this real history.

[40] We can scarcely attribute to the Persian monarchy the sea coast of Gedrosia or Macran, which extends along the Indian Ocean from Cape Jask (the promontory Capella) to Cape Goadel. In the time of Alexander, and probably many ages afterwards, it was thinly inhabited by a savage people of Ichthyophagi, or Fishermen, who knew no arts, who acknowledged no master, and who were divided by inhospitable deserts from the rest of the world. (See Arrian de Reb. Indicis [26].) In the twelfth century, the little town of Taiz (supposed by M. d'Anville to be the Tesa of Ptolemy) was peopled and enriched by the resort of the Arabian merchants. (See Geographia Nubiens. p. 58, and d'Anville Géographie Ancienne, tom. ii. p. 283.) In the last age the whole country was divided between three princes, one Mahometan and two Idolaters, who maintained their independence against the successors of Shaw Abbas. [(Voyages de Tavernier, part i. l. v. p. 635.)

[41] Chardin, tom. iii. c. 1, 2, 3. [The number seems too high. At the

house of Sassan with that of the house of Sesi, the political influence of the Magian with that of the Mahometan religion, we shall probably infer that the kingdom of Artaxerxes contained at least as great a number of cities, villages, and inhabitants. But it must likewise be confessed that in every age the want of harbours on the sea coast, and the scarcity of fresh water in the inland provinces, have been very unfavourable to the commerce and agriculture of the Persians; who, in the calculation of their numbers, seem to have indulged one of the meanest, though most common, artifices of national vanity.

As soon as the ambitious mind of Artaxerxes had triumphed over the resistance of his vassals, he began to threaten the neighbouring states, who, during the long slumber of his predecessors, had insulted Persia with impunity. He obtained some easy victories over the wild Scythians and the effeminate Indians; but the Romans were an enemy who, by their past injuries and present power, deserved the utmost efforts of his arms. A forty years' tranquillity, the fruit of valour and moderation, had succeeded the victories of Trajan. During the period that elapsed from the accession of Marcus to the reign of Alexander, the Roman and the Parthian empires were twice engaged in war; and, although the whole strength of the Arsacides contended with a part only of the forces of Rome, the event was most commonly in favour of the latter. Macrinus, indeed, prompted by his precarious situation and pusillanimous temper, purchased a peace at the expense of near two millions of our money;[42] but the generals of Marcus, the emperor Severus, and his son, erected many trophies in Armenia, Mesopotamia, and Assyria. Among their exploits, the imperfect relation of which would have unseasonably interrupted the more important series of

present time the population of Iran and Turan (including Afghanistan, Beluchistan, &c.) is said to be between fifteen and sixteen millions.]

[42] Dion, l. lxxviii. p. 1335 [27. Two hundred million sesterces. Yet the coins of 218 A.D. boast of a Victoria Parthica.]

domestic revolutions, we shall only mention the repeated calamities of the two great cities of Seleucia and Ctesiphon.

Seleucia, on the western bank of the Tigris, about forty-five miles to the north of ancient Babylon, was the capital of the Macedonian conquests in Upper Asia.[43] Many ages after the fall of their empire, Seleucia retained the genuine characters of a Grecian colony — arts, military virtue, and the love of freedom. The independent republic was governed by a senate of three hundred nobles; the people consisted of six hundred thousand citizens; the walls were strong, and, as long as concord prevailed among the several orders of the state, they viewed with contempt the power of the Parthian: but the madness of faction was sometimes provoked to implore the dangerous aid of the common enemy, who was posted almost at the gates of the colony.[44] The Parthian monarchs, like the Mogul sovereigns of Hindostan, delighted in the pastoral life of their Scythian ancestors; and the Imperial camp was frequently pitched in the plain of Ctesiphon, on the eastern bank of the Tigris, at the distance of only three miles from Seleucia.[45] The innumerable attendants on luxury and despotism resorted to the court, and the little village of Ctesiphon insensibly swelled into a great city.[46] Under the reign of Marcus, the Roman generals penetrated as far as Ctesiphon and Seleucia.[47] They were received as

[43] For the precise situation of Babylon, Seleucia, Ctesiphon, Modain, and Bagdad, cities often confounded with each other, see an excellent Geographical Tract of M. d'Anville, in Mém. de l'Académie, tom. xxx.

[44] Tacit. Annal. vi. 42. Plin. Hist. Nat. vi. 26.

[45] This may be inferred from Strabo, l. xvi. p. 743.

[46] That most curious traveller, Bernier (see Hist. de Voyages, tom. x.), who followed the camp of Aurengzebe from Delhi to Cashmir, describes with great accuracy the immense moving city. The guard of cavalry consisted of 35,000 men, that of infantry of 10,000. It was computed that the camp contained 150,000 horses, mules, and elephants; 50,000 camels, 50,000 oxen, and between 300,000 and 400,000 persons. Almost all Delhi followed the court, whose magnificence supported its industry.

[47] [These successes were achieved by Avidius Cassius. He took Nisibis, and Dausara near Edessa. The Parthians were defeated at Europos in Cyrrhestica.]

friends by the Greek colony; they attacked as enemies the seat of the Parthian kings; yet both cities experienced the same treatment. The sack and conflagration of Seleucia, with the massacre of three hundred thousand of the inhabitants, tarnished the glory of the Roman triumph.[48] Seleucia, already exhausted by the neighbourhood of a too powerful rival, sunk under the fatal blow; but Ctesiphon, in about thirty-three years, had sufficiently recovered its strength to maintain an obstinate siege against the emperor Severus. The city was, however, taken by assault; the king, who defended it in person, escaped with precipitation; an hundred thousand captives and a rich booty rewarded the fatigues of the Roman soldiers.[49] Notwithstanding these misfortunes, Ctesiphon succeeded to Babylon and to Seleucia as one of the great capitals of the East.[50] In summer, the monarch of Persia enjoyed at Ecbatana the cool breezes of the mountains of Media; but the mildness of the climate engaged him to prefer Ctesiphon for his winter residence.

From these successful inroads the Romans derived no real or lasting benefit; nor did they attempt to preserve such distant conquests, separated from the provinces of the empire by a large tract of intermediate desert. The reduction of the kingdom of Osrhoene was an acquisition of less splendour indeed, but of a far more solid advantage. That little state occupied the northern and most fertile part of Mesopotamia, between the Euphrates and the Tigris. Edessa, its capital, was situated about twenty miles beyond the former of those rivers, and the inhabitants, since the time of Alexander, were

[48] Dion, l. lxxi. p. 1178 [2]. Hist. August. p. 38 [v. 8]. Eutrop. viii. 10. Euseb. in Chronic. [ann. 2180]. Quadratus (quoted in the Augustan History) attempted to vindicate the Romans by alleging that the citizens of Seleucia had first violated their faith.

[49] Dion, l. lxxv. p. 1263 [9]. Herodian, l. iii. p. 120 [9]. Hist. August. p. 70 [x. 16. *Hiemali prope tempore*, which fixes the capture to end of 197 or beginning of 198 A.D.]

[50] [Ctesiphon was restored by Sapor II.]

a mixed race of Greeks, Arabs, Syrians, and Armenians.[61] The feeble sovereigns of Osrhoene, placed on the dangerous verge of two contending empires, were attached from inclination to the Parthian cause; but the superior power of Rome exacted from them a reluctant homage, which is still attested by their medals.[62] After the conclusion of the Parthian war under Marcus, it was judged prudent to secure some substantial pledges of their doubtful fidelity. Forts were constructed in several parts of the country, and a Roman garrison was fixed in the strong town of Nisibis. During the troubles that followed the death of Commodus, the princes of Osrhoene attempted to shake off the yoke; but the stern policy of Severus confirmed their dependence,[63] and the perfidy of Caracalla completed the easy conquest. Abgarus, the last king[64] of Edessa, was sent in chains to Rome, his dominions reduced into a province, and his capital dignified with the rank of colony;[65] and thus the Romans, about ten years before the fall of the Parthian monarchy, obtained a firm and permanent establishment beyond the Euphrates.[66]

Prudence as well as glory might have justified a war on the side of Artaxerxes, had his views been confined to the defence or the acquisition of a useful frontier. But the ambitious Persian openly avowed a far more extensive design of conquest; and he thought himself able to support his lofty pre-

[61] The polished citizens of Antioch called those of Edessa mixed barbarians. It was, however, some praise, that, of the three dialects of the Syriac, the purest and most elegant (the Aramæan) was spoken at Edessa. This remark M. Bayer (Hist. Edess. p. 5) has borrowed from George of Malatia, a Syrian writer.

[62] [Compare Eckhel, iii. 514.]

[63] Dion, l. lxxv. p. 1248, 1249, 1250 [1, 2, 3]. M. Bayer has neglected to use this most important passage.

[64] [*Basileus* was the title.]

[65] [Caracalla promoted Carrhæ to be a Roman colony. Eckhel, iii. 508. He seems to have formed the design of annexing Armenia as a province.]

[66] This kingdom, from Osrhoes, who gave a new name to the country, to the last Abgarus, had lasted 353 years. See the learned work of M. Bayer, Historia Osrhoena et Edessena.

tensions by the arms of reason as well as by those of power. Cyrus, he alleged, had first subdued, and his successors had for a long time possessed, the whole extent of Asia, as far as the Propontis and the Ægean Sea; the provinces of Caria and Ionia, under their empire, had been governed by Persian satraps; and all Egypt, to the confines of Æthiopia, had acknowledged their sovereignty.[87] Their rights had been suspended, but not destroyed, by a long usurpation;[88] and, as soon as he received the Persian diadem, which birth and successful valour had placed upon his head, the first great duty of his station called upon him to restore the ancient limits and splendour of the monarchy. The Great King, therefore (such was the haughty style of his embassies to the emperor Alexander), commanded the Romans instantly to depart from all the provinces of his ancestors, and, yielding to the Persians the empire of Asia, to content themselves with the undisturbed possession of Europe. This haughty mandate was delivered by four hundred of the tallest and most beautiful of the Persians; who, by their fine horses, splendid arms, and rich apparel displayed the pride and greatness of their master.[89] Such an embassy was much less an offer of negotiation than a declaration of war. Both Alexander Severus and Artaxerxes, collecting the military force of the Roman and Persian monarchies, resolved in this important contest to lead their armies in person.

If we credit what should seem the most authentic of all records, an oration, still extant, and delivered by the emperor himself to the senate, we must allow that the victory of Alexander Severus was not inferior to any of those formerly obtained over the Persians by the son of Philip. The army of

[87] Xenophon, in the preface to the Cyropædia, gives a clear and magnificent idea of the extent of the empire of Cyrus. Herodotus (l. iii. c. 79, &c.) enters into a curious and particular description of the twenty great *Satrapies* into which the Persian empire was divided by Darius Hystaspis.

[88] [Dion, lxxx. 4, 1.]

[89] Herodian, vi. 209, 212 [2 and 4].

the Great King consisted of one hundred and twenty thousand horse, clothed in complete armour of steel; of seven hundred elephants, with towers filled with archers on their backs; and of eighteen hundred chariots armed with scythes. This formidable host, the like of which is not to be found in Eastern history, and has scarcely been imagined in Eastern romance,[60] was discomfited in a great battle, in which the Roman Alexander approved himself an intrepid soldier and a skilful general. The Great King fled before his valour: an immense booty and the conquest of Mesopotamia were the immediate fruits of this signal victory. Such are the circumstances of this ostentatious and improbable relation, dictated, as it too plainly appears, by the vanity of the monarch, adorned by the unblushing servility of his flatterers, and received without contradiction by a distant and obsequious senate.[61] Far from being inclined to believe that the arms of Alexander obtained any memorable advantage over the Persians, we are induced to suspect that all this blaze of imaginary glory was designed to conceal some real disgrace.

Our suspicions are confirmed by the authority of a contem-

[60] There were two hundred scythed chariots at the battle of Arbela, in the host of Darius. In the vast army of Tigranes, which was vanquished by Lucullus, seventeen thousand horse only were completely armed. Antiochus brought fifty-four elephants into the field against the Romans: by his frequent wars and negotiations with the princes of India, he had once collected an hundred and fifty of those great animals; but it may be questioned, whether the most powerful monarch of Hindostan ever formed a line of battle of seven hundred elephants. Instead of three or four thousand elephants, which the Great Mogul was supposed to possess, Tavernier (Voyages, part ii. l. i. p. 198) discovered, by a more accurate inquiry, that he had only five hundred for his baggage, and eighty or ninety for the service of war. The Greeks have varied with regard to the number which Porus brought into the field; but Quintus Curtius (viii. 13), in this instance judicious and moderate, is contented with eighty-five elephants, distinguished by their size and strength. In Siam, where these animals are the most numerous and the most esteemed, eighteen elephants are allowed as a sufficient proportion for each of the nine brigades into which a just army is divided. The whole number, of one hundred and sixty-two elephants of war, may sometimes be doubled. Hist. des Voyages, tom. ix. p. 260. [See below, vol. vi. p. 229, note [11].]

[61] Hist. August. p. 133 [xviii. 55].

porary historian, who mentions the virtues of Alexander with respect, and his faults with candour. He describes the judicious plan which had been formed for the conduct of the war. Three Roman armies were destined to invade Persia at the same time, and by different roads. But the operations of the campaign, though wisely concerted, were not executed either with ability or success. The first of these armies, as soon as it had entered the marshy plains of Babylon, towards the artificial conflux of the Euphrates and the Tigris,[62] was encompassed by the superior numbers, and destroyed by the arrows, of the enemy. The alliance of Chosroes, king of Armenia,[63] and the long tract of mountainous country, in which the Persian cavalry was of little service, opened a secure entrance into the heart of Media to the second of the Roman armies. These brave troops laid waste the adjacent provinces, and by several successful actions against Artaxerxes gave a faint colour to the emperor's vanity. But the retreat of this victorious army was imprudent, or at least unfortunate. In repassing the mountains, great numbers of soldiers perished by the badness of the roads and the severity of the winter season. It had been resolved that whilst these two great detachments penetrated into the opposite extremes of the Persian dominions, the main body, under the command of Alexander himself, should support their attack by invading the centre of the kingdom. But the unexperienced youth, influenced by his mother's counsels, and perhaps by his own fears, deserted the bravest troops and the fairest prospect of victory; and, after consuming in Mesopotamia an inactive

[62] M. de Tillemont has already observed that Herodian's geography is somewhat confused.

[63] Moses of Chorene (Hist. Armen. l. ii. c. 71) illustrates this invasion of Media, by asserting that Chosroes, King of Armenia, defeated Artaxerxes, and pursued him to the confines of India. The exploits of Chosroes have been magnified, and he acted as a dependent ally to the Romans. [But Chosroes really inflicted a serious defeat on Ardeshir in 228, drove him back from Armenia, and invaded his realm, pressing as far as Ctesiphon, if not to the borders of Arabia. The Romans had not yet appeared on the scene.]

and inglorious summer, he led back to Antioch an army diminished by sickness, and provoked by disappointment. The behaviour of Artaxerxes had been very different. Flying with rapidity from the hills of Media to the marshes of the Euphrates, he had everywhere opposed the invaders in person; and in either fortune had united with the ablest conduct the most undaunted resolution. But in several obstinate engagements against the veteran legions of Rome the Persian monarch had lost the flower of his troops. Even his victories had weakened his power. The favourable opportunities of the absence of Alexander, and of the confusions that followed that emperor's death, presented themselves in vain to his ambition. Instead of expelling the Romans, as he pretended, from the continent of Asia, he found himself unable to wrest from their hands the little province of Mesopotamia.[64]

The reign of Artaxerxes, which from the last defeat of the Parthians lasted only fourteen years, forms a memorable era in the history of the East, and even in that of Rome. His character seems to have been marked by those bold and commanding features that generally distinguish the princes who conquer, from those who inherit, an empire. Till the last period of the Persian monarchy, his code of laws was respected as the groundwork of their civil and religious policy.[65] Several of his sayings are preserved. One of them in particular discovers a deep insight into the constitution of government. "The authority of the prince," said Artaxerxes,

[64] For the account of this war, see Herodian, l. vi. p. 209, 212 [5]. The old abbreviators and modern compilers have blindly followed the Augustan History. [Though no very glorious exploit was wrought in this campaign of Alexander, it is clear that the Persians were completely checked in their advance westward, and that the Romans gained some victories. Cp. Aurelius Victor, Cæsar. 24, 2, and Eutropius, viii. 23. Not an inch of ground was lost to the empire.]

[65] Eutychius, tom. ii. p. 180, vers. Pocock. The great Chosroes Noushirwan sent the code of Artaxerxes to all his satraps, as the invariable rule of their conduct.

"must be defended by a military force; that force can only be maintained by taxes; all taxes must, at last, fall upon agriculture; and agriculture can never flourish except under the protection of justice and moderation." [66] Artaxerxes bequeathed his new empire, and his ambitious designs against the Romans, to Sapor, a son not unworthy of his great father; but those designs were too extensive for the power of Persia, and served only to involve both nations in a long series of destructive wars and reciprocal calamities.

The Persians, long since civilised and corrupted, were very far from possessing the martial independence, and the intrepid hardiness, both of mind and body, which have rendered the Northern barbarians masters of the world. The science of war, that constituted the more rational force of Greece and Rome, as it now does of Europe, never made any considerable progress in the East. Those disciplined evolutions which harmonise and animate a confused multitude were unknown to the Persians. They were equally unskilled in the arts of constructing, besieging, or defending regular fortifications. They trusted more to their numbers than to their courage; more to their courage than to their discipline. The infantry was a half-armed, spiritless crowd of peasants, levied in haste by the allurements of plunder, and as easily dispersed by a victory as by a defeat. The monarch and his nobles transported into the camp the pride and luxury of the seraglio. Their military operations were impeded by a useless train of women, eunuchs, horses, and camels; and in the midst of a successful campaign the Persian host was often separated or destroyed by an unexpected famine.[67]

[66] D'Herbelot, Bibliothèque Orientale, au mot *Ardshir*. We may observe that, after an ancient period of fables, and a long interval of darkness, the modern histories of Persia begin to assume an air of truth with the dynasty of the Sassanides.

[67] Herodian, l. vi. p. 214 [5]. Ammianus Marcellinus, l. xxiii. c. 6. Some differences may be observed between the two historians, the natural effects of the changes produced by a century and a half.

But the nobles of Persia, in the bosom of luxury and despotism, preserved a strong sense of personal gallantry and national honour. From the age of seven years they were taught to speak truth, to shoot with the bow, and to ride; and it was universally confessed that in the two last of these arts they had made a more than common proficiency.[68] The most distinguished youth were educated under the monarch's eye, practised their exercises in the gate of his palace, and were severely trained up to the habits of temperance and obedience in their long and laborious parties of hunting. In every province the satrap maintained a like school of military virtue. The Persian nobles (so natural is the idea of feudal tenures) received from the king's bounty lands and houses on the condition of their service in war. They were ready on the first summons to mount on horseback, with a martial and splendid train of followers, and to join the numerous bodies of guards, who were carefully selected from among the most robust slaves and the bravest adventurers of Asia. These armies, both of light and of heavy cavalry, equally formidable by the impetuosity of their charge and the rapidity of their motions, threatened, as an impending cloud, the eastern provinces of the declining empire of Rome.[69]

[68] The Persians are still the most skilful horsemen, and their horses the finest, in the East.

[69] From Herodotus, Xenophon, Herodian, Ammianus, Chardin, &c., I have extracted such *probable* accounts of the Persian nobility, as seem either common to every age, or particular to that of the Sassanides.

CHAPTER IX

The State of Germany till the Invasion of the Barbarians, in the Time of the Emperor Decius

THE government and religion of Persia have deserved some notice from their connection with the decline and fall of the Roman empire. We shall occasionally mention the Scythian or Sarmatian tribes, which, with their arms and horses, their flocks and herds, their wives and families, wandered over the immense plains which spread themselves from the Caspian Sea to the Vistula, from the confines of Persia to those of Germany. But the warlike Germans, who first resisted, then invaded, and at length overturned, the Western monarchy of Rome, will occupy a much more important place in this history, and possess a stronger, and, if we may use the expression, a more domestic, claim to our attention and regard. The most civilised nations of modern Europe issued from the woods of Germany, and in the rude institutions of those barbarians we may still distinguish the original principles of our present laws and manners. In their primitive state of simplicity and independence, the Germans were surveyed by the discerning eye, and delineated by the masterly pencil, of Tacitus, the first of historians who applied the science of philosophy to the study of facts. The expressive conciseness of his descriptions has deserved to exercise the diligence of innumerable antiquarians, and to excite the genius and penetration of the philosophic historians of our own times. The subject, however various and important, has already been so frequently, so ably, and so successfully discussed, that it is now grown familiar to the reader, and difficult to the writer. We shall therefore content ourselves with observing, and indeed with repeating, some of the most important circumstances of climate, of manners, and of institutions, which rendered the wild barbarians of Germany such formidable enemies to the Roman power.

Ancient Germany, excluding from its independent limits the province westward of the Rhine, which had submitted to the Roman yoke, extended itself over a third part of Europe.[1] Almost the whole of modern Germany, Denmark, Norway, Sweden, Finland, Livonia, Prussia, and the greater part of Poland were peopled by the various tribes of one great nation, whose complexion, manners, and language denoted a common origin, and preserved a striking resemblance. On the west, ancient Germany was divided by the Rhine from the Gallic, and on the south by the Danube from the Illyrian, provinces of the empire. A ridge of hills, rising from the Danube, and called the Carpathian Mountains, covered Germany on the side of Dacia or Hungary. The eastern frontier was faintly marked by the mutual fears of the Germans and the Sarmatians, and was often confounded by the mixture of warring and confederating tribes of the two nations. In the remote darkness of the north the ancients imperfectly described a frozen ocean that lay beyond the Baltic Sea and beyond the peninsula, or islands,[2] of Scandinavia.

[1] [Though the author exaggerates the extent of ancient Germany towards the east, he is not so far wrong as has sometimes been supposed. Speaking roughly, German tribes occupied the whole of Europe between the Rhine and the Vistula, the Northern Sea and the Danube. Vandals, Burgundians, Turcilingi, Skiri, and Gutones held the land between the Oder and Vistula.]

[2] The modern philosophers of Sweden seem agreed that the waters of the Baltic gradually sink in a regular proportion, which they have ventured to estimate at half an inch every year. Twenty centuries ago, the flat country of Scandinavia must have been covered by the sea; while the high lands rose above the waters, as so many islands of various forms and dimensions. Such indeed is the notion given us by Mela, Pliny, and Tacitus, of the vast countries round the Baltic. See in the Bibliothèque Raisonnée, tom. xl.

Some ingenious writers[3] have suspected that Europe was much colder formerly than it is at present; and the most ancient descriptions of the climate of Germany tend exceedingly to confirm their theory. The general complaints of intense frost and eternal winter are perhaps little to be regarded, since we have no method of reducing to the accurate standard of the thermometer the feelings or the expressions of an orator born in the happier regions of Greece or Asia. But I shall select two remarkable circumstances of a less equivocal nature. 1. The great rivers which covered the Roman provinces, the Rhine and the Danube, were frequently frozen over, and capable of supporting the most enormous weights. The barbarians, who often chose that severe season for their inroads, transported, without apprehension or danger, their numerous armies, their cavalry, and their heavy waggons, over a vast and solid bridge of ice.[4] Modern ages have not presented an instance of a like phenomenon. 2. The reindeer, that useful animal, from whom the savage of the North derives the best comforts of his dreary life, is of a constitution that supports, and even requires, the most intense cold. He is found on the rock of Spitzberg, within ten degrees of the pole; he seems to delight in the snows of Lapland and Siberia; but at present he cannot subsist, much less multiply, in any country to the south of the Baltic.[5]

and xlv., a large abstract of Dalin's History of Sweden, composed in the Swedish language.

[3] In particular, Mr. Hume, and the Abbé du Bos, and M. Pelloutier, Hist. des Celtes, tom. i.

[4] Diodorus Siculus, l. v. p. 340, edit. Wessel [25]. Herodian, l. vi. p. 221 [7]. Jornandes, c. 55. On the banks of the Danube, the wine, when brought to table, was frequently frozen into great lumps, *frusta vini*. Ovid Epist. ex Ponto, l. iv. 7, 7–10. Virgil Georgic. l. iii. 355. The fact is confirmed by a soldier and a philosopher, who had experienced the intense cold of Thrace. See Xenophon, Anabasis, l. vii. p. 560, edit. Hutchinson [4]. [Milman in his note on this passage refers to an incident in the Thirty Years' War. In 1635 "Jan van Werth, an Imperialist partisan, crossed the Rhine from Heidelberg on the ice with 5000 men, and surprised Spires."]

[5] Buffon, Historie Naturelle, tom. xii. p. 79, 116.

In the time of Cæsar, the reindeer, as well as the elk and the wild bull, was a native of the Hercynian forest, which then overshadowed a great part of Germany and Poland.[6] The modern improvements sufficiently explain the causes of the diminution of the cold. These immense woods have been gradually cleared, which intercepted from the earth the rays of the sun.[7] The morasses have been drained, and, in proportion as the soil has been cultivated, the air has become more temperate.. Canada, at this day, is an exact picture of ancient Germany. Although situate in the same parallel with the finest provinces of France and England, that country experiences the most rigorous cold. The reindeer are very numerous, the ground is covered with deep and lasting snow, and the great river of St. Lawrence is regularly frozen, in a season when the waters of the Seine and the Thames are usually free from ice.[8]

It is difficult to ascertain, and easy to exaggerate, the influence of the climate of ancient Germany over the minds and bodies of the natives. Many writers have supposed, and most have allowed, though, as it should seem, without any adequate proof, that the rigorous cold of the North was favourable to long life and generative vigour, that the women were more fruitful, and the human species more prolific, than in warmer or more temperate climates.[9] We may assert, with greater confidence, that the keen air of Germany formed the large and masculine limbs of the natives, who were, in general, of a more lofty stature than the people of the South,[10]

[6] Cæsar de Bell. Gallic. vi. 23, &c. The most inquisitive of the Germans were ignorant of its utmost limits, although some of them had travelled in it more than sixty days' journey.

[7] Cluverius (Germania Antiqua, l. iii. c. 47) investigates the small and scattered remains of the Hercynian Wood.

[8] Charlevoix, Histoire du Canada.

[9] Olaus Rudbeck asserts that the Swedish women often bear ten or twelve children, and not uncommonly twenty or thirty; but the authority of Rudbeck is much to be suspected.

[10] In hos artus, in hæc corpora, quæ miramur, excrescunt. Tacit. Germania, c. 20. Cluver. l. i. c. 14.

gave them a kind of strength better adapted to violent exertions than to patient labour, and inspired them with constitutional bravery, which is the result of nerves and spirits. The severity of a winter campaign, that chilled the courage of the Roman troops, was scarcely felt by these hardy children of the North,[11] who, in their turn, were unable to resist the summer heats, and dissolved away in languor and sickness under the beams of an Italian sun.[12]

There is not anywhere upon the globe a large tract of country, which we have discovered destitute of inhabitants, or whose first population can be fixed with any degree of historical certainty. And yet, as the most philosophic minds can seldom refrain from investigating the infancy of great nations, our curiosity consumes itself in toilsome and disappointed efforts. When Tacitus considered the purity of the German blood, and the forbidding aspect of the country, he was disposed to pronounce those barbarians *Indigenæ*, or natives of the soil. We may allow with safety, and perhaps with truth, that ancient Germany was not originally peopled by any foreign colonies already formed into a political society;[13] but that the name and nation received their existence from the gradual union of some wandering savages of the Hercynian woods. To assert those savages to have been the spontaneous production of the earth which they inhabited would be a rash inference, condemned by religion, and unwarranted by reason.

[11] Plutarch. in Mario. The Cimbri, by way of amusement, often slid down mountains of snow on their broad shields.

[12] The Romans made war in all climates, and by their excellent discipline were in a great measure preserved in health and vigour. It may be remarked that man is the only animal which can live and multiply in every country from the equator to the poles. The hog seems to approach the nearest to our species in that privilege.

[13] Tacit. German. c. 3. The emigration of the Gauls followed the course of the Danube, and discharged itself on Greece and Asia. Tacitus could discover only one inconsiderable tribe that retained any traces of a Gallic origin. [The Cotini, c. 43. They were certainly not Gallic.]

Such rational doubt is but ill suited with the genius of popular vanity. Among the nations who have adopted the Mosaic history of the world, the ark of Noah has been of the same use, as was formerly to the Greeks and Romans the siege of Troy. On a narrow basis of acknowledged truth, an immense but rude superstructure of fable has been erected; and the wild Irishman,[14] as well as the wild Tartar,[15] could point out the individual son of Japhet from whose loins his ancestors were lineally descended. The last century abounded with antiquarians of profound learning and easy faith, who, by the dim light of legends and traditions, of conjectures and etymologies, conducted the great-grandchildren of Noah from the Tower of Babel to the extremities of the globe. Of these judicious critics, one of the most entertaining was Olaus Rudbeck, professor in the university of Upsal.[16] Whatever is celebrated either in history or fable, this zealous patriot ascribes to his country. From Sweden (which formed so considerable a part of ancient Germany) the Greeks themselves derived their alphabetical characters, their astronomy, and their religion. Of that delightful region (for such it appeared to the eyes of a native) the Atlantis of Plato, the country of the Hyperboreans, the gardens of the Hesperides, the Fortunate Islands, and even the Elysian Fields, were all but faint and imperfect transcripts. A clime so profusely favoured by Nature could not long remain desert after the

[14] According to Dr. Keating (History of Ireland, p. 13, 14), the giant Partholanus, who was the son of Seara, the son of Esra, the son of Sru, the son of Framant, the son of Fathaclan, the son of Magog, the son of Japhet, the son of Noah, landed on the coast of Munster, the 14th day of May, in the year of the world one thousand nine hundred and seventy-eight. Though he succeeded in his great enterprise, the loose behaviour of his wife rendered his domestic life very unhappy, and provoked him to such a degree, that he killed — her favourite greyhound. This, as the learned historian very properly observes, was the *first* instance of female falsehood and infidelity ever known in Ireland.

[15] Genealogical History of the Tartars by Abulghazi Bahadur Khan.

[16] His work, entitled Atlantica, is uncommonly scarce. Bayle has given two most curious extracts from it. République des Lettres, Janvier et Février, 1685.

flood. The learned Rudbeck allows the family of Noah a few years to multiply from eight to about twenty thousand persons. He then disperses them into small colonies to replenish the earth, and to propagate the human species. The German or Swedish detachment (which marched, if I am not mistaken, under the command of Askenaz the son of Gomer, the son of Japhet) distinguished itself by a more than common diligence in the prosecution of this great work. The northern hive cast its swarms over the greatest part of Europe, Africa, and Asia; and (to use the author's metaphor) the blood circulated back from the extremities to the heart.

But all this well-laboured system of German antiquities is annihilated by a single fact, too well attested to admit of any doubt, and of too decisive a nature to leave room for any reply. The Germans, in the age of Tacitus, were unacquainted with the use of letters;[17] and the use of letters is the principal circumstance that distinguishes a civilised people from a herd of savages, incapable of knowledge or reflection. Without that artificial help the human memory soon dissipates or corrupts the ideas entrusted to her charge; and the nobler faculties of the mind, no longer supplied with models or with materials, gradually forget their powers:

[17] Tacit. Germ. ii. 19. Literarum secreta viri pariter ac foeminæ ignorant. We may rest contented with this decisive authority, without entering into the obscure disputes concerning the antiquity of the Runic characters. The learned Celsius, a Swede, a scholar and a philosopher, was of opinion, that they were nothing more than the Roman letters, with the curves changed into straight lines for the ease of engraving. See Pelloutier, Histoire des Celtes, l. ii. c. 11. Dictionnaire Diplomatique, tom. i. p. 223. We may add, that the oldest Runic inscriptions are supposed to be of the third century, and the most ancient writer who mentions the Runic characters, is Venantius Fortunatus (Carm. vii. 18), who lived towards the end of the sixth century.

Barbara fraxineis pingatur RUNA tabellis. [See Zacher, Das Gothische Alphabet Vulfilas und das Runenalphabet; Mr. Isaac Taylor, Greeks and Goths; Stephen's Runic Monuments. Mr. Taylor's theory that the Runic alphabet was originally derived from the Greeks by the trade route, which existed at a very early age between the Euxine and the Baltic, is gaining ground. It was certainly developed in Scandinavia, not in Germany. The number of Runic inscriptions found in Germany is very small.]

the judgment becomes feeble and lethargic, the imagination languid or irregular. Fully to apprehend this important truth, let us attempt, in an improved society, to calculate the immense distance between the man of learning and the *illiterate* peasant. The former, by reading and reflection, multiplies his own experience, and lives in distant ages and remote countries; whilst the latter, rooted to a single spot, and confined to a few years of existence, surpasses but very little his fellow-labourer the ox in the exercise of his mental faculties. The same and even a greater difference will be found between nations than between individuals; and we may safely pronounce, that without some species of writing no people has ever preserved the faithful annals of their history, ever made any considerable progress in the abstract sciences, or ever possessed, in any tolerable degree of perfection, the useful and agreeable arts of life.

Of these arts the ancient Germans were wretchedly destitute. They passed their lives in a state of ignorance and poverty, which it has pleased some declaimers to dignify with the appellation of virtuous simplicity. Modern Germany is said to contain about two thousand three hundred walled towns.[18] In a much wider extent of country the geographer Ptolemy could discover no more than ninety places which he decorates with the name of cities;[19] though, according to our ideas, they would but ill deserve that splendid title. We can only suppose them to have been rude fortifications, constructed in the centre of the woods, and designed to secure the women, children, and cattle, whilst the warriors of the tribe marched out to repel a sudden invasion.[20] But Tacitus

[18] Recherches Philosophiques sur les Américains, tom. iii. p. 228. The author of that very curious work is, if I am not misinformed, a German by birth. [De Pauw.]

[19] The Alexandrian Geographer is often criticised by the accurate Cluverius.

[20] See Cæsar, and the learned Mr. Whitaker in his History of Manchester, vol. i.

asserts, as a well-known fact, that the Germans, in his time, had *no* cities;[21] and that they affected to despise the works of Roman industry as places of confinement rather than of security.[22] Their edifices were not even contiguous, or formed into regular villas;[23] each barbarian fixed his independent dwelling on the spot to which a plain, a wood, or a stream of fresh water had induced him to give the preference. Neither stone, nor brick, nor tiles were employed in these slight habitations.[24] They were indeed no more than low huts of a circular figure, built of rough timber, thatched with straw, and pierced at the top to leave a free passage for the smoke. In the most inclement winter, the hardy German was satisfied with a scanty garment made of the skin of some animal. The nations who dwelt towards the north clothed themselves in furs; and the women manufactured for their own use a coarse kind of linen.[25] The game of various sorts with which the forests of Germany were plentifully stocked supplied its inhabitants with food and exercise.[26] Their monstrous herds of cattle, less remarkable indeed for their beauty than for their utility,[27] formed the principal object of their wealth. A small quantity of corn was the only produce exacted from the earth: the use of orchards or artificial meadows was unknown to the Germans; nor can we expect any improvements in agriculture from a people whose property every year experienced a general change by

[21] Tacit. Germ. 16.

[22] When the Germans commanded the Ubii of Cologne to cast off the Roman yoke, and with their new freedom to resume their ancient manners, they insisted on the immediate demolition of the walls of the colony. "Postulamus a vobis, muros coloniæ, munimenta servitii, detrahatis; etiam fera animalia, si clausa teneas, virtutis obliviscuntur." Tacit. Hist. iv. 64.

[23] The straggling villages of Silesia are several miles in length. See Cluver. l. i. c. 13.

[24] One hundred and forty years after Tacitus a few more regular structures were erected near the Rhine and Danube. Herodian l. vii. p. 234.

[25] Tacit. Germ. 17.

[26] Tacit. Germ. 5.

[27] Cæsar de Bell. Gall. vi. 21.

a new division of the arable lands, and who, in that strange operation, avoided disputes by suffering a great part of their territory to lie waste and without tillage.[28]

Gold, silver, and iron were extremely scarce in Germany. Its barbarous inhabitants wanted both skill and patience to investigate those rich veins of silver, which have so liberally rewarded the attention of the princes of Brunswick and Saxony. Sweden, which now supplies Europe with iron, was equally ignorant of its own riches; and the appearance of the arms of the Germans furnished a sufficient proof how little iron they were able to bestow on what they must have deemed the noblest use of that metal. The various transactions of peace and war had introduced some Roman coins (chiefly silver) among the borderers of the Rhine and Danube; but the more distant tribes were absolutely unacquainted with the use of money, carried on their confined traffic by the exchange of commodities, and prized their rude earthen vessels as of equal value with the silver vases, the presents of Rome to their princes and ambassadors.[29] To a mind capable of reflection such leading facts convey more instruction than a tedious detail of subordinate circumstances. The value of money has been settled by general consent to express our wants and our property, as letters were invented to express our ideas; and both these institutions, by giving more active energy to the powers and passions of human nature, have contributed to multiply the objects they were designed to represent. The use of gold and silver is in a great measure factitious; but it would be impossible to enumerate the important and various services which agriculture, and all the arts, have received from iron, when tempered and fashioned by the operation of fire and the dexterous hand of man. Money, in a word, is the most universal incitement, iron the most powerful instrument, of human industry; and it is very difficult to conceive by what means a people, neither

[28] Tacit. Germ. 26. Cæsar, vi. 22.

[29] Tacit. Germ. 5.

actuated by the one nor seconded by the other, could emerge from the grossest barbarism.[30]

If we contemplate a savage nation in any part of the globe, a supine indolence and a carelessness of futurity will be found to constitute their general character. In a civilised state every faculty of man is expanded and exercised; and the great chain of mutual dependence connects and embraces the several members of society. The most numerous portion of it is employed in constant and useful labour. The select few, placed by fortune above that necessity, can, however, fill up their time by the pursuits of interest or glory, by the improvement of their estate or of their understanding, by the duties, the pleasures, and even the follies, of social life. The Germans were not possessed of these varied resources. The care of the house and family, the management of the land and cattle, were delegated to the old and the infirm, to women and slaves. The lazy warrior, destitute of every art that might employ his leisure hours, consumed his days and nights in the animal gratifications of sleep and food. And yet, by a wonderful diversity of nature (according to the remark of a writer who had pierced into its darkest recesses), the same barbarians are by turns the most indolent and the most restless of mankind. They delight in sloth, they detest tranquillity.[31] The languid soul, oppressed with its own weight, anxiously required some new and powerful sensation; and war and danger were the only amusements adequate to its fierce temper. The sound that summoned the German to arms was grateful to his ear. It roused him from his uncomfortable lethargy, gave him an active pursuit, and, by strong exercise of the body, and violent emotions of the mind, restored him to a more lively sense of his existence. In the

[30] It is said that the Mexicans and Peruvians, without the use of either money or iron, had made a very great progress in the arts. Those arts, and the monuments they produced, have been strangely magnified. See Recherches sur les Américains, tom. ii. p. 153, &c.

[31] Tacit. Germ. 15.

dull intervals of peace these barbarians were immoderately addicted to deep gaming and excessive drinking; both of which, by different means, the one by inflaming their passions, the other by extinguishing their reason, alike relieved them from the pain of thinking. They gloried in passing whole days and nights at table; and the blood of friends and relations often stained their numerous and drunken assemblies.[32] Their debts of honour (for in that light they have transmitted to us those of play) they discharged with the most romantic fidelity. The desperate gamester, who had staked his person and liberty on a last throw of the dice, patiently submitted to the decision of fortune, and suffered himself to be bound, chastised, and sold into remote slavery, by his weaker but more lucky antagonist.[33]

Strong beer, a liquor extracted with very little art from wheat or barley, and *corrupted* (as it is strongly expressed by Tacitus) into a certain semblance of wine, was sufficient for the gross purposes of German debauchery. But those who had tasted the rich wines of Italy, and afterwards of Gaul, sighed for that more delicious species of intoxication. They attempted not, however (as has since been executed with so much success), to naturalise the vine on the banks of the Rhine and Danube; nor did they endeavour to procure by industry the materials of an advantageous commerce. To solicit by labour what might be ravished by arms was esteemed unworthy of the German spirit.[34] The intemperate thirst of strong liquors often urged the barbarians to invade the provinces on which art or nature had bestowed those much envied presents. The Tuscan who betrayed his country to the Celtic nations attracted them into Italy by the prospect of the rich fruits and delicious wines, the productions of a happier climate.[35] And in the same manner the German auxiliaries,

[32] Tacit. Germ. 22, 23.

[33] Id. 24. The Germans might borrow the *arts* of play from the Romans, but the *passion* is wonderfully inherent in the human species.

[34] Id. 14.

[35] Plutarch. in Camillo. T. Liv. v. 33.

invited into France during the civil wars of the sixteenth century, were allured by the promise of plenteous quarters in the provinces of Champagne and Burgundy.[86] Drunkenness, the most illiberal, but not the most dangerous of *our* vices, was sometimes capable, in a less civilised state of mankind, of occasioning a battle, a war, or a revolution.

The climate of ancient Germany has been mollified, and the soil fertilised, by the labour of ten centuries from the time of Charlemagne. The same extent of ground, which at present maintains, in ease and plenty, a million of husbandmen and artificers, was unable to supply an hundred thousand lazy warriors with the simple necessaries of life.[87] The Germans abandoned their immense forests to the exercise of hunting, employed in pasturage the most considerable part of their lands, bestowed on the small remainder a rude and careless cultivation, and then accused the scantiness and sterility of a country that refused to maintain the multitude of its inhabitants. When the return of famine severely admonished them of the importance of the arts, the national distress was sometimes alleviated by the emigration of a third, perhaps, or a fourth part of their youth.[88] The possession and the enjoyment of property are the pledges which bind a civilised people to an improved country. But the Germans, who carried with them what they most valued, their arms, their cattle, and their women, cheerfully abandoned the vast silence of their woods for the unbounded hopes of plunder and conquest. The innumerable swarms that issued, or

[86] Dubos, Hist. de la Monarchie Françoise, tom. i. p. 193.

[87] The Helvetian nation, which issued from the country called Switzerland, contained, of every age and sex, 368,000 persons (Cæsar de Bell. Gall. i. 29). At present, the number of people in the Pays de Vaud (a small district on the banks of the Leman Lake, much more distinguished for politeness than for industry) amounts to 112,591. See an excellent Tract of M. Muret, in the Mémoires de la Société de Berne.

[88] Paul Diaconus, c. 1, 2, 3. Machiavel, Davila, and the rest of Paul's followers represent these emigrations too much as regular and concerted measures.

seemed to issue, from the great storehouse of nations, were multiplied by the fears of the vanquished and by the credulity of succeeding ages. And from facts thus exaggerated, an opinion was gradually established, and has been supported by writers of distinguished reputation, that, in the age of Cæsar and Tacitus, the inhabitants of the North were far more numerous than they are in our days.[39] A more serious inquiry into the causes of population seems to have convinced modern philosophers of the falsehood, and indeed the impossibility, of the supposition. To the names of Mariana and of Machiavel[40] we can oppose the equal names of Robertson and Hume.[41]

A warlike nation like the Germans, without either cities, letters, arts, or money, found some compensation for this savage state in the enjoyment of liberty. Their poverty secured their freedom, since our desires and our possessions are the strongest fetters of despotism. "Among the Suiones (says Tacitus) riches are held in honour. They are *therefore* subject to an absolute monarch, who instead of entrusting his people with the free use of arms, as is practised in the rest of Germany, commits them to the safe custody, not of a citizen, or even of a freedman, but of a slave. The neighbours of the Suiones, the Sitones, are sunk even below servitude; they obey a woman."[42] In the mention of these exceptions, the great historian sufficiently acknowledges the general theory of government. We are only at a loss to conceive by what means riches and despotism could penetrate into a remote corner of the North, and extinguish the generous flame that blazed with such fierceness on the frontier of the

[39] Sir William Temple and Montesquieu have indulged, on this subject, the usual liveliness of their fancy.

[40] Machiavel, Hist. di Firenze, l. i. Mariana, Hist. Hispan. l. v. c. 1.

[41] Robertson's Cha. V. Hume's Politic. Ess.

[42] Tacit. Germ. 44, 45. Freinshemius (who dedicated his supplement to Livy, to Christina of Sweden) thinks proper to be very angry with the Roman who expressed so very little reverence for Northern queens.

Roman provinces, or how the ancestors of those Danes and Norwegians, so distinguished in later ages by their unconquered spirit, could thus tamely resign the great character of German liberty.[43] Some tribes, however, on the coast of the Baltic, acknowledged the authority of kings, though without relinquishing the rights of men;[44] but in the far greater part of Germany the form of government was a democracy, tempered, indeed, and controlled, not so much by general and positive laws as by the occasional ascendant of birth or valour, of eloquence or superstition.[45]

Civil governments, in their first institutions, are voluntary associations for mutual defence. To obtain the desired end it is absolutely necessary that each individual should conceive himself obliged to submit his private opinion and actions to the judgment of the greater number of his associates. The German tribes were contented with this rude but liberal outline of political society. As soon as a youth, born of free parents, had attained the age of manhood, he was introduced into the general council of his countrymen, solemnly invested with a shield and spear, and adopted as an equal and worthy member of the military commonwealth. The assembly of the warriors of the tribe was convened at stated seasons, or on sudden emergencies. The trial of public offences, the election of magistrates, and the great business of peace and war were determined by its independent voice.

[43] May we not suspect that superstition was the parent of despotism? The descendants of Odin (whose race was not extinct till the year 1060) are said to have reigned in Sweden above a thousand years. The temple of Upsal was the ancient seat of religion and empire. In the year 1153 I find a singular law prohibiting the use and possession of arms to any, except the king's guards. Is it not probable that it was coloured by the pretence of reviving an old institution? See Dalin's History of Sweden in the Bibliothèque Raisonnée, tom. xl. and xlv.

[44] Tacit. Germ. c. 43. [The Gotones, that is, the Goths, who in the time of Tacitus lived on the right bank of the lower Vistula; but in the third century we find them on the Black Sea. Pliny also mentions the Guttones, Nat. Hist. iv. 14.]

[45] Id. c. 11, 12, 13, &c.

Sometimes, indeed, these important questions were previously considered and prepared in a more select council of the principal chieftains.[46] The magistrates might deliberate and persuade, the people only could resolve and execute; and the resolutions of the Germans were for the most part hasty and violent. Barbarians accustomed to place their freedom in gratifying the present passion, and their courage in overlooking all future consequences, turned away with indignant contempt from the remonstrances of justice and policy, and it was the practice to signify by a hollow murmur their dislike of such timid councils. But, whenever a more popular orator proposed to vindicate the meanest citizen, from either foreign or domestic injury, whenever he called upon his fellow-countrymen to assert the national honour, or to pursue some enterprise full of danger and glory, a loud clashing of shields and spears expressed the eager applause of the assembly. For the Germans always met in arms, and it was constantly to be dreaded lest an irregular multitude, inflamed with faction and strong liquors, should use those arms to enforce, as well as to declare, their furious resolves. We may recollect how often the diets of Poland have been polluted with blood, and the more numerous party has been compelled to yield to the more violent and seditious.[47]

A general of the tribe was elected on occasions of danger; and, if the danger was pressing and extensive, several tribes concurred in the choice of the same general. The bravest warrior was named to lead his countrymen into the field, by his example rather than by his commands. But this power, however limited, was still invidious. It expired with the war,

[46] Grotius changes an expression of Tacitus, *pertractantur*, into *praetractantur*. The correction is equally just and ingenious. [Germ. 11, *apud principes pertractentur*. No change is necessary; *pertractentur* means "be thoroughly discussed." But the general meaning is the same.]

[47] Even in *our* ancient parliament, the barons often carried a question not so much by the number of votes as by that of their armed followers.

and in time of peace the German tribes acknowledged not any supreme chief.[48] *Princes* were, however, appointed, in the general assembly, to administer justice, or rather to compose differences,[49] in their respective districts. In the choice of these magistrates as much regard was shown to birth as to merit.[50] To each was assigned, by the public, a guard, and a council of an hundred persons, and the first of the princes appears to have enjoyed a pre-eminence of rank and honour which sometimes tempted the Romans to compliment him with the regal title.[51]

The comparative view of the powers of the magistrates, in two remarkable instances, is alone sufficient to represent the whole system of German manners. The disposal of the landed property within their district was absolutely vested in their hands, and they distributed it every year according to a new division.[52] At the same time they were not authorised to punish with death, to imprison, or even to strike a private citizen.[53] A people thus jealous of their persons, and careless of their possessions, must have been totally destitute of industry and the arts, but animated with a high sense of honour and independence.

The Germans respected only those duties which they imposed on themselves. The most obscure soldier resisted with disdain the authority of the magistrates. "The noblest youths blushed not to be numbered among the faithful companions of some renowned chief, to whom they devoted their arms and service. A noble emulation prevailed among the companions to obtain the first place in the esteem of their chief; amongst the chiefs, to acquire the greatest number of valiant companions. To be ever surrounded by a band of

[48] Cæsar de Bell. Gall. vi. 23.

[49] Minuunt controversias, is a very happy expression of Cæsar's.

[50] Reges ex nobilitate, duces ex virtute sumunt. Tacit. Germ. 7.

[51] Cluver. Germ. Ant. l. i. c. 38.

[52] Cæsar, vi. 22. Tacit. Germ. 26.

[53] Tacit. Germ. 7.

select youths was the pride and strength of the chiefs, their ornament in peace, their defence in war. The glory of such distinguished heroes diffused itself beyond the narrow limits of their own tribe. Presents and embassies solicited their friendship, and the fame of their arms often ensured victory to the party which they espoused. In the hour of danger it was shameful for the chief to be surpassed in valour by his companions; shameful for the companions not to equal the valour of their chief. To survive his fall in battle was indelible infamy. To protect his person, and to adorn his glory with the trophies of their own exploits, were the most sacred of their duties. The chiefs combated for victory, the companions for the chief. The noblest warriors, whenever their native country was sunk in the laziness of peace, maintained their numerous bands in some distant scene of action, to exercise their restless spirit, and to acquire renown by voluntary dangers. Gifts worthy of soldiers, the warlike steed, the bloody and ever victorious lance, were the rewards which the companions claimed from the liberality of their chief. The rude plenty of his hospitable board was the only pay that *he* could bestow, or *they* would accept. War, rapine, and the free-will offerings of his friends supplied the materials of this munificence."[84] This institution, however it might accidentally weaken the several republics, invigorated the general character of the Germans, and even ripened amongst them all the virtues of which barbarians are susceptible — the faith and valour, the hospitality and the courtesy, so conspicuous long afterwards in the ages of chivalry. The honourable gifts, bestowed by the chief on his brave companions, have been supposed, by an ingenious writer, to contain the first rudiments of the fiefs, distributed after the conquest of the Roman provinces, by the barbarian lords among their vassals, with a similar duty of homage and military service.[85] These

[84] Tacit. Germ. 13, 14.

[85] Esprit des Loix, l. xxx. c. 3. The brilliant imagination of Montesquieu

conditions are, however, very repugnant to the maxims of the ancient Germans, who delighted in mutual presents, but without either imposing or accepting the weight of obligations.[86]

"In the days of chivalry, or more properly of romance, all the men were brave, and all the women were chaste;" and, notwithstanding the latter of these virtues is acquired and preserved with much more difficulty than the former, it is ascribed, almost without exception, to the wives of the ancient Germans. Polygamy was not in use, except among the princes, and among them only for the sake of multiplying their alliances. Divorces were prohibited by manners rather than by laws. Adulteries were punished as rare and inexpiable crimes; nor was seduction justified by example and fashion.[87] We may easily discover that Tacitus indulges an honest pleasure in the contrast of barbarian virtue with the dissolute conduct of the Roman ladies; yet there are some striking circumstances that give an air of truth, or at least of probability, to the conjugal faith and chastity of the Germans.

Although the progress of civilisation has undoubtedly contributed to assuage the fiercer passions of human nature, it seems to have been less favourable to the virtue of chastity, whose most dangerous enemy is the softness of the mind. The refinements of life corrupt while they polish the intercourse of the sexes. The gross appetite of love becomes most dangerous, when it is elevated, or rather, indeed, disguised, by sentimental passion. The elegance of dress, of motion, and of manners gives a lustre to beauty, and inflames the

is corrected, however, by the dry cold reason of the Abbé de Mably. Observations sur l'Histoire de France, tom. i. p. 356.

[86] Gaudent muneribus, sed nec data imputant, nec acceptis obligantur. Tacit. Germ. c. 21.

[87] The adulteress was whipped through the village. Neither wealth nor beauty could inspire compassion, or procure her a second husband. [Tacit. Germ.] 18, 19.

senses through the imagination. Luxurious entertainments, midnight dances, and licentious spectacles present at once temptation and opportunity to female frailty.[58] From such dangers the unpolished wives of the barbarians were secured by poverty, solitude, and the painful cares of a domestic life. The German huts, open on every side to the eye of indiscretion or jealousy, were a better safeguard of conjugal fidelity than the walls, the bolts, and the eunuchs of a Persian harem. To this reason another may be added of a more honourable nature. The Germans treated their women with esteem and confidence, consulted them on every occasion of importance, and fondly believed that in their breasts resided a sanctity and wisdom more than human. Some of these interpreters of fate, such as Velleda, in the Batavian war, governed, in the name of the Deity, the fiercest nations of Germany.[59] The rest of the sex, without being adored as goddesses, were respected as the free and equal companions of soldiers; associated even by the marriage ceremony to a life of toil, of danger, and of glory.[60] In their great invasions, the camps of the barbarians were filled with a multitude of women, who remained firm and undaunted amidst the sound of arms, the various forms of destruction, and the honourable wounds of their sons and husbands.[61] Fainting armies of Germans have more than once been driven back upon the enemy by the generous despair of the women, who dreaded death much less than servitude. If the day was irrecoverably lost, they well knew how to deliver themselves and their children, with their

[58] Ovid employs two hundred lines in the research of places the most favourable to love. Above all he considers the theatre as the best adapted to collect the beauties of Rome, and to melt them into tenderness and sensuality.

[59] Tacit. Hist. iv. 61, 65.

[60] The marriage present was a yoke of oxen, horses, and arms. See Germ. c. 18. Tacitus is somewhat too florid on the subject.

[61] The change of *exigere* into *exugere* is a most excellent correction [c. 7. *Exugere plagas* would hardly be possible. *Exigere plagas* is right, "to examine, probe the wounds."]

own hands, from an insulting victor.[69] Heroines of such a cast may claim our admiration; but they were most assuredly neither lovely nor very susceptible of love. Whilst they affected to emulate the stern virtues of *man*, they must have resigned that attractive softness in which principally consist the charm and weakness of *woman*. Conscious pride taught the German females to suppress every tender emotion that stood in competition with honour, and the first honour of the sex has ever been that of chastity. The sentiments and conduct of these high-spirited matrons may, at once, be considered as a cause, as an effect, and as a proof of the general character of the nation. Female courage, however it may be raised by fanaticism, or confirmed by habit, can be only a faint and imperfect imitation of the manly valour that distinguishes the age or country in which it may be found.

The religious system of the Germans (if the wild opinions of savages can deserve that name) was dictated by their wants, their fears, and their ignorance.[70] They adored the great visible objects and agents of Nature, the Sun and the Moon, the Fire and the Earth; together with those imaginary deities who were supposed to preside over the most important occupations of human life. They were persuaded that, by some ridiculous arts of divination, they could discover the will of the superior beings, and that human sacrifices were the most precious and acceptable offering to their altars. Some applause has been hastily bestowed on the sublime notion entertained by that people of the Deity whom they neither confined within the walls of a temple, nor represented by any human figure; but when we recollect that the Ger-

[69] Tacit. Germ. c. 7. Plutarch. in Mario. Before the wives of the Teutones destroyed themselves and their children, they had offered to surrender, on condition that they should be received as the slaves of the vestal virgins.

[70] Tacitus has employed a few lines, and Cluverius one hundred and twenty-four pages, on this obscure subject. The former discovers in Germany the gods of Greece and Rome. The latter is positive that, under the emblems of the sun, the moon, and the fire, his pious ancestors worshipped the Trinity in unity.

mans were unskilled in architecture, and totally unacquainted with the art of sculpture, we shall readily assign the true reason of a scruple, which arose not so much from a superiority of reason as from a want of ingenuity. The only temples in Germany were dark and ancient groves, consecrated by the reverence of succeeding generations. Their secret gloom, the imagined residence of an invisible power, by presenting no distinct object of fear or worship, impressed the mind with a still deeper sense of religious horror;[64] and the priests, rude and illiterate as they were, had been taught by experience the use of every artifice that could preserve and fortify impressions so well suited to their own interest.

The same ignorance which renders barbarians incapable of conceiving or embracing the useful restraints of laws exposes them naked and unarmed to the blind terrors of superstition. The German priests, improving this favourable temper of their countrymen, had assumed a jurisdiction even in temporal concerns which the magistrate could not venture to exercise; and the haughty warrior patiently submitted to the lash of correction, when it was inflicted, not by any human power, but by the immediate order of the god of war.[65] The defects of civil policy were sometimes supplied by the interposition of ecclesiastical authority. The latter was constantly exerted to maintain silence and decency in the popular assemblies; and was sometimes extended to a more enlarged concern for the national welfare. A solemn procession was occasionally celebrated in the present countries of Mecklenburgh and Pomerania. The unknown symbol of the *Earth*, covered with a thick veil, was placed on a carriage drawn by cows; and in this manner the goddess, whose common residence was in the isle of Rugen, visited several adjacent tribes of her worshippers. During her progress, the sound of war was

[64] The sacred wood, described with such sublime horror by Lucan, was in the neighbourhood of Marseilles; but there were many of the same kind in Germany.

[65] Tacit. Germania, c. 7.

hushed, quarrels were suspended, arms laid aside, and the restless Germans had an opportunity of tasting the blessings of peace and harmony.[66] The *truce of God*, so often and so ineffectually proclaimed by the clergy of the eleventh century, was an obvious imitation of this ancient custom.[67]

But the influence of religion was far more powerful to inflame than to moderate the fierce passions of the Germans. Interest and fanaticism often prompted its ministers to sanctify the most daring and the most unjust enterprises, by the approbation of Heaven, and full assurances of success. The consecrated standards, long revered in the groves of superstition, were placed in the front of the battle;[68] and the hostile army was devoted with dire execrations to the gods of war and of thunder.[69] In the faith of soldiers (and such were the Germans) cowardice is the most unpardonable of sins. A brave man was the worthy favourite of their martial deities; the wretch who had lost his shield was alike banished from the religious and the civil assemblies of his countrymen. Some tribes of the North seem to have embraced the doctrine of transmigration,[70] others imagined a gross paradise of immortal drunkenness.[71] All agreed that a life spent in arms, and a glorious death in battle, were the best preparations for a happy futurity, either in this or in another world.

The immortality so vainly promised by the priests was, in some degree, conferred by the bards. That singular order of men has most deservedly attracted the notice of all who have attempted to investigate the antiquities of the Celts, the

[66] Tacit. Germania, c. 40.

[67] See Dr. Robertson's History of Charles V. vol. i. note 10.

[68] Tacit. Germ. c. 7. These standards were only the heads of wild beasts.

[69] See an instance of this custom, Tacit. Annal. xiii. 57.

[70] Cæsar, Diodorus, and Lucan seem to ascribe this doctrine to the Gauls, but M. Pelloutier (Histoire des Celtes, l. iii. c. 18) labours to reduce their expressions to a more orthodox sense.

[71] Concerning this gross but alluring doctrine of the Edda, see Fable xx. in the curious version of that book, published by M. Mallet, in his Introduction to the History of Denmark.

Scandinavians, and the Germans. Their genius and character, as well as the reverence paid to that important office, have been sufficiently illustrated. But we cannot so easily express, or even conceive, the enthusiasm of arms and glory which they kindled in the breast of their audience. Among a polished people, a taste for poetry is rather an amusement of the fancy than a passion of the soul. And yet, when in calm retirement we peruse the combats described by Homer or Tasso, we are insensibly seduced by the fiction, and feel a momentary glow of martial ardour. But how faint, how cold is the sensation which a peaceful mind can receive from solitary study! It was in the hour of battle, or in the feast of victory, that the bards celebrated the glory of heroes of ancient days, the ancestors of those warlike chieftains who listened with transport to their artless but animated strains. The view of arms and of danger heightened the effect of the military song; and the passions which it tended to excite, the desire of fame and the contempt of death, were the habitual sentiments of a German mind.[73]

Such was the situation and such were the manners of the ancient Germans. Their climate, their want of learning, of arts, and of laws, their notions of honour, of gallantry, and of religion, their sense of freedom, impatience of peace, and thirst of enterprise, all contributed to form a people of military heroes. And yet we find that, during more than two hundred and fifty years that elapsed from the defeat of Varus to the reign of Decius, these formidable barbarians made few considerable attempts, and not any material impression, on the luxurious and enslaved provinces of the

[73] See Tacit. Germ. c. 3. Diodor. Sicul. l. v. [29]. Strabo, l. iv. p. 197. The classical reader may remember the rank of Demodocus in the Phaeacian court, and the ardour infused by Tyrtaeus into the fainting Spartans. Yet there is little probability that the Greeks and the Germans were the same people. Much learned trifling might be spared, if our antiquarians would condescend to reflect that similar manners will naturally be produced by similar situations.

empire. Their progress was checked by their want of arms and discipline, and their fury was diverted by the intestine divisions of ancient Germany.

I. It has been observed, with ingenuity, and not without truth, that the command of iron soon gives a nation the command of gold. But the rude tribes of Germany, alike destitute of both those valuable metals, were reduced slowly to acquire, by their unassisted strength, the possession of the one as well as the other. The face of a German army displayed their poverty of iron. Swords and the longer kind of lances they could seldom use. Their *frameæ* (as they called them in their own language) were long spears headed with a sharp but narrow iron point, and which, as occasion required, they either darted from a distance, or pushed in close onset. With this spear and with a shield their cavalry was contented. A multitude of darts, scattered[73] with incredible force, were an additional resource of the infantry. Their military dress, when they wore any, was nothing more than a loose mantle. A variety of colours was the only ornament of their wooden or their osier shields. Few of the chiefs were distinguished by cuirasses, scarce any by helmets. Though the horses of Germany were neither beautiful, swift, nor practised in the skilful evolutions of the Roman manage, several of the nations obtained renown by their cavalry; but, in general, the principal strength of the Germans consisted in their infantry,[74] which was drawn up in several deep columns, according to the distinction of tribes and families. Impatient of fatigue or delay, these half-armed warriors rushed to battle with dissonant shouts and disordered ranks; and sometimes, by the effort of native valour, prevailed over the constrained and more artificial bravery of the Roman mercenaries. But as the barbarians poured forth their whole souls on the first

[73] Missilia spargunt, Tacit. Germ. c. 6. Either that historian used a vague expression, or he meant that they were thrown at random.

[74] It was the principal distinction from the Sarmatians, who generally fought on horseback.

onset, they knew not how to rally or to retire. A repulse was a sure defeat; and a defeat was most commonly total destruction. When we recollect the complete armour of the Roman soldiers, their discipline, exercises, evolutions, fortified camps, and military engines, it appears a just matter of surprise how the naked and unassisted valour of the barbarians could dare to encounter in the field the strength of the legions and the various troops of the auxiliaries, which seconded their operations. The contest was too unequal, till the introduction of luxury had enervated the vigour, and a spirit of disobedience and sedition had relaxed the discipline, of the Roman armies. The introduction of barbarian auxiliaries into those armies was a measure attended with very obvious dangers, as it might gradually instruct the Germans in the arts of war and of policy. Although they were admitted in small numbers and with the strictest precaution, the example of Civilis was proper to convince the Romans that the danger was not imaginary, and that their precautions were not always sufficient.[78] During the civil wars that followed the death of Nero, that artful and intrepid Batavian, whom his enemies condescended to compare with Hannibal and Sertorius,[79] formed a great design of freedom and ambition. Eight Batavian cohorts, renowned in the wars of Britain and Italy, repaired to his standard. He introduced an army of Germans into Gaul, prevailed on the powerful cities of Treves and Langres to embrace his cause, defeated the legions, destroyed their fortified camps, and employed against the Romans the military knowledge which he had acquired in their service. When at length, after an obstinate struggle, he yielded to the power of the empire, Civilis secured himself and his country by an honourable treaty. The Batavians still

[78] The relation of this enterprise occupies a great part of the fourth and fifth books of the History of Tacitus, and is more remarkable for its eloquence than perspicuity. Sir Henry Saville has observed several inaccuracies.

[79] Tacit. Hist. iv. 13. Like them, he had lost an eye.

continued to occupy the islands of the Rhine,[77] the allies, not the servants, of the Roman monarchy.

II. The strength of ancient Germany appears formidable when we consider the effects that might have been produced by its united effort. The wide extent of country might very possibly contain a million of warriors, as all who were of an age to bear arms were of a temper to use them. But this fierce multitude, incapable of concerting or executing any plan of national greatness, was agitated by various and often hostile intentions. Germany was divided into more than forty independent states; and even in each state the union of the several tribes was extremely loose and precarious. The barbarians were easily provoked; they knew not how to forgive an injury, much less an insult; their resentments were bloody and implacable. The casual disputes that so frequently happened in their tumultuous parties of hunting or drinking were sufficient to inflame the minds of whole nations; the private feud of any considerable chieftains diffused itself among their followers and allies. To chastise the insolent, or to plunder the defenceless, were alike causes of war. The most formidable states of Germany affected to encompass their territories with a wide frontier of solitude and devastation. The awful distance preserved by their neighbours attested the terror of their arms, and in some measure defended them from the danger of unexpected incursions.[78]

"The Bructeri (it is Tacitus who now speaks) were totally exterminated by the neighbouring tribes,[79] provoked by their insolence, allured by the hopes of spoil, and perhaps inspired by the tutelar deities of the empire. Above sixty thousand

[77] It was contained between the two branches of the old Rhine, as they subsisted before the face of the country was changed by art and nature. See Cluver. German. Antiq. l. iii. c. 30, 37.

[78] Cæsar de Bell. Gall. l. vi. 23.

[79] They are mentioned however in the ivth and vth centuries by Nazarius, Ammianus, Claudian, &c., as a tribe of Franks. See Cluver. Germ. Antiq. l. iii. c. 13.

barbarians were destroyed, not by the Roman arms, but in our sight, and for our entertainment. May the nations, enemies of Rome, ever preserve this enmity to each other! We have now attained the utmost verge of prosperity,[80] and have nothing left to demand of fortune except the discord of the barbarians."[81] These sentiments, less worthy of the humanity than of the patriotism of Tacitus, express the invariable maxims of the policy of his countrymen. They deemed it a much safer expedient to divide than to combat the barbarians, from whose defeat they could derive neither honour nor advantage. The money and negotiations of Rome insinuated themselves into the heart of Germany, and every art of seduction was used with dignity to conciliate those nations whom their proximity to the Rhine or Danube might render the most useful friends as well as the most troublesome enemies. Chiefs of renown and power were flattered by the most trifling presents, which they received either as marks of distinction or as the instruments of luxury. In civil dissensions, the weaker faction endeavoured to strengthen its interest by entering into secret connections with the governors of the frontier provinces. Every quarrel among the Germans was fomented by the intrigues of Rome; and every plan of union and public good was defeated by the stronger bias of private jealousy and interest.[82]

The general conspiracy which terrified the Romans under the reign of Marcus Antoninus comprehended almost all the nations of Germany, and even Sarmatia, from the mouth of the Rhine to that of the Danube.[83] It is impossible for us to

[80] *Urgentibus* is the common reading, but good sense, Lipsius, and some MSS. declare for *Vergentibus*. [An unnecessary correction.]

[81] Tacit. Germania, c. 33. The pious Abbé de la Bléterie is very angry with Tacitus, talks of the devil who was a murderer from the beginning, &c., &c.

[82] Many traces of this policy may be discovered in Tacitus and Dion; and many more may be inferred from the principles of human nature.

[83] Hist. August. p. 31 [iv. 22]. Ammian. Marcellin. l. xxxi. c. 5. Aurel. Victor. [Cæs. 16]. The emperor Marcus was reduced to sell the rich fur-

determine whether this hasty confederation was formed by necessity, by reason, or by passion; but we may rest assured, that the barbarians were neither allured by the indolence or provoked by the ambition of the Roman monarch. This dangerous invasion required all the firmness and vigilance of Marcus. He fixed generals of ability in the several stations of attack, and assumed in person the conduct of the most important province on the Upper Danube. After a long and doubtful conflict, the spirit of the barbarians was subdued. The Quadi and the Marcomanni,[84] who had taken the lead in the war, were the most severely punished in its catastrophe. They were commanded to retire five miles [85] from their own banks of the Danube, and to deliver up the flower of the youth, who were immediately sent into Britain, a remote island, where they might be secure as hostages and useful as soldiers.[86] On the frequent rebellions of the Quadi and Marcomanni, the irritated emperor resolved to reduce their country into the form of a province.[87] His designs were disappointed by death. This formidable league, however, the only

niture of the palace, and to enlist slaves and robbers. [This war is generally called the Marcomannic, but its proper name, at first, was the *Bellum Germanicum*. At a later stage, when the Sarmatians made common cause with the Germans, it was called the *Bellum Germanicum Sarmaticum*. The Romans took the field in 167, and hostilities lasted, with a short interval of peace, till the accession of Commodus, 180. The following German peoples took part in it:— Marcomanni, Quadi, Narisci, Victovali, Hermunduri, Vandals, Buri; also the (Sarmatian) Jazyges, who dwelt between the Theiss and Danube. Large settlements of the conquered barbarians were made within the limits of the Empire, so that this period has importance for the history of the Roman *colonatus*. It has been well treated by Heisterbergk in his work, Die Entstehung des Colonats.]

[84] The Marcomanni, a colony, who, from the banks of the Rhine, occupied Bohemia and Moravia, had once erected a great and formidable monarchy under their king Maroboduus. See Strabo, l. vii. [290]. Vell. Pat. ii. 105 [108]. Tacit. Annal. ii. 63.

[85] Mr. Wotton (History of Rome, p. 166) increases the prohibition to ten times the distance. His reasoning is specious but not conclusive. Five miles were sufficient for a fortified barrier.

[86] Dion, l. lxxi. [11 *et sqq.*] and lxxii. [2].

[87] [He intended to form two new provinces, Marcomannia and Sarmatia.]

one that appears in the two first centuries of the Imperial history, was entirely dissipated without leaving any traces behind in Germany.

In the course of this introductory chapter, we have confined ourselves to the general outlines of the manners of Germany, without attempting to describe or to distinguish the various tribes which filled that great country in the time of Cæsar, of Tacitus, or of Ptolemy.[88] As the ancient, or as new tribes successively present themselves in the series of this history, we shall concisely mention their origin, their situation, and their particular character. Modern nations are fixed and permanent societies, connected among themselves by laws and government, bound to their native soil by arts and agriculture. The German tribes were voluntary and fluctuating associations of soldiers, almost of savages. The same territory often changed its inhabitants in the tide of conquest and emigration. The same communities, uniting in a plan of defence or invasion, bestowed a new title on their new confederacy. The dissolution of an ancient confederacy restored to the independent tribes their peculiar but long-forgotten appellation. A victorious state often communicated its own name to a vanquished people. Sometimes crowds of volunteers flocked from all parts to the standard of a favourite leader; his camp became their country, and some circumstance of the enterprise soon gave a common denomination to the mixed multitude. The distinctions of the ferocious invaders were perpetually varied by themselves, and confounded by the astonished subjects of the Roman empire.[89]

Wars and the administration of public affairs are the principal subjects of history; but the number of persons interested in these busy scenes is very different, according to the different condition of mankind. In great monarchies millions of

[88] [For our authorities on early German History, see vol. ii. App. 1.]

[89] See an excellent dissertation on the origin and migrations of nations, in the Mémoires de l'Académie des Inscriptions, tom. xviii. p. 48-71. It is seldom that the antiquarian and the philosopher are so happily blended.

obedient subjects pursue their useful occupations in peace and obscurity. The attention of the writer, as well as of the reader, is solely confined to a court, a capital, a regular army, and the districts which happen to be the occasional scene of military operations. But a state of freedom and barbarism, the season of civil commotions, or the situation of petty republics[90] raises almost every member of the community into action and consequently into notice. The irregular divisions and the restless motions of the people of Germany dazzle our imagination, and seem to multiply their numbers. The profuse enumeration of kings and warriors, of armies and nations, inclines us to forget that the same objects are continually repeated under a variety of appellations, and that the most splendid appellations have been frequently lavished on the most inconsiderable objects.

[90] Should we suspect that Athens contained only 21,000 citizens, and Sparta no more than 39,000? See Hume and Wallace on the number of mankind in ancient and modern times. [See above, chap. ii. note 22.]

APPENDIX

ADDITIONAL NOTES BY THE EDITOR

1. AUTHORITIES

CASSIUS DIO COCCEIANUS belonged to a good family of the Bithynian town of Nicæa. His father Apronianus had been entrusted with the governorships of Dalmatia and Cilicia, and he himself achieved a more distinguished career in the civil service. Arriving at Rome in the year in which the Emperor Marcus died (180), he advanced step by step to the prætorship (193), and subsequently held the office of consul twice (see lxxiii. 12; lxxx. 2; Corp. Insc. Lat. iii. 5587). He was prefect (ἐπεστάτησα, lxxix. 7) of Pergamum and Smyrna in the reign of Macrinus; and under Alexander Severus was at first proconsul of Africa, and was afterwards transferred to Dalmatia and thence to Upper Pannonia (lxxx. 1). After the year 229 he retired from public life, owing to an ailment of his feet (lxxx. 5).

A work on dreams and a monograph on the reign of the Emperor Commodus having elicited words of encouragement from Septimius Severus, Dion conceived the idea of writing a Roman history from the earliest time to his own day. During the intervals between his public employments abroad he used to retire to Capua and devote his leisure to this enterprise. He completed it in eighty Books, bringing the history down as far as the year of his second consulship, 229 A.D. Of this work we possess in a complete form only Books xxxvi. to lx., which cover the important period from 68 B.C. to 60 A.D. The earlier books were largely used by Zonaras whose Epitome we possess, and we have also a considerable number of fragments, preserved in the Excerpta de virtutibus et vitiis, and the Excerpta de legationibus (compilations made from Constantine VII. in the tenth century).[1] For the last twenty Books we have the abridgment by Xiphilin (eleventh century), but in the case of the lxxviiith and lxxixth a mutilated MS. of the original text. For the reign of Antoninus Pius, however (bk. lxx.), even Xiphilin deserts us; there seems to have been a lacuna in his copy.

For the history of the early Empire we have few contemporary literary sources, and thus the continuous narrative of Dion is of inestimable value. Living before the Principate had passed away, and having had personal experience of affairs of state, he had a grasp of constitutional matters which was quite impossible for later writers; though in describing the institutions of Augustus he falls into the error of making statements which applied to his own age but not to the beginning of the Principate. He affected to be an Attic stylist and aspired to write like Thucydides. (The text of Dindorf — an important contribution to the study of Dion — is now being admirably re-edited by J. Melber; the first two volumes have already appeared.)

[1] The Excerpta de Sententiis contain not direct extracts from Dion, but passages founded on his work. The Planudean Excerpta (fifteenth century) are spurious. See preface to Melber's edition.

The history of Dion was continued by an ANONYMOUS author, of whose work we have some fragments (collected in vol. iv. of Müller's Fragmenta Hist. Græc. p. 191 *sqq.*), and know something further through the fact that it was a main source of Zonaras when he had no longer Dion to follow. [Compare vol. ii. Appendix 10 ad. init.]

HERODIAN was of Syrian birth, and, like Dion, was employed in the civil service, but in far humbler grades. If he had ever risen to the higher magistracies, if he had ever held the exalted position of a provincial governor, he would certainly have mentioned his success; the general expression which he employs, "Imperial and public offices" (i. 2), shows sufficiently that he had no career. The title of his work was "Histories of the Empire after Marcus," and embraced in eight Books the reigns from the accession of Commodus to that of Gordian III. His own comments on the events which he relates are tedious; and the importance of his book rests on the circumstance that he was an honest contemporary; he has none of the higher qualities of an historian. (Kreutzer's dissertation, De Herodiano rerum Rom. scriptore, 1881, may be referred to.)

The HISTORIA AUGUSTA is a composite work, in which six several authors, who lived and wrote in the reigns of Diocletian and Constantine, had a hand. These authors however were not collaborators and did not write with a view to the production of the work which we possess. The Historia Augusta seems, in the light of recent criticism, to have been an eclectic compilation from a number of different, originally independent histories.

Ælius Spartianus wrote, by the wish of the Emperor Diocletian, whom he often addresses, a series of Imperial biographies (including Cæsars as well as Augusti) from the death of the dictator (post Cæsarem dictatorem; ii. 7, 5). He came down at least as far as Caracalla.

Vulcacius Gallicanus likewise addressed to Diocletian a work on the lives of all the Emperors who bore the full title of Augustus, whether by legitimate right or as tyrants. See vi. 3, 3.

The series of *Trebellius Pollio* was on a more limited scale. It began with the two Philips, and embracing all Emperors, whether renowned or obscure, reached as far as Claudius and his brother Quintillus. It was not dedicated to Diocletian but was written in his reign, before Constantius Chlorus had been raised to the dignity of Augustus, that is before 1st May 305 (cp. xxiii. 7, 1, where Claudius is described as the ancestor *Constanti Cæsaris nostri*; cp. too, *ib.* 14, 3, where *Constantinus* is an error for *Constantius*, and xxiv. 21, 7, where we get the prior limit of 302). It is probable that the work of Pollio was a continuation of another series of Lives which ended with the accession of Philip; and it is possible that this presumable series may have been actually that of Spartian or Vulcacius, but it is quite uncertain.

Flavius Vopiscus of Syracuse professedly continued the work of Pollio, and carried it down as far as the death of Carinus and accession of Diocletian. He wrote, at least, the life of Aurelian between 1st May 305 and 25th July 306, the period in which Constantius was Emperor; et est quidem iam Constantius imperator, xxvi. 44, 5.

Julius Capitolinus wrote another series of Imperial biographies, of which some were composed under, and dedicated to, Diocletian, while others were written at a later period for Constantine. Where he began is uncertain; the earliest Life from his pen which we possess is that of Antoninus Pius, the latest those of Maximus and Balbinus. Of the Lives which are extant under his name, those of Marcus, Lucius Verus, and Macrinus contain the name of Diocletian. Those of Albinus and the Maximins have internal notes of their dedication to Constantine. As Albinus comes chronologically between Verus and Macrinus, both dating from the reign of Diocletian, it is impossible, if the ascription of *Macrinus* to Capitolinus is right, to draw the conclusion that all the earlier Lives were written in the earlier period, and all the later Lives in the later. But to this point I shall return.

Ælius Lampridius dedicated his Imperial biographies to Constantine. He began with Commodus, if not earlier, and intended to include Diocletian and Maximian. The latest of his Lives that exists is that of Alexander Severus.

The original MS. of the Historia Augusta, from which our MSS. are derived, contained a complete series of Imperial biographies, from Hadrian to Carinus, put together from the works of these six writers. The work of Pollio, and its continuation by Vopiscus, were included in their entirety. The contributions drawn from the various biographers may be conveniently seen in the following table: —

Spartian:	Hadrian . .	i.	(date: before May 305).
	Aelius Verus .	ii.	
	Didius Julianus .	ix.	
	Severus . .	x.	
	Pescennius Niger	xi.	
	Caracallus . .	xiii.	
Vulcacius:	Avidius Cassius .	vi.	(date: before May 305).
Capitolinus:	Antoninus Pius .	iii.	(date: before May 305).
	M. Antoninus .	iv.	
	Verus . .	v.	
	Pertinax . .	viii.	
	Clodius Albinus .	xii.	(date: reign of Constantine).
	Maximini duo .	xix.	
	Gordiani tres .	xx.	
	Maximus et Balbinus	xxi.	
Lampridius:	Commodus . .	vii.	(date: reign of Constantine).
	Diadumenus .	xvi.	
	Heliogabalus .	xvii.	
	Alexander Severus	xviii.	
Pollio:	Philip to Claudius	—— to xxv.	(date: before May 305).
Vopiscus:	Aurelian to Carinus	xxvi. to xxx.	(date: after May 305, and begun before July 306).

I. The Life of Geta (xiv.) I have not included in this list. The name of the author is not given in the MSS.; the *editio princeps* assigned it to Spartianus. There is, however, a serious objection against attributing it to Spartian in the lack of decisive external evidence. For it is dedicated to Constantine, whereas the Lives written by Spartian are dedicated to Diocletian. The fact that Spartian intended to write a life of Geta (see xiii. 11, 1) proves nothing; for there is nothing to show that separate Lives of Geta were not also included in the collections of Lampridius and Capitolinus, and that the compiler of the Historia Augusta did not prefer one of them to the *Geta* of Spartian.

II. The Life of Opilius Macrinus (xv.) I have also omitted, although the

MSS. ascribe it to Capitolinus. But it is highly probable that the Inscriptio is not genuine. For the author of this Life only knows of two Gordians (3, 5, nec inter Antoninos referendi sunt duo Gordiani), herein agreeing with Lampridius (xvi. 32, and xvii. 34, 6); whereas Capitolinus is not only aware of the three Gordians, whose lives he wrote (xx.), but criticises the ignorant writers who only speak of two (xx. 2, 1, Gordiani non, ut quidam imperiti scriptores locuntur, duo sed tres fuerunt). This flagrant contradiction, which imperatively forbids us to ascribe the *Gordians* and *Macrinus* to the same writer, is borne out by the fact that *Macrinus* is dedicated to Diocletian, whereas *Albinus* is addressed to Constantine. It is natural to suppose that Capitolinus wrote his Lives in chronological order, and completed in the reign of Constantine the biographical series which he had begun in that of Diocletian. If we decide that our *Macrinus* is not really his work, we restore the natural order. We cannot, however, suppose that *Macrinus* was the composition of Lampridius, who wrote under Constantine. We must attribute it either to Spartian or to Vulcacius.

III. The archetype of our MSS. was mutilated, and, unfortunately for the history of a very difficult period, there is a lacuna extending from the end of *Maximus* and *Balbinus* into the *Two Valerians*, of which only a congeries of fragments remains. Thus the Lives of Philip, Decius, and Gallus by Trebellius Pollio are lost. The subscription at the end of *Maximus* and *Balbinus* attributes the *Valerians* to Capitolinus, but this is clearly an insertion made after the lost Lives had fallen out.

IV. In general the Lives are arranged in chronological order. There are three remarkable deviations. (1) Didius Julianus comes after Verus and before Commodus, in the place where we should expect Avidius Cassius, while Avidius comes where we expect Julianus. (2) Albinus comes after Macrinus instead of following Pescennius; and (3) Heliogabalus, Diadumenus, Macrinus takes the place of the proper order Macrinus, Diadumenus, Heliogabalus. In all three cases Peter has corrected the MSS. in his edition. These misplacements cannot be explained by mistakes in the binding of the sheets (quaternions) of the archetype, though such mistakes certainly occurred and led to minor misplacements, notably that in the Life of Alexander, c. 43 (see Peter's ed.).

All these writers have much the same idea of historical biography. They give a great many personal details, and are fond of trivial anecdotes; but they have no notion of perspicuous arrangement, and no apprehension of deeper historical questions. Their chief source for the earlier Lives was Marius Maximus (used by Spartian, Vulcacius, Capitolinus, and Lampridius, and criticised by Vopiscus as homo omnium verbosissimus, xxix. 1), who continued the work of Suetonius, from Nerva to Elagabalus. He lived about 170–230 A.D. (See, for a daring attempt to reconstruct the history of Marius, Müller's essay in Büdinger's Untersuchungen zur römischen Kaisergeschichte, vol. iii. The tract of J. Plew, Marius Maximus als directe und indirecte Quelle der Scriptores Hist. Aug., 1878, is of much greater value.) Capitolinus and the author of the Vita Macrini, also used a work of Junius Cordus who devoted himself to the elucidation of the obscurer reigns (xv. 1). But there were other stray sources both Latin and Greek. For example Acholius, master of ceremonies to the Emperor Valerian, described the journeys of Alexander Severus and was consulted by Lampridius (xviii. 64). The same writer wrote Acta, in the ninth Book of which he dealt with the reign of Valerian (xxvi. 12). For other sources see Teuffel, Gesch. der röm. Litt., § 387. The introduction of Vopiscus to his Life of Aurelian is well worth reading. It throws some light on the way in which these lives were written and the sources which the writers commanded. We learn that Aurelian's daily acts were written by his own orders in *libri lintei*, and the historian could obtain them from the numbered cases[1] of the Ulpian Library. The war of Aurelian then was an official account (*characters historico digesta*).

The citation of original documents (both genuine and spurious) is a feature of the Historia Augusta. Vopiscus, and perhaps the others in some cases, took these directly from the originals in the Ulpian Library, but in the case of the earlier Lives it is highly probable that they were drawn, at second hand, from Marius Maximus, who included such *pièces justicatifs* in his work.

The uncertainty which prevailed in the reign of Diocletian as to leading events which happened as late as the reign of Aurelian is illustrated instructively by the dispute among historical students, recorded by Vopiscus, as to whether Firmus, the tyrant of Egypt, had been invested with the purple, and reigned as an Emperor, or not (xxix. 2).

A special word must be said about the Lives of Trebellius Pollio. It has been shown with tolerable certainty, by the investigations of H. Peter, that all the original documents which he inserts, whether transactions, or letters, or speeches, are forgeries. He has also been convicted of unfairness in his presentation of the personality of Gallienus. When Gibbon says (chap. x. note 156), that the character of that unfortunate prince has been fairly transmitted to us, on the ground that "the historians who wrote before the elevation of the family of Constantine, could not have the most remote interest to misrepresent the character of Gallienus," he overlooks the internal evidence in the Biographies of Pollio (as pointed out above) which proves that this writer was actuated by the wish to glorify Constantius indirectly by a glorification of Claudius. He had thus a distinct motive for disparaging the abilities and actions of Gallienus. For, by portraying that monarch as incapable of ruling and utterly incompetent to cope with the dangers which beset the Empire, he was enabled to suggest a contrast between the contemptible prince and his brilliant successor. Through such a contrast the achievements of Claudius seemed more striking. (Recently F. Rothkegel in a treatise on Die Regierung des Gallienus, of which the first part has appeared, 1894, has endeavoured to do justice to Gallienus, and show that he was not so bad or incompetent as he has been made out.)

The best text of the Historia Augusta is that of H. Peter, who is the chief authority on the subject. Out of the large literature, which bears on these biographies, I may refer to Gemoll's Die Script. Hist. Aug., 1886, which has been largely used in this account of the Augustan Biographies. Dessau has recently proved (Hermes, 1889) that the Lives were seriously interpolated in the age of Theodosius. His daring thesis that they are entirely forgeries is rejected by Mommsen, who admits the interpolations (*ib.* 1890).

When the Historia Augusta deserts us, our sources, whether Greek or Latin, are either late or scrappy. We can extract some historical facts from a number of contemporary PANEGYRICAL ORATIONS, mostly of uncertain authorship, composed for special occasions under Maximian and his successors. These will be best consulted in the xii. Panegyrici Latini edited by Bährens. No. 2 in praise of Maximian is doubtfully ascribed to Claudius Mamertinus; it was composed at Trier in 289 A.D. for 21st April, the birthday of Rome. No. 3, said to be by the same author, is a *genethliacus* for Maximian's birthday in 291. No. 4 is the plea of Eumenius of Augustodunum *pro restaurandis*

[1] Cp. xxvii. 8, 1, where an "ivory volume in the sixth armarium" is referred to. Decrees of the Senate, relating to the Emperors, used to be written in ivory books, as we learn in the same place.

scholis pronounced in the end of 297 before the *praeses provinciae*. No. 5, of uncertain authorship, but probably by Eumenius, is a panegyric on Constantius, delivered in the spring of the same year at Trier. No. 6 extols Maximian and Constantine, on the occasion of the marriage of Constantine with Fausta, Maximian's daughter, 307. No. 7 (probably by Eumenius), is a panegyric on Constantine, delivered at Trier, shortly after the execution of Maximian, 310. No. 8 (also plausibly ascribed to Eumenius), is a speech of thanksgiving to Constantine for benefits which he bestowed upon Autun, 311. No. 9 is a eulogy of Constantine pronounced at Trier, early in 313, and contains a brief account of his Italian expedition. No. 10 bears the name of Nazarius, and is likewise a panegyric of Constantine, dating from the fifteenth year of his reign, 321. (On Eumenius, cp. Brandt, Eumenius von Augustodunum, &c., 1882.)

SEXTUS AURELIUS VICTOR was appointed (Ammianus tells us, xxi. 10, 6) governor of the Second Pannonia by the Emperor Julian in 361; and at a later period became Prefect of the City. Inscriptions confirm both statements (see C.I.L. 6, 1186, and Orelli-Henzen, 3715). He was of African birth (see his Cæs. 20, 6), and a pagan. Some think that the work known as Cæsares was composed in its present form by Victor himself; but in the two MSS. (Bruxell. and Oxon.) the title is Aurelii Victoris historiæ abbreviatæ, and Th. Opitz (Quæstiones de Sex. Aurelio Victore, in the Acta Societ. Philol. Lips. ii. 2) holds that it is an abridgment of a larger work—an opinion which is shared by Wölfflin and others. (A convenient critical edition has been recently brought out by F. Pichlmayer, 1892.) The Epitome (*libellus de vita et moribus imperatorum breviatus ex libris Sex. Aurelii Victoris a Cæsare Aug. usque ad Theodosium*) seems dependent on the Cæsares as far as Domitian, but afterwards differs completely. Marius Maximus was very probably one of the chief sources.

EUTROPIUS held the office of *magister memoriae* at the court of Valens (365–378 A.D.), to whom he dedicated his Short Roman History (Breviarium ab urbe condita). He had taken part, as he tells us, in the fatal expedition of Julian, 363 A.D. (x. 16, 1). His handbook, which comes down to the death of Jovian, was a success, and had the honour of being translated into Greek about 380 A.D. by the Syrian Paeanius, a pupil of Libanius (see above, p. 237). It contrasts favourably with other books of the kind, both in matter and in style. His chief sources were Suetonius, the writers of the Historia Augusta, and the work of the unknown author who is generally designated as the "CHRONOGRAPHER OF 354."

This work, unknown to Gibbon, was published and commented on by Mommsen in the Abhandlungen der sächs. Gesellschaft der Wissensch. in 1850, and has been recently published by the same editor in vol. i. of the Chronica Minora in the M.H.G. It contains a number of various lists, including Fasti Consulares up to 354, the praefecti urbis of Rome from 258 to 354, the bishops of Rome up to Liberius (352). The MSS. contain later additions, especially the so-called Chronicon Cuspiniani (published by Cuspinianus in 1552 along with the Chronicle of Cassiodorus), which is a source of value for the reigns of Leo and Zeno and the first years of Anastasius.

Another historical epitome dedicated to Valens was that of (Rufus) FESTUS, who seems also to have been a *magister memoriae*. The time at which his book was composed can be precisely fixed to 369 A.D. by his reference to "this great victory over the Goths" (c. 29) gained by Valens in that year and by the fact that he is ignorant of the province of Valentia, which was formed in the same year. Festus has some valuable notices for the history of the fourth century.

L. Cælius Lactantius Firmianus lived at Nicomedia under Diocletian and Constantine, and taught rhetoric. In the later years of his life he had the honour of acting as the tutor of Constantine's son, Crispus. Our chief authority for his life is Jerome; cp. esp. De Viris Illust., 80. His works were mainly theological, and the chief of them is the Divine Institutions in seven Books. But the most important for the historian is the treatise De Mortibus Persecutorum,[1] — concerning the manners of death which befell the persecutors of Christianity from Nero to Maximin. It was composed in 314–315 A.D. Its authorship has been a matter of dispute, for it does not bear the name Lactantius, but L. Cæcilius. It is, however, by no means improbable that L. Cæcilius is Lactantius, and that the treatise is that enumerated by Jerome (*loc. cit.*) among his works as de persecutione librum unum. There is a remarkable resemblance in vocabulary and syntax with the undoubted works of Lactantius, and differences in style can be explained by the difference of subject. The author of the De Mortibus is accurately informed as to the events which took place in Nicomedia, and he dedicates his work to Donatus, to whom Lactantius addressed another treatise, De Ira Dei. Due allowance being made for the tendency of the De Mortibus, it is a very important contemporary source.

Other authorities which, though referred to in the present volume, are more concerned with the history of subsequent events, such as Ammianus Marcellinus, the Anonymous known as Anon. Valesianus, Eusebius, Zosimus, will be noticed in the Appendix to vol. ii.

Modern Works. For the general history: Schiller's Geschichte der römischen Kaiserzeit (2 vols., from Augustus to Theodosius I.), up to date and very valuable for references. Mommsen, Römische Geschichte, vol. v. Die Provinzen von Cäsar bis Diocletian (also in Eng. trans. in 2 vols.). Hoeck's Römische Geschichte (reaching as far as Constantine) is now rather antiquated; Duruy's History of Rome (to Theodosius the Great) may also be mentioned. For the general administration, including the military system of which Gibbon treats in chap. i.: Marquardt, Handbuch der römischen Alterthümer (Staatsverwaltung. vols. iv.–vi.); and Schiller's summary in Ivan Müller's Handbuch der klass. Alterthumswissenschaft. For manners, social life, &c., under the early empire: Friedländer's Darstellungen aus der Sittengeschichte Roms in der Zeit von Augustus bis zum Ausgang der Antonine. For chronology: Clinton's Fasti Romani, and Goyau's short Chronologie de l'Empire romain; Klein's Fasti Consulares.

A few special monographs (in addition to those referred to elsewhere) may be mentioned here. Hundertmark, de Imperatore Pertinace. Höfner, Untersuchungen zur Gesch. des Kaisers L. Septimius Severus; A. de Ceuleneer, Essai sur la vie et la règne de Septime Sevère; Wirth, Quaestiones Severianae. A. Duncker, Claudius Gothicus. Preuss, Kaiser Diokletian und seine Zeit; Vogel, Der Kaiser Diokletian.

2. CONQUEST OF BRITAIN — (P. 4 AND P. 45)

It may be well to note more exactly how Roman arms progressed in Britain after Claudius. (Our chief authority is the Agricola of Tacitus.) The first legatus sent by Vespasian was Petillius Cerealis, who fought against the Brigantes and subdued the eastern districts of the island as far north as Lin-

[1] For the De Mortibus Persecutorum compare vol. ii. Appendix 10, p. 357–358.

coln (Lindum). A line drawn from Chester (Deva) to Lincoln would rightly mark the limits of Roman rule at this time. Cerealis was succeeded by Frontinus (whose treatise on the science of warfare is extant), and he reduced the Silures (in the west). Then came Agricola, whose government lasted from 78 to 85 A.D. He attempted to extend the Roman frontiers both northward and westward, but failed to consolidate his conquests. The only lasting fruit of the enterprises of Agricola was the acquisition of York (Eburacum), — a fact which Tacitus does not record and which we have to infer.

On p. 45, n. 34, Gibbon mentions nine colonies in Britain, on the authority of Richard of Cirencester, which has no value. The only towns, which we know to have had the rank of *coloniae*, are Camalodunum, Eburacum, Glevum, Lindum. Verulamium was a municipium.

3. THE CONQUESTS OF TRAJAN, AND POLICY OF HADRIAN — (P. 7)

The first Dacian war of Trajan lasted during 101 and 102 A.D. and Trajan celebrated his triumph at the end of the latter year, taking the title of Dacicus. The second war began two years later, and was concluded in 107 by the dissensions of the barbarians and the suicide of Decebalus. Our only contemporary sources for these wars are monumental, — the sculptures on the Pillar of Trajan and some inscriptions. Unfortunately Trajan's own work on the war has perished. (Arosa and Froehner have published in a splendid form photographic reproductions of the scenes on the column of Trajan, Paris, 1872–1874. For details of the war, see Jung, Römer und Romanen in den Donauländern; a paper of Xenopol in the Revue Historique, 1886; and an interesting Hungarian monograph by Király on Sarmizegetusa, Dacia fővárosa, 1891. On the reign of Trajan, consult Dierauer's paper in Büdinger's Untersuchungen, vol. i., and De la Berge, Essai sur la règne Trajan. I may also refer to the Student's Roman Empire.)

Trajan's Dacia must be carefully distinguished from *Dacia ripensis* south of the Danube, a province formed, as we shall see, at a much later date. The capital of northern Dacia was Sarmizegetusa, a Dacian town, which was founded anew after Trajan's conquest under the name of Ulpia Trajana. The traveller in Siebenbürgen may now trace the remains of this historic site at Várhely, as the Hungarians have named it. H. Schiller lays stress on one important result of the Dacian war: "The military centre of gravity of the Empire" was transferred from the Rhine to the Danube (Gesch. der röm. Kaiserzeit, i. 554).

Gibbon omits to mention as a third "exception," besides Britain and Dacia, the acquisition of new territory in the north of Arabia (east of Palestine), and the organisation of a province of "Arabia" by Cornelius Palma (106 A.D.). This change was accomplished peacefully; the two important towns of Petra and Bostra had been already Roman for a considerable time. The chief value of the province lay in the fact that the caravans from the East on their way to Egypt passed through it. There are remarkable ruins at Petra which testify to its importance.

Hadrian, as Gibbon explains, narrowed the boundaries of the Empire in the East (it may be disputed whether he was right in resigning Great Armenia); but he was diligent in making strong the defences of what he retained. The Euphrates was a sufficient protection in itself; but in other quarters Hadrian found work to do, and did it. He built forts on the northern frontier of Dacia; he completed the rampart which defended the exposed corner between the Danube and Rhine; and it is probable that he built the great wall in

Britain, from the mouth of the Tyne to the Solway. He visited Britain in 122 A.D. (The chronology of his travels given by Merivale must be modified in the light of more recent research. See J. Dürr, Die Reisen des Kaisers Hadrian, 1881, and the Student's Roman Empire.)

It has been said that under no Emperor was the Roman army in better condition than under Hadrian. Dion Cassius regarded him as the founder of what might be almost called a new military system, and from his time the character of the army becomes more and more "cosmopolitan" (Schiller, i. 609).

4. THE ROMAN ARMY—(P. 15)

In his account of the army Gibbon closely followed Vegetius, whose statements must be received with caution. I may call attention here to a few points.

(*a*) The legion contained ten cohorts; and the cohort, which had its own standard (*signum*), six centuries. Each century was commanded by a centurion. Under the early Empire, each legion was commanded by a *tribunus militum Augusti* (under the republic, *trib. mil. a populo*), who, however, was subject to the authority of a higher officer, the *legatus legionis*, who was supreme commander of both the legion and the auxiliary troops associated with it. In later times (as we learn from Vegetius) the sphere of the tribune was reduced to the cohort. The number of soldiers in a legion was elastic, and varied at different times. It is generally reckoned at six thousand foot, and one hundred and twenty horsemen (four *turmae*).

(*b*) The *auxilia* included all the standing troops, except the legions, the volunteers (*cohortes Italicae civium Romanorum voluntariorum*), and of course the prætorian guards. They were divided into cohorts, and were under the command of the *legati*. Cavalry and infantry were often combined, and constituted a *cohors equitata*. Each cohort (like the legionary cohort) had its standard, and consisted of six or ten centuries, according to its size, which might be five hundred or a thousand men. To be distinguished from the *auxilia* were a provincial militia, which appear in certain provinces (such as Rætia, Britain, Dacia). They were not imperial, and were supported by provincial funds (Mommsen, Die röm. Provinzialmilizen, Hermes, xxii. 4).

(*c*) The use of "artillery" on a large scale was due to Greek influence. It played an important part in the Macedonian army. The fixed number of engines mentioned in the text (ten *onagri* and fifty-five *carroballistae*) was perhaps introduced in the time of Vespasian. Vegetius, ii. 25; Josephus, Bell. Jud. 5, 6, 3.

(*d*) As for the distribution of the troops, Gibbon arrived at his statement by combining what Tacitus tells of the reign of Tiberius, and what Dion Cassius tells of the reign of Alexander Severus; always a doubtful method of procedure, and in this case demonstrably leading to erroneous results. Under Tiberius in 23 A.D. there were four legions in Upper Germany, four in Lower Germany, three in Spain, two in Egypt, four in Syria, two in Pannonia, two in Dalmatia, two in Moesia, two temporarily removed from Pannonia to Africa. New legions were created by Claudius, Nero, Domitian, &c.; on the other hand, some of the old legions disappeared, or their names were changed. Three new legions (i., ii., and iii. Parthica) were instituted by Septimius Severus. Each legion had a special name. A list of the legions (thirty in number) in the time of Marcus Aurelius will be found in Marquardt, Röm. Alterthümer, iii. 2, 356. The history of the Roman legions is a very difficult subject, and the conclusions of Pfitzner (Geschichte der römischen

Kaiserlegionen) are extremely doubtful (see Mr. E. G. Hardy in the Journal of Philology, xxiii. 29 *sqq*.).

(*e*) The *cohortes urbanae* had their headquarters in the *Forum Suarium* (Pig-market) at Rome. They were at first four in number, of one thousand men each, until the time of Claudius, who seems to have increased the number to six; Vespasian perhaps added another. Some of these regiments were sometimes stationed elsewhere; for example, at Lyons, Ostia, Puteoli.

See further article Exercitus in Smith's Dictionary of Antiquities, new edition.

5. THE ROMAN NAVY—(P. 23)

The fleets of Ravenna and Misenum were called the *classes praetoriae*, a fitting name, as they were the naval guards of the Emperor as long as he resided at Old Rome.

The fleet at (1) Forum Julium was discontinued soon after the time of Augustus. The other lesser naval stations under the Empire were (2) Seleucia, for the *classis Syriaca;* (3) Alexandria, for the *classis Augusta Alexandreae;* (4) the Island of Carpathos; (5) at the beginning of the fifth century, Aquileia, for the *classis Venetum*. Besides these there were (6) the *classis Pontica*, stationed in the Euxine or in the Propontis, and (7) the *classis Britannica*, both mentioned in the author's text. There were also fleets on the three great rivers of the Empire; (8) the *classis Germanica* on the Rhine; (9) the *classis Pannonica* and *Moesica* on the Danube; and (10) a fleet on the Euphrates (mentioned by Ammianus Marcellinus, xxiii. 3, 9).

6. THE PROVINCES OF THE ROMAN EMPIRE IN 180 A.D.—(P. 24)

For a general view of the provinces, the reader must be referred to Mommsen's brilliant volume Die Provinzen von Cäsar bis Diocletian (translated into English in two vols.). For the general administration, including the military system, see Marquardt, Handbuch der römischen Alterthümer (Staatsverwaltung, vols. iv.–vi.).

1. Sicilia, the first Roman province, 241 B.C. It became a *senatorial* province in 27 B.C.

2. Sardinia and Corsica, 231 B.C. Senatorial in 27 B.C., but became imperial in 6 A.D. Again senatorial under Nero; once more *imperial* under Vespasian, and governed by a *procurator et praeses*. (Given to senate again by M. Aurelius but resumed by Commodus.)

3. Hispania citerior, or Tarraconensis, 197 B.C.; *imperial*. (Divided into 3 dioceses, each under a leg. Augusti.)

4. Baetica, *senatorial*. 5. Lustania, *imperial*.	These formed one province under the Republic, Hispania ulterior (197 B.C.), which was divided soon after the foundation of the Empire (27 B.C.).

6. Gallia Narbonensis, after 121 B.C. (At first, imperial, after) 22 B.C. *senatorial*.

7. Aquitania, 27 B.C. 8. Lugdunensis, 27 B.C. 9. Belgica, 27 B.C.	Called collectively *tres Galliae*, at first under one imperial governor; after 17 A.D. each had its own *imperial* governor.

Novempopuli, a province cut off from Aquitania by Trajan.

10. Germania superior, 17 A.D. (?). 11. Germania inferior 17 A.D. (?).	The civil administration of these frontier districts was united with that of Belgica. The military commanders were consular legati.

12. Alpes Maritimæ, 14 B.C., made an *imperial* province, governed by a (prefect, afterwards a) procurator.

13. Alpes Cottiæ, under Nero, *imperial* (under a *procurator et praeses*).

14. Alpes Poeninæ (or A. Poeninæ et Graiæ); in second century became an *imperial* province (under a procurator).

15. Britannia, 43 A.D., *imperial*.

16. Rætia, 15 B.C., *imperial* (under a procurator); but after Marcus Aurelius governed by the legatus pro prætore of the legion *Concordia*.

17. Noricum, 15 B.C., *imperial*, under a procurator. After Marcus, under the general of the legion *Pia*. (Dion Cassius, lv. 24, 4.)

18. Pannonia superior. 19. Pannonia inferior. 20. Dalmatia, or Illyricum.	After its conquest Pannonia was added to the province of Illyria (44 B.C.), *imperial;* which was broken up into Pannonia and Dalmatia, 10–14 A.D.; Dalmatia under a consular legatus. Pannonia was broken up by Trajan (102–107 A.D.) into the two Pannoniæ, each under a consular legatus (at least under Marcus).
21. Moesia superior. 22. Moesia inferior.	Moesia, 6 A.D., an *imperial* province, was broken up into the two Moesias by Domitian under consular legati.
23. Dacia Porolissensis. 24. Dacia Apulensis. 25. Dacia Maluensis.	Dacia, 107 A.D., was at first one province (*imperial*). Hadrian broke it up into two (superior and inferior). Marcus made a new triple division (not later than 168 A.D., not earlier than 158 A.D.), and placed the provinces under consular legati.

26. Thracia, 46 A.D., *imperial* (at first under a procurator, but from Trajan forward) under a legatus.

27. Macedonia, 146 B.C.; senatorial in 27 B.C.; from Tiberius to Claudius, imperial and united with Achaia; after Claudius, *senatorial*.

28. Achaia. 29. Epirus.	Included in Macedonia, 146 B.C.; together formed a senatorial province, 27 B.C.; after having been united with Macedonia (15 and 44 A.D.), restored to the senate, and declared free by Nero, it was made *senatorial* by Vespasian. This Emperor probably separated Epirus (including Acarnania), *imperial*, under a procurator.

30. Asia, 133 B.C.; *senatorial* 27 B.C. (under a consular).

31. Bithynia and Pontus, 74 and 65 B.C.; senatorial 27 B.C., became under Hadrian *imperial*.

32. Galatia (including Pontus Polemoniacus), 25 B.C. *imperial;* united twice and twice severed from Cappadocia; finally separated by Trajan and placed under a praetorian legatus.

33. Cappadocia (including Lesser Armenia), 17 A.D. *imperial;* (procuratorial till Vespasian, 70 A.D., gave it a consular legatus).

34. Lycia and Pamphylia, 43 A.D.; after various changes definitely constituted as imperial by Vespasian, 74 A.D., but transferred to the *senate* by Hadrian.

35. Cilicia, 102 B.C. At one time apparently united with Syria, but independent since Vespasian. From Hadrian (including Trachea) *imperial* under legatus; Severus transferred Isauria and Lycaonia from Galatia to Cilicia.

36. Cyprus, 58 B.C.; at first united with Cilicia; 22 B.C., became an independent *senatorial* province.

37. Syria, 64 B.C.; *imperial* under consular legatus, 27 B.C.

38. Syria Palaestina (=Judæa), separated from Syria 70 A.D., *imperial* under legatus.

39. Arabia, 106 A.D., *imperial*.

40. Aegyptus 30 B.C., *imperial* domain under *praefectus Aegypti*.

41. Creta and Cyrene, at first one province (67 B.C. and 74 B.C. respectively); united 27 B.C. as a *senatorial* province (under a praetor).

42. Africa, 146 B.C., *senatorial* under a consular proconsul; seems to have included Numidia from 25 B.C.

43. Mauretania Caesariensis. } 40 A.D., *imperial* (under procurators).
44. Mauretania Tingitana. }

It is important to note some changes that were made between the death of Marcus and the accession of Diocletian. (1) The diocese of Asturia et Gallaecia was cut off as a separate imperial province from Tarraconensis (216 or 217 A.D.); (2) Britannia was divided by Septimius Severus (197 A.D.) into Brit. superior and Brit. inferior (each probably under a *praeses*); (3) Septimius made Numidia a separate province (under a legatus till Aurelian, afterwards under a *praeses*); (4) Syria was divided by the same Emperor (198 A.D.) into Syria Cœle (Magna) and Syr. Phœnice; (5) Arabia was divided in the third century into Ar. Bostræa and Arabia Petræa, corresponding to the two chief towns of the province; (6) Mesopotamia (made a province by Trajan, and resigned by Hadrian) was restored by Lucius Verus. (7) For Dacia see vol. ii., p. 73.

7. CHANGES IN SOUTH-EASTERN EUROPE SINCE GIBBON WROTE — (Pp. 28, 29)

Gibbon's account of the political geography of the Illyrian lands brings home to us the changes which have taken place within the last century. When he wrote, Servia and Bulgaria were "united in Turkish slavery"; Greece herself was under the same bondage as well as Moldavia, Walachia and Bosnia; the Dalmatian coast was a province of the Venetian State. Since then (1) the Turkish realm in Europe has been happily reduced, and (2) Austria has advanced at the expense of Venice. (1) Now Greece and Servia are each a kingdom, wholly independent of the Turk; Bulgaria is a free principality, only formally dependent on the Sultan. Moldavia and Walachia form the independent kingdom of Roumania. Even a portion of Thrace, south of the Balkans, known as Eastern Roumelia, has been annexed to Bulgaria. Macedonia and the greatest part of Epirus are still Turkish. (2) All the Dalmatian coast, including Ragusa, belongs to Austria, but Antivari and Dulcigno belong to the independent Slavonic principality of Tzernagora or Montenegro (which was founded in the middle of the fifteenth century, preserved its independence against the Turks with varying success ever since, and in our own time played a conspicuous part in the events of 1876 to 1878, which so effectually checked the power of the Turk). Austria also acquired (by the treaty of Berlin, 1878) the protectorate of Bosnia and Herzegovina.

8. COLONIES AND MUNICIPIA, IUS LATINUM — (P. 46)

The distinction between colonies and municipal towns, and the history of *ius Latinum*, are explained briefly in the following passage of the Student's Roman Empire, pp. 76, 77:—

"It is to be observed that these communities were either *coloniæ* or *municipia*. In the course of Italian history the word *municipium* had completely changed its meaning. Originally it was applied to a community possessing *ius Latinum*, and also to the *civitas sine suffragio*, and thus it was a term of contrast to those communities which possessed full Roman citizenship. But when in the course of time the *civitates sine suffragio* received political rights and the Roman states received full Roman citizenship, and thus the *municipium* proper disappeared from Italy, the word was still applied to those communities of Roman citizens which had originally been either Latin *municipia* or independent federate states. And it also, of course, continued to be applied to cities outside Italy which possessed *ius Latinum*. It is clear that originally *municipium* and *colonia* were not incompatible ideas. For a colony founded with *ius Latinum* was both a *municipium* and a *colonia*. But a certain opposition arose between them, and became stronger when *municipium* came to be used in a new sense. *Municipium* is only used of communities which existed as independent states before they received Roman citizenship, whether by the deduction of a colony or not. *Colonia* is generally confined to those communities which were settled for the first time as Roman cities, and were never states before. Thus *municipium* involves a reference to previous autonomy.

"Besides Roman cities, there were also Latin cities in the provinces. Originally there were two kinds of *ius Latinum*, one better and the other inferior. The old Latin colonies possessed the better kind. The inferior kind was known as the *ius* of Ariminum, and it alone was extended to provincial communities. When Italy received Roman citizenship after the Social war, the better kind of *ius Latinum* vanished for ever, and the lesser kind only existed outside Italy. The most important privilege which distinguished the Latin from peregrine communities was that the member of a Latin city had a prospect of obtaining full Roman citizenship by holding magistracies in his own community. The Latin communities are of course autonomous and are not controlled by the provincial governor; but like Roman communities they have to pay tribute for their land, which is the property of the Roman people, unless they possess immunity or *ius Italicum* as well as *ius Latinum*."

9. THE MINE OF SOUMELPOUR — (P. 69)

In an appendix to the second volume of his translation of Tavernier's Travels in India, Mr. V. Ball has pointed out (p. 457), that the diamond mine of Soumelpour on the Gouel is not to be identified, as hitherto, with Sambulpur on the Mahánadi, but is the same as "Semah or Semulpur on the Koel, in the Sub-Division of Palámau."

In the original, and all subsequent editions of Gibbon, the name was spelt "Jumelpur." Mr. Ball rightly remarks that this is merely a misprint; and I have corrected it in the text.

10. THE CONSTITUTION OF THE ROMAN EMPIRE — (CHAPTER III.)

The constitutional history of Rome (both Republican and Imperial) has been set on a new basis since Gibbon. The impulse was given by Niebuhr; and this branch of history has progressed hand in hand with the study of inscriptions on stone and metal. No one has done so much for the subject as

Mommsen, whose Römisches Staatsrecht (3 vols.) occupies the same position for Roman constitutional history as the work of Bishop Stubbs for English. Another recent work of importance is E. Herzog's Geschichte und System der römischen Staatsverfassung (2 vols.). Madvig's Verfassung und Verwaltung des römischen Staates was retrogressive. The works of Mispoulet and Willems may also be mentioned. Of great value for details is O. Hirschfeld's Untersuchungen auf dem Gebiete der römischen Verwaltungsgeschichte. For the imperial procurators see "Procurator" in Smith's Dictionary of Antiquities, new edition.

It would be endless to enumerate the writers from whom material for the constitutional history is drawn; but attention must be called to the importance of inscriptions and coins which fill up many gaps in our knowledge. It would hardly be an exaggeration to say that the Corpus Inscriptionum Latinarum (edited by Mommsen and others) is the keystone of Mommsen's Staatsrecht. The Corpus is not yet complete, and must be supplemented by the collections of Orelli-Henzen and Wilmanns.

The most important collections of coins are Eckhel's Doctrina Numorum Veterum (8 vols.), which appeared in 1792 — some years too late for Gibbon, — and Cohen's Descriptions des monnaies frappées sous l'Empire romain communément appelées Médailles impériales, 2nd ed. 1880–92.

For a short account of the Imperial constitution I may refer to Mr. Pelham's article on the Principate in Smith's Dictionary of Antiquities, and to the Student's Roman Empire, chaps. ii. and iii. Here it will be enough to draw attention to a few important points in which Gibbon's statements need correction or call for precision.

(1) P. 76. — "He was elected censor."

The censorship of Augustus was only temporary; it was not considered one of the necessary prerogatives of the princeps, for that, as Gibbon says, would have meant the destruction of the independence of the senate. It must be remembered that in the *theory* of the principate the independence of the senate was carefully guarded, though practically the influence of the princeps was predominant. Augustus discharged the functions of censor repeatedly; not, however, under that name, but as *præfectus morum*. Gibbon is wrong in stating (p. 83) that the censorship was one of the Imperial prerogatives. He was followed in this by Merivale.

(2) P. 77. — "Prince of the Senate."

The view that the name *princeps* meant *princeps senatus* held its ground until a few years ago, when it was exploded by Mr. Pelham. *Princeps*, the general, non-official designation of the emperors, meant "first of the Roman citizens" (*princeps civium Romanorum* or *civitatis*), and had nothing to do with the Senate.

(3) P. 80. — "Lieutenants of the Emperor."

The provinces fell into two classes according as consulars or prætorians were admitted to the post of governor. But this distinction must not be confounded with that of the titles *pro consule* and *pro prætore*, which were borne by the governors of senatorial and Imperial provinces respectively. The representative of the emperor could not be *pro consule*, as his position depended on the proconsular imperium of the emperor himself. A *vir consularis* might be *pro prætore*. The full title of the Imperial lieutenant was *legatus Augusti pro prætore*.

In the dependent kingdoms were placed *procuratores*, of equestrian rank.

(4) P. 82. — "Consular and tribunitian powers."

Gibbon's statements here require correction, though the question of the exact constitution of the power of the princeps is still a matter of debate.

Augustus at first intended to found the principate as a continuation of the proconsular imperium with the consulate, and he held the consulate from 27 to 23 B.C. But then he changed his mind, as this arrangement gave rise to some difficulties, and replaced the consular power by the tribunitian power, which had been conferred on him for life in 36 B.C., after his victory over Sextus Pompeius. Thus the principate depended on the association of the proconsular with the tribunitian power; and Augustus dated the years of his reign from 23, not from 27 B.C. After this he filled the consulship only in those years in which he instituted a census.

(5) P. 83. — "Supreme pontiff."

He became Pontiff in 12 B.C. Besides being Pont. Max., Augustus belonged to the other sacerdotal colleges. He was *augur*, *septemvir*, *quindecimvir*.

11. THE CONSTITUTIONAL SIGNIFICANCE OF THE PRINCIPATE OF SEPTIMIUS SEVERUS — (Pp. 154–161)

The name of Septimius Severus marks an important stage in the development of the Principate of Augustus into the absolute monarchy of Diocletian. If he had been followed by emperors as strong and far-sighted as himself, the goal would have been reached sooner; and, moreover, the tendencies of his policy would have been clearer to us. But the administration of his immediate successors was arbitrary; and the reaction under Alexander threw things back. Severus had no Tiberius or Constantine to follow him; and like Augustus he committed the error of founding a dynasty. His example was a warning to Diocletian.

The records of his reign show that he took little account of the senate, and made much of the army. This has been brought out by Gibbon. But it would be a mistake to call his rule a military despotism. He did not apply military methods to civil affairs. He was more than a mere soldier-emperor: he was a considerable statesman.

His influence on constitutional history concerns three important points. (1) He furthered in a very marked way the tendency, already manifest early in the second century, to remove the line of distinction between Italy and the provinces. (*a*) He recruited the Prætorian guards, hitherto Italians, from the legionaries, and so from the provinces. (*b*) He encroached on the privileges of Italy by quartering one of three new legions, which he created, in a camp on Mount Alba near Rome. (*c*) He assumed the proconsular title in Italy. (*d*) By the bestowal of *ius Italicum* he elevated a great many provincial cities (in Dacia, Africa, and Syria) to a level with Italy. (2) He increased the importance of the Prætorian prefect. We can see now this post undergoing a curious change from a military into a civil office. Held by Papinian, it seemed to be the summit in the career not of a soldier but of a jurist. (3) The financial policy of Severus in keeping the *res privata* of the princeps distinct from his *fiscus*, — crown property as distinguished from state revenue (cp. p. 126, footnote 52).

There is no doubt that the tendency to give effect to the *maius imperium* of the princeps in controlling the governors of the senatorial provinces and the republican magistrates (consuls) was confirmed and furthered under Severus. For example, governors of senatorial provinces are brought before his court, Hist. Aug. x. 4, 8. The *maius imperium*, used with reserve by the earlier emperors, was one of the chief constitutional instruments by which the princeps ousted the senate from the government and converted the "dyarchy" into a monarchy.

Note. — In regard to the prefecture of the Pretorian guards, the rule that it should be held by two colleagues was generally observed from Augustus to Diocletian. We can quote cases of (1) *two* prefects under Augustus, Tiberius, Gaius, Claudius, Nero, Otho, Vitellius, Domitian, Trajan, Hadrian, Pius, Marcus, Commodus, Julianus, Severus, Caracalla, Elagabalus, Macrinus, Alexander, Gordian; (2) of *one* prefect under Augustus (Seius Strabo), Tiberius (Sejanus Macro), Claudius and Nero (Burrus), Galba, Vespasian (Clemens, Titus), Pius, Alexander (Ulpian), Probus; (3) of *three* prefects under Commodus, Julianus, Alexander (Ulpian as superior colleague and two others).

12. CHRONOLOGY OF 238 A.D. — (P. 229)

The chronological difficulties of the year 238, which exercised Tillemont, Clinton, Eckhel (vii. 293 *sqq.*) and Borghesi, have been recently discussed with care by O. Seeck in a paper in the Rheinisches Museum, xli. (p. 161 *sqq.*) 1886, and by J. Löhrer in his monograph de Julio Vero Maximino.

The Chronicler of 354 gives as the length of the reign of Maximin three years, four months, two days, which would give 17th March 235 to 18th July 238 (Hist. Aug. xxi. i.). The latter date cannot be right (for Alexandrian coins show that the seventh trib. year of Gordian III. ran from 30th August 243, to 29th August 244, proving that Gordian was elected before 29th August 238; the latest possible date for the dethronement of Maximus and Balbinus would therefore be 1st August, and in the thirteen days between 18th July and that day, there is not room for the arrival of the news of Maximin's death at Rome, for the journey of Maximus to Aquileia and his stay there); hence Seeck emends menses iii. (for menses iiii.), which gives 17th June for Maximin's death. He calculates that the siege of Aquileia began in the beginning or middle of May.

The Chronicler of 354 gives ninety-nine days for the reign of Maximus and Balbinus; and twenty days for that of the two Gordians, but Seeck shows from Zonaras (622 D.), and Glycas (243 C.) that this number should be twenty-two. Allowing roughly 130 days from the elevation of the Gordians to the fall of Maximus and Balbinus, we get 24th March, as the *latest possible* date for the elevation of the Gordians. This calculation would suit Cod. Just. vii. 26, 5 (Imp. Gordianus A. Marino), which is subscribed xii. Kal. April Pio et Pontiano Coss., and would prove that the reign of Gordianus began before 21st March. But we should have to emend Impp. Gordiani.

It must be remembered that this plausible reconstruction of Seeck depends on the emendation of a text.

13. AUTHORITIES FOR ORIENTAL AFFAIRS — (CHAPTER VIII.)

The Armenian writers: Moses of Chorene, History of Armenia; Agathangelus, History of the Reign of Tiridates and the Preaching of Gregory Illuminator (Müller, F.H.G. v. 2; transl. by V. Langlois); Faustus of Byzantium, Historical Library (*ib.*). The credibility of Moses of Chorene is examined in an important article by Gutschmid in the Berichte der kön. sächs. Gesellschaft d. Wissensch., 1876. A. Carrière has recently attempted to show (Nouvelles Sources de Moïse de Khoren, 1893) that the work of Moses belongs not to the latter half of the fifth, but to the beginning of the eighth century.

Agathias, the Greek historian, who wrote at the end of the sixth century, made a special study of Sassanid history, and, through a friend, derived information from Persian documents. His digression on the origin of the new Persian kingdom (bk. ii. 26, 27) is important.

Rawlinson's Sixth and Seventh Oriental Monarchies treat of the Parthian and new Persian periods respectively. Gutschmid, Geschichte Irans von Alexander dem Grossen bis zum Untergang der Arsaciden, 1888. Justi, Geschichte Persiens. Nöldeke, Geschichte der Perser und Araber zur Zeit der Sassaniden, 1879. Schneiderwirth, Die Parther, 1874. Drexler, Caracallas Zug nach dem Orient.

14. THE ZEND AVESTA — (P. 253 *sqq.*)

The first European translation of the Avesta was made by Anquetil du Perron, and appeared (in 3 vols.) in 1771, just in time for Gibbon to make use of. The appearance of this work aroused a storm of controversy, chiefly in England, and it is interesting to observe that Gibbon was among those who accepted the Avesta as genuine documents of the Zoroastrian religion. It is unnecessary to say that in the present century their antiquity has been abundantly confirmed.

The Avesta is a liturgical collection of fragments from older texts, and is (as M. Darmesteter remarks) more like a prayer-book than a Bible. It consists of two parts, of which the first (1) contains the Vendîdâd, the Visperâd, and the Yasna. The Vendîdâd (a corruption of *vîdaêvô-dâtem* = "antidemoniac law") consists of religious laws and legendary tales; the Visperâd, of litanies for sacrifice; and the Yasna, of litanies also, and five hymns in an older dialect than the rest of the work. The second part (2) is the Small Avesta, a collection of short prayers.

Two questions arise: (*a*) When was the Avesta compiled? (*b*) What is the origin of the older texts which supplied the material?

(*a*) It is generally supposed that the Avesta was first collected under the Sassanids. But it is stated in a Pahlavi authority that the collection was begun under the Arsacids (having been ordered by King Valkash or Vologeses) and completed under the Sassanid Shapûr II. in the fourth century (A.D. 309–380). If this is true, we must modify the usual view of the revival of Mazdeism by Ardeshîr the first Sassanid, and regard his religious movement as merely the thorough realisation of an idea derived from the Parthian princes. M. Darmesteter concludes his discussion of the question thus (Introduction to his translation of the Zend Avesta, p. xxxv.): "It can be fairly admitted, that even in the time and at the court of the Philhellenic Parthians a Zoroastrian movement may have originated, and that there came a time when they perceived that a national religion is a part of national life. It was the merit of the Sassanids that they saw the drift of this idea which they had the good fortune to carry out." It would of course be vain to attempt to determine which of the four or five kings named Vologeses originated the collection. The completion under Shapûr II. is an established fact.

(*b*) As to the older texts from which the Avesta was put together, Darmesteter concludes that "the original texts of the Avesta were not written by the Persians. . . . They were written in Media by the priests of Ragha and Atropatene in the language of Media, and they exhibit the ideas of the sacerdotal class under the Achaemenian dynasty."

There is a Parsi tradition that of twenty-one original books the Vendîdâd is the sole remaining one. But Zend scholars seem uncertain as to how far this tradition is to be accepted. For the original religion of Ahura-mazda, as it existed under the Achaemenians, our sources are (1) the inscriptions of Darius and his successors, and (2) Herodotus and other Greek writers.

Those who wish to know more of the Avesta and the Zoroastrian religion may be sent to M. Darmesteter's translation of the Vendîdâd (vol. iv. of the "Sacred Books of the East") and his admirable Introduction, to which I am indebted for the summary in this note. This translation has superseded those of Spiegel and De Harlez; but it must be observed that the students of the sacred books of the Persians constantly disagree in a very marked way, in translation as well as in interpretation.

Lightning Source UK Ltd.
Milton Keynes UK
UKHW011416060122
396675UK00002B/54

9 785519 707817